World Literature

Volume II: Italian, French, Spanish, German
and Russian Literature since 1300

COLLEGE OUTLINE SERIES

World

About the Author

Professor of English at the University of Alabama, Buckner B. Trawick was graduated from Emory University and received both his M.A. and Ph.D. from Harvard University, where he has undertaken additional study on a Ford Foundation Fellowship. Prior to his present position, he held teaching positions at Clemson College, the University of Mississippi, and Temple University. Professor Trawick is also the author of *The Bible as Literature: The Old Testament and the Apocrypha* and *The Bible as Literature: The New Testament*, both in the College Outline Series.

Literature

*Volume II   Italian, French, Spanish, German
and Russian Literature since 1300*

BUCKNER B. TRAWICK

NEW YORK
BARNES & NOBLE, Inc.

Preface

For several years there have been available a number of admirable anthologies of world literature and continental European literature. There has been a need, however, for a convenient handbook to supplement these anthologies and to serve the student both as a guide through the great mass of writings and as a ready-reference work for factual information. It is the purpose of this outline to supply that need.

The objective of the author has been twofold: first, to provide enough biography, synopsis, and criticism to make the book useful to students who are employing the "great-works" approach, and, second, by means of copious introductions and cross-references, to render the outline serviceable to the students of comparative literature who are especially interested in trends and influences, including the interrelationships with English and American literature.

It has been difficult to decide which authors and works to exclude. In writing a short survey of nearly five thousand years of European and Oriental literature, there are only two alternatives: to give an extremely brief account of nearly all authors, or to omit many minor figures and thereby allow space for a more adequate coverage of the major writers. The latter alternative has been adopted in this outline. The selection of authors to be treated has been guided by two considerations: first, the contents of the five or six most popular anthologies now in use, and second, the influence that authors and their works have exerted on national and world literature. The great writings in the fields of history, philosophy, science, and literary criticism have been omitted except in a few cases where their intrinsic literary value has justified inclusion.

In a work of this sort, consistency in the use of foreign and English forms is virtually impossible. Both forms of the names of authors have been given in most cases. When an anglicized form (such as Virgil or Petrarch) has attained popular usage, that form has been employed in the discussions. The names of historical persons other than authors have usually been anglicized. As for titles of works, both original and translated versions have been given wherever they have seemed useful, especially in medieval Italian, French, Spanish, and German. Feeling that inclusion of foreign forms in such literatures as ancient Hebrew would be useless, pedantic, and precious, the author has given only the English titles.

The author has tried to give the most authentic dates available for authors' biographies and for their works. When a date has been found to be controversial, for sake of consistency *Webster's Biographical Dictionary* has been used as the authority. The *c.* preceding two dates (for example, *c.* 429–378 B.C.) applies to both figures.

There has been no attempt to make the bibliographies exhaustive. At the end of each part is a list of the biographical, historical, and critical material in English which has appeared to be most useful for the average student of world literature.

Attention is called to the index, which lists authors, foreign and English titles, and some special genres; to the index to characters; and to the quiz and examination questions.

The author wishes to express his gratitude to Professors Werner P. Friederich (see *History of German Literature*) and Urban T. Holmes, both of the University of North Carolina, for their many suggestions and corrections, and to thank Professor Jerome W. Schweitzer and Miss Barbara Terry, both of the University of Alabama, for their assistance with the section on French literature of the twentieth century.

—B.B.T.

Acknowledgments

The author of this outline is grateful to the publisher of each of the following books for permission to quote extensively:

Butler, Kathleen T. *A History of French Literature.* New York: E. P. Dutton & Co., 1921. 2 vols.

Fletcher, Jefferson Butler. *Literature of the Italian Renaissance.* New York: Macmillan Co., 1934.

Kuhns, Levi Oscar. *The Great Poets of Italy.* Boston: Houghton, Mifflin Co., 1903.

Lange, Victor. *Modern German Literature, 1870–1940.* Ithaca, N. Y.: Cornell University Press, 1945.

Mérimée, Ernest. *A History of Spanish Literature.* Translated and revised by S. Griswold Morley. New York: H. Holt & Co., 1930.

Mirsky, D. S. *A History of Russian Literature.* Edited and abridged by Francis J. Whitfield. New York: A. A. Knopf, 1949.

Nitze, William A., and E. Preston Dargan. *A History of French Literature.* 3rd ed. New York: H. Holt & Co., 1950.

Northrup, George Tyler. *An Introduction to Spanish Literature.* Chicago: University of Chicago Press, 1925.

Olgin, Moissaye J. *A Guide to Russian Literature (1820–1917).* New York: Harcourt, Brace, & Howe, 1920.

Phelps, William Lyon. *Essays on Russian Novelists.* New York: Macmillan Co., 1926.

Priest, George Madison. *A Brief History of German Literature.* New York: Charles Scribner's Sons, 1932.

Robertson, John G. *A History of German Literature.* Revised edition. Edinburgh: Blackwood, 1949.

Saintsbury, George. *A Short History of French Literature.* 5th edition, revised. Oxford: Clarendon Press, 1897.

Sellery, George Clark. *The Renaissance: Its Nature and Origins.* Madison, Wisconsin: University of Wisconsin Press, 1950.

Spector, Ivar. *The Golden Age of Russian Literature.* Revised edition. Caldwell, Idaho: Caxton Printers, 1943.

Strachey, Giles Lytton. *Landmarks in French Literature.* New York: Oxford University Press, 1912.

Thomas, Calvin. *A History of German Literature.* New York: D. Appleton & Co., 1909.

Weatherly, Edward H., and Others. *The Heritage of European Literature.* Boston: Ginn & Co., 1948–1949. 2 vols.

Willoughby, L. A. *The Classical Age of German Literature, 1748–1805.* Oxford: Oxford University Press, 1926.

Wright, C. H. C. *A History of French Literature.* New York: Oxford University Press, 1925.

Table of Contents

Part One: Modern Italian Literature

Part Two: Modern French Literature

Part Three: Modern Spanish Literature

Part Four: Modern Germanic Literature

Part Five: Modern Russian Literature

Part One
Modern Italian Literature

The Renaissance

(1321–1600)

Historical Background. The political history of Italy during the fourteenth, fifteenth, and sixteenth centuries is bewildering and chaotic. The peninsula knew little peace and no unity; the petty kingdoms, the powerful city-states (often under the control of some eminent family, such as the Medici in Florence and the Este in Ferrara), and foreign monarchs squabbled and fought continually. The popes, too, continued their bid for temporal power and were rewarded for their pains by having the seat of the papacy removed in 1309 to Avignon, where it was maintained till 1377 under the protection of the king of France. When Charles I of Spain led a successful expedition against Italy and was crowned Emperor Charles V of the Holy Roman Empire in 1530, virtually every semblance of Italian independence disappeared, and the name *Italy*, as some commentator expressed it, became only a geographical designation.

Most of these matters are of little concern to the student of literature. Of incalculable importance, on the contrary, is the cultural and intellectual transformation known as the Renaissance, which began in Italy about 1321[1] and lasted till about 1600.

The word *Renaissance* connotes far more than "rebirth" of interest in classical Greek and Latin literature. Jules Michelet, who coined the term, defined it as the "Discovery of the world and man."[2] It means, furthermore, the reawakening of individualism and of secularism.

There has been a tendency to label certain movements or events (for example, the invention of the telescope) as either causes or results of the Renaissance when, in reality, they are "constituent elements."[3] Perceiving the difficulty — and even the illogicality — of making such distinctions, one may list the following as some of the main elements or contributory influences.

Geographical Explorations. Explorations of the Polos the Crusaders, Diaz, Columbus, da Gama, Magellan, and others brought
about freedom from prejudice plus a thirst for more knowledge.
The comforts and luxuries of the Saracens and other foreign peoples
suggested new standards of living. And the center of the world
was shifted from the Mediterranean; Ptolemy's maps, standard for
twenty generations, were now objects of condescending amusement.

Scientific Discoveries. Discoveries in medicine, mathematics,
physics, and astronomy; Newton's theories about gravitation; and
the findings of Galileo, Copernicus, and Kepler about the stars
and the planets, all helped to change the medieval conception of
man's role in the universe.

The Invention and Spread of Printing. Johann Gutenberg of Mainz
(*c.* 1400–1468) is generally given credit for the invention (in Europe)
of movable type (*c.* 1440–1450). By making the acquisition of
books comparatively cheap and easy, the invention greatly increased
the percentage of people who could read. Acquisition of knowledge
led to thirst for still more knowledge and thus fostered the questioning attitude. Bibles printed in the vernacular reduced people's
dependence on the clergy for spiritual teachings and thereby encouraged independent thinking on religious matters. Finally, the
general increase in reading fostered broadmindedness, tolerance,
and philosophizing.

The Fall of Constantinople. The Turks' conquest of Constantinople
in 1453 caused many Greek scholars to flee to Italy, where they
helped to spread enthusiasm for the Greek classics — an enthusiasm
which had been alive since the days of Petrarch.

Humanism.[4] "Humanism" is a term which strictly should apply —
and perhaps originally applied — to the rebirth of interest in
ancient Greek and Latin literature. In the middle of the fourteenth
century Petrarch and Boccaccio had begun and had sponsored this
interest, and in 1397 the Greek scholar Chrysoloras brought to Italy
"the intellectual contagion which is characteristic of the Greek
spirit."[5] Humanism has come to mean a revolt against medieval
asceticism. In the Middle Ages the highest moral attitude had
been a perpetual denial of the claims of society and of the needs of
the flesh. Man had had a pessimistic view of life, which he considered a fearful struggle between good and evil; original sin had
brought misery of all sorts upon the world. "The pristine perfection of the Garden of Eden could never be recovered save after

death, and then only by a portion of mankind."[6] Because death
provided the only escape from the miserable and hopeless world,
medieval man had emphasized preparing for heaven.   The Renaissance man shifted his emphasis.   Discoveries of new lands; new
luxuries; new social, political, and economic freedoms; and new
intellectual horizons brought about a new interest in man and this
world as opposed to God and the next world.   Man began to discover that "the present world is interesting and beautiful, real and
God-given"[7] and that "whatever may be the validity of the claims
of the other world, simple human joys and loves on this side of the
grave have a legitimate right to a large part of man's endeavor."[8]
The belief in this right is humanism.

Discovery of the Individual (closely akin to, and perhaps even part
of, humanism).   In the Middle Ages individuality had been lost.
The Church had taught that individuality was sinful and that one
must divest oneself of selfhood, imitate Christ and the saints, and
strive for self-abnegation.   Feudalism had encouraged this attitude.
"The story of the Renaissance is the story of the revival of the individual — in science, [in] invention, in discovery, in art, in literature,
and in religion.   The deep underlying cause of the Renaissance was the revival of the individual."[9]   Individuality generated
intense energy — intellectual, physical, and artistic — and it laid
emphasis on the complete man (*l'uomo universale*), learned and skillful
in many fields — such a man as Castiglione's Courtier (p. 27) or
Leonardo da Vinci, who was a scientist, anatomist, engineer,
sculptor, and painter.

The Questioning Spirit.   Individuality also led men to question
conventional attitudes and standards and to burst the bonds of
authority.   A man once again dared to ask questions and to attempt
to discover truth for himself.   He refused to accept blindly old
theories — scientific, artistic, moral, or religious.   He developed
an attitude of stubborn intellectual honesty, well illustrated by
Galileo's conduct at his trial for heresy.   Before ten cardinals he
was forced to recant his belief that the earth was not the immovable
center of the universe; then as he arose, he muttered: "*Eppur si
muove*" ("Nevertheless, it moves").

Religious Reactions.   A combination of the new, questioning attitude, of widespread reading (especially of the Bible), of the new
knowledge about the universe, of humanism, of acquaintance with
pagan lore, and of the growing dissatisfaction with the corruption

within the Church — all these caused many men to reconsider and re-evaluate their beliefs about God and the afterlife. One group forsook Christianity.* Of this group some turned to paganism, recognizing that the pagan gods were patrons of the enjoyment of life; others simply disregarded religious matters; and still others, feeling that all standards were overthrown and that retribution was a mere fiction, embraced outright immorality. Nothing seemed wrong — sexual excesses, sensuality, even murder. A second group tried (sometimes unsuccessfully) to reconcile Christianity with the new trends — in art, in ethics, and in religion. A third group revolted against the paganism, the liberalism, and the excesses of the Renaissance. In this group there was a revival of conscience. In Italy, Spain, and France the group brought about reform principally within the Church; in Germany, Switzerland, and Holland the abuses within the Church plus the immorality and paganism of the humanists provoked the Protestant Reformation. The Catholic Church as a necessary divine agency was repudiated, and more emphasis was placed on the individual's conscience, on his direct relationship with God, and on Christian ethics.

In Italy the spirit of the Renaissance soon made itself manifest in many fields. In science, da Vinci and Galileo; in art, da Vinci, Michelangelo, Raphaelo, del Sarto, Correggio, and Tintoretto; in government and diplomacy, Machiavelli; and in philosophy, Ficino, Poliziano, and della Mirandola — these are only a few of the men who helped to make Italy once again the intellectual and cultural center of the world. One of the principal fields in which Italians were leaders was literature, but that topic deserves separate discussion.

General View of the Literature. If we exclude the classical Latin era, the Renaissance is incomparably the most glorious literary period that Italy has ever known. Italian authors achieved greatness in many types of literature.

In the fourteenth century the most prominent men of letters (exclusive of Dante, who perhaps belonged more to the Middle

---

* Douglas Bush, in *The Renaissance and English Humanism* (Toronto: University of Toronto Press, 1939), shows the fallacy of the overemphasis which has been placed on the paganism of the Renaissance. He points out that Petrarch, Boccaccio, Erasmus, More, and most of the other important humanists in Italy as well as in England were practicing Christians. Bush also believes that the asceticism of the Middle Ages has been stressed too much.

Ages than to the Renaissance) were Petrarch and Boccaccio; both were zealous sponsors of the ancient classics and of humanism in general. Petrarch's lyrics (especially his sonnets) and Boccaccio's short prose tales and long narratives in verse set the style for all Europe.

For nearly a hundred years after the death of Boccaccio virtually no great literature was written in Italy. Then in the latter part of the fifteenth century there was a revival of literary activity when Lorenzo de Medici gathered about himself a brilliant group of scholars, philosophers, and poets. One of the group was Luigi Pulci, who wrote *Morgante Maggiore*, a metrical romance. Two other poems of the same genre soon followed: *Orlando Innamorato*, by Matteo Boiardo, and *Orlando Furioso*, by Ludovico Ariosto. Jacopo Sannazaro wrote *Arcadia*, a pastoral romance which was extraordinarily influential in Spain, France, and England.

In the sixteenth century the most notable literary productions were in prose and in the epic. Niccolo Machiavelli wrote *The Prince*, an important document in political science; Baldassare Castiglione wrote *The Courtier*, a presentation of "the Renaissance ideal of living as a fine art,"[10] Benvenuto Cellini wrote his famous *Autobiography*; and Torquato Tasso wrote *Jerusalem Delivered*, a romantic epic.

Two other genres written during Italy's Renaissance need to be mentioned. One is the *novella*, or short prose tale. Boccaccio's *Decameron* (c. 1353) set the style; it was followed by several important and influential collections: GIOVANNI FIORENTINO's *Simpleton* (*Il Pecorone*, c. 1378–1380), FRANCO SACCETTI's tales (1388–1395), SALERNITANO MASSUCCIO's *Little Story* (*Il Novellino*, 1476), MATTEO BANDELLO's tales (1554), GIRALDI CINTHIO's *Hundred Tales* (*Ecatommithi*, 1565), and others.

Finally, there was drama. Though Italian plays of the Renaissance were not so great as those of England and Spain, there were tragedies, comedies, and pastoral plays. The tragedies were modeled after those of Seneca and were generally poor. Some of the comedies were in the tradition of Plautus and Terence; the principal authors of this type were Ariosto and Machiavelli. The pastoral drama was a new type, written by Tasso and Guarini. Finally, there was a fourth sort of drama known as the *commedia dell'arte*, an informal production that was made up largely of improvisation.

PETRARCH

Francis Petrarch (Francesco Petrarca) (1304–1374), "the first modern man,"[11] was born in Arezzo of an exiled Florentine family, who in 1313 moved to Avignon in southern France; there young Francis received his early education.   In 1319 he began the study of law, which he pursued first at the University of Montpellier and later (1323–1326) at the University of Bologna.   The death of his father (1326), followed by the trustees' dishonest administration of the estate, left Petrarch comparatively poor, and apparently he took holy orders as a means to a livelihood.   Soon afterwards there occurred an event "which controlled the whole course of Petrarch's life.   On April 6, 1327, he first saw the lady Laura in the church of Santa Clara at Avignon, and became enamoured of the beautiful vision."[12]   Till her death on April 6, 1348, and for more than ten years after that, Laura was the object of the poet's adoration and the source of his highest poetic inspiration.*

In 1328 Petrarch renewed his acquaintance with Giacomo Colonna, whom he had known at Bologna.   The Colonnas were a powerful and influential Roman family; Giacomo himself became Bishop of Lombez.   A journey to Toulouse which Petrarch made with Giacomo in 1330 probably brought them into contact with the troubadours, who undoubtedly influenced Petrarch's later poetry.[13]   The Colonna family became patrons of the young poet and used their influence to aid him in his scholarly and artistic endeavors. Petrarch was for a while a member of the household of Cardinal Giovanni Colonna, brother of Giacomo.

After much traveling (to Paris, the Netherlands, Cologne, Ardennes, Rome, Prague, and possibly the English Channel), Petrarch established himself in Vaucluse (1337), about fifteen miles from Avignon.   Here he lived (except for numerous trips and visits elsewhere) till 1353.   During these years he was in great demand as a scholar, critic, and poet; and many honors were heaped upon him. The most notable was his coronation as poet laureate in Rome in

---

* The identity of Laura is still a matter of scholarly dispute, and some commentators have even thought that she was not a real person — only a fabrication of Petrarch's imagination.   The almost overwhelming evidence, however, indicates that Laura was a real human being, that she was the daughter of Audibert de Noves, and that she was the wife of Hugues (Hugo, Ugo) de Sade. For a thorough discussion of the question, see the appendix in Francis Petrarch, *Some Love Songs of Petrarch*, ed. and intro. by William Dudley Foulke (London: Oxford University Press, 1915).

1341.* He also took part in various political activities; he even encouraged the ill-fated republican activities of Cola da Rienzi (1342–1348). In 1350 Petrarch began his friendship with Boccaccio, which was to continue the rest of his life.

In 1353 he gave up his residence in Vaucluse and returned to Italy. He lived at several different places — at Garignano near Milan (1357–1362), at Venice (1362–1367), at Padua (1367–1369), and at Arquà (1369–1374). On July 18, 1374, he was found dead in his library, his head lying upon an opened book.

Works. Petrarch's fame as an author rests on his one volume of Italian poetry, the *Song-Book* (*Canzoniere*). This volume, however, is about one-twentieth of his total literary production, which was principally in Latin. He himself valued his Latin works far above the Italian ones, to which he slightingly referred as " 'little trifles' and 'juvenile fooleries.' "[14] Today few of the Latin compositions are read at all, and these few are primarily of autobiographical or historical interest.

LATIN.

AFRICA (begun *c.* 1337, completed *c.* 1347). A long epic poem concerning the struggle between ancient Carthage and Rome; Scipio Africanus is its hero. It reflects Petrarch's interest in antiquity and his patriotic belief in the future of Rome. He believed this poem to be his masterpiece, but most readers find it dull.

LETTERS. A large number of letters — some (347) collected by himself, some (1,365) by later editors — give an intimate picture of Petrarch and a valuable account of the life of his time. Many letters are addressed to eminent men, such as popes, emperors, and bishops. Perhaps the most important is the "Letter to Posterity" ("Epistola ad Posteros"), which is an unfinished autobiography; it portrays Petrarch as he wanted future ages to know him. Although some critics have thought this letter vain, others have considered it simple, charming, noble, and pathetic.

GRISELDA (*c.* 1373). A translation of the famous "Patient Griselda" tale from Boccaccio's *Decameron*. Chaucer used Petrarch's translation, he says,[15] as the source of his *Clerk's Tale*.

ITALIAN.

THE SONG–BOOK (*Canzoniere*) (written at various times between

---

* Petrarch tells us that he was offered the laurel crown of France and that of Italy on the same day. His passion for things Roman and Latin led him to choose the Italian laureateship.

1327 and 1373; sent in manuscript to Pandolfo Malatesta, lord of Pesaro, in 1373). A collection of 367 poems: "317 sonnets, 29 odes, nine sestines,* seven ballads, and 4 madrigals, besides the epic poem, *I Trionfi. . . .*"[16] These poems show the influence of the classical Latin poets, the troubadours, and the Italian poets of the late Middle Ages, especially Dante and Cavalcante.

All but thirty sonnets and five odes are concerned with Petrarch's love for Laura. The whole *Song-Book* was divided by sixteenth-century editors into two parts: the first (266 poems), written "during the life of Madonna Laura"; the second, written after her death. The poems about Laura have been called "an epitomized encyclopedia of passion."[17] They run "the whole gamut of emotions and passions of a lover, from the highest elation to the deepest despair. In this full scale only one note is missing . . .: the exaltation of physical consummation."[18] One can trace roughly the course of Petrarch's love — a course marked by "a steady elevation of sentiment."[19] At first there are the impatient complaints of an impetuous lover. Then the lady's virtue sobers him and engenders his respect. Next he discovers that his love for her is an ennobling influence on him, and he decides to make himself worthy of her admiration by modeling his own nature after hers. The poems written after Laura's death show the same trend. Like Dante's Beatrice, Laura becomes a symbol of, and a guide toward, heavenly love; Dante's worship of Beatrice, however, was always remote and idealized, whereas Petrarch's passion was sometimes (especially in the early poems) distinctly physical; and the portrait of Laura is more humanized than that of Beatrice.

The *Song-Book* ends with *The Triumphs* (*I Trionfi*), a series of six allegorical poems in *terza rima*,† in which, successively, Love triumphs over Petrarch, Laura's Chastity over Love, Death over Laura, Fame over Death, Time over Fame, and Eternity over Time.

The thirty-five poems in the *Song-Book* which do not deal with Petrarch's love affair are on various subjects; some are personal, some topical, some religious. Three of the best known are those beginning as follows: "Choice Spirit! that dost stir the mortal

---

* A *sestine* (*sestina*) is a poem made up of six six-line stanzas and a three-line envoy, with a complicated repetition of end words.

† A three-line stanza form (usually iambic pentameter) in which the second line of each stanza rhymes with the first and third lines of the succeeding stanza: *aba, bcb, cdc,* and so on.

clay"[20] ("Spirto gentil," no. 53), a patriotic ode addressed to some eminent political leader, possibly one of the Colonnas or Busone da Gubbio, a Roman senator; "My Italy" ("Italia mia," no. 128), another patriotic ode; and "O Virgin fair" ("Virgine bella," no. 366), an ode to the Virgin Mary, which Macaulay calls "perhaps the finest hymn in the world."[21]

Summary of Criticism. The world owes Petrarch a twofold debt: first, as a humanist, and second, as a poet; it is difficult to say which part of the debt is the greater.

He has been called not only the first modern man but also "the first humanist,"[22] "the first modern literary dictator,"[23] "the inaugurator of the Revival of (classical) Learning,"[24] and "the founder of modern civilization."[25] His industry, his passion for Greek and Latin literature, and his devotion to learning in general have led most scholars to agree that he did more than any other person to help bring the Renaissance into being.

But Petrarch is memorable, too, as an artist. Many songs and sonnets from the *Song-Book* are included in every anthology of the world's great lyrics. To be sure, they have some faults. There is much repetition in rhyme and meter. Sometimes the occasion for a single sonnet is so trivial as to suggest that at the moment the poet, instead of being inspired by love, was simply eager to turn a clever phrase. As one critic puts it: "It is all beautiful, — or at the least, pretty, — but too often less love than gallantry. There is too often an intonation of smartness, even of smugness . . . [to use Gabriel Harvey's phrase] nothing but neat Wit and refined Elegance."[26] Another commentator adds: "Often the very cleverness seems inconsistent with real passion."[27]

Other critics, however, have been more eulogistic, and even Everett (quoted directly above) admits that "Petrarch was a very great man and a very great poet, who ranks in his best work with the kings of song. . . ."[28] Garnett is even more enthusiastic: "The best is transcendently excellent. . . ."[29] And, finally, Joseph Auslander, one of the best translators of Petrarch, has said, "The sonnets to Laura in life and Laura in death constitute a portrait unique in fullness and variety and assuredly stand with the few sustained and memorable sonnet sequences of the world."[30]

Influence. Of all the poets who have written in the Italian language — Dante not excepted — Petrarch has had the most influence on later literature. He did not invent the sonnet, but he brought it close to perfection, and he made it immensely popular. "It has been estimated that more than three hundred thousand individual sonnets were composed in western Europe in the sixteenth century, a striking testimony to the power of the movement known as *Petrarchism*."[31] This movement (in Italy, Portugal, France, Spain, and England) followed Petrarch's glorification of rather Platonic love and his use of conceits, puns, and violent protestations of passion for a virtuous lady or reluctant (usually married) mistress. Some of the poets most influenced by Petrarch were Boccaccio, Ronsard, du Bellay, Chaucer, Wyatt, Surrey, Sidney, Spenser, and Shakespeare.

BOCCACCIO

Giovanni Boccaccio (1313–1375), the "greatest story-teller in the world,"[32] was born probably in Paris. He was the illegitimate son of a rather wealthy merchant of Certaldo, a small town near Florence. His mother (according to most biographers) was a French-woman named Jeanne. When the boy was twelve,[33] his father apprenticed him to a merchant in Naples. After six years, Boccaccio was permitted to drop this uncongenial task and take up the study of canon law; this also proved unpleasant for him, but he continued it about six years. These twelve years in the gay city of King Robert were probably the happiest in Boccaccio's life. He apparently was welcomed in high society; and about 1333 he began a liaison with Maria d'Aquino, the natural daughter of King Robert himself. Like Dante's Beatrice and Petrarch's Laura, Maria (whom Boccaccio calls Fiammetta, or "Little Flame") was the wife of another man and also the inspiration of many of Boccaccio's works. If we can believe Boccaccio, after the romance had continued for about a year or so, Maria jilted him for another lover.

In 1338 his father's financial difficulties made it necessary for Giovanni to return to Certaldo, much against his will. Here, however, he devoted himself to literature, which — along with love — had been his chief interest in Naples. During the next ten years he was a prolific writer; his literary productions soon made him famous, and he was in great demand as an envoy. One mission (1351) was to Petrarch (whom he had met the year before) for the purpose of offering the older poet a professorial chair in the Academy of Florence — which, incidentally, Petrarch refused; the friendship of the two poets continued till Petrarch died (1374).

Boccaccio's latter years were troubled by poverty, failing vitality, a snub by a rich and pretty widow to whom he had made some advances (1354), and anxiety about religious matters. In 1362 a warning sent to him by a dying saint almost persuaded him to destroy his secular writings, but a letter from Petrarch restrained him. His last two years were brightened by his appointment to lecture on Dante at the University of Florence. He died at Certaldo.

Works. Despite the fact that Dante and Boccaccio were antipodal in temperament and attitude, the younger man proclaimed the older as his master;* and he revered Petrarch almost as much as he did Dante. Other important literary influences on him were Cicero, Virgil, Ovid, Juvenal, Apuleius, Benoît de Ste Maure, Guido della Colonna, and many medieval tales, romances, and fabliaux.

Though most famous as a teller of tales, Boccaccio also wrote eclogues, sonnets, prose romances, metrical romances, an epic, biographies, and a satire. Some of his work was in Italian, some in Latin.†

ITALIAN PROSE.

THE FILOCOLO, or THE FILOCOPO (*c.* 1333)‡. Boccaccio's first major work, undertaken, he says, at the request of Maria d'Aquino. It is a long romance (seven books) based on the medieval lay of Flore and Blanchefleur. Boccaccio modernizes the old tale to suit the tastes of Renaissance Naples; he adds multitudes of new characters, new events, and new descriptions. The characterization is unconvincing, and the style is affected — prolix, florid, full of long Ciceronian periods. The romance is of little interest to the average reader, but to the specialist it is important as Boccaccio's first serious attempt to write artistic prose. It was influential on Chaucer.

FIAMMETTA (*c.* 1341). "A step away from the romance toward the psychological novel."[34] Fiammetta tells her own story: Panfilo, her lover, is forced by his father to desert her. She vainly waits for his return and even considers suicide. Her husband takes

* In addition to giving lectures on Dante, Boccaccio also wrote a biography of him.

† Since nearly all Boccaccio's works are known by their Italian or Latin names, translations will be given only when the meaning of the title is especially significant.

‡ The dates given here are those of composition, not publication.

her away for a while, but to no avail. She returns and continues to pine, but finally tries to console herself by remembering that she is not the only woman who has been deserted so.

Whether Boccaccio was trying to avenge himself vicariously on his own Fiammetta or simply attempting a sympathetic picture of a jilted lover is still a matter of dispute.

THE PASTORAL OF AMETO (*Ninfale d'Ameto*) (*c.* 1343). An allegorical prose tale, interspersed with bits of poetry. The nymph Lia introduces her huntsman-lover to a group of other nymphs, who take turns telling their experiences of love. Then it is revealed that the nymphs are really personified virtues and that their husbands and lovers are vices whom they have redeemed. The whole work is "an unsuccessful attempt to reconcile idyll and allegory, pagan fable and Christian moral, which things are past reconciling."[35] Artistically, then, the *Ameto* is a failure, but it is historically important as the first modern pastoral romance and as a step toward the successful storytelling framework of *The Decameron.* It was influential on Sannazaro and Guarini.

THE DECAMERON (*Il Decamerone*)[36] (*c.* 1348–1353). Boccaccio's masterpiece, a collection of one hundred tales bound together by a framework.

Plan. The proem tells how seven young women and three young men flee from Florence to escape the Black Death which ravaged that city in 1348. The ten young people retire to the villa of one of them, where for ten days, during the heat of each day, they beguile the time by telling stories, each person telling one tale a day. The first day there was no prearranged program, but each tale suggested the next so that by the end of the period of narration it was perceived that all the tales that day had revolved around one theme — "peril averted by ready wit."[37] Thereupon Pampinea, the unofficial leader of the group, suggested that some particular theme be chosen for the tales of each successive day. The ninth day — left open — was an exception. The themes for the other days were as follows: (2) "evil fortune unexpectedly turned to good"; (3) "how patience and perseverance win out"; (4) and (5) "issues of love — unhappy and happy"; (6) "the saving grace of wit"; (7) "treasons, stratagems and spoils of wives"; (8) "the witty war of sex"; and (10) "love's magnanimities."

Sources. Boccaccio originated few, if any, of his plots. Instead he drew them from a legion of sources — Oriental tales; Ovid;

Apuleius; fabliaux; chronicles; medieval romances; several famous collections of medieval Latin narratives: the *Gesta Romanorum* (*Deeds of the Romans*), *Vitae Patrum* (*Lives of the Fathers*), and the *Legenda Aurea* (*Golden Legend*); the Italian *Cento Novelle Antichi* (*Hundred Old Tales*), also known as *Il Novellino* (*The Little Tale*); oral traditions; and, finally, contemporary events. Whatever his material, in every case Boccaccio transformed it into something new. He poured into each tale his own enthusiasm, his own broad interests, and his own frank delight in the things of this world, especially the things of the senses.

Content. In *The Decameron* the "whole variety of human society from lowest to highest is given in form and feature. . . . At one moment, we rub elbows with the scum of the earth . . ., the next moment, we breathe a rarefied air of chivalry and courtesy . . .; soon again we are among hearty, healthy, plain people. . . ."[38] The breadth and variety of Boccaccio's canvas has led historians to describe it as the *Human Comedy* — as opposed to Dante's *Divine* one.

Tone, Style, and Humor. In *The Decameron* Boccaccio threw off the subjectivity found in most of his earlier works. He makes no attempt to moralize or to analyze. The characters of the stories usually display their natures dramatically; some of them we get to know intimately, others not so well. When Boccaccio does find it necessary to elaborate a character for purposes of the plot, that character often becomes a type — the embodiment of a Jonsonian humor, such as Craftiness, Greed, or Stupidity.[39] The stories vary in tone — some sad, some merry, some uproarious. None are deeply philosophical, but all are clever. Some border on sentimentality; many are cynical. Boccaccio delights in depicting lecherous monks and friars, stupid husbands, and wanton wives; but he also enjoys painting pictures of loyal and chivalrous knights and of patient ladies (though "Boccaccio was unsuccessful in depicting virtuous womanhood"[40]).

Much censure has been directed at Boccaccio's indecency. It cannot be denied that some of the tales are bawdy and salacious. Their indecency has been defended, however, on several grounds. Some critics say that the difference between the attitudes of Boccaccio's era and ours must be taken into account; but some of the tales were indecent even for the Renaissance, as a letter of mild reproval from Petrarch indicates. Other critics say that *The Decameron* represents only a world of make-believe and therefore is not to be judged by ordinary standards. At any rate, it is safe to say that the indecent stories were written for the sake not of indecency but of humor.

In *The Decameron* Boccaccio finds his mature style. Now he is writing about the things which he knows and likes best. He is at ease; there is no affectation, no florid figure such as one finds in *Il Filocolo.* He achieves "a truly classic prose, — a prose that was to be *the* model of the Renaissance."[41]

Specific Tales. Some of the best-known tales are "Masetto the Gardener" (III, 1); "Gilletta of Narbonne" (III, 9), the source of Shakespeare's *All's Well That Ends Well;* "Lizabetta and the Pot of Basil" (IV, 5); "The Falcon of Federigo" (V, 9); "The Lover in the Vat" (VII, 2); and "The Patient Griselda" (X, 10).

Influence. The Decameron has been one of the "four or five most influential books in literary history."[42] In addition to all the Italian authors and compilers of *novelle,* the book has influenced Hans Sachs, Lessing, Lope de Vega, Chaucer, Shakespeare, Dryden, Keats, Tennyson, Molière, La Fontaine, de Musset, Longfellow, and many others.

THE CORBACCIO (*c.* 1354). A savage satire both against the widow who rejected Boccaccio's advances and against womankind in general. It shows the influence of Juvenal. The work does little credit to the author, but is noteworthy because it marks the beginning of a new stage in his life — the desertion of the world and its pleasures.

LIFE OF DANTE (*Vita di Dante*) (*c.* 1357–1362). Valuable because it preserves some of the early oral traditions concerning the author of the *Divine Comedy.* It is the "first biography of an artist."[43]

ITALIAN POETRY.

THE TESEIDE (*c.* 1341). A long epic poem (twelve books) in *ottava rima.** The sources are Homer, Virgil, Statius, and probably a lost Greek or Oriental romance. Boccaccio attempted to write an account of the exploits of ancient Greek heroes, but he "was not at home upon the battle-field, and knew not how to sound the heroic trumpet."[44] As might be expected, by far the most important part of the poem deals with a love affair: Two friends, Palemone and Arcita, fall in love with Emilia. When they fight

---

* *Ottava rima,* or octave rhyme, is a stanza of eight lines, rhyming *abababcc.* Each line has eleven syllables.   It is now believed that Boccaccio did not invent the form.

for her, Arcita wins, but he is killed by a fall from his horse.   Palemone gets Emilia.

Poetically the poem is not a success (Snell calls it "an invertebrate, inorganic composition"[45]), but it has served as the source for Chaucer's *Knight's Tale* and his *Palemon and Arcite*, Shakespeare and Fletcher's *Two Noble Kinsmen*, and Dryden's *Palemon and Arcite*. Furthermore, the *ottava rima* has been used by many poets, including Pulci, Poliziano, Boiardo, Ariosto, Byron, and Keats.

THE FILOSTRATO (*c.* 1344[46]).   A long metrical romance (nine parts, 5,704 lines), composed in *ottava rima*.   The sources are the accounts of the Troy story found in the epitomes of Dictys Cretensis and Dares Phrygius, Benoît's *Romance of Troy*, and Guido della Colonna's *Trojan History*, a Latin version of Benoît's romance.   The *Filostrato* tells the famous Troilus and Cressida story, later retold (with variations) by Chaucer, Shakespeare, and Dryden.   In Boccaccio's version Troilo, with the aid of Pandaro, woos the widow Griseida, who later deserts to the Greek camp and gives her love to Diomede.   Troilo seeks Diomede in battle, but is killed by Achille (Achilles).   Manifestly a reflection of Boccaccio's own affair with Maria d'Aquino, the poem contains some excellent psychological portraits and some passionate love poetry.   ("In its inmost essence the poem is neither a romance nor a drama, but a lyric."[47])

THE AMOROSA VISIONE (*c.* 1344).   A long, dream-vision allegory (fifty cantos) in *terza rima*.   A fair lady (Virtue) leads Boccaccio to a castle with two gates, the narrow one leading to spiritual values, the other to worldly ones.   Characteristically, the poet chooses the second.   After a tour of the regions of Wealth, Fame, Love (wherein Boccaccio meets and tries to kiss Fiammetta), and the like, he is brought back to the narrow gate, and the poem ends.   "[It] is an allegory of earthly love — the only sort that Boccaccio understood — and its lesson is that learning and natural love give beatitude."[48]   About fifteen cantos are little more than a paraphrase of parts of Ovid's *Metamorphoses*.   Furthermore, the work is obviously indebted to Dante for both form and meter — neither of which is suitable for Boccaccio's theme.   He is trying "to pour the new wine of the Renaissance into the old bottles of medieval allegory."[49]   Despite these shortcomings, the poem "must be allowed the merits of fertile invention and glowing color."[50]

THE PASTORAL OF FIESOLE. (*The Ninfale Fiesolano*) (*c.* 1341).   An idyllic narrative in *ottava rima*.   The nymph Mensola and her lover Affrico are punished for their loss of chastity by being changed into rivers. The poem also tells about Prunello, the founder of Fiesole, and his progeny; but Boccaccio's chief interest is in the love affair of Mensola and Affrico, which takes up about 85 per cent of the poem. The work probably influenced Boiardo, Ariosto, Tasso, and Spenser.

LATIN.

ON THE GENEALOGY OF THE GODS OF THE GENTILES (*De Genealogia Deorum Gentilium*) (begun *c.* 1351, completed 1360). In fifteen books, this is an encyclopedia of mythology drawn chiefly from Ovid. It is memorable for its defense of poetry (Books XIV and XV).

ON THE FALLS OF FAMOUS MEN (*De Casibus Virorum Illustrium*) (begun *c.* 1356, completed 1364). Boccaccio has the shades of various great men — from Adam down to the author's contemporaries — come to his study and relate their tragedies. The purpose is "to show the fragility and emptiness of human grandeur."[51] The work is remembered because it is the main source of Chaucer's *Monk's Tale* and because it influenced, in addition, Lydgate's *Falls of the Princes* and Ferrers and Baldwin's *Mirror for Magistrates.*

ON FAMOUS WOMEN (*De Claris Mulieribus*) (begun *c.* 1356). A hundred and four sketches of illustrious women (saints excluded), from Eve through Queen Giovanna of Naples. The implication of the work is that women are weak and inferior creatures and should recognize the superiority of the other sex. The work influenced Chaucer's *Legend of Good Women.*

Summary of Criticisms. Like Petrarch, Boccaccio is significant both as a promoter of the Renaissance ideals and as a literary artist. In the first capacity he joined Petrarch in proclaiming the merits of Greek and Latin literature. He was reputedly the first modern Western European to learn to read Greek; he was influential in persuading the University of Florence to establish a chair of Greek; and he made the Greek scholar Leonzio Pilato a guest in his own household for a long period. As a poet, he never achieved greatness, but he did perfect the *ottava rima* stanza, and he wrote several poems which had tremendous influence on later writers.

It is as a prose master, of course, that he showed his real genius. Although the style of his early prose works was prolix, artificial, and flowery, his *Decameron* "added consistency to Italian syntax and harmony to Italian prose, and it made the final contribution to the establishment of the Florentine dialect as the literary language of Italy."[52] Here he "combined . . . brevity . . . with rhetorical smoothness and intricacy,"[53] and he attained "an ornate and smoothly rhythmic suavity of manner, now and then relieved by spicy and colloquial dialogue."[54] Although "he lacked moral greatness [and was] deficient in philosophical depth and religious earnestness, his devotion to art was serious, intense, profound, absorbing."[55] And, finally, as for his masterpiece, it possesses "undying freshness,"[56] and in the "quality of breadth he is rivalled by Dante and Shakespeare alone."[57]

THE ROMANTIC EPIC

The three "matters" of medieval romance (see Vol. I) enjoyed great vogue in Italy, especially in Lombardy and Tuscany. Minstrels accompanying pilgrims and Crusaders to the Holy Land helped to spread the lore about ancient heroes, King Arthur's knights, and "paladins and Paynims." In the fifteenth century such lore, along with biblical, legendary, and historical stories, became the stock repertoire of the *cantastorii*, or professional street-minstrels, who sang or recited to crowds in the city squares and who often were called upon to furnish entertainment for private social gatherings. One of the most popular themes was that concerning Charlemagne (Carlo), Roland (Orlando), Oliver (Uliviere), and Ganelon (Gan, Gano). The character of Charlemagne had suffered a great deal of impairment since the time of the *Song of Roland* (*c.* 1100); he was usually depicted by the *cantastorii* as a senile old king who could be persuaded all too readily to believe evil of his followers, even of Roland, whose family (Clermont) was eternally feuding with that of Ganelon (Mayence). Roland also performed many prodigious feats of arms against the Saracens.

Such a romantic tradition was the heritage of Pulci, Boiardo, and Ariosto, who were the first in Italy to create real literature out of the material.

Luigi Pulci (1432–1484). "The jester and the jest"[58] of the circle of Lorenzo the Magnificent. Only a few facts about his life are known. Apparently his family at one time had been well-to-do, but Luigi himself was nearly always in debt and always in bad luck. He wrote his one great poem, *The Greater Morgante*, at the request of Lorenzo's mother, Lucrezia Tornabuoni.

THE GREATER MORGANTE (*Il Morgante Maggiore*)[59] (twenty-three cantos composed between 1460 and 1470; five more added in 1482; the whole published the following year).   Written in *ottava rima*, the story is, briefly, as follows: The self-exiled Orlando encounters three pagan giants, kills two, and converts the third, Morgante, who becomes his devoted servant.   Morgante performs many great feats, including acting as the mast of a ship, slaying a whale, and driving away singlehandedly a whole herd of wild hogs. He himself is slain by a crab that bites him on the toe (Canto 23). His companion is Margutte, a stunted giant, a baboon of a creature who delights chiefly in eating and in bragging about his crimes; he is the literary descendant of Plautus' Sosia and the "ancestor of Rabelais' Panurge."[60]   He literally laughs himself to death over the antics of an ape.   Orlando is conducted back to Paris by Astarotte, a friendly devil, who supplies him with a winged horse and who discourses Platonism.   The last five cantos are more serious and retell Orlando's defeat at Roncevaux and Carlo's revenge on Gano.

The Greater Morgante is made up of three strains: (1) the main Morgante story (Cantos I–XXIII), derived chiefly from a late fourteenth-century Italian metrical romance; (2) the Roncevaux story (Cantos XXIV–XXVIII), drawn principally from a Spanish tale, the *Spagna in rima;* and (3) Pulci's own satirical and humorous comments plus his two great interpolations of the Margutte and Astarotte material.

The poem is significant for three main reasons.   First, it is intrinsically entertaining, especially the brilliant flashes of wit and satire contributed by Pulci.   Secondly, it reflects Florentine tastes and customs of the time of Lorenzo.   And third, it has been of enormous influence; the Margutte episodes are perhaps the forerunner of the picaresque novel, and Ariosto, Rabelais, Cervantes, Spenser, and Byron have all been greatly influenced by it.   The last named translated one canto of the *Morgante* and used the poem as his model in *Beppo* and *Don Juan.*

Matteo Maria Boiardo (1434[61]–1494).   Count of Scandiano, Governor of Reggio and Modena, "the Homer of Chivalry,"[62] he was an important official at the court of the Este family, the Dukes of Ferrara.   In 1469 he fell in love with Antonia Caprara, to whom he wrote a sonnet sequence and whom he invokes to inspire his *Orlando in Love.*   It is significant that he chose as his motto *Amor*

vincit omnia ("Love conquers all things"), the same that Chaucer's
Prioress wore on her brooch; in Boiardo's case (as perhaps in that
of the Prioress) the love referred to was romantic, not spiritual.
Boiardo's one memorable work is the romantic epic *Orlando in Love*.
   ORLANDO IN LOVE (*Orlando Innamorato*).   Written in *ottava
rima*.   Boiardo published two books (sixty cantos) in 1484 and had
finished only nine and a fraction cantos of the third book at the time
of his death.   There is no evidence that he even knew of the existence of Pulci's *Morgante*, and Boiardo's poem is entirely unlike
Pulci's epic in tone, style, and content.   In the *Orlando in Love* the
titular character is a lovesick hero, who abandons everything else —
even the defense of his king and his country — to pursue the reluctant Angelica, a paynim princess of Cathay; and Boiardo implies
that Orlando is entirely right to exalt love above all else.   But
Orlando is not the only one smitten by the charms of Angelica;
nearly the whole French court, including Orlando's cousin Rinaldo
and the ancient Nano, are enamored.   Both Orlando and Rinaldo
join in the pursuit of the maiden — a pursuit which extends to
China and back.   En route the knights engage in countless battles
with other knights, lady-knights, wizards, and demons.   These
adventures are full of magical happenings and magical paraphernalia — springs of water, rings, swords, and many others.
The poem breaks off where Carlo is besieged in Paris by the Saracens.
   Despite the roughness and provinciality of Boiardo's language,
his poem has many merits.   The several threads of the complicated
plot are cleverly interwoven.   The characterization is amusing
though sometimes exaggerated.   Perhaps the main "charm of
Boiardo's poetry consists in its firm grasp on truth and nature, the
spontaneity and immediateness of its painting."[63]
   The *Orlando in Love* was very popular for a while, but the change
in the temper of the times[64] and the inelegance of its language caused
the sixteenth century to forget the poem almost entirely.   Francesco
Berni polished up the style and diction of the poem in 1541, thereby
changing its whole tone.
   Boiardo was particularly influential on Ariosto and Spenser.
   Ludovico Ariosto (1474–1533).   The greatest of the three
writers of romantic epics.   He was born in Reggio near Florence.
Upon the death of his father in 1500 he had to assume the support
of a large family.   At first he attached himself to Cardinal Ippolito
and later to Duke Alfonso of Ferrara — both of the Este family and

both rather niggardly patrons.   In 1522 Alfonso made him governor of Garfagnana, a remote and bandit-infested village.   He returned to Ferrara three years later and there bought a house of his own, where he lived the remainder of his life.

Ariosto wrote some lyrics and elegies in Latin and some madrigals, sonnets, satires, and dramas in Italian.   From *The Substitutes* (*I Suppositi*), his most famous drama, Gascoigne adapted his *Supposes*, and Ariosto's play probably gave Shakespeare the subplot of *The Taming of the Shrew*.   Ariosto's fame, however, rests almost entirely on his *Orlando Insane*.

ORLANDO INSANE (*Orlando Furioso*).   A sequel to Boiardo's *Orlando in Love*.   Forty cantos were published in 1516; a revised edition (forty-six cantos) came out in 1532.   Besides Boiardo, Ariosto drew on Virgil, Ovid, Statius, Boccaccio, Pulci, and the whole corpus of medieval romance.

Themes.   In the *Orlando Insane* there are hundreds of events and episodes more or less loosely attached to one or more of the main themes, which are three.   (1) The first is the siege of Paris by the Saracens under Agramante, King of Africa; some of his principal allies are Marsilio, King of Spain, and the warriors Rodomonte, Manricardo, and Ruggiero.   (2) The second is the madness of Orlando, from which the poem derives its name.   Angelica escapes from the French and succeeds in getting outside the walls of the city.   There she discovers the wounded Moorish youth Medoro. After nursing him back to health, she falls in love with him and marries him.   When Orlando learns of the marriage, his jealous rage completely deprives him of his senses.   He wanders naked over the country and fights many battles against man and beast. (3) The last is the love of Ruggiero and Bradamante.   The former is converted to Christianity and falls in love with Bradamante, the sister of the French knight Rinaldo.   This theme is of great importance — especially to Ariosto — because Ruggiero and Bradamante were supposed to be the ancestors of the great family of Este, for whose sake the poet was in large measure writing the poem.   The three threads are brought together at the end of the poem.   Orlando is cured of his madness — and, incidentally, of his love for Angelica — when Astolfo, a British knight, journeys to the moon, there recovers Orlando's senses, then returns to earth and injects the recovered senses into Orlando's nostrils.   Orlando kills Agramante, the siege is lifted, and Ruggiero and Bradamante are married.

Summary of Criticism. Ariosto's poem is neither a burlesque of chivalry (such as Pulci's *Morgante* came near being) nor sympathetic idealization of it (such as Boiardo's *Orlando in Love* was). As Symonds says: "Ariosto jests. . . . His philosophy inclined him to watch the doings of humanity with a genial half-smile, an all-pervasive irony that had no sting in it. . . . [He paints] mankind, not as he thinks it ought to be, but as he finds it."[65]

The *Orlando Insane* has several rather serious flaws or shortcomings. Perhaps the most noticeable is the profusion of not very subtle flattery which it heaps upon the Este family. As has been pointed out, one of the main themes of the poem is the founding of the noble house and the tracing of its pedigree back to A.D. 800. But Ariosto does more: he seizes many opportunities to praise the Duke of Ferrara and his kinsmen. "Stanza after stanza is poured out in genealogical and monarchical panegyrics which would have almost seemed fulsome to James I and Lewis XIV —and Ariosto must go into the list of those who have sunk the noblest genius in the adulation of a courtier."[66]

A second flaw is repetitiousness. Like Spenser's *Faerie Queene*, the *Orlando Insane* wearies us with endless descriptions of forlorn ladies and of ferocious battles — descriptions that are all too much alike.

A third adverse criticism is that the poem is lacking in deep moral or ethical content. Professor Foligno remarks that it is Ariosto's "means of giving expression to the beautiful" but that "while it influenced life, [it] did not have its roots in it."[67] Sellery adds that this censure applies to Pulci and Boiardo as well as Ariosto and says: "As a consequence, their masterpieces lack universality, and time has withered them."[68] "No thrilling cry from the heart of humanity is heard; no dreadful insight into moral woe disturbs the rhythmic dance."[69]

These defects, which prevent the *Orlando Insane* from being ranked with the greatest masterpieces of world literature, are to a large extent the defects of the age in which Ariosto lived, and "he remains its best interpreter."[70]

The poem, however, has many real merits. Rapidity of movement, fancy, lightheartedness, variety, humor, "plastic beauty"[71] — all of these have been proclaimed by the critics. Even if the poem does not "have its roots in life," its author has a "sagacity of insight"[72] into human motives and smiles ironically at them. The one merit that nearly all commentators have agreed upon is technical perfection. Ariosto has a sureness of touch and a mastery of his material which are lacking in Pulci and Boiardo. He spent twenty-six years composing and revising the poem, and the result "is that there cannot be found a rough or languid or inharmonious passage in an epic of 50,000 lines."[73]   Everett adds: "The verse of Ariosto is absolutely perfect for his subject: it is melodious, yet not luscious; free, yet not slovenly; manly, yet not austere. Only Homer ever applied to a great body of poetry a measure more perfectly wedding sound to sense."[74]

Influence. The vogue and influence of the *Orlando Insane* were enormous. In the sixteenth century alone it went through 180 editions. "It was translated into all languages, imitated in every literature."[75]   Some of the later authors most indebted to it were Tasso, Cervantes, Spenser, Shakespeare, Milton, Byron, and Shelley.

THE PASTORAL ROMANCE

Jacopo Sannazaro (1458–1530). Poet and prose romancer. Sannazaro was born in Naples; of Spanish descent, he was a loyal adherent to the Aragonese rulers of Naples, especially Federigo, whom he followed into exile in France in 1501. When Federigo died in 1504, Sannazaro returned to Naples and lived there till his death.

He wrote some eclogues (*Piscatory Eclogues,* or *Eclogae Piscatoriae*), some lyrics, and one epic in Latin; and he composed many lyrics in the vernacular. He is remembered principally, however, for his pastoral romance *Arcadia.*

ARCADIA (published 1504). Part prose, part poetry. Indebted chiefly to Boccaccio's *Filocolo* and *Ninfale d'Ameto* for style, diction, and subject matter, the work borrowed also from Theocritus, Bion, Moschus, Catullus, Virgil, Ovid, Apuleius, and Petrarch. Although "the whole work would appear to be an intricately built-up mosaic of borrowed bits,"[76] it also reflects his own unrequited devotion to Carmosina Bonifacio: Sincero loves Amaranta, who, alas, does not love him. He tries to forget her — even goes away for that purpose. A premonition of disaster drives him home, where he learns that Amaranta is dead. On such a slight narrative frame Sannazaro hangs the descriptions which have made him famous — descriptions of peaceful Arcadia, an idealized rural never-never land inhabited by shepherds and shepherdesses who do little more than sing songs and make love.

This work started a fashion which soon spread all over western Europe and which lasted, in some countries, till almost the end of the eighteenth century. Guarini's *Faithful Shepherd* (*Pastor Fido*), Montemayor's *Diana*, Sidney's *Arcadia*, and D'Urfé's *Astrée* are direct descendants. A few of the other authors who were influenced by Sannazaro are Tasso, du Bellay, Spenser, Marlowe, Shakespeare, Phineas Fletcher, Milton, and Keats.

POLITICAL PHILOSOPHY

Niccolo Machiavelli (1469–1527). Statesman, political philosopher, and dramatist, Machiavelli was born in Florence. His father was a lawyer, his mother, a poet. Niccolo was given a good humanistic education. In 1498 he was appointed a member of the Council of Ten, the chief legislative body of the Florentine Republic. He was sent on many "foreign" missions, including several to the court of the notorious Cesare Borgia. In 1512 he lost his position when the Medici returned to power in Florence. He retired to his farm at San Casciano near Florence, where he remained seven years and where he wrote *The Prince* and the *Discourses on the First Decade of Titus Livy*. In 1519 he was restored to Mediccan favor and commissioned to draw up a plan for political reform in Florence, and from 1520 to 1525 he was engaged in writing a history of the city. The following two years he devoted to perfecting a plan for the Florentine militia. In May, 1527, the Medici were again driven out of Florence, the city was once more declared a republic, and Machiavelli was again in ill favor. He died a month later.

Like most of the other late Renaissance writers, Machiavelli wrote many things — a verse-chronicle, letters, reports, a history, military documents, and several dramas (one of the dramas, *Mandrake* [*Mandragola*], superlatively cynical and immoral,* has been called "the finest play of the Renaissance"[77]) — but he is famous for only one work, *The Prince*.

THE PRINCE (*Il Principe*) (written *c.* 1513, published 1516). Perhaps the first modern treatise on political philosophy. Its thesis, briefly, is as follows: A republican government is the best

---

* In the play a friar and Callimaco, a young man, connive to trick an old man and have Callimaco seduce Lucrezia, the old man's wife. Lucrezia loses her scruples and decides that it was all the will of heaven.

kind;* however, in a world where deceit and selfishness and greed are rife and strong, sometimes it is necessary for a powerful leader (or prince) to assume control, fight fire with fire, and ruthlessly put down all opposition. The wise prince *prefers* to practice the traditional virtues, but should not hesitate to depart from them when considerations of state demand. He may resort to any means, including breach of faith and even murder, to attain his end — a strong state. Machiavelli implies that when the state has been made strong and stable, the prince should let it become a republic or at least a constitutional monarchy.

Ever since Machiavelli's day *The Prince* has been considered by some to be a diabolical production, and its author's name has been held synonymous with Satan (hence, according to Samuel Butler, "Old Nick"). Passages have been quoted out of context to prove their author depraved and immoral. Although such a practice is unfair and does not do justice to Machiavelli's whole thesis, it must be admitted that he exalts the state above the individual; that the most enthusiastic exponents of his theories have been Napoleon, Bismarck, Hitler, Mussolini, and Stalin; and that his "state is exempt from the obligations of religion and morality."[78] But one must remember that Machiavelli's chief aim was a strong and unified Italy and that *The Prince* was written at a time when the peninsula was divided into small, autonomous, squabbling states, beset by greedy and powerful foreign neighbors. The last chapter of the book, entirely different in tone from the cold practicality of the earlier chapters, is an emotional and eloquent appeal for an independent and united Italy.

Machiavelli's prose style is clear, straightforward, forceful, and entirely lacking in ornamentation.

COURTESY LITERATURE†

Baldassare Castiglione (1478–1529). "The arbiter elegantiarum for all Renaissance Europe."[79] He was born in Mantua. For a long time he served the Duke of Urbino; he went as an envoy to England and later to the court of Pope Leo X. Later still he entered the service of Pope Clement VII, whose accusation of him

---

* This precept is implied in the *Discourses* rather than in *The Prince*, but it may be considered an integral part of Machiavelli's political philosophy.

† "Courtesy" literature is literature which attempts to establish rules and standards of conduct, manners, and education of a person in polite society.

as a poor diplomat is said to have broken his heart and killed him. Castiglione himself was considered by his contemporaries to be the exemplar of all the attributes with which he endows his ideal courtier.

THE COURTIER (*Il Cortegiano*) (1528). A report of imaginary conversations held at the court of the Duke of Urbino. These conversations are concerned with the qualities and abilities which a gentleman of the court should have; secondarily, they touch on the attributes of the ideal court-lady, too. Castiglione depicts his courtier as the universal man, *"l'uomo universale"* — a man skilled and learned in nearly all fields. He must be an accomplished soldier, statesman, diplomat, athlete, artist, and man of letters. "He must be high-minded as well as broad-minded,"[80] and he must be gentle, sensitive, and tactful. He is brought to his highest development by love for a beautiful woman. This love is Platonic in the original sense of the word, and the woman beloved must be a " 'golden mean of reserve,' — must be not a wanton, nor yet a prude."[81]   *The Courtier* has much to say about love and Platonism, of which Cardinal Pietro Bembo is (in the conversations) the chief interpreter.

Castiglione's book immediately became popular in western Europe. It was translated into English (by Sir Thomas Hoby) only thirty-three years after it was written, and it influenced especially the works of Sidney and Spenser.

AUTOBIOGRAPHY

Benvenuto Cellini (1500–1571).   Cellini was born in Florence. Though (according to his own account) in great demand as a silversmith and a sculptor, he spent a considerable portion of his adult life wandering — or escaping — from one place to another, especially Rome, Florence, and Paris.   He died in Florence.

His *Autobiography* (not published till 1728) is one of the world's greatest and most entertaining self-portraits. Although he may be guilty of egotism and exaggeration, Cellini gives a frank account of his many crimes, including theft, sexual immorality, and the brutal treatment of his mistresses.   In portraying himself Cellini gives us "the composite photograph, as it were, of Renaissance Italy, — its serene self-confidence now and then extending and descending to *bravado* and *braggadochio*, its unaffected passion for the beautifully right, its elegance and chivalry, its callous cruelty."[82]   The *Auto-*

biography furthermore gives valuable accounts of contemporary Italy and France and of many of the interesting people of the time, especially King Francis I of France and Duke Cosimo de Medici of Florence — both of them great patrons of the arts.

DRAMA

During the Renaissance in Italy there were a few vestigial remains of the medieval drama, as was the case in most of the other western European countries. As late as 1472 ANGELO AMBROGINO POLIZIANO (1454–1494) wrote *La Favola di Orfeo*, a secular mystery play (*sacra rappresentazione*) on the old Orpheus legend, which anticipated the pastoral drama. And about 1494 Boiardo (above) composed *Timone*, a dramatic version of the well-known Timon of Athens story; this drama has some allegorical characters (e.g., Poverty and Wealth), which make it one of the last descendants of the morality play.

Besides these carry-overs from the Middle Ages, there were tragedies, comedies, and pastoral plays.

Tragedy. There were no truly great tragedies. Most of the tragic plays that were composed were modeled on Seneca's dramas and followed Horace's precepts about decorum. The plot was most often lurid and melodramatic, and it usually represented a reversal of fortune — the fall of some nobleman from prosperity to adversity; most of the action took place offstage and was reported by some sort of messenger. This type of drama was known as *tragedia erudita*, "learned tragedy." The earliest example is *Sofonisba* (*c.* 1515), by GIANGIORGIO TRISSINO; others are *Orbecche* (*c.* 1541), by GIRALDI CINTHIO; *Orazio* (1546), by PIETRO ARETINO; *Marianna* (1565), by LODOVICO DOLCE; and *Torrismondo* (1586), by Tasso.

Comedy. Comedy was a little better than tragedy. One may distinguish three main types.

COMEDY OF MANNERS (*commedia erudita* or "learned comedy"). *Commedia erudita* was modeled on the plays of Plautus and Terence. The first "learned comedy" to be written in the Renaissance was Ariosto's *Cassaria* (*c.* 1508); it was followed by four others by the same author: *The Substitutes* (*I Suppositi*, 1509), *The Necromancer* (*Il Negromante*, 1520), *Lena* (1529), and *The Students* (*Gli Studenti* or *Scholastica*, left unfinished at his death in 1533). Other important comedies were Machiavelli's *Mandrake* (*Mandragola, c.* 1512) (above, p. 25); BERNARDO DOVIZI's *Calandria*

(1513), on the same theme as Shakespeare's *Comedy of Errors;* and Aretino's *Cortegiana* (1525), a satire on Castiglione's "high society."

FARCE. The farce was a genre comparable to the English interlude. It was a short "spicy episode originally introduced — or *stuffed* — into a solemn mystery for comic relief";[83] later it became a separate production. The humor was broad and often coarse. The characters were at first rude rustics or clowns; in the later farces "type" characters (e.g., the boastful soldier and the pedant) were popular. The most famous author of the early Italian farce was GIOVANNI MARIA CECCHI (1518–1587).

COMMEDIA DELL'ARTE ALL'IMPROVISO ("improvised art [or guild] comedy"). Historically and influentially the most important of the three types of Renaissance comedy. As the name indicates, it was produced by a group of professional actors. Given only the outline of a plot, these actors ad-libbed all the dialogue. The plot itself was derived from a variety of sources. The characterizations were sometimes similar to the "types" in the *commedia erudita.* "An original feature . . . was the gradual investing of these stock-characters from the old comedy with satirical local traits of new Italy."[84] The characters wore masks indicative of their natures. Three favorites were Pantalone, a typical father and businessman, and a pair of lovers, Arlecchino (Harlequin) and Columbina (preserved in Leoncavallo's opera *I Pagliacci*). The *commedia dell'arte* influenced Lope de Vega, Shakespeare, Jonson, and Molière.

Pastoral Drama. The pastoral drama did not come into being till the middle of the sixteenth century. In 1545 CINTHIO wrote *Egle* (based on Euripides' *Cyclops* and elements from Ovid), which has a forest setting but no shepherds for actors. In 1554 AGOSTINO BECCARE presented *Il Sacrificio* (*The Sacrifice*), which is often considered the first full-fledged pastoral play. In this genre the plot nearly always revolves around "a love tangle, . . . in which the wrong people love the wrong people, and have to be unsnarled."[85] Often such devices as lost or hidden identities, recognitions, and substitutions of one person for another are employed.

Besides Tasso's *Aminta* (below) the most important Italian pastoral drama is BATTISTA GUARINI's *Faithful Shepherd* (*Pastor Fido*, 1590). In this clever and complicated play, Silvio and Amarilli are supposed to marry in order to fulfill an old prophecy. But Silvio loves only hunting, and Amarilli and Mirtillo love each other. The latter shows himself to be "the faithful shepherd" by offering his life to save Amarilli when she is condemned (by means of a trick played by Corisca, who also loves Mirtillo) to die. Then it is discovered that Mirtillo and Silvio were exchanged as babies. Silvio marries Dorinda, who has vainly loved him for a long time; Mirtillo marries Amarilli, and Corisca is forgiven.

This play was so popular that eighty editions of it were published between 1600 and 1800. It had a great vogue abroad as well as in Italy, and its Italian successors had a tremendous influence on English pastoral literature of the Elizabethan and Jacobean periods. John Fletcher's *Faithful Shepherdess* imitated it, and Greene, Marlowe, and Shakespeare were either directly or indirectly indebted.

TASSO

Torquato Tasso (1544–1595), lyricist, dramatist, and epic poet, was born at Sorrento. He received an elementary education at a Jesuit school and continued his studies at Bergamo, Urbino, Venice, and Rome. Like Petrarch and Boccaccio, Tasso was urged by his father to study law, but he soon gave it up for literature. He entered the service of Cardinal Luigi d'Este, but later shifted his allegiance to the Cardinal's brother, Duke Alfonso of Ferrara. In 1575 he finished his great epic *Jerusalem Delivered*. The four critics to whom it was submitted were so violent in their disapproval — on both literary and religious grounds — that Tasso's sensitive and conscientious nature was severely shaken, and he suffered a "storm of nerves."[86] For three years he wandered from place to place, eventually returning to Ferrara. Here his condition grew much worse, and he became violently insane in 1579. For seven years he was confined in the hospital of Santa Anna and then released. In the meanwhile his epic had been widely printed, and he had become famous. He spent the remainder of his life wandering from city to city, where he was treated with great generosity and honor. He died a few days before he was to receive the laurel crown with which Petrarch alone had been honored.

Works. Tasso was a rather prolific writer. He composed lyrics, dialogues, essays, dramas, epics, and letters. Only two of these works are worthy of detailed treatment.

AMINTA (1573). A pastoral drama, its plot is simple and romantic: Aminta woos Silvia in vain, even after he has saved her from a lascivious satyr. In despair Aminta throws himself from a cliff. Silvia repents and mourns. Then it is discovered that Aminta has been caught by a bush. The lovers are united, and all ends happily. Despite the ingenuous plot and the conventional characters, the *Aminta* contains warm and beautifully dainty poetry. It was a great success in Tasso's day — and it is still worth reading — because it presented a "genuine yearning for the golden age"[87] and because its "central motive . . . is the contrast between the actual world of ambition, treachery, and sordid strife, and the ideal world of pleasure, loyalty, and tranquil ease."[88] The play probably influenced Guarini, Sidney, Spenser, Greene, Shakespeare, John Fletcher, and Milton.

JERUSALEM DELIVERED (*Gerusalemme Liberata*) (1575). Tasso's masterpiece, an epic in twenty cantos, written in *ottava rima*. While Tasso was confined for insanity, the poem was brought out in two pirated editions; his own authorized version was printed in 1581. In 1593 he brought out a drastically changed version entitled *Jerusalem Conquered* (*Gerusalemme Conquistata*) — inferior to the earlier form.

The theme of the epic is the capture of Jerusalem in 1099 by Godfrey of Bouillon and his followers in the First Crusade. This was a timely topic in the last quarter of the sixteenth century because the Turks were again threatening western Europe and actually making occasional raids on Italy. Tasso considered his poem an epic of Christendom. As one might expect, it contains accounts of many valorous battles. These combats, however, are not the main attraction of the epic; its chief appeal has always been its accounts of three love affairs involving Sophronia and Olindo, Dorinda and Tancredo, Armida and Rinaldo.

Sophronia and Olindo. These two Christians who live in Jerusalem love each other. When Sophronia offers herself to be burned at the stake to save the other Christians in the city, Olindo tells a lie in order to substitute himself in her place. Both are then condemned to die, but both are released at the last moment by the intercession of Dorinda.

Dorinda and Tancredo. The former, a Saracen lady-knight, is beloved by the latter, a Christian; but she scorns his love. Without recognizing her, Tancredo engages her in combat and wounds her fatally; but she forgives him, receives baptism, and later communicates with him after she reaches heaven.

*Armida and Rinaldo.** Armida, a pagan enchantress, is sent to work a spell on fifty of the leading Christian knights. She succeeds, but falls in love with Rinaldo, one of the bravest of the Christians. She carries him away to a retreat on the island of Teneriffe. When Goffredo (Godfrey) learns that only Rinaldo (whom he has virtually exiled for slaying the Christian Gernando in a duel) can bring about the fall of Jerusalem, he sends messengers to find and release Rinaldo, who then returns to the siege. The city falls, and an Egyptian army sent to break the siege is defeated. So also are men sent by Armida to kill Rinaldo, who overtakes Armida, converts her to Christianity, and marries her.

Summary of Criticism. Tasso has been censured for allowing romantic love to take up so large a part of his epic — to the neglect of the heroic matter. Readers today, however, are happy to accept the siege of Jerusalem as a mere backdrop for the drama of the love affairs; and so, perhaps, were most of the courtly circle to whom the poem was originally addressed. At any rate, Tasso's genius was in the realm of "the pathetic, the picturesque, and the romantic, [rather] than towards the sublime and majestic,"[89] and in *Jerusalem Delivered* he gave that genius free rein.

Tasso has been accused of preciosity, artificiality, lack of sense of humor, and too great lushness. On the other hand, he has been praised for his superb technique in drawing portraits, especially of women; for completeness and coherence of the action of the poem; for "delicacy and elevation of tone";[90] for "profound religious feeling";[91] for pathos; and for the melody of his verse.

He influenced Spenser and Byron.

* The portrait of Rinaldo was Tasso's tribute to the Este family. According to the poem, Rinaldo was the ancestor of the Estes. Tasso's portrait, however, is anachronistic, because Rinaldo d'Este was not born till late in the twelfth century.

2

The Seventeenth–Twentieth Centuries

Historical Background. Before the middle of the nineteenth century there was — politically speaking — no such thing as an Italian nation. Spain, Austria, France, and the pope kept the peninsula in a continual round of wars; and throughout those centuries most of the territory was actually under the control of foreign powers. Independent thought was discouraged by the Catholic Counter-Reformation and by the Jesuits, who were vigorous opponents of any new ideas which might be somewhat heretical. In the nineteenth century such patriots as Mazzini, Cavour, and Garibaldi made valiant attempts (the *Risorgimento*) to throw off all foreign yokes and to unite the various sections and political factions into a nation. The Kingdom of Italy was proclaimed in 1861, and at length in 1870, while the French were at war with the Prussians, Victor Emmanuel was able to march on Rome, defeat the pope's French forces, and effectively establish himself as king of a unified Italy.[1] From then till 1939 the nation grew steadily as a world power. In 1916 she entered the First World War on the side of the Allies. Benito Mussolini and his Fascist party gained control of the country during the 1920's, enlarged her empire, and increased her military strength. In 1940 Italy entered the Second World War — this time against France and England.

General View of the Literature. Italian literature of the seventeenth century hardly deserves to be mentioned. Most of the poetry was artificial, unnatural, verbose, and bombastic. Conceits and other extravagant figures of speech were the fashion. The most representative poet of the century was Giovanni Battista Marino (1569–1625), whose "preciosity and poetical fireworks . . . became the touchstone of art; and Marino had many imitators."[2] In drama, the *commedia dell'arte* continued but was of little literary value; pastoral comedy was imitative and lacked vitality; and "tragedy could not flourish. . . ."[3] Giovanni Battista Andreini

33

(1578–1650) wrote one tragedy, *Adamo*, which was of some merit and which influenced Milton.

In the eighteenth century there was some improvement. Wearied by the specious productions of the preceding era, the men of letters sought elsewhere for models and inspiration. They turned especially to the ancient classics and to French authors. Goldoni was the leader in neoclassicism, and Alfieri effected some important reforms in drama.

Romanticism, which had its feeble beginnings near 1800, was given a temporary backset by the conservative reaction to the Napoleonic wars; but eventually the romanticists prevailed. The movement was abetted by the optimism, patriotism, and nationalism engendered by the struggle for national independence and unity. Toward the end of the nineteenth century there was the inevitable swing of the pendulum toward realism and naturalism. One group of extremists, the so-called Futurists, reacted violently against the romantic tendency to revere the past; they rebelled against old institutions, old conventions, old art, and old literature. Influenced by Nietzsche and somewhat resembling Walt Whitman, they found inspiration and beauty in "wealth, and the wealth-building machinery of industry, motion, as the expression of energy, noise, dust, [and] war."[4]

GOLDONI

Carlo Goldoni (1707–1793), "the Italian Molière,"[5] was born in Venice. He practiced law and served as a diplomat for some time, but his heart had always been in the theater: at the age of eight he had written a play! In 1748 he gave up all other pursuits in order to write for the Venetian stage. His best Italian work was done in Venice between 1748 and 1762. Then he went to Paris, where, during the remainder of his life, he wrote some plays in French.

Goldoni's significance lies in his perception that the old masked play, the *commedia dell'arte*, was outmoded and sterile. Returning to classicism, he introduced a comedy of manners modeled on the works of Molière. His two aims were to make the characters human beings and to make the situations representative of real life. Many of his best plays are based on his own observations of the middle-class people of Venice. Though not so satirical, forceful, philosophical, or psychologically profound as his master Molière, he rivals the

French dramatist "in dialogue, in development of plot, and in comic talent."[6]

Goldoni did not succeed in reforming Italian comedy; he "had no successor."[7] His reforms were opposed successfully by the dramatists Pietro Chiari (1711–1785) and Carlo Gozzi (1720–1806) and by the critic Giuseppe Baretti (1719–1789).

Goldoni wrote approximately 120 comedies and 80 librettos for operas. Three of the best known comedies are *The Coffee Shop* (*La Bottega di Cafee*), *The Innkeeper* (*La Locandiera*), and *The New House* (*La Casa Nuova*).

ALFIERI

Vittorio Alfieri (1749–1803), dramatist, lyricist, satirist, "the apostle of neo-classicism,"[8] was born in Asti, near Turin, of a noble and well-to-do family. During his younger years he devoted most of his time, energy, and money to the indulgence of his passions for horses, traveling, and women. In 1777 he met Louise Stolberg, Countess of Albany and wife of Charles Edward Stuart, the Young Pretender to the throne of England; soon thereafter she became Alfieri's mistress. They dwelt in Paris from 1785 till 1792, when the excesses of the Revolution drove them to Florence; there they stayed till Alfieri's death in 1803.

After composing a fairly successful play, *Cleopatra*, in 1774, Alfieri "was fired with [a] fierce and consuming desire to win a really deserved triumph on the stage."[9] Suddenly aware that his education was deficient for such a task, he ardently set about to remedy the situation; eventually he learned Italian (his native Piedmontese was very different from classical Tuscan), Latin, and Greek; and he read widely in all three languages.

Between 1777 and 1789 Alfieri wrote nineteen tragedies. Most of his subjects were drawn from classical mythology, from the Bible, and from history. These topics he treated subjectively. His purpose was not so much to amuse as "to promulgate those great principles of liberty which inspired his own life. A deep, uncompromising hatred of kings is seen in each of his plays. . . . Alfieri was the first to speak of a fatherland, a united Italy; he practically founded the patriotic school of literature."[10]

His tragedies observe the three unities meticulously. "His plays begin when the plot is already far advanced";[11] consequently his plots are extremely simple. They are also almost entirely lacking in action.   Most of his dramas are very short — only one extending to more than 1,500 lines.   There are few characters, and these never change throughout the play.   The tone is invariably somber, "utterly unrelieved by that tender sympathy, — the pity of it all, — which softens the tragic effect in Shakespeare's plays.   Horror is the keynote. . . ."[12]   The style is concise, austere, and harsh.

His best tragedies are the following: (1) *Saul,* which depicts the biblical king's spiritual struggle resulting from his jealousy of David;[13] (2) *Filippo,* which deals with the marriage of Philip II of Spain to his own son's sweetheart and the subsequent death of the two young lovers; (3) *Bruto Secondo,* which retells the tale of the murderer of Julius Caesar; (4) *Mirra,* which is a dramatic account of the incestuous love of Myrrha (from classical mythology) for her father; and (5) and (6) *Agamennone* and *Oreste,* which retell part of the story of Aeschylus' *Oresteia* trilogy.

In addition to tragedies, Alfieri wrote an unusually entertaining autobiography, four comedies (of little merit), some satires, and some lyrics.

Like Goldoni, Alfieri had no literary disciples.   After his death French sentimental comedy (*comédie larmoyante*) replaced tragedy in Italy.

MANZONI

Alessandro Manzoni (1785–1873), lyricist, dramatist, and novelist, was born in Milan of an aristocratic family.   In 1805 he and his mother moved to Paris, where they were associated with the famous literary circle of Madame de Condorcet.   He was converted to Roman Catholicism about 1811 and developed strong Jansenist sympathies which were to permeate his later writings.   Soon after his conversion, he returned to Milan; there and at his country home at Brusuglio a few miles away, he lived the remainder of his long life.   He was always a mild but loyal supporter of the cause of Italian independence.

Lyrics.   Manzoni's earliest literary productions were lyrical poems.   In 1806 he wrote in blank verse a defense of his mother and her late lover, Carlo Imbonati; the poem is important for its sincere statement of Manzoni's own ideals.   Between 1812 and 1822 he wrote five hymns celebrating festivals of the Church: the Annunciation, the Advent, the Passion (Crucifixion), the Resurrection, and the Pentecost.   Expressed in plain but forceful language, these hymns contain much genuine and powerful emotion. More famous, however, was the "Fifth of May" ("Cinque Maggio"), an ode on the death of Napoleon, written in 1821.

Drama. Manzoni wrote two tragedies on historical subjects, memorable more for the theories of drama which they illustrate than for their intrinsic merit. *Il Conte di Carmagnola* (1820) tells the story of the famous fifteenth-century Venetian soldier Francesco Bussone, who was executed for treason; *Adelchi* (1822) tells about the struggle of the Lombards against Charlemagne. Their author, an ardent admirer of Shakespeare and a thoroughgoing romantic, refused to observe the unities of time and place. Unlike Shakespeare, however, he would not alter historical facts, even for the exigencies of a dramatic situation. Consequently the tragedies are dramatically unsuccessful; "[at] best they are only closet dramas."[14] They have, nevertheless, some good points: their style is clear, simple, and noble; they contain some admirable and thought-provoking scenes; and some of the choruses are excellent lyrics expressive of Manzoni's own patriotic sentiments.

The Novel.

THE BETROTHED (*I Promessi Sposi*). This has been called "the one great Italian novel."[15] It was finished in 1823 but not published till 1827. Later Manzoni revised it, replacing Milanese dialectal forms with pure and idiomatic Tuscan; the revised edition was published serially between 1840 and 1842.

The action of the novel begins in Lecco, a village near Milan, on Lake Como, in the second quarter of the seventeenth century, while the region was under the harsh domination of the Spaniards. Don Rodrigo has unworthy designs on the peasant girl Lucia, who is engaged to Lorenzo, another peasant. The plot consists chiefly of their flight from Rodrigo.

The novel has several faults. In an attempt to be historically accurate, Manzoni allows documentation to interfere with the flow of the narrative. Some descriptions (e.g., of a bread riot) are too long. And some critics have considered the hero and heroine colorless. On the other hand, the merits far outbalance the shortcomings. The plot is exciting. The characterization, especially of the Lombard peasants, is admirable. The theme of the book is noble: "a struggle between right and might, in which God is on the side of the former."[16] There are many touches of delightful humor. The clear, clean style of the novel has caused it to be considered a classic. Finally, "[as] a picture of human nature the book is above criticism."[17] It was praised elaborately by Scott, Goethe, and Chateaubriand.

LEOPARDI

Giacomo Leopardi (1798–1837), lyricist, philosopher, critic, and essayist; "unquestionably the greatest Italian poet since Tasso."[18] He was born at Recanati, a small town in the Apennines, near Bologna. Here his early years were rendered miserable by ill health, a stern and unsympathetic father, and a bigoted and parsimonious mother. An almost fanatic application to study made him an accomplished Greek and Latin scholar before he was twenty; he also became proficient in French, German, and Hebrew. Such fervent study, however, probably aggravated his physical ailments, which, in turn, increased his tendency toward pessimism. From 1822 till 1833 he went from city to city in Italy in a futile attempt to find love, happiness, and health. He died poor and miserable in Naples in 1837.

Leopardi wrote many interesting and self-revelatory letters, a commentary on Petrarch (1826), some essays in literary criticism, and some treatises (*Moral Works, Operette Morali*, 1824–1828) advocating pessimism as the only tenable philosophy.

His chief claim to fame, however, is a small volume of about forty odes (*canzoni*), classical in their poetic restraint, "in the close union of concept and imagination, form and content,"[19] and sometimes in their use of ancient Greek material, but romantic in their expression of Leopardi's own pessimism and individualism. Some of the odes are patriotic (e.g., "To Italy" ["All'Italia"] and "On the Monument to Dante" ["Sopra il Monumento di Dante"]); some are concerned with romantic love (e.g., "The First Love" ["Il Primo Amore"], "To Silvia" ["A Silvia"], and "Aspasia"); and some are philosophical and reflective (e.g., "Sappho's Last Song" ["L'Ultimo Canto di Saffo"] and "The Broom" ["La Ginestra"]). Almost all — even the love poems — are imbued with the direst pessimism — "sincere, profound, crushing."[20] In Leopardi's opinion, happiness was the greatest good, but it was seldom attainable and then only for brief moments. "Not only is the world in misery now, but it always has been so and is destined to be so to the end of time."[21] Leopardi's restlessness, love of liberty, hatred of tyranny, and pessimism remind us of Byron and

Shelley; his love for beauty and the Greek classics and his yearning for a woman's love recall Keats.

Sainte-Beuve thought Leopardi "the 'noblest, calmest, most austere of poets,' Matthew Arnold says he is worthy to be 'named with Milton and Dante,' . . . [and it] is the common opinion . . . of the world at large, that he is the greatest poet of modern Italy."[22]

CARDUCCI

Giosuè Carducci (1835–1907), senator, orator, professor, critic, and poet, was born at Val di Castello in Tuscany. As a boy he went to school in Florence and later at the University of Pisa, where he took a degree in 1856. After doing some editorial work and teaching in secondary school, he was offered a professorship at the University of Bologna; he held the position from 1860 till 1904.

Although Carducci never developed any coherent system of philosophy, he had very strong and definite opinions in political, religious, and aesthetic matters.

In politics he began as a monarchist, a supporter of Victor Emmanuel of the House of Savoy. For a while, when he felt that the king was negligent in carrying out his obligations to the nation, he became a Republican; but later he reverted somewhat toward monarchism and toward the end of his life was a good friend of Queen Margherita.

In religion he was virtually a pagan. The Church was to him a symbol of Austrian rule,* feudalism, medievalism, and slavery. What was more important, perhaps, was his conviction, like that of Swinburne, that Christianity was too ascetic. He turned instead to the myths of the ancient Greek and Roman deities, whom he felt to be "no mere poetical machinery, but something alive and real. . . . He had all a pagan's delight in life for its own sake, a simple frugal, healthy, hardworking life on the beautiful earth, where all the virtues and patriotism and self-sacrifice in a noble cause found full scope. . . ."[23] Carducci did not, however, repudiate Christian ethics, and its effect on him was probably greater than he himself recognized.

In aesthetics he was a classicist. He loathed romanticism, which he felt went hand in hand with Christianity, medievalism, and foreign domination. His models were Virgil, Horace, Petrarch,

* For many years the pope had sided with Austria against those who were trying to unify and free Italy.

and Boccaccio. He admired Dante, too, for he felt that Dante had been a champion of Italian liberty; but he disagreed with the earlier poet, of course, about religious matters. This fervent classicism was partially a result of Carducci's patriotism. He exulted in the fact that he was a descendant of the ancient Romans and an heir not only of their literary tradition but also of the glorious Italian countryside which had so inspired such poets as Virgil and Horace.

Paganism, humanism, classicism, and patriotism — these are the ever-recurrent themes of Carducci's poetry. He treated them emotionally rather than philosophically or didactically, for he was pre-eminently a lyrical poet. His lyrics are aggressive, vigorous, individualistic, and optimistic. Although these are romantic characteristics, the form of Carducci's poetry is classical. He reverts to many of the meters of Greece and Rome, and his diction is pure and economical. In fact, sometimes his thought is so compact as to make understanding difficult, and this difficulty is aggravated by a wealth of rather erudite allusions. Consequently his poetry has never been widely popular.

Some of his most significant volumes are *Poesy* (*Poesie*, 1871); *New Rhymes* (*Rime Nuove*, 1873); *Barbaric Odes* (*Odi Barbari*, three series, 1877, 1882, and 1889); and *Rhymes and Rhythms* (*Rime e Ritme*, 1899).

Carducci is remembered not only for his poetry but also for his prose — especially lectures and orations. Perhaps his greatest speech is the one on Garibaldi (1882).

D'ANNUNZIO

Gabriele d'Annunzio (1863–1938), poet, novelist, playwright, aviator, and soldier, was born in Pescara. He was educated at the college in Prato. After a precocious youth, he engaged in editorial work for a short while and then decided to earn his living as an author. Most of his long life was characterized by daring, recklessness, indulgence of his passions, and irregularity. In World War I, despite his age, he became an aviator and lost an eye in aerial combat. In 1919 he led a successful expedition against Fiume, in violation of the Treaty of Versailles.

He gained recognition first as a poet. Carducci, the English romanticists, Swinburne, Wilde, Flaubert, de Maupassant, Baudelaire, Rimbaud, Verlaine, Nietzsche, and the Russian novelists of his own day all influenced his poetry, which has been called a combination of primitivism and decadence; it is primitive in its violence and frequent coarseness, decadent in its surrender to sensuality, its satiety, its dilettantism, its revolt against moral fetters, and its paganism. D'Annunzio makes no attempt to hold a mirror up to nature. "His purpose is almost entirely aesthetic. His desire is to set beauty before us rather than to describe life. By beauty he means sensual beauty, for depth of feeling or of thought is beyond his reach."[24] His descriptions are lush; their "general impression . . . is one of dazzling splendour and intoxicating perfume, . . . [but] the too uniform splendour satiates and fatigues."[25] Sometimes he exhibits a predilection for the indecent, the immoral and the vicious — "foul and slimy things. . . ."[26] These criticisms are especially applicable to his earlier poetry, of which the most famous volumes are *Truly the First* (*Primo Vere*, 1879), *New Songs* (*Canti Nuovi*, 1881), *Intermezzo of Rhymes* (*Intermezzo di Rime*, 1884), *The Chimaera* (*La Chimera*, 1888), and a series of *Praises of the Sky, of the Sea, of the Land, and of the Heroes* (*Laudi del Cielo, del Mare, della Terra, e degli Eroi*, 1903–1904). Some later poems (after 1914) are on patriotic themes.

The faults of d'Annunzio's poetry may be found in his prose. Many of his novels illustrate a Nietzschean philosophy and depict a hero similar to d'Annunzio himself — "a hedonist with an intense, lawless, almost heroic sense of beauty."[27] The most famous are *The Child of Pleasure* (*Il Piacere*, 1889); *The Innocent* (*L'Innocente*, 1892); *The Triumph of Death* (*Il Trionfo della Morte*, 1894); *The Virgins of the Rocks* (*Le Vergini delle Rocce*, 1895); and *The Fire* (*Il Fuoco*, 1900) — allegedly an account of his own liaison with the actress Eleanora Duse.

"D'Annunzio is at his worst as a dramatist."[28] In addition to the faults common to his poetry and novels, the dramas have virtually no action and are too subjective. The best known are *Francesca da Rimini* (1902) and *Fedra* (1909).

Today d'Annunzio's popularity has waned. He is remembered chiefly as the "typical poet of the adolescence of the new Italian nation . . . to whom he appealed with his superhumanism and sensuality, with the crudeness of his passions and the exuberance of his style."[29]

PIRANDELLO

Luigi Pirandello (1867–1936) was born at Girgenti (Agrigento) in Sicily, and there he spent his childhood. His father was the

wealthy owner and operator of a sulphur mine.   After a short trial
in the world of business, Luigi turned to academic pursuits and
attended the Universities of Rome and Bonn.   He married in 1894
and for several years thereafter devoted his life to his family and his
writing.   From 1897 till 1921 he held the position of Professor of
Italian Literature at the Normal College for Women in Rome.   In
1925 he undertook the founding of a national theater; the movement was sponsored by Mussolini himself; and the troupe, after a
successful stand in Rome, toured England, France, and Germany.
In 1934 Pirandello received the Nobel Prize for his drama.   His
last few years were spent in writing and in traveling in South America, France, and the United States.

Pirandello's earliest literary productions were not dramas.   He
began composing poetry in 1883; during his early married life he
contributed several articles of literary criticism to the periodical
Marzocco; and he wrote many novels and short stories prior to 1914.
During World War I he became interested in the theater, and it was
his output of dramas after 1915 that won him world fame.

His Philosophy.   These dramas reflect Pirandello's own embittered attitude.*   His bitter pessimism was probably caused by his
unhappy domestic affairs: his wife was mentally deranged from
1904 till her death in 1918 and was subject to furious outbursts of
jealousy; and his daughter, persecuted by her mother, was saved
from suicide only by the bullet's lodging in the pistol barrel.   Saddened by such tribulations and impressed by the belief that man's
life is to a large extent determined by his heredity and environment
over which he has little control, Pirandello concluded that man's lot
is worse than that of a lower animal, for the animal may find happiness by giving way to natural impulses, whereas "as soon as man
yields to instinct, he sets in motion the so-called intellect which is
nothing more, in the majority of cases, than a mechanism of deception through which he attempts to give idealistic motives and
terms to his instinctive actions."[30]   Although man perceives the
ideal, he never is able to attain it, for he is guided by his "instincts."
The intellect deceives him into believing that his motives are idealis-

* Domenico Vittorini, *The Drama of Luigi Pirandello* (Philadelphia: University of Pennsylvania Press, 1935), p. 10, says: "In Luigi Pirandello, the
artist and the man are so closely interwoven as to make it imperative to know
him intimately in order to understand his art."   On p. vii a foreword by
Pirandello himself says that Vittorini's book is a mirror in which the dramatist
beholds himself "with gratification."

tic, but the ideal eventually is discovered to be an illusion. The contrast between the beauty of the ideal and the ugliness of life as it is, plus the awareness of the irreconcilability of the two, is the basis of Pirandello's pessimism.

His Dramatic Method. Perhaps it is the failure to understand Pirandello's preoccupation with the conflict between the real and the ideal that has given rise to the accusation that his plays are "unreal" and have little to do with "real" human beings. Ruth Shepard Phelps, for example, says that his plays "have a superficial effect of realism, but the *dénouement*, since it is . . . brought about by logic, has nothing realistic about it, it is too perfect. It is not like life. . . . They [his plays] tell us nothing about human emotion or circumstances, or the interplay of character. They are purely metaphysical."[31]   This accusation is denied by Vittorini, who claims that "the outstanding characteristic of Pirandello's thought is that of being constantly close to life. . . . In Pirandello , . . the two planes of reality, that of the actual and that of the imaginary life, are tragically fused into one."[32]

Tragic though they may be, his dramas contain many humorous passages, but the laughter which they provoke is usually hysterical, grotesque, or satirical. Lander MacClintock says that Pirandello "is such a humorist as laughs only to keep from weeping at the disillusionments of life and the crudity of existence."[33]   According to Pirandello himself, the humorist should adopt the motto of Giordano Bruno: "*In tristitia hilaris, in hilaritate tristis* — Hilarious in sadness, sad in hilarity."[34]

Having found no solution for the problems of life, Pirandello brings many of his plays to an end at a point which at first glance may seem to be *in medias res*. But their very inconclusiveness — their lack of either a happy ending or a tragic catastrophe — is his philosophical point, " 'that there is nothing to conclude, because it is so,' which is a conclusion itself."[35]

His Dramas. Vittorini divides the thirty-eight dramas into five groups: I, In the Wake of Naturalism; II, The Drama of Being and Seeming; III, Social Plays; IV, The Drama of Womanhood; and V, Art and Life.[36]   Among the most significant plays are *Right You Are if You Think You Are* (*Così è se vi pare*, 1918); *Six Characters in Search of an Author* (*Sei personaggi in cerca d'autore*, 1921); *Henry IV* (*Enrico IV*, 1922); *Tonight We Improvise* (*Questa sera si recita a soggetto*, 1932); and *All for the Best* (*Tutto per bene*, 1937).

By far the best known of these dramas is *Six Characters in Search of an Author*.   It is a good illustration of Pirandello's ideas and methods, for it is concerned with the grotesque sorrows of humanity and with the relation of the ideal (in the brain of the author) to the real (in the lives of the characters).   The Six Characters (a father, a mother, and four children) appear before a company of Actors, state that they are incomplete creations of the author's brain and ask the Actors to give them reality by performing the drama implicit in their (the Characters') lives.   The Actors acquiesce, and the Characters agree to re-enact their past existence.   In the first scene of the re-enactment, the Father leaves his wife after he has had one Son by her; he encourages her affair with his secretary, by whom she thereafter has three children.   After the death of the secretary, the family disappears, and the Father becomes lonesome.   The second scene shows the Father in a bawdy house seeking to buy the services of his Step-daughter (whom he does not recognize).   The actions are so shameful that the Characters forget that they are participating in a mere re-enactment, and they also rebel at the Actors' ineffective attempts to reproduce their lives.   In the final scene the Characters are seen in the home of the Father, who now regards his life as dull and useless; the Son is morose and indifferent to his Mother, whom he makes miserable; the Step-daughter, despite her shame, is arrogant and offensive; the Little Girl is drowned in a pool; and the Adolescent shoots himself.

Pirandello's aesthetic and philosophical conclusions — if they may be so called — are that art can never be more than a dim and imperfect representation of reality and that life is hopelessly tragic.

Bibliography for Modern Italian Literature

Bush, Douglas. *The Renaissance and English Humanism*. Toronto: University of Toronto Press, 1939.

Collison-Morley, Lacy. *Modern Italian Literature*. Boston: Little, Brown and Co., 1912.

Everett, William. *The Italian Poets since Dante*. New York: Charles Scribner's Sons, 1904.

Fletcher, Jefferson Butler. *Literature of the Italian Renaissance*. New York: Macmillan Co., 1934.

Foligno, Cesare. *Epochs of Italian Literature*. Oxford: Clarendon Press, 1930.

Gardner, Edmund G. (ed.). *Italy: A Companion to Italian Studies*. London: Methuen and Co., 1934.

Garnett, Richard. *A History of Italian Literature*. New York: D. Appleton and Co., 1898.

Hulme, Edward Maslin. *The Renaissance, the Protestant Revolution, and the Catholic Reformation in Continental Europe*. Revised ed. New York: Century Co., 1920.

Hutton, Edward. *Giovanni Boccaccio*. London: J. Lane, 1910.

Kennard, Joseph Spencer. *The Italian Theatre*. New York: W. E. Rudge, 1932. 2 vols.

Krutch, Joseph Wood. *Five Masters*. New York: J. Cape and H. Smith, 1930.

Kuhns, Levi Oscar. *The Great Poets of Italy*. Boston: Houghton, Mifflin Co., 1903.

Lucas, Henry S. *The Renaissance and the Reformation*. New York: Harper Brothers, 1934.

MacClintock, Lander. *The Contemporary Drama of Italy*. Boston: Little, Brown, and Co., 1920.

Petrarch, Francis. *Some Love Songs of Petrarch*. Translated and edited by William D. Foulke. London: Oxford University Press, 1915.

———. *Sonnets and Songs*. Translated by Anna Maria Armi, with an introduction by Theodor E. Mommsen. New York: Pantheon, 1946.

45

————. *The Sonnets of Petrarch.* Translated and edited by Joseph Auslander. London: Longmans, Green and Co., 1932.

Phelps, Ruth Shepard. *Italian Silhouettes.* New York: A. A. Knopf, 1924.

Riccio, Peter M. *Italian Authors of Today.* New York: S. F. Vann, 1938.

Sellery, George Clarke. *The Renaissance: Its Nature and Origins.* Madison, Wis.: University of Wisconsin Press, 1950.

Smith, Winifred. *The Commedia dell'Arte: A Study in Italian Popular Comedy.* New York: Columbia University Press, 1912.

Snell, Frederick J. *The Fourteenth Century.* New York: Charles Scribner's Sons, 1899.

Symonds, John Addington. *Renaissance in Italy,* Part I, *The Age of Despots.* New York: H. Holt and Co., 1881.

————. *Renaissance in Italy,* Part IV, *Italian Literature.* New York: H. Holt and Co., 1888. 2 vols.

Thompson, Stith, and John Gassner. *Our Heritage of World Literature.* New York: Dryden Press, 1942.

Vittorini, Domenico. *The Drama of Luigi Pirandello.* Philadelphia: University of Pennsylvania Press, 1935.

Weatherly, Edward H., and Others. *The Heritage of European Literature.* Boston: Ginn and Co., 1948–1949. 2 vols.

Part Two
Modern French Literature

3
The Renaissance[1]
(1494–1600)

Historical Background.   When Charles VIII of France invaded Italy
in 1494, what he saw (according to Jules Michelet[2]) was as much a
discovery to him as America had been to Christopher Columbus two
years earlier.   During the fourteenth and fifteenth centuries wars,
plagues, and famines had all but prohibited intercourse with foreign
countries and had discouraged literary and cultural activity; consequently medievalism, which had very nearly spent its force, had
still not been replaced by the social and intellectual currents which
had for a hundred and fifty years been so strong in Italy — the
currents known as the Renaissance.   To be sure, some knowledge of
Petrarch and Boccaccio had come to France, and many Italian silk
merchants had brought some of the humanistic attitude to Lyons by
1450 or 1460.   But it was not till the period of the so-called Italian
Wars (1494–1525) that the Renaissance really arrived in France.
Noblemen and soldiers of Charles VIII and Louis XII (who led
an expedition into Italy in 1500) were deeply impressed with Italian
culture and elegance, and they wished to reproduce it in their own
country.   Francis I (who reigned 1515–1547), the "Father of the
French Renaissance,"[3] gave an immense impetus by patronizing
literature and the arts and especially by bringing into France many
Italian artists, scientists, and men of letters — for example, Leonardo
da Vinci, Andrea del Sarto, and Benvenuto Cellini.   Francis I also
greatly increased the Royal Library, which became the nucleus of
the great Bibliothèque Nationale; and in 1530 he established a new
institution of learning, the Collège des trois Langues,[4] where Greek,
Latin, Hebrew, and mathematics were taught.   During this king's
reign three other colleges came into existence: Trinité Collège at
Lyons (1529), the Collège de Guyenne at Bordeaux (1533), and the
Université de Nîmes (1539).

Francis I's sister, Queen Marguerite de Navarre (known also as
Marguerite d'Angoulême, Marguerite de Valois, and Marguerite

d'Alençon), was an equally enthusiastic sponsor of the new learning. She attracted to her court many men of letters, whom she infected with her zeal and whom she persuaded to do a great deal of reading, writing, and translating (especially of Plato, Dante, Boccaccio, and Ficino). She herself wrote some prose and a large amount of poetry (see below).

The successors of Francis I were also great exponents of Italian Renaissance culture. The queen of Henry II (who reigned 1547–1559) was Catherine de' Medici of the famous Florentine family; she filled her court with Italians. And her sons, Francis II (who reigned 1558–1559), Charles IX (who reigned 1560–1574), and Henry III (who reigned 1574–1589), were thoroughly imbued with Italian culture. Toward the end of the century, however, there was a strong nationalistic reaction against that culture.

Opposed to the humanistic currents were the religious reformers, of whom the most important was John Calvin. Although the majority of French people never adopted Calvin's stern views and although humanism triumphed over the Reformation in France, the reformers were far more influential there than in Italy and succeeded in infusing into French literature "a moral purpose and a high seriousness which it lacked south of the Alps."[5] In the last half of the century the clash between the Protestants and the Catholics became violent; eight religious wars were fought between 1562 and 1598. The worst single incident was the massacre of Saint Bartholomew's Day (1572), when many Protestants (Huguenots) were slain by zealous Catholics at the instigation of Charles IX; this massacre strengthened the reaction against Italian influence. In 1598 Henry IV brought the wars to an end by the famous Edict of Nantes, which granted to the Protestants liberty of conscience, permission for schools, permission to hold public office, and many facilities for worship.

General View of the Literature. The literature of the French Renaissance had many of the characteristics of Italian Renaissance literature. Individualism, humanism, a spirit of adventure, and a careful attention to form and technique were usually evident.

Miss Butler divides the era of the Renaissance in France into four parts: (1) 1494–1515, The Period of Origins; (2) 1515–1550, The National Period; (3) 1550–1572, The Italian Period; and (4) 1572–1598, The Age of Montaigne.[6]

In The Period of Origins no literature of importance was written. At the beginning of The National Period, the so-called "Grands Rhétoriqueurs" ("Great Rhetoricians") were dominating poetry; as the name suggests, they emphasized technique, rhetoric, and intricacy of versification and of rhythm. They were opposed by CLÉMENT MAROT (*c.* 1497–1544), who aimed at simplicity, clarity, and elegance. The poetry of MARGUERITE DE NAVARRE falls into this period. Her best poems are either religious or personal; her *Prisons* (*Les Prisons*) is an allegorical poem in which Christianity and Platonism are blended, and her *Mirror of the Sinful Soul* (*Miroir de l'âme pécheresse*) is a series of theological discussions. Finally (among the poets of The National Period) there were the members of the School of Lyons — neo-Platonists and Petrarchists, who produced no great poetry. In prose there were, in addition to several translations of Greek and Italian works, the great masterpieces of Rabelais and Calvin, and Marguerite de Navarre wrote the *Heptameron*, a collection of short tales modeled on Boccaccio.

The Italian Period is dominated by the *Pléiade*, a group of poets who stressed the importance of the ancient Greek and Roman classics and who attempted successfully to defend and enrich the French language.

Montaigne was, of course, the greatest figure in the last period of the Renaissance. During that period there were also two disciples of the *Pléiade:* PHILIPPE DESPORTES (1542–1606) and GUILLAUME DU BARTAS (1544–1590), whose *Semaine* (an epic about the Creation) influenced Anne Bradstreet, Milton, Thomas Moore, and Byron. The religious troubles of the time inspired both poetry and prose; the most notable pieces are by AGRIPPA D'AUBIGNÉ: *The Tragic Ones* (*Les Tragiques*) — seven cantos of poetry giving the Protestant view of the religious wars — and the *Menippean Satire* (*Satire Menippée*), a piece of religious and political satire written by Catholics but supporting the moderate party and preferring a French Protestant to a foreign Catholic as king of France.

Drama became important about the middle of the century.

RABELAIS

François Rabelais (*c.* 1494–1553), satirist and humorist, was born at Chinon in Touraine. From about 1509 till 1524 he was a Franciscan monk in the monastery of Fontenay le Comte, where he studied Greek. In 1524 he changed to the Benedictine order — probably because it was less narrow and pedantic than the Franciscan. Before long, however, he gave up the cloister entirely and became a priest. In 1530 he began the study of medicine at Montpellier, and two years later was an assistant at the hospital in Lyons. The following year he became physician to Jean (later Cardinal) du Bellay and went with him to Rome. He returned to Montpellier, received his doctor's degree there in 1537, and began practice in Lyons. About 1546 or 1547 he moved to Metz — probably driven there because of his writings. In 1550 he was given the parish of Meudon, which apparently he held till his death three or four years later.

Works.

THE GREAT AND INESTIMABLE CHRONICLES OF THE GREAT AND ENORMOUS GIANT GARGANTUA (*Les Grands et inestimables chroniques du grand et énorme géant Gargantua**). An anonymous chapbook which appeared in 1532. It seems likely that Rabelais was the editor rather than the author of this work, which gives the genealogy of Gargantua, a giant in the service of King Arthur; the whole book is a burlesque of the romances of chivalry.

THE DEEDS AND HEROIC SAYINGS OF THE GOOD PANTAGRUEL, SON OF GARGANTUA (*Les Faits et dits héroiques du bon Pantagruel, fils de Gargantua*). A continuation of *The Great and Inestimable Chronicles*, published in late 1532 or 1533, by "Alcofribas Nasier" (an anagram of François Rabelais). This work, which was later to become Book II of the whole series, recounts the birth and education of the hero, and it introduces his servant and companion Panurge, a prototype of Don Quixote's Sancho Panza. The book discusses many burning questions of the day; it ridicules again the chivalric romances; it derides pedantry; and it upholds the Renaissance ideas of education.

THE INESTIMABLE LIFE OF THE GREAT GARGANTUA, FATHER OF PANTAGRUEL (*La Vie inestimable du grand Gargantua, père de Pantagruel*). In 1534 Rabelais apparently felt that the chapbook of 1532 was an unworthy predecessor of *The Deeds and Heroic Sayings* and so completely recast it, under this new title. This work, too, he signed Alcofribas Nasier. The revision gives an account of Gargantua's birth, education, and visit to Paris, where he steals the

* The French custom of capitalizing only the first words of titles will be observed throughout this Part.

bells of Notre Dame to hang around his horse's neck. Again Rabelais attacks the old type of schooling and upholds humanism. He also attacks war in his account of the battles between Grandgousier (Gargantua's father) and Picrochole. One of the most important parts of the book is that which tells about Gargantua's building of the Abbey of Thélème, a sort of Utopia, in which the only rule is "Do what thou wilt" ("Fais ce que voudras"). It is highly significant, however, that the Thélèmites are never idle; their lives are distinguished by freedom plus activity plus cheerfulness in the face of adversity — Rabelais' own philosophy. The liberality of the rules of the Abbey reflect the author's own aversion for the strict monastic life of his youth.

BOOK III (*Le Tiers Livre*). In 1546 Rabelais wrote (and signed with his own name) Book III, devoted almost entirely to the "knotty problem" of whether Panurge should marry. He asks numbers of people, but none are able to give a satisfactory answer. Finally the court fool suggests that he consult the Oracle of the Holy Bottle ("Dive Bouteille"). This book is more serious and trenchant than the earlier ones — less youthfully enthusiastic. It contains a broad treatment of sex and a medievalistic indictment of woman. Rondibilis, a physician, seems to be speaking for Rabelais in this passage: "When I say 'woman,' I mention a sex so fragile, so variable, so changeable, so inconstant and imperfect that Nature seems to me — speaking with all honor and reverence — to have been deprived of that good sense (with which she formerly created and formed all things) when she created woman."[7]

BOOK IV (*Le Quart Livre, c.* 1552–1553). This tells of the voyage of Pantagruel and Panurge — to Cathay and India via the Northwest Passage — to find the Holy Bottle. They visit a series of islands, in each of which some human foible is held up to ridicule.

THE SOUNDING ISLE (*L'Île sonnante;* Book V). Brought out in 1562, about eight or nine years after the death of Rabelais. Although Rabelais' authorship has been doubted, most scholars now think that the book was made up of scraps and notes which Rabelais left in manuscript. In this last portion of the tale, Panurge and Pantagruel visit more islands, including the Sounding (or Sonorous) Isle, which represents Rome; and they engage in more adventures. Finally Lanterne (Study) leads them to the long-sought Oracle of the Bottle, where, in answer to their question, they hear only one word: "Drink!" — "which interpreted means: drink deeply of life, truth, and knowledge, but which, as Panurge points out, leaves him as wise as he was before on the subject of his marriage."[8]

Summary of Criticisms. There is both much to blame and much to praise in the works of Rabelais. On the adverse side of the ledger, it may be said that there are many coarse and obscene passages. In order partially to explain these passages, one must take into consideration the great difference between the tastes and sensibilities of the French people in the time of the Renaissance and those of twentieth-century Americans. Furthermore, Rabelais' coarseness and obscenity never lead to immorality; their excesses either leave one unmoved or excite to disgust. A second accusation is that Rabelais usually — but not always — lacks a reverence for lofty and spiritual matters.

There is much to be said, on the other hand, in praise of Rabelais. In the first place, one must admire his prodigious learning. "The vast erudition of the Renaissance is literally there on the printed page. The wonder is that it is so well fused, so flowing, so much a part of the common purpose. Titanic is the suitable word."[9] In the second place, Rabelais exposes many real evils — the evils of hypocrisy, pedantry, narrowness, cruelty, bigotry, intolerance, and many others. In the third place, the characterization is extraordinarily well done, especially of Panurge, who "has almost all intellectual accomplishments but is totally devoid of morality. He is a coward, a drunkard, a lecher, a spiteful trickster, a spendthrift, but all the while infinitely amusing."[10] Finally — and most important — there is the broad humanity of Rabelais' message. His works are "an affirmation of life itself: the resolve to live it and the courage to see it through. For experience alone can keep us sound and sane; whereas speculation, abstraction, monastic rule, and self-abnegation — when placed in control — wreck Nature and are its negation."[11] Rabelais' philosophy — "Pantagruelism" — may be defined as "humor. . . . It consists in the extension of a wide sympathy to all human affairs, together with a comprehension of their vanity."[12] Or, to use Rabelais' own words: "To laugh is a privilege peculiar to man" ("Rire est le propre de l'homme").

CALVIN

John Calvin or Jean Caulvin (1509–1564) was born at Noyon in Picardy. He studied theology at the Sorbonne and law at Orléans and Bourges. Early in his life he was converted to Protestantism, and in 1534 he fled to Basle in Switzerland, where he became a dictator of theocracy. Two years later he published the Latin version of his greatest work, *The Institutes of the Christian Religion*, which he translated into French (*L'Institution de la religion chrétienne*) in 1541. After a visit to Italy, he settled in Geneva, where he lived most of the remainder of his life.

For two reasons *The Institutes* is of the greatest importance. First, it has had the profoundest influence on theological thought. John Knox, the Puritans, Milton, Bunyan, and Jonathan Edwards are only a tiny percentage of those who have been affected. The cornerstones of Calvin's beliefs may be outlined as follows: (1) predestination, (2) original sin (that is, innate wickedness and perversity of man), (3) omniscience and omnipotence of God, (4) God's election of the few (to heaven) and damnation of the many, (5) salvation by God's grace alone, and (6) superiority of faith to good works.

The second reason for Calvin's importance (and the reason he is of special interest to students of literature) is that *The Institutes* is "a landmark in the history of French prose. . . . It is the first piece of close reasoning in the French language, and its admirable method and style have caused F. Brunetière to call it '*le premier de nos livres qu'on puisse appeler classique.*'"[13] It is a masterpiece of lucid and orderly thinking; and its style is terse, precise, plain, vigorous, and — often — eloquent.

Calvin and his contemporary Rabelais are antipodes. Whereas the latter is the embodiment of humanism, Calvin is "the very incarnation of the Reformation."[14]

THE PLEIAD

In the middle of the sixteenth century, when Italian and humanistic influence was at its height, a group of young poets, led by Pierre de Ronsard, launched a movement for the improvement of the French language and French literature. The manifesto of their views, *The Defense and Glorification of the French Language* (*La Défense et Illustration de la langue française*, 1549), written by Joachim du Bellay (below), is in two parts. The first part scoffs at those who insist on employing Latin for serious writing and defends French as a suitable language for literary and philosophical composition. The second part aims at improving the vernacular tongue, and the best way, it proclaims, is to read and imitate the ancients, especially Homer,

Virgil, and Horace.   It suggests abandoning medieval literary forms (e.g., the rondeau and the ballade) and returning to the ancient ones (e.g., the epic and the ode).   This part of the manifesto urges also following the style of the old classics.

The young poets who espoused and put into practice these views were known as the Pleiad (La Pléiade).*   Its members were Pierre de Ronsard, Joachim du Bellay, Ponthus de Thyard, Étienne Jodelle, Remi Belleau, Antoine de Baïf, and Jean Dorat.†

Although the Pleiad have been accused of blind adoration of the classics — even of the inferior works of the ancients — of bookishness, of allowing erudition to smother some poems, and of lack of self-restraint, the literature of France is indebted to them for several great achievements.   They succeeded in ennobling and elevating the language, they exalted poetry and the poet's mission, they popularized the sonnet in France, and they laid the foundation for the classical literature of the seventeenth century.

PIERRE DE RONSARD (1524–1585).   Ronsard, "Prince of Poets," was born at the Château de la Poissonnière near Vendôme. After studying a short while at the Collège de Navarre in Paris, he became a page, first to the Duc d'Orléans and later to Madeleine de France, whom he accompanied to Scotland when she married James V.   He remained in Scotland about two years and in England about six months.   After returning to France, he accompanied several noblemen on diplomatic missions and seemed destined himself to become a diplomat, when he was stricken with deafness. Thereupon he took holy orders, but soon devoted most of his energies to the study of Latin and Greek.   Along with Antoine de Baïf he studied for about six years under the great humanist Jean Dorat — part of the time at the Collège de Coqueret, where he knew du Bellay, Jodelle, and Belleau.   After 1550 he divided his time between Paris and Touraine.   He was always a great favorite of the monarchs — Henry II, Francis II, Charles IX, and Henry III.

Works.   As leader of the Pleiad, Ronsard took as his models the Greek and Latin epic and lyric poets and Petrarch.   Versatile and prolific, he wrote poetry of almost every sort except dramatic.   His

* The name was borrowed from a group of Alexandrian poets of the third century B.C., among whose members was Theocritus.   This earlier group had, of course, taken its name from the constellation.

† Various authorities list different members.   All, however, agree on the first four named.   Other poets thought by some historians to have been members are Peletier, Des Autels, and La Péruse.

works may be divided into three distinct periods: (1) from 1550 to 1560, "the innovating epoch of Hellenistic and Petrarchian imitation";[15] (2) from 1560 to 1574, when he "is the official court poet . . . the *poète oratoire*. . . .";[16] and (3) from 1574 to 1584, the period of his tranquil retirement, when he writes some calm poetry about nature and love.

His most important works are as follows:

ODES (Books I–IV, 1550; Book V, 1552). On the whole, unsuccessful imitations of Pindar. "In trying to reproduce the sentiment and sing the modern equivalents of the old demi-gods and heroes, Ronsard crammed his poems with historical and mythological allusions, resulting in a noble but quite superfluous disorder. . . ."[17] The *Odes* were, nevertheless, popular in Ronsard's own day.

LOVE POETRY. Ronsard's love poetry often is filled with a mild melancholy — a wistful regret that beauty is so short-lived and that life itself is so short. He wrote several groups of love poems:

Loves of Cassandra (*Amours de Cassandre* or *Amours de P. Ronsard,* 1552). A collection of 181 sonnets, addressed to Cassandre Salviati of Blois. These show some influence of Horace, but are chiefly Petrarchistic.* They generally lack originality but have some exquisite lines. Along with the *Loves of Marie* they established Ronsard's fame and won for him the unofficial title of "*Prince des poètes français.*"

Loves of Marie (*Amours de Marie* or *Continuation des Amours,* 1555–1556). These are indebted to Anacreon, Theocritus, and Petrarch. They are addressed to Marie Dupin, a village girl of Anjou, and, like Petrarch's sonnets to Laura, celebrate the beloved before and after her death. They are somewhat deeper in feeling than the *Loves of Cassandra,* but still rather shallow.

Sonnets for Helen (*Sonnets pour Hélène, c.* 1574–1584). A series of sonnets to Hélène de Surgères, the maid of honor to Catherine de'

* "The characteristics of Petrarchism were: Forced metaphor and similes running into each other, so that often the original subject of interest was quite lost to view; constant allegory, not of personified qualities as in the Middle Ages, but of hearts driven to and fro like barks in distress; over-indulgence in mythological allusions, so that the explanations of commentators seemed often necessary; repeated antitheses and, later, *pointes;* laments of the unhappy lover and complaints about the cruel coquette who makes him suffer agony so long that he seems to take joy in his woe; elaborate and sensuous descriptions of the beauty adored" (Wright, pp. 194–195).

Medici.   The poems are among Ronsard's more original, personal, and sincere work.

POLITICAL POETRY.   During the first of the civil wars of religion (1562–1563), Ronsard wrote (in alexandrines) three "Discourses" in support of the Catholics: *Discourse on the Miseries of the Times* (*Discours des misères de ce temps*), *Continuation of the Discourse* (*Continuation du discours*), and *Remonstrance to the People of France* (*Rémontrance au peuple de France*).   Here he discards mythology and speaks sincerely, powerfully, and sometimes ironically.

AN EPIC: *THE FRANCIADE* (1372).   "A dull epic."[18]   Ronsard wrote only four of the proposed twenty-four books of an epic which was intended to relate the origins of the French people.   His models were Homer and Virgil; his principal source was the *Illustrations of the Gauls and Singularities of Troy*, by the minor poet Jehan Lemaire de Belges (1473–1525).   The *Franciade* was a complete failure, because it was artificial and lacked "an unquestioning feeling of human destiny to guide it."[19]

Evaluation.   Ronsard's greatest faults are prolixity and an eruditeness which often leans toward pedantry.   His merits are versatility, liveliness, skill in rhythm and meter (later French poetry is indebted to him for his metrical experiments), and an occasional genuine lyricism.   He is poorest in his odes and epic, best in his amorous and political poetry, where he gives vent to his own emotions.

Three of his best known single poems are "Darling, Let's Go See if the Rose" ("Mignonne, allons voir si la rose") — an excellent expression of the *carpe diem* theme; "When I Have Gone Twenty or Thirty Months" ("Quand je suis vingt ou trente mois"); and "When You Are Very Old" ("Quand vous serez bien vieille") — an admirable sonnet to Hélène.

JOACHIM DU BELLAY (1525–1560).   Next to Ronsard the greatest of the Pleiad, he was born at Liré in Anjou.   After studying law for a short time at Poitiers, he met Jacques Peletier and Ronsard, became a member of the Collège de Coqueret, and devoted himself to literature.   Like Ronsard, he became deaf (1549); and like Rabelais, he went to Rome with Jean du Bellay, his kinsman (1553).   He returned to France in 1557 and died there of apoplexy when he was only thirty-five years old.

In addition to his famous *Defense and Glorification* (above), du Bellay wrote "the first sonnet-sequence in the French language"[20] — *The*

Olive (*L'Olive*, 1550), a rather close imitation of Petrarch and Ariosto which contains a considerable amount of Platonic epistemology. *The Antiquities of Rome* (*Les Antiquités de Rome*, 1558)[21] celebrates the former glories of the Eternal City; and *The Regrets* (*Les Regrets*) satirizes and laments the contemporary corruption of Rome.

MONTAIGNE

Michel Eyquem, Seigneur de Montaigne (1533–1592), was born at Périgord, one of eleven children. His father, a rich merchant of wine and fish, was endowed with a considerable amount of originality and ambition; he was also an enthusiastic humanist. Michel's mother was of Spanish-Jewish descent. At the age of six the boy was sent to the Collège de Guyenne at Bordeaux, which he attended till 1546. For several years after leaving Bordeaux, he studied law, probably at Toulouse (1547–1554). In 1568 his father died and Michel succeeded to the family estate and his father's title. For seventeen years he spent an active life as a soldier, courtier, and traveler; and for four years (1581–1585) he served as mayor of Bordeaux. In 1585 he retired to the Château de Montaigne, where he spent the remainder of his life reading, writing, revising, and publishing. He died of a quinsy (grippe).

Works.

TRAVEL JOURNAL (*Journal de Voyage*, 1574). Montaigne wrote an account of a trip he made through Switzerland, Germany, and Italy. It is remarkable mainly for its dullness — in contrast to his essays.

ESSAYS (*Essais*).

Dates of Publication. In 1580 Books I and II were published. New editions were brought out in 1582, 1587, and 1588. The definitive edition (107 essays) was edited in 1595 — three years after his death — by his *fille d'alliance*, Marie de Gournay.

Nature and Content. The *Essays* are, as their name indicates, "attempts" — that is, expressions of the author's multifarious opinions. They appear to be made up of marginalia and notes jotted down while Montaigne was reading (he was a voracious reader and had a library of about a thousand books). The purpose of the essays is self-exploration: "I myself am the matter of my book. . . . It is myself that I depict."[22] But he also explores humanity at large, of which he feels himself merely a typical representative, a microcosm.

Unlike Rabelais and Calvin, Montaigne maintains no one point of view, but instead gives many points of view in different essays. Although there is no consistency in his mental attitude, some historians and critics have found a progression from stoicism to skepticism and on to dilettantism as one goes from his earlier essays to the last ones. Others have defended him by holding that he is not a dilettante but simply an intellectually honest, conservative inquirer, who prefers not to pass final judgment on anything till all the facts are in. His motto is "Que sais-je?" ("What do I know?"). His skepticism (most fully expressed in "The Apology of Raymond Sébond," II, 12) is never bitter — nearly always wise, tolerant, and sane.

Evaluation. Montaigne's essays have been censured for dilettantism (discussed above), disregard of grammatical correctness, and utter lack of order, plan, and consistency. They have been praised — and universally read — for their spirit of inquiry and especially for their revelation of the author's self.

Montaigne's influence has been very great. His skepticism has affected Pascal, Robert Burton, Thomas Browne, Rousseau, and Nietzsche; his diction (through the Florio translation, 1603) was repeated by Shakespeare; his attitude was adopted by Lamb; and his form — the essay, which he invented — has been copied by Bacon and many later writers.

DRAMA

The medieval forms of drama were still flourishing in the early years of the sixteenth century. The Pleiad and the humanists, of course, were eager to replace them with classical tragedy and comedy, and both Catholics and Protestants objected to the profane elements in the mysteries. In 1548 an edict by the Parlement relegated the sacred mysteries to the provinces. The rise of classical drama began soon afterward. Some secular mysteries, moralities, and farces continued, however, till 1599.

Tragedy

Between 1537 and 1550 both Italians and Frenchmen translated into French some of the tragedies of Euripides and Sophocles. It was Seneca, however, whose techniques were followed.

Étienne Jodelle (1532–1573). Jodelle composed the first regular tragedy in French. That tragedy was *Cléopâtre* (1552), which covers about the same material as the fifth act of Shakespeare's *Antony and Cleopatra*. Jodelle's drama has almost no action, but it employs the classical devices of division into five acts, observance of the unities, use of a chorus, and restriction of the number of characters. Jodelle's second tragedy, *Dido the Suicide* (*Didon se sacrifiant, c.* 1558) has similar characteristics.

Robert Garnier (1534–1590). Garnier wrote eight tragedies, most of them on classical topics (e.g., *Hippolytus* [*Hippolyte,* 1573], *Mark Antony* [*Marc Antoine,* 1578], and *Antigone* [1585]). He lets dialogue replace some long speeches (such as are found in Seneca's and Jodelle's plays), he increases the action and the number of characters, he injects an element of real conflict into the plot, and he makes "some attempt at psychological treatment."[23]

Antoine de Montchrétien (*c.* 1575–1621). Montchrétien wrote six plays which have a smoother style and more polished diction than those of Garnier, but which are dramatically inferior. The best of these plays is *The Scotchwoman, or Mary Stuart* (*L'Écossaise ou Marie Stuart,* published 1601).

Comedy

As Seneca was the model of the earliest tragedy, so Plautus and Terence were the classical dramatists who set the style for French comedy; and after 1570 a strong Italian influence was perceptible.

The comic playwrights of the Renaissance made four steps forword in French drama. They learned (1) "to divide comedies into acts and scenes . . .," (2) "to bring the author in touch with his audience by means of prologue . . .," (3) "to work out a comic intrigue or to twist and then unravel an imbroglio . . .," and (4) "to substitute prose for the traditional octosyllabic line of farce."[24]

The most significant writers of comedy are ÉTIENNE JODELLE (above), who wrote the first French comedy as well as the first tragedy, PIERRE LARIVEY (*c.* 1540–1611), and ODET DE TURNÈBE (died *c.* 1585). Jodelle's *Eugène* (1552) is a rather farcical account of how a roué tricks the stupid husband of a not-too-virtuous young woman. Larivey wrote twelve plays in prose, noteworthy for their lively and witty dialogue. His comedy, *The Ghosts* (*Les Esprits,* 1579) has been called "the best sixteenth-century comedy in French."[25] Turnèbe's *Contented Ones* (*Les Contents, c.* 1584) has received highest praise by another critic. Miss Butler calls it "the best comedy of the French Renaissance."[26]

4

The Seventeenth Century

Historical Background. The seventeenth century was the *grand siècle* for France. She became the leading political and military power in Europe, and she enjoyed a period of intellectual and artistic activity which made her recognized as the cultural center of the world.

At the beginning of the century Henry IV (who ruled 1589–1610) blessed the country with an era of peace and prosperity. His Edict of Nantes (1598) put an end to internal religious squabbles, and the Treaties of Vervins (1588) with Spain and of Paris (1600) and Lyons (1601) with Savoy terminated the international strife of the sixteenth century. The last ten years of Henry's reign and the first twenty-five of the reign of Louis XIII (1610–1643) were an epoch of rest. Both Henry IV and Cardinal Richelieu, Louis XIII's prime minister, reduced the power of the nobles; and Richelieu virtually destroyed the political importance of the Protestants. In 1636 France's successful entry into the Thirty Years' War (1618–1648) enhanced her prestige abroad. The might and splendor of the monarchy reached its peak about 1685 under Louis XIV, who ruled 1643–1715. During the last thirty years of this reign, the fortunes of France began to decline. The revocation of the Edict of Nantes in 1685 drove thousands of Protestants abroad, and the nation thereby lost a great deal in wealth, culture, and technical skills. Louis' autocratic methods (he is reputed to have coined the expression "L'état c'est moi" — "I am the state"), his outrageous expenditures, and his dangerous political ambitions (which met with serious reverses in his last years) — all these caused Frenchmen as well as the people of other nations to breathe a sigh of relief when his long reign came to an end.

The first half of the seventeenth century was a period of transition from baroque literature to classicism. The trend was away from the enthusiasm, the individualism, and the skepticism of the sixteenth century and in the direction of rationalism, conformity, orthodoxy, order, refinement, and etiquette.

A strong influence on the refinement of society was the rise of the literary *salons*. Perceiving that the court of Henry IV was rather crude and lacking in the social graces, Catherine de Vivonne, Marquise de Rambouillet, invited to her own house the leading artists and men of letters as well as noblemen, so that literature and the arts became fashionable. Other noblewomen followed Madame de Rambouillet's example and welcomed learned and cultivated gatherings in their own *salons*. Eventually the activities of the *salons* led to the abuses of preciosity and affectation.

Conformity in intellectual matters was encouraged by the "centralized absolutism" of the courts of Louis XIII and Louis XIV. Both monarchs, as well as Richelieu, were patrons of literature, and as such were powerful forces for uniformity. The Royal Academy (granted letters patent by Louis XIII in 1635) became a steadying and restraining influence and gave dignity and prestige to men of letters.

The philosophy of René Descartes (1596–1650) had a deep and enduring effect on French thought of the seventeenth and eighteenth centuries. This skeptical thinker took as the foundation of his beliefs the one thing he could accept without doubting — his own existence ("Je pense; donc je suis" — "I think; therefore I exist"). His method was to reject all data except those supplied by observation and experience; then these data were to be tested by reason, which was the final criterion of truth. When applied to aesthetics and literature, these principles tended to identify truth and beauty — a tendency away from emotionalism, imagination, romanticism, and revelation and toward classicism.

A very different system of beliefs was also influential on some seventeenth-century thought. That system was Jansenism. Cornelius Jansen (1585–1638) agreed with Calvin about original sin and predestination but rejected the doctrine of justification by faith and emphasized the individual's personal relationship with God through the agency of the Catholic Church. Racine and Pascal were profoundly affected by Jansenism.

General View of the Literature. The same trends that have been noticed in the manners and attitudes of society and in philosophy may also be found in seventeenth-century literature. FRANÇOIS DE MALHERBE (1555–1628) violently attacked the mannerisms, affectation, and exaggeration of the later poets of the French baroque period — especially du Bartas and Desportes. His emphasis on impersonality, sobriety, clarity, and purity and precision of diction virtually killed lyricism and substituted eloquence.

The destructive criticism of Malherbe, the rationalism of Descartes, the absolutism of the court, the elegance and refinement of the *salons*, and the stabilizing influence of the Academy — all these combined to clear the way for French classicism (or neoclassicism), which was triumphant in the last half of the century. NICOLAS BOILEAU-DESPRÉAUX (1636–1711), who succeeded Malherbe as literary dictator, continued his predecessor's work of purifying diction; and — more important — he propounded the literary dogma of French classicism: "Truth alone is beautiful. The poet should imitate nature*, which is true. Reason should dominate the poet's work. Poetical expression should conform to good taste. Imitation of the ancients should be cultivated. . . . And originality is not novelty of idea, but . . . the perfect expression of an idea. . . ."[1] "Nature seen through the eyes of reason and expressed in the forms of antiquity, this, in a condensed form, was his literary creed."[2] Boileau's *Poetic Art* (*Art Poétique*) was of immense influence in England as well as in France, and his supreme importance as the literary dictator of neoclassicism can hardly be exaggerated.

During the last few years of the century the classical spirit and the influence of the old classics dwindled. The famous Quarrel of the Ancients and the Moderns (1687–1715) (over whether the ancient authors were superior to the modern ones) succeeded in showing that reason and tradition are not identical (as the French classicists maintained), and the Quarrel also directed attention to "the idea of progress, i.e., 'the idea that civilization has moved, is moving, and will move in a desirable direction.' "[3] Eventually this idea was accepted without questioning, and this acceptance led to eighteenth-century intellectual and emotional individualism.

As might be guessed, little good lyrical poetry was written in the seventeenth century. The most important forms were satire, the drama, and the fable. There were, in addition, the pastoral romance *Astrée*, by HONORÉ D'URFÉ (1568–1625); the heroic romances of LA CALPRENÈDE (1614–1663) and of GEORGES (1601–1667) and MADELEINE (1607–1701) DE SCUDERY; the Jansenist *Thoughts* (*Pensées*) of BLAISE PASCAL (1623–1662); the brilliant and bitter

* For the French as well as the English neoclassicists, the word *nature* denotes man's nature, the whole universe, and the system of laws by which the two are governed.

Maxims (*Maximes*) of FRANÇOIS, DUC DE LA ROCHEFOUCAULD (1613–1680); the learned and historically significant letters of MARIE, MARQUISE DE SÉVIGNÉ (1626–1696); the satirical novel of ANTOINE FURETIÈRE (1619–1688); the psychological novels of MADAME DE LA FAYETTE (1634–1693); the eloquent and sonorous sermons of JACQUES BOSSUET (1627–1704); the character sketches of JEAN DE LA BRUYÈRE (1645–1696); and the narratives and critical works of FRANÇOIS DE LA MOTHE FÉNELON (1651–1715).

DRAMA
Tragedy

At the end of the sixteenth century French tragedy was a dull and lifeless thing made up principally of oratory. In 1599 Alexandre Hardy (*c.* 1570–1631) came to Paris and introduced some important reforms: he did away with the chorus and long declamations, and he substituted action and spectacle. In 1634 *Sophonisbe*, by Jean de Mairet (1604–1686), strictly observed the three unities. Two years later Corneille's *The Cid* caused a violent controversy over whether a play should violate the unities and decorum. The "regulars," backed by the Academy and the *salon* of Madame de Rambouillet, won; and the neoclassic "rules" were thereafter followed by most dramatists, including Corneille.

PIERRE CORNEILLE (1606–1684). Born at Rouen, he studied law and actually practiced it for more than twenty years, but his greatest interest was always the theater. *The Cid* (1636), although it was bitterly attacked, made him famous, and he wrote many other well-received tragedies, comedies, and tragicomedies during the following twenty-four years. He became a member of the Academy in 1647. After 1660 several of his plays were unsuccessful; the complete failure of *Suréna* in 1674 led him to cease writing for the stage. Ten years later he died poor and almost forgotten.

Dramatic Theories. Corneille's age "was an age of action, of strength, of rapid and simple decisions; when men were struggling to realize an ideal, and intelligence and will-power were in the ascendency. Of such a view of humanity, the dramas of Corneille are the quintessence. . . ."[4] He conceived of tragedy as a psychological study, a portrayal of the conflict of man's will and some strong passion. Man's reason directs his choice of actions, and then his will — often opposed by his own emotions or by the wills of others — attempts to put those actions into effect. "The glorification of reasoned will-power is the motive of all Corneille's tragedies."[5] Love plays comparatively little part in these tragedies; what love there is is controlled by the reason.

Corneille draws most of his subjects from history and from classical mythology. When dealing with a historical topic, he does not feel compelled to adhere strictly to fact, but makes whatever changes are necessary to carry out his dramatic purpose. Furthermore, he declares that "the subject of a beautiful tragedy should not be probable."[6] In other words, the protagonist should be heroically rather than realistically portrayed. Somewhat like Marlowe, Corneille is concerned with the extraordinary, the superlative, the tremendous; and he has little interest in the average human being.

Style and Technique. Corneille's diction is well adapted to his themes; it is noble, eloquent, grandiose, and sometimes bombastic. His dramas, like those of Hardy, are full of action. After the Quarrel of *The Cid* he attempted to observe the unities, but such restrictions were galling to his genius. His plots are generally well motivated, and the unstable situation which is the core of each plot arises naturally out of the conflicts of his characters' wills. These characters are drawn with bold rather than subtle strokes, and they "arouse admiration rather than pity, for their power of resistance is stronger than their capacity for suffering."[7]

Specific Plays. In addition to eighteen tragedies, Corneille wrote eight comedies and seven tragicomedies (which are sometimes called merely tragedies). *The Liar* (*Le Menteur*, 1643) is his best comedy; the best of his tragedies are summarized below.

THE CID (1636). Actually a tragicomedy, but grouped along with the tragedies. This is one of the few dramas of Corneille in which romantic love plays an important part, and even here it is no irresistible passion which sweeps all else before it. The story concerns the love of Chimène and Rodrigue, the hero of the great Spanish epic (see Vol. I). Like Romeo and Juliet, the lovers suffer from a feud between their fathers. To avenge an insult to his own father, Rodrigue kills Chimène's father. Chimène then asks the king to execute Rodrigue; the king appoints a champion to battle against Rodrigue, but Rodrigue is victorious. Moved by his valor, Chimène relents and forgives; her future wedding to Rodrigue is implied.

HORACE (1640). This tragedy tells the story (derived from Livy) of the Horatii and the Curiatii, two feuding Roman families bound together by love and marriage. Horace slays his own sister for cursing the patriotism which led Curiace, her beloved, to his death. This play, unlike *The Cid*, observes the unities.

CINNA (1640). Another Roman play, it depicts the internal struggle of Augustus Caesar over whether to punish or to forgive Cinna and his conspirators. Caesar's magnanimity wins.

POLYEUCTE (1641 or 1642). Still another Roman play, this time glorifying religion. Pauline, the wife of the Christian martyr Polyeucte, is wooed by Sévère, her former sweetheart. The devoutness and self-abnegation of Polyeucte, however, completely win her over to himself and to God; and she then leads others to Christianity.

Estimate. Many shortcomings of Corneille's tragedies have been pointed out by his critics. It has been said that his plays lack verisimilitude, that they violate propriety and good taste, that they abound in bombast, and that many lines are banal and grotesque. The dramatist's admirers, however, claim that these defects are forgivable when one remembers his inevitable high moral purpose, his nobility, and his magnificence. Though his dramas are of uneven workmanship, one must judge him by his most successful efforts. He "was both the creator of classical French tragedy and [at his best] 'the greatest romantic poet of France.' "[8]

JEAN RACINE (1639–1699). Racine was born at La Ferté-Milon. Both his parents died while he was a young child, and he was reared by his grandmother. In 1649 he began to attend the Jansenist elementary school known as the Collège de Beauvais. When he was fifteen, he transferred to the Jansenist school at Port-Royal, where he remained till 1658. Then he entered the Collège d'Harcourt in Paris and studied philosophy. In the gay capital he soon made the acquaintance of La Fontaine and several actors and actresses. In 1660 or 1661, fearing that he might be corrupted, his aunts decided that he should go to Uzès to study theology under his uncle. After two years of this uncongenial pursuit he returned to Paris. He was welcomed into the circle of La Fontaine, Molière, and Boileau. Now he began to write plays. His first, *The Thébaïde*, was produced at the Palais-Royal in 1664; this was soon followed by *Alexandre le Grand* (1665). These were fair, but it was not till the production of *Andromaque* in 1667 that he became famous. Other plays followed in quick succession: *The Pleaders* (*Les Plaideurs*, 1668), his only comedy, which is an entertaining satire (indebted to Aristophanes' *Wasps*) on courts, judges, and legal procedure; *Britannicus* (1669); *Bérénice* (1670); *Bajazet* (1672); *Mithridate* (1673); *Iphigénie* (1674); and *Phèdre* (1677).   In 1673 he was elected to membership in the Academy.   After the production of *Phèdre* he apparently became convinced that drama was an immoral influence, renounced it completely, and became one of the royal historiographers.   It was not till 1689 that he wrote another play, *Esther*, at the instigation of Madame de Maintenon, mistress of Louis XIV; this was followed in 1691 by another biblical drama, *Athalie*.   The last few years of his life were made melancholy by a coolness (probably caused by Racine's Jansenism) on the part of the king, who had hitherto been his enthusiastic patron for about a quarter of a century.

Style and Technique.   Although Corneille was Racine's model in the first two tragedies, the younger playwright thereafter began to throw off the Corneillian influence; and in his later tragedies his style and technique are in almost every way antithetical to those of his former master.   Whereas nearly every one of Corneille's dramas is complicated and comprehensive, each of Racine's is simple and concentrated.   Corneille's tragedies abound in physical action; Racine's are almost static.   Corneille has a miserable time trying to observe the unities; Racine considers them no restriction at all. Corneille's plays are lacking in verisimilitude and probability; Racine's "are true to life even when they are not true to fact."[9] Corneille delights in demonstrating the clash of the will against external circumstances and against the wills of others; Racine restricts his field to the emotional struggle taking place within the human heart.   In Corneille's dramas love plays little part; in nearly all of Racine's the tender passion is the main motive force. Corneille's diction is colorful and flamboyant; Racine's is quiet and commonplace.   And finally, whereas Corneille's protagonists are extraordinary, strongwilled, coolly rational, almost superhuman figures, Racine's heroes and heroines are human beings — subject to the storms of passion common to the average man.

"Singleness of purpose is the dominating characteristic of the French classical drama, and of Racine's in particular."[10]   His policy is to allow his tragedy to begin well along in the story — very near a great emotional crisis.   The action is kept simple and free of irrelevancies, and it is subordinated to characterization.   He shows us every indecision, every emotion, every pang in the heart of the protagonist.   It is in this psychological probing that he achieves *vraisemblance*, which (he tells us in the preface to *Bérénice*) is the principal aim of tragedy.

Racine draws his stories from mythology, the Bible, and ancient Greek, Roman, and Oriental history.* Most of his protagonists are women, for it is their emotions that he is best at analyzing.

Specific Plays.

ANDROMAQUE (1667). Here Racine treats the themes of motherly love and of passion. After the fall of Troy, Andromaque, the widow of Hector, pretends love for the Greek Pyrrhus in order to save her son Astyanax. But Pyrrhus, though enamored of Andromaque, is engaged to Hermione, who loves him with a consuming passion. Hermione, in turn, is beloved by Oreste. When Pyrrhus threatens to kill Astyanax unless Andromaque marries him, she agrees but secretly plans suicide. Hermione persuades Oreste to murder Pyrrhus, then renounces him for the murder, and commits suicide. Oreste goes mad.

The portraits of the maternal Andromaque and of the passionate and jealous Hermione, "a splendid tigress,"[11] are the chief attractions of the play.

BÉRÉNICE (1670). A drama "so devoid of physical action or violence as to be a tragedy only by implication . . . a dramatic elegy."[12] The Roman Emperor Titus reluctantly gives up his beloved Bérénice because Roman laws forbid the emperor's marrying a foreigner.

This play is the best illustration of Racine's inventive ability — "to make something out of nothing" ("faire quelque chose de rien") — to sense a powerful dramatic situation in an emotional crisis which would ordinarily be overlooked. The entire plot was created out of six words from Suetonius: "Titus, unwilling, relinquished Queen Berenice, [also] unwilling" — or, as Victor Hugo arranged them: "Act I, *Titus;* Act II, *reginam Berenicen;* Act III, *invitus;* Act IV, *invitam;* Act V, *dimisit.*"[13]

PHÈDRE (1677). A tragedy of jealousy and remorse, it is a complete reworking of Euripides' *Hippolytus*, with a shift of emphasis from the chaste and cold Hippolytus to the passionate and jealous Phèdre, who, though she remains Greek, is given "a searching, Jansenist conscience."[14] The play was at first a failure because the

---

* *Bajazet* is an exception. The titular Turkish hero lived in the early seventeenth century.

Duchesse de Bouillon engaged Pradon, a rival playwright, to compose another *Phèdre* and present it at the same time; the Duchesse filled the front rows in Racine's theater with hissers and those in Pradon's theater with a vociferous claque.   Despite its initial failure, Racine's *Phèdre* is usually regarded as his masterpiece.   "As an expression of passion on a grand scale it is probably unsurpassed in literature."[15]

ATHALIE (1691).   This play retells the biblical story (II Kings 11) of Athaliah, the daughter of Ahab and Jezebel, who, when her own son Ahaziah is slain, kills all the "seed royal" (except Joash, who escapes) and takes over the throne.   Six years later Athaliah herself is slain and Joash is restored as sovereign.

Racine makes the story an illustration of how God (who is the protagonist of the drama) wreaks vengeance on the wicked — especially on the enemies of the Church and the state.   The power of the drama lies not only in its moral earnestness (enhanced by the setting in the temple at Jerusalem) but also in the superb characterizations of the "frenzied Athalie"; of Joad (Jehoiada), the fanatical priest of Jehovah; of Mathan (Mattan), the wily priest of Baal; and of the "bluff general Abner."

Although only Boileau among Racine's contemporaries recognized the excellence of *Athalie*, later critics have become increasingly aware of its merits.   Nitze and Dargan proclaim it Racine's "most perfect dramatic poem,"[16] and Wright says that it is his "greatest drama and the culmination of French classicism.   His poetry here reaches its supreme melody and harmony."[17]

Summary of Criticisms.   Many English critics have refused to rank Racine as a very great dramatist.   They have considered him dull, cold, and narrow in range; they have objected to the dearth of action in his plays; and they have found his vocabulary too small. Saintsbury, one of his severest critics, condemned him for ingratitude toward his friends and benefactors and thought him guilty of imitativeness — "an almost unlimited capacity for writing from models."[18]   Elsewhere[19] this same critic indicted him as a mere "poetical artificer" who "does not even attempt the highest poetry at all" and who takes as his subject "only a narrow artificial and conventional fraction" of the world.

Most critics — not only French ones — have placed him at the head of all the literary artists of France.   They praise him for his inventiveness, for the careful construction of his plots, for his verisimilitude, and for the "elegance, precision, balance, harmony, purity, and polish"[20] of his style. They praise him for his diction, because "every word, every phrase, goes straight to its mark, and the impression produced is ineffaceable."[21] Most of all they praise him for his psychological penetration — his brilliant portraits of passionate people. At his best, "the imaginative grandeur of the loftiest poetry and the supreme force of dramatic emotion are mingled in a perfect whole" and earn for him "a right to walk beside Sophocles in the highest places of eternity."[22]

Comedy

In the first half of the *grand siècle* French comedies were still farces — little more than adaptations of Spanish romances and of Italian *commedia dell'arte* and comedies of intrigue. After Jodelle and Larivey, Corneille and Racine wrote some comedies, but their genius was primarily in tragedy. It remained for Molière to write French comedy which would be placed beside the works of Shakespeare.

MOLIÈRE (stage-name of Jean Baptiste Poquelin, 1622–1673). He was born in Paris, where his father was an upholsterer and a *valet de chambre* to Louis XIV. In 1637 Jean was sent to the Jesuit Collège de Clermont, where he studied science, grammar, Plautus, and Terence. Six years later, renouncing his succession to his father's position in the royal household, he became an actor and impresario, and he formed a theatrical company, the Illustre Théâtre, with several friends, of whom three were members of the Béjart family. After a year or so of unsuccessful production, Molière had to be rescued by his father from a debtor's prison. From 1645 till 1658 he and his troupe made a barnstorming tour of the provinces, during which time he gained a great deal of valuable experience. In 1658 he returned to Paris, won the favor of the king and of Boileau, married Armande Béjart, and for fifteen years continued as a successful producer, playwright, and actor. Though extremely popular in most circles, he was under incessant attacks by the clergy, physicians, courtiers, bores, and *précieuses* whom he ridiculed in his plays; only the protection and the patronage of the king saved him. In 1673 while playing the title role of his *Imaginary Invalid* (*Le Malade imaginaire*), he was stricken with a hemorrhage and died a few hours later.

Purpose. Molière claims that his purpose is "to represent in general all the defects of men, and principally of the men of our century."[23]

Sources. Although Molière finds most of his material in the society of his day, he is indebted to several literary sources for some of his content and also some of his technique. Plautus, Terence, Spanish drama and tales, Italian comedy, French fabliaux and fables, and earlier French comedy all proved useful.

Characteristics. Molière's drama is essentially a comedy of manners. Sometimes he relies on intrigue and sometimes on farcical predicaments, but most often he creates a comedy of character rather than of situation. He uses characterization to attack some common human weakness, most often some kind of hypocrisy. In order to make a character trait stand out, he uses exaggeration — almost caricature — and his characters are often types. Sometimes the result is bubbling laughter, but sometimes there is an admixture of pathos and of trenchant criticism — sometimes "an aftertaste of bitterness and sadness which is the reflection of Molière's own existence. . . . It was the tragedy of life amid its comedy that he tried to show."[24]

Specific Plays. Twenty-seven of Molière's comedies are extant. Some of the most significant are as follows:

THE AFFECTED MISSES[25] (*Les Précieuses ridicules*, 1659). Molière's first great comedy, it pokes fun at the preciosity and affectation of the ladies of the cultural *salons*, such as the Hôtel de Rambouillet. Two gentlemen, rejected as suitors because they do not make love according to the "cultivated" rules, disguise their servants as noblemen and have them pay court to the "affected misses." When the servants' vulgarity and boorishness are accepted as mere idiosyncrasies of the well-bred, the real lovers divulge their trick.

DON JUAN, OR THE FEAST OF PIERRE (*Don Juan, ou le festin de Pierre*, 1665). Really a tragicomedy on the subject of the loves of the famous hero of Spanish legend, whom Molière depicts as an arrogant, hypocritical, atheistic, and yet fascinating villain.

THE DOCTOR IN SPITE OF HIMSELF (*Le Médecin malgré lui*, 1666). One of Molière's four attacks on the hypocrisy of the medical profession.* The source of this rollicking farce is the old

---

* The other three are *Love as a Doctor* (*L'Amour médecin*, 1665), *Monsieur de Pourceaugnac* (1669), and *The Imaginary Invalid* (*Le Malade imaginaire*, 1673).

fabliau "The Peasant Doctor." Mistakenly believed to be a great physician, Sganarelle, a faggot-binder, is engaged to cure Lucinde of dumbness. When he discovers that the dumbness is merely feigned because Lucinde's father, Géronte, is trying to force her to marry somebody she does not love, Sganarelle secretely prescribes elopement. Lucinde and Léandre, her chosen lover, flee; and Sganarelle is exposed and condemned to be hanged. Unexpectedly Léandre learns that he has inherited a fortune; Géronte accepts him as a prospective son-in-law, and even Sganarelle is forgiven. The humor — and satire — of the play lie in the faggot-binder's ability to hoodwink the gullible Géronte and his messengers. The dénouement is entirely unmotivated.

THE MISANTHROPE (*Le Misanthrope*, 1666). "Molière's nearest approach to tragedy,"[26] " 'the French Hamlet.' "[27] Alceste, the sensitive though somewhat cross-grained and impatient hero, loves the worldly coquette Célimène, who "will not give up the world for the sake of Alceste; and he will not take her on any other terms. And that is all."[28] The play ends with Alceste left melancholy and disillusioned. Many critics have seen in the play a reflection of Molière's own unhappy marriage to Armande Béjart in 1662.

TARTUFFE, OR THE IMPOSTOR (*Tartuffe, ou l'imposteur*, 1664; reworked 1669). Molière's attack on hypocrisy in religion. When first produced in 1664, the play so antagonized the clergy that they had it prohibited. It is not, however, a criticism of religion in general but an exposé of the impostors who pretend piety for their own selfish purposes. Tartuffe deceives the wealthy Orgon and his mother, Madame Pernelle, into believing him (Tartuffe) devout and self-sacrificial. The deception is so complete that Orgon deeds all his property to Tartuffe and plans to make his daughter, Mariane, marry the impostor. Orgon is finally made to see the light when he catches Tartuffe making love to Elmire, Orgon's own wife. A royal decree restores his property and punishes Tartuffe.

THE MISER (*L'Avare*, 1668). A delightful comedy based on the character of the rich miser Harpagon, who practices usury on his own son Cléante; tries to marry Mariane, Cléante's betrothed; and attempts to make his own daughter Elise marry Anselme, a rich old man whom she does not love. His plans are all defeated when Cléante's valet steals the miser's money-box and refuses to return it unless Cléante is permitted to marry Mariane. Elise is also allowed to marry Valère, her beloved, when he is revealed as the son and heir of Anselme.

Summary of Criticism. Most of the defects of Molière's comedies are the results of hastiness. Perhaps their most obvious fault is their weak dénouements. Far too often, as in *The Doctor in Spite of Himself*, Molière clears up a bad predicament by introducing an entirely unmotivated and fortuitous event. Furthermore, there are too many improbable situations, too much trickery, too much farce. And finally, the minor characters are not individualized. They reappear too often — under various names — and they resemble each other too much.

All these shortcomings, however, are of minor significance when one considers Molière's many excellencies. In the first place, there is his profundity. Boileau calls him "the great contemplator," and Nitze and Dargan add — "which is another way of saying that he looked human nature through and through. . . . With a flash he penetrates the absurdity and presents it to us in a phrase, an attitude, a gesture."[29] His second merit is common sense, combined with sanity. His point of view mingles tragedy and comedy in such a way as to achieve balance, measure, and universality. A third merit is naturalness or verisimilitude, especially in dialogue. Fourth, there is his superb gallery of characters. Although most of these characters are types and are therefore lacking in complexity, they are drawn with consummate skill and force. Tartuffe will probably be remembered longer than Dickens' Pecksniff, and Harpagon as long as Shakespeare's Shylock. Finally, as a critic of society, Molière is unsurpassed. "As a painter of the foibles of his age, Molière is supreme . . . and is not excelled in pure comedy by Shakespeare,"[30] and "it is no exaggeration to say that . . . he is . . . the greatest comic genius among the moderns."[31]

THE FABLE

JEAN DE LA FONTAINE (1621–1695). Born at Château-Thierry. After a desultory early education, supplemented by wide independent reading, he tried, in turn, to learn theology and law at Rheims, but soon gave up each pursuit. In 1647 he returned to his native town, succeeded his father as Master of Waters and Forests, and married the sixteen-year-old Marie Héricart. He neglected — and at length deserted — both his family and his occupation, and in 1657 went to Paris, where he was received into the circle of

Racine, Molière, and Boileau. In 1683 he was elected to membership in the Academy. During most of his Parisian life he was the protégé of various patrons: Fouquet, the minister of Louis XIV; the Duchesse d'Orléans; the Duchesse de Bouillon; Madame de la Sablière; and finally Monsieur d'Harvart, at whose home he died.

La Fontaine wrote some lyrics, elegies, ballades, epistles, comedies, and clever though licentious tales (*Contes*); but the only works for which he is famous are the *Fables*.

FABLES. (Books I–VI, 1668; Books VII–XI, 1678; Book XII, 1694). There are 241 fables in all, varying in length from a few to a few hundred lines. All are in verse, of which La Fontaine changes the line length and rhyme scheme, even within one poem. "It is *vers libre* in the sense merely that each Fable has its particular verse, each idea or mood its particular line — adapted, in all cases, to the thought to be expressed."[32]

Like Boccaccio and Molière, La Fontaine invented few of his subjects. He borrowed from Aesop, Phaedrus, and whatever other Oriental, Greek, Latin, and French sources suited his fancy. His originality lies in his technique: "A suggestion of background or landscape, a swift narrative interspersed with dramatic dialogue, a dénouement often in one line, a maxim of worldly wisdom or a brief personal reflexion, and the tale is told or rather the scene is enacted before our very eyes."[33] Unlike Aesop, who appears to have written each of his apologues mainly for the sake of its moral, La Fontaine seems to have used each moral as a mere excuse for telling the tale. "From an apologue, tending to an express moral, he converted the fable into a *conte*, in which narrative, description, observation, satire, dialogue have an independent value, and the moral is little more than an accident."[34] The "wordly wisdom" is the rationalistic, realistic wisdom of the age of Louis XIV.

Many of the characters of the fables are animals. But these are neither real animals nor human beings disguised as beasts; "they are animals with the minds which human beings would certainly have, if one could suppose them transformed into animals."[35]

The following are some of the best and most characteristic fables: (1) "The Oak and the Reed" ("Le Chêne et le roseau"), in which the oak twits the reed for its fragility but is uprooted by a storm, before which the reed saves itself by bending with the wind; (2) "The Wolf and the Lamb" ("Le Loup et l'agneau"), in which the wolf proves that might is right by eating the lamb; (3) "The

Grasshopper and the Ant" ("La Cigale et la fourmi"), in which the ant offers no pity to the frivolous grasshopper who dances all summer but who starves when winter comes; and (4) "The Cobbler and the Financier" ("Le Savetier et le financier"), in which the poor but happy cobbler is given a large sum by the rich man. The former is so fearful that the money will be stolen that he is no longer happy and therefore returns the money to the financier.

5

The Eighteenth Century, the "Enlightenment"

Historical Background. For France the eighteenth century was a period of great changes. In 1700 and even in 1715, when Louis XIV died, the monarchy was still strong; Catholicism was still by far the predominant religion; classicism still prevailed in aesthetics; and rationalism was still the touchstone of philosophical thought. By 1800 the king and queen had been beheaded; France had been proclaimed a republic; deism had made serious inroads into Catholicism; classicism was virtually dead and had to some extent been superseded by romanticism; and rationalism, found wanting, had given way before emotionalism.

The accession of Louis XV was an occasion of great rejoicing. The people of France had high hopes that the extravagance and despotism which had characterized the preceding reign were now at an end. Their hopes were disappointed. Oppression of the common people by the clergy and the nobility was continued, and the burden of taxation remained almost insupportable. Governmental matters, especially those pertaining to finances and international diplomacy, were conducted with the grossest ineptitude. Participation in three wars — the War of the Spanish Succession (1701–1713), the War of the Austrian Succession (1741 and 1748), and the Seven Years' War (1756–1763) — cost France vast sums of money, many men, a great deal of national prestige, and all colonial possessions.

Louis XV, who during the first few years of his reign was the "well beloved" ("bien aimé"), was at length recognized to be "a selfish, irresponsible, and dissolute being, who shamelessly took as his motto, 'Après moi le déluge' "[1] ("After me the deluge"). His successor, Louis XVI, who ruled 1774–1789, was also at first hailed as a liberator. But he was weak, lazy, and ignorant; and Marie Antoinette, his wife, was frivolous and pleasure-bent. The people once more despaired of reform from within the monarchy.

The clamor for reform continually grew louder. It received a tremendous impetus from the writings of Rousseau, Diderot, and others who proclaimed the inherent goodness of man, the equality of all people, and the importance of the individual. In 1789 the people took matters into their own hands, stormed the Bastille (the symbol of despotism and oppression), deposed the king, and set up a republic. In 1793 the king was executed. Six years later Napoleon Bonaparte was made consul, and in 1804 he had himself crowned emperor.

In addition to governmental affairs, there were during the century several trends, conditions, and events of which note must be taken.

First, there was the trend of the intellectual, the philosophical, and the artistic to drift away from the court at Versailles, which could no longer offer them leadership. Once again the *salons* began to flourish. Now, however, they were more catholic in interest and less esoteric than in the days of Madame Rambouillet. Politics, science, economics, business, and practical philosophy were added to literature, art, and etiquette as the topics for discussion. Virtually all the literati were habitués of one or more of the *salons*. The cafés, too, became important gathering places for the best society of the day, who were eager to discuss current events and new theories.

The enthusiasm for — and dependence on — rationalism continued throughout most of the century. In science this belief led to the abandonment of many traditional ideas, to open-mindedness, and to much original investigation. In religion it led to deism* or to atheism. In philosophy it led to an apathy toward theoretical metaphysics and to an emphasis on practical ethics.

By the third quarter of the century Rousseau and others had begun to raise a doubt whether all questions could be answered purely by means of reason. Beginning with the premise that man is inherently good, they argued that his emotions as well as his reason could be relied on, that each individual was important, and that each individual was endowed with certain natural rights, including life, liberty, equality, fraternity, and the pursuit of happiness. These beliefs gave a great impetus to democracy and

---

* Deism is the belief in a benevolent God who made the universe, set it running according to a system of natural laws, and then allowed it to run without His interference. Immortality is the reward of the good. Deism rejects belief in miracles and special divine revelations, including divine inspiration of the Bible.

humanitarianism. Many thinkers, including Diderot and some of the other Encyclopedists, clung to rationalism but combined it with humanitarianism.

Two more tendencies during the century must be considered. One is the tendency of French thought, literature, and institutions to be influenced by foreign nations. The Huguenot refugees were the first to translate English books into French and to interest Frenchmen in English culture. Later, almost every eminent French writer except Diderot visited across the Channel, and Englishmen responded by visiting France. Horace Walpole, Burke, Gibbon, Bolingbroke, Chesterfield, and Hume were frequent attendants at the *salons*. In addition to these, Locke, Swift, Pope, Addison, Defoe, and Richardson were influential on French letters. German culture also began to make itself felt. Leibniz, Lessing, Schiller, Herder, and Kant were the most influential figures. And finally, the Italians Metastasio, Goldoni, and Alfieri had a considerable following in France.

Any survey of the tendencies of the Age of Enlightenment must mention the enormous role that women played in national affairs. The wives and mistresses of the kings (especially Madame de Pompadour, Madame du Barry, and Marie Antoinette) exercised a great deal of control over governmental and social matters; and the ladies who maintained the *salons* were the virtual arbiters of intellectual activities.

General View of the Literature. Unlike the literary productions of the seventeenth century, the literature of the Age of Enlightenment was more concerned with content than with form and technique. Much of it was utilitarian, purposive, and didactic. It "was dominated by a sceptical philosophy, a hatred of any form of authority or tradition, and an intense desire for political and social reform. . . . The watchwords of the age were reform, freedom of thought, and tolerance."[2] Seventeenth-century authors superseded the ancients as models, but classical forms and genres were still employed, and the rules of Boileau were not questioned. Wit and cosmopolitanism were frequent ingredients; and after the middle of the century "sensibility"* became popular.

Quite understandably, practically all memorable eighteenth-

* In the eighteenth century *sensibility* meant emotional sensitivity, especially with regard to the "noble" emotions of love, pity, generosity, and the like.

century French literature is prose. Voltaire, it is true, wrote many types of poetry, and at the end of the century ANDRÉ CHÉNIER (1762–1794) wrote some lyrical, philosophical, political, and satirical poems. But these were works of minor importance.

The literary giants of the age were Voltaire and Rousseau; their works will be discussed in detail below. For the other writers, a brief summary must suffice.

In the field of the essay, CHARLES-LOUIS DE SECONDAT, BARON DE MONTESQUIEU, (1689–1755) was one of the leaders. His *Persian Letters* (*Lettres persanes*, 1721) were satires on Parisian institutions and customs. Of more importance was his *Spirit of the Laws* (*De L'Esprit des lois*, 1748), an analysis of various governments which demonstrates that they are the results of the moral, economic, and physical conditions and that human laws are relative. Another famous essayist was GEORGES LOUIS LECLERC, COMTE DE BUFFON (1707–1788). He wrote a thirty-six volume *Natural History* (*Histoire naturelle*, 1749–1788) and a famous critical essay, a *Discourse on Style* (*Discours sur le style*, 1753), in which he advocates careful planning and plain diction.

Perhaps the most famous and certainly one of the most influential of all literary undertakings of the eighteenth century was the *Encyclopedia, or Practical Dictionary of the Sciences, of the Arts, and of the Trades* (*Encyclopédie, ou dictionnaire raisonné des sciences, des arts, et des métiers*, 1750–1777), in thirty-four volumes. Its editor-in-chief and principal author was DENIS DIDEROT (1713–1784), and among its chief contributors were nearly all the great men of the time — Voltaire, d'Alembert,* Rousseau, Montesquieu, Buffon, and many others. The *Encyclopedia* attempted to gather and systematize all knowledge about the sciences, arts, and trades. Its contributors used it, however, for attacking tyranny in all its forms and for championing individual liberty, human reason, and human perfectibility. The work played a very large part in forming the ideas which led to the French Revolution.

Most eighteenth-century French comedies were mediocre. There were four types:[3] (1) comedy of character, written chiefly by PHILIPPE NICOLAS DESTOUCHES (1680–1754); (2) sentimental psychological comedy, written principally by PIERRE DE MARIVAUX (1688–1763); (3) comedy of intrigue and manners, of whom the main composer was PIERRE-AUGUSTIN DE BEAUMARCHAIS (1732–

---

* Jean le Rond d'Alembert (1717–1783), mathematician and scientist.

1799) — author of *The Barber of Seville* (*Le Barbier de Séville*, 1772) and *The Marriage of Figaro* (*Le Mariage de Figaro*, 1778); and (4) sentimental and domestic comedy (*comédie larmoyante et domestique*), of whom the most famous authors were NIVELLE DE LA CHAUSÉE (1692–1754), DIDEROT, MICHEL-JEAN SEDAINE (1719–1797), and LOUIS SÉBASTIEN MERCIER (1740–1814).

Tragedy was even poorer than comedy. Besides Voltaire, only FRANÇOIS JOLYOT DE CRÉBILLON (1674–1762) is worth mentioning as a writer of tragedies. He composed nine melodramatic plays, memorable chiefly for their horror.

The French novel reached its maturity in the eighteenth century. The narratives of the Scudéry and of La Calprenède (p. 64) hardly deserve to be called novels. Perhaps it is accurate to say that the first French novelist was ALAIN RENÉ LE SAGE (1668–1747). His *Lame Devil* (*Le Diable boiteux*, 1707) is rather plotless but contains some excellent analyses of human characters; and his *Gil Blas* (1715–1735) is a real picaresque novel which traces the adventures of the wandering hero. MARIVAUX began two novels (both were finished by other authors) of which the main feature was psychological analysis of the characters; these were *The Life of Marianne* (*La Vie de Marianne*, 1731–1741) and *The Upstart Peasant* (*Le Paysan parvenu*, 1735–1736). L'ABBÉ PRÉVOST (1697–1763) wrote several enormous novels, but his fame rests on *The History of the Chevalier des Grieux and of Manon Lescaut* (*L'Histoire du Chevalier des Grieux et de Manon Lescaut*, 1731), the seventh installment of *Memoirs of a Man of Quality* (*Mémoires d'un homme de qualité*, 1728–1732); *Manon Lescaut* is "a story of fatal and overmastering passion, . . . one of the world's masterpieces."[4] The other noteworthy novelist of the period was Rousseau, whose works are discussed below.

Finally, there was the prose tale. Besides Voltaire, only one writer achieved distinction in that genre. That writer was BERNARDIN DE SAINT-PIERRE (1737–1814), a disciple of Rousseau and a precursor of romanticism. His *Paul and Virginia* (*Paul et Virginie*, 1787) is a sentimental tale full of exotic descriptions of nature.

VOLTAIRE

Voltaire,* or François-Marie Arouet, le jeune (1694–1778), " 'the personification of the Age of Enlightenment,' "[5] was born in

* The pseudonym *Voltaire* is probably an anagram of *Arouet l*[*e*] *j*[*eune*] — the *u* being equivalent (as in Latin) to a *V* and the *j* to an *i*.

Paris of a middle-class family. He was educated at the Jesuit Collège Louis-le-Grand. In 1717 he was thrown into the Bastille for two satires on the Regent which were falsely attributed to him. Later two of his comedies won him the favor of Queen Marie Leczinska, the wife of Louis XV. In 1725 he was again imprisoned in the Bastille, this time for an insult to the Chevalier de Rohan. Upon his release he fled to England, where he remained for about three years (1726–1729), and where he met most of the distinguished Englishmen of the day, e.g., the Walpoles, Congreve, Gay, Swift, Pope, Bolingbroke, Thomson, and Chesterfield. He was also deeply impressed with the philosophy of Newton and Locke and with the dramas of Shakespeare. The publication in England of his epic, the *Henriade* (1728), brought him considerable revenue, which was the beginning of the large fortune he was eventually to acquire.

After his return to France he published his *Philosophical Letters* (*Lettres Philosophiques*, 1734), in which he attacked the political, social, and religious institutions of France by contrasting them with those of England. The *Letters* were burned by the executioner, and Voltaire was again forced to flee. He took refuge at Cirey, the home of Madame du Châtelet; there he lived, except for occasional visits elsewhere, till the death of his benefactress (1749). In 1746 he was elected a member of the French Academy.

In 1750 he accepted the invitation of Frederick the Great of Prussia to come to Potsdam. At first he and the monarch were very intimate, but after a while their temperaments began to clash; and furthermore Voltaire engaged in some shady financial affairs and also quarreled with a court favorite. In 1753 he left Prussia for Switzerland, where he stayed five years, principally at Geneva. In 1758 he purchased an estate at Ferney in Burgundy, almost on the border between Switzerland and France. Here he spent the remaining twenty years of his life in incessant activity. In 1778 he went to Paris to witness the performance of his *Irène*. His reception was overwhelming, but the exertion was too much for him. Soon afterwards he died — only a few months before his eighty-fourth birthday.

Works. Voltaire was not only about the most versatile but also one of the most prolific of all authors who have ever lived. From his early childhood till almost the day of his death there poured from his pen a profuse stream of tragedies, comedies, histories, satires, tales, epics, epigrams, letters, essays — virtually every genre then in vogue. His total output runs (in two different editions) to ninety-seven volumes. Most of his major works fall into one of the following groups:

DRAMA. Voltaire's comedies are among his most unsuccessful efforts and merit no further comment. His tragedies, however, were considered by some contemporaries to be on a par with those of Corneille and Racine. Although in his youth he admired Shakespeare's tragedies, he later deplored their violation of the classical rules, and he himself stuck to "the seventeenth-century idea of concentration upon the passions of characters developed as types."[6] Some of his most representative tragedies are *Oedipe* (1718), on the old Oedipus legend; *Brutus* (1730), drawn from Roman history; *Zaïre* (1732), a study of jealousy, modeled to some extent on *Othello;* and *Mérope* (1743), based on classical mythology.

Few of his plays are actable today.

POETRY. Voltaire wrote all sorts of poems — odes, satires, narratives, epigrams, sonnets, madrigals, and epistles. His most ambitious poem is the *Henriade* (1728), an epic influenced by Virgil and based on the times of Henry IV (reigned 1589–1610). The poem contains some vivid accounts of the wars of religion; but it is "entirely lacking in grandeur, inspiration, and imagination,"[7] and it is decidedly artificial. Like most of his other works, the *Henriade* contains virulent attacks on superstition and fanaticism. Similar attacks appear in the *Poem on the Disaster of Lisbon* (*Poème sur le désastre de Lisbonne*, 1756). The lighter verse is characterized by grace, wit, and cleverness.

HISTORY. Voltaire was "among the first to conceive of history as material for the formulation of general ideas. . . . [He tried] to deduce the underlying principles which explain the past and give due proportion to hidden motives as well as to concrete phenomena."[8] He wrote history of three main types:

Biographical. The best example of this type is the *History of Charles XII* (*Histoire de Charles XII*, 1731). The author is more concerned with the character of the hero than with his military strategy.

Annalistic. The Century of Louis XIV (*Le Siècle de Louis XIV*, 1751) gives a great deal of information about the arts and sciences as well as about the king and his court. This work probably had more effect than any other history on the formation of world opinion about the seventeenth century in France.

Philosophical. The *Essay on the Customs and Spirit of the Nations*

(*Essaie sur les moeurs et l'esprit des nations*, 1756) is not only "an exposition of the tendencies and feelings of the human race at the different periods of its history and of the lessons to be derived therefrom,"[9] but also a violent attack on hypocrisy and tyranny of all kinds.   It was an important influence in fomenting the Revolution.

LITERARY CRITICISM.   Voltaire's theories and opinions about literature are scattered throughout many of his works, including his poetry, his histories, and his letters.   As a literary critic he is an "ultra-conservative pseudo-Classicist. . . .   Racine and Boileau are his deities. . . ."[10]   An important work devoted entirely to literary criticism is the *Commentary on Corneille* (*Commentaire sur Corneille*, 1764), which praises the dramatist but takes him to task for "submitting to petty fashions of taste and of language, many of which had not been accepted when the plays were composed."[11]

TALES.   It is Voltaire's short prose narratives (he wrote no long ones) that have been the most widely popular of all his writings. Every one of his tales has a purpose — moral, social, political, or theological.[12]   "The characters leave us cold because we cannot forget that they are merely the vehicles for conveying lessons of good sense."[13]   Furthermore, the plots are often poorly constructed and contain the most incredible adventures.   Yet the tales make delightful reading.   They are full of wit and satire — "satire of good sense impatient against folly, and armed with the darts of wit."[14] The two most famous tales are *Zadig* and *Candide*.

ZADIG, OR DESTINY (*Zadig, ou la Destinée*, 1747).   This tells how a righteous man of Babylon falls from prosperity to adversity and then regains prosperity.   The moral, like that of the Biblical book of Job, is that the ways of Providence are hidden from men.

CANDIDE, OR OPTIMISM (*Candide, ou l'Optimisme*, 1759). The most popular of all Voltaire's works, this is an attack on the optimism of the deists and especially of the German philosopher Gottfried Wilhelm von Leibniz (1646–1716).   The hero, Candide, and his Leibnizian mentor, Pangloss, suffer an incredible series of hardships, while Pangloss doggedly asserts that this is the "best of all possible worlds."   Candide himself is finally disillusioned and concludes that it is *not* the best possible world and that whatever is, is not necessarily right.   He decides that man's role is to bear ills bravely, to be tolerant, and to do the very best with what he has — "It is necessary to cultivate our garden."[15]   Here Voltaire is at his satirical best, and he takes a few shots at all his pet hates.   "Religion, political government, national peculiarities, human weakness, ambition, love, loyalty, all come in for the unfailing sneer."[16]

LETTERS. Voltaire was probably the world's most indefatigable letter writer. More than ten thousand of his epistles have been preserved, and more are continually being discovered. His seven hundred addressees ranged from the highest to the lowest people in Europe; among the most notable were Frederick the Great, Catherine the Great of Russia, Diderot, Rousseau, d'Alembert, Horace Walpole, and Goldoni. Although a few were obviously written for publication, the great majority were not and were therefore frank and spontaneous. All together they form an excellent autobiography and a priceless commentary on the eighteenth century.

Thought. Most of Voltaire's opinions have already been touched on. It is necessary to add that he was neither a deep nor an original thinker, but a clever assimilator and popularizer of other men's ideas. Moreover, he had no coherent system of belief; it has been said that his mind was a chaos of clear ideas. He was a destroyer and not a builder of systems. He valiantly smashed whatever idols he found to be false, but he was unable to set up true ones. He was a conservative in virtually everything but religion; there he was a liberal. He believed in a God who was a creator and a punisher of evil; but he assailed any religion that he felt to be guilty of superstition, intolerance, or persecution.* In conclusion, "though his social and political criticism was eminently destructive, preaching hatred of intolerance and oppression, the reforms he indirectly advocated were all within the sphere of practical politics, and could have been realized without a revolution."[17]

Estimate. Although Voltaire had no deep or positive philosophy, and although his eagerness for reason, truth, tolerance, and humanity often led to "window-smashing," he had a great spirit of "truth-seeking," and he was an inveterate enemy of hypocrisy, injustice, tyranny, fanaticism, and superstition. Despite the fact that in no single form of literature did he attain the first rank, his near-excellence in so many forms has assured him of a high and permanent place in French literature.

---

* His famous slogan "Écrasez l'infâme!" ("Crush the infamous thing!") "means not, as has been erroneously thought 'Crush Christianity,' but 'Crush persecuting superstition.' " (Saintsbury, *Short History of French Literature,* p. 451).

ROUSSEAU

Jean-Jacques Rousseau (1712–1778) was born in Geneva, Switzerland, of Protestant parents. His mother died at his birth, and during his first ten years he was reared by his romantic and impractical father, who was a watchmaker. In 1722 his father became entangled in an argument with a fellow-citizen and was forced to flee from Geneva. The boy was then sent to school to the pastor Lambercier at Boissy. Two years later he stopped school and served as an apprentice, first to a notary and then to an engraver. In 1728 he ran away, wandered in Savoy, embraced Roman Catholicism (which he later abjured), and then became footman to Madame de Vercellis. Between 1731 and 1740 he lived with Madame de Warens at Annecy and at Chambéry. For several years he supported himself as a tutor (in Lyons) and as a music-copyer and secretary (in Paris and Venice). In 1745 he formed a liaison with Thérèse le Vasseur, an ignorant servant girl, who (he claims) bore him five children; each of these he consigned to a foundling home as soon as it was born.

From 1741 to 1757 Rousseau was on friendly terms with Diderot and contributed several articles to the *Encyclopedia*. He became famous overnight for his *Discourse on the Sciences and the Arts* (below). The last half of his life was made up principally of writing, quarreling with one patron after another, and fleeing from place to place to escape real or imaginary persecution. In 1747 he became a member of the circle of Madame d'Épinay, who placed at his disposal the Hermitage, a cottage in Montmorency. A quarrel led to his departure in the winter of 1757–1758; he remained in the neighborhood, however, and there wrote most of his major works between 1758 and 1762. He stayed briefly at Yverdon, Motiers, and Île St. Pierre — all in Switzerland. In 1766, at the invitation of David Hume, he went to England, where he remained about a year and a half. After returning to France, he lived at various places, including Trye and Paris. He died at Ermenonville.

The last ten or fifteen years of his life were clouded by a mania of persecution.

Thought. Although Rousseau was neither a very original nor a very logical thinker, it was his theories and beliefs that established his fame and that were such important influences on democracy, the French Revolution, and the romantic movement in Europe and America.

Most of his theories stem from his Swiss-Protestant, Republican-bourgeois background. It is his conviction that man is fundamentally and inherently good and that he has been depraved by civilization, conventions, and social environment. It follows, then, according to Rousseau, that man's emotions and intuitions are trustworthy. External nature alone has escaped the ruinous influences of civilization, and it is therefore a suitable object of man's adoration.

These beliefs and the more specifically social, political, educational, and religious ones are contained in the works discussed below.

Works.

DISCOURSE ON THE SCIENCES AND THE ARTS (*Discours sur les sciences et les arts*, 1750). This essay won the prize offered by the Academy of Dijon for the best discussion of the question whether the sciences and arts had improved morals and customs. Possibly at the suggestion of Diderot, Rousseau took the negative and let fly his first great blast at civilization. The *Discourse* glorifies the simple life and the ancient Roman virtues.

DISCOURSE ON THE ORIGIN AND THE FOUNDATIONS OF INEQUALITY AMONG MEN (*Discours sur l'origine et les fondements de l'inégalité parmi les hommes*, 1755). A supplement to the discourse written five years earlier. Here Rousseau depicts the "noble savage" — natural man (such as the American Indian) in a state of primitive but blissful culture. Inequality arose when some man first began to lust for a little more property and a little more power than his fellows; and inequality led to corruption, oppression, and slavery.

JULIE, OR THE NEW ELOISE (*Julie, ou la nouvelle Héloïse*, 1761). An epistolary novel derived partially from Richardson's *Clarissa Harlowe* and partially from Rousseau's own amour with Madame d'Houdetot, the sister-in-law of Madame d'Épinay. As the title indicates, the plot somewhat resembles the affair of the famous medieval lovers Héloïse and Abelard: Julie becomes the mistress of Saint-Preux, her tutor. When the affair is discovered, Julie is forced to marry Monsieur de Wolmar, and her lover travels to help himself forget. When he returns, Julie almost gives herself to him again, but is prevented by her death.

The novel is to a large extent autobiographical and subjective. Rousseau reiterates his belief in the goodness of emotions and of individualism, and he condemns society rather than Julie or Saint-Preux for the lovers' misdeeds.

THE SOCIAL CONTRACT (*Le Contrat social*, 1762). In this philosophical treatise Rousseau vigorously expounds his belief in the individual's "inalienable rights" and in democratic government. Government, he says, is a "contract" entered into by the governed, who willingly surrender some of their rights for the good of the state. Law "is the expression of the 'infallible' general will,"[18] and each individual is equal before the law.

The treatise, the work of a Genevan rather than of a Frenchman, is inconsistent in its emphasis on individualism on the one hand and its insistence on the infallibility of the "general will" on the other, which, if carried to its logical conclusion, subordinates the individual to the state.

ÉMILE (1762). A didactic novel which contains Rousseau's theories about education and religion. Like *Julie*, it is semiautobiographical and subjective. Émile is reared as a "child of nature" — almost entirely without restraint or compulsion. He is encouraged to engage in physical exercise, and as an adolescent he is persuaded to read "historians of the soul," such as Plutarch, so that "his sentiments will be awakened."[19] Upon reaching adulthood he marries Sophie, "who has been trained mainly to please Émile."[20]

Despite the impracticality of Émile's education and despite Rousseau's own irresponsibility as a parent and incompetence as a teacher, the work was amazingly popular. It paved the way to the establishment of kindergartens and to the twentieth-century doctrine of "progressive education."

"The Profession of Faith of the Savoyard Vicar" ("Le Profession de foi du Vicaire Savoyard," Book IV) contains Rousseau's religious views, which have been called "sentimental deism." Rousseau believes in God, but bases his belief on emotion rather than reason. He finds God's spirit manifest in all nature.

This section of *Émile* was especially influential on the romantic authors of the next century, Chateaubriand and Wordsworth in particular.

THE CONFESSIONS (*Les Confessions*, written *c.* 1765–1770, published 1781–1788). A frank though inaccurate account of the first fifty-three years of the author's life. Although his purpose is to defend his own course of actions, he candidly tells about many of his follies and sins. The work is in the main a faithful revelation of

Rousseau's emotions. It is usually considered his masterpiece, and by some critics is regarded as one of the greatest books of confessions ever written.

Evaluation. As has been intimated above, it is as a propagator of ideas and not as an originator that Rousseau is so important. The times were ready for his message, and he delivered it to them vigorously and eloquently. His emotional appeal was so strong that people overlooked his false premises and his illogicality. His social and political theories were one of the main causes of the French Revolution; and — together with his individualism, his sentimentalism, and his love for nature — they caused him to be known as the father (Sainte-Beuve calls him the grandfather) of the romantic movement. Today, more than two centuries after the publication of his first discourse, his ideas are still exerting inestimable influence on people's thought.

6

The Romantic Age
1800–1842

Historical Background.* Many exciting political events which helped determine national thought and literature took place in France in the first half of the nineteenth century. As has been mentioned, Napoleon Bonaparte was made consul in 1799 and emperor in 1804. It soon became clear that he was not merely continuing a revolution which had once aimed at freedom from tyranny and oppression, but that he was waging an aggressive war of conquest. His fortunes continued to rise till his unsuccessful invasion of Russia in 1812. He met disaster again at the Battle of Leipzig (1813), was exiled to Elba (1814), but escaped (March, 1815) — only to lose his final battle at Waterloo (June, 1815). He was exiled again — this time to the island of St. Helena, where he died in 1821.

The Bourbons were restored to the throne in the person of Louis XVIII, who ruled from 1815 till 1824. He was succeeded by Charles X, whose despotic methods led to another revolution (July, 1830). France was proclaimed a constitutional monarchy, and Louis Philippe was called to the throne. Another revolution (1848) overthrew this monarchy, and the Second Republic was proclaimed. Louis Napoleon, a nephew of Napoleon I, served as president from 1848 till 1851. Then by a *coup d'état* he established himself as dictator, declared France an empire again, and was crowned Emperor Napoleon III in December, 1851.

The political unrest is, of course, reflected in the temper of the times. Both the failure of the French Revolution to establish and maintain a just and democratic government and the defeat of Napoleon I were inevitably followed by periods of disillusionment among many groups. The liberals and democrats were kept well in check by Bonaparte, and the reactionaries and monarchists triumphed after his fall. The general trend during the half-century,

* Although the romantic age may be said to have ended about 1842, it is more convenient to discuss the history of the first half of the century as a unit.

90

however, was toward liberalism, as shown in the overthrow of Charles X and of Louis Philippe.

There were conservatives and liberals in religion, too. The conservatives revolted against the deism and rationalism of the eighteenth century and reverted to Catholicism and mysticism. There were others who, impressed by the strides made in the natural sciences, turned away from orthodox religious beliefs and emotionalism and embraced materialism, mechanism, and perhaps atheism.

Belief in the innate goodness of man survived both the Revolution and Bonaparte; but now, through some waning of individualism, it was transmuted into humanitarianism.

One eminent thinker, AUGUSTE COMTE (1798–1857) combined humanitarianism with a firm trust in scientific methods to form the new "science" of sociology. Holding that only the knowledge gained by observation and experimentation was positive or real (positivism), he attempted to develop a science as well as a religion from his observations of human behavior. He rejected belief in all absolutes, and he held that the only way to improve conditions on earth was to strive increasingly to apply scientific methods to the study of human problems.

Other thinkers suggested various political, economic, and social schemes for bettering man's lot. Among the most noteworthy was CHARLES FOURIER (1772–1837), "an ultra-Rousseauist,"[1] who proposed breaking society up into small agricultural communities, where the passions and wills of men would be free. Some of his ideas were put into practice in the Brook Farm experiment in America. Another theorist was Pierre-Joseph Proudhon (1809–1865), also a Rousseauist, who advocated the abolition of private property and eventually — as soon as society was sufficiently benevolent — of government itself. A third reformer was Louis Blanc (1811–1882), who wanted to establish national workshops in order to improve labor conditions.

Such was the social, philosophic, and political *milieu* in which French *littérateurs* found themselves between 1800 and 1842.

General View of the Literature. The French Revolution and the Napoleonic wars retarded the romantic movement of which Rousseau and Saint-Pierre had been the harbingers. Napoleon I discouraged freedom of the press and tried to absorb the most talented men into his political or military machinery. Consequently, little literature of the first rank was written between 1800 and 1815. There were some political oratory and political journalism, but these hardly deserve to be called literature.

Romanticism began to blossom as soon as Napoleon fell, and it reached its height between 1827 and 1842. By the middle of the century realistic elements were making a strong bid for supremacy.

The meaning of romanticism is at the same time too complex and too familiar to justify more than the briefest treatment here. The following may be listed as its main characteristics: revolt against authority of all kinds, including all literary traditions and forms; faith in man, individualism, and personal liberty; love for nature; interest in the long ago, the far away, and the supernatural; giving of free reign to the emotions and the imagination; melancholy; cosmopolitanism; egoism; humanitarianism; and escapism.

The principal literary forms in vogue during the romantic period were lyric poetry, drama, the novel, the short tale, history, and literary criticism.

THE NOVEL

Professor Butler quotes Sainte-Beuve as designating Rousseau the grandfather, Saint-Pierre the uncle, and Chateaubriand the father of the romantic movement; and then she herself nominates Madame de Staël the aunt.[2] Perhaps it is accurate to say that the novels of Madame de Staël and Chateaubriand are the first really romantic pieces of French literature. All the novels of the first half of the century may be classified as sentimental novels, historical novels, novels of adventure, novels of manners, and realistic novels. The chief literary influences on the French romantic novel were Rousseau, Richardson, Sterne, Scott, and Goethe.

The Sentimental Novel

MADAME DE STAËL (née Anne Marie Germaine Necker, 1766–1817). The daughter of the great Swiss financier and prime minister of France, she was born in Paris. During her childhood she spent much time in her mother's *salon*, where she met many famous and brilliant guests and where she developed an early interest in literature. She became a thoroughly devoted Rousseauist. In 1792 the Reign of Terror forced her to flee to Geneva, but she returned to Paris in 1797 and set up her own *salon*. Her opposition to Napoleon led to her second banishment from Paris in 1803.

For ten years she traveled in Germany, Switzerland, Austria, and Italy. Especially impressed by the German romanticists, she wrote *On Germany* (*De l'Allemagne*, 1813), which earned for her a banishment from all France — not merely Paris. In 1815 she was once more allowed to return to Paris, where she spent the last two years of her life entertaining in her *salon* and editing some of her works.

Novels. Madame de Staël wrote two semiautobiographical, sentimental novels, both dealing with "heroines [who] are superior beings in conflict with their environment."[3] *Delphine* (1802), which is deeply indebted to Rousseau for its philosophy and its epistolary form, attacks the conventions, mores, and prejudices which blight the love affair of the heroine. The book depicts a misunderstood woman of spirit (*la femme incomprise*) who defies public opinions. *Corinne, or Italy* (*Corinne, ou l'Italie*, 1807) is a sentimental tale of Corinne, another *femme incomprise*, who releases her English fiancé from his engagement to her so that he can marry her half-sister. Corinne dies of a broken heart. The book contains many descriptions of the beauties of Italy and some clever discussions of the national characteristics of Englishmen, Italians, and Frenchmen.

Critical Works. Far more important than her novels are her two critical treatises. In the first, *On Literature Considered in Its Relation to Social Institutions* (*De la Littérature considérée dans ses rapports avec les institutions sociales*, 1800), she suggests a new method of criticism: one must not judge a work by an objective and absolute standard, but instead one must take into consideration the social, political, philosophical, and religious environment in which it was written. "In a word, Madame de Staël is the Montesquieu of literary criticism."[4] She suggests that the new social and political order resultant from the Revolution should produce a new sort of literature. The second critical treatise is *On Germany* (*De l'Allemagne*, 1813), in which she examines German customs, literature, philosophy, ethics, and religion. She pays special attention to Lessing, Goethe, Schiller, Herder, Kant, and Fichte, and she urges a closer intellectual relationship between France and Germany. Her enthusiasm popularized German romanticism in France and in other countries of Europe and was a most potent force in bringing about the French romantic triumph.

FRANÇOIS–RENÉ DE CHATEAUBRIAND (1768–1848). Chateaubriand was born in Saint-Malo in Brittany of a noble family. In 1791 he visited the United States, where he gathered material for *Atala* and *René*. The following year he joined the *émigré* army and later was wounded at Thionville (1792). He fled to England, where for seven years he earned a living as a teacher and translator. In 1798 he was reconverted to an ardent form of Christianity. In 1806–1807 he traveled in Egypt and the Near East. He became a member of the French Academy in 1811. After the restoration of the Bourbons he was active for several years (1815–1830) in political affairs. After 1830 he lived in retirement and wrote his *Memoirs*.

Works. It has been said that Chateaubriand wrote on only three topics: "Christianity, Nature, and himself."[5] Actually, all three of these appear in almost every one of his major works.

ABOUT NATURE. Like so many other romantics, he found solace in natural scenery; he was especially moved by "its grander and lonelier aspects, associating it with his woes and either adoring it for its beauty or cursing it for its indifference. His descriptions . . . are . . . subjective . . . and have a richness of color, a glow and a sense of mystery."[6] Like Rousseau, he saw in the Red Indian a pure, unspoiled child of nature, and he idealized him in his three works whose scenes are laid in America.

ATALA (1801). A short novel (or long tale) originally intended as part of *The Genius of Christianity* (below), but published separately and earlier. Chactas, a young Indian, falls in love with Atala, a Christian maiden who has saved his life. He agrees to allow himself to be converted to Christianity if she will marry him. But she has promised her dying mother to become a nun. The plot is resolved by Atala's suicide. The story is told by Chactas to René, a Frenchman. The tale is filled with violent romantic love. The style is majestic: the tone, melancholy.

RENÉ (1802). A sequel to *Atala*, published first as part of *The Genius of Christianity* and later (1805) as a separate tale. "The hero is another Chateaubriand, an ill-fated young Frenchman, who can find happiness neither in the civilization of Europe nor beyond the sea."[7] Here the turn is changed, and René tells Chactas, now an old man, about his own life — his unhappy boyhood; his affection and concern for his unfortunate sister, who finally becomes a nun; his futile attempts to find in travel some answer to the cosmic questions which torture his soul; and at last his journey into the American wilderness. "The *mal de René* consists in the perpetual disappointment which confronts insatiable desires, whether concerning the sympathy of women, the consolation of nature, or the venture of life as a whole."[8] This *"mal,"* derived from Rousseau and from Goethe's *Sorrows of Young Werther*, is characteristic not only of Chateaubriand but also of a great many of the romantic poets and prose writers of France, England, and Germany.

THE NATCHEZ (1826). A long "nature epic," as Chateaubriand calls it, in which the fortunes of René are continued. The moody hero marries an Indian maiden, who believes him to be a traitor to her tribe, the Natchez. Interwoven with this story is that of the massacre of the Natchez in 1727. Both threads of the story end in murder and suicide. The author has included many absurdly inappropriate epic conventions, such as invocations, ghosts, and the participation of both angels and Indian gods in the battles.

ABOUT CHRISTIANITY. Chateaubriand's Christianity is aesthetic rather than devotional. He was not especially interested in creeds and faith as such, but he deplored the drabness of deism and was "eager to restore the Christian religion generally and Catholicism in particular to that place in art and literature which since the Renaissance had been usurped by pagan mythology."[9]

THE GENIUS OF CHRISTIANITY (*Le Génie du Christianisme*, 1802). The work which brought to its author not only general acclaim but also the good will of Napoleon. The thesis of the work is that Christianity has "supreme emotional, imaginative, and artistic value, and . . . that this religion is the source and mainspring of all progress in the modern world."[10] He calls to witness the great Christian poems, such as Dante's *Divine Comedy* and Milton's *Paradise Lost*, and also the glorious Gothic architecture of the Middle Ages.

THE MARTYRS (1809). A prose epic on the subject of the persecution of the third-century Christians by Diocletian. Like *Atala* and *René*, it is full of local color and of glowing descriptions of natural scenes; and like *The Natchez*, it is marred by ludicrous epic paraphernalia. It contains, however, some valuable pictures of the ancient world.

ABOUT HIMSELF. Perhaps the topic that Chateaubriand was most interested in was Chateaubriand. Like Byron, he enjoyed his egoistic pessimism, and he liked to display it. *René* is largely a self-portrait; and his *Memoirs from beyond the Tomb* (*Mémoires d'outre-*

tombe, composed 1811–1841, published 1848–1850) "contain all of Chateaubriand, his beauties and defects, his power, egomania and puerilities."[11]   They give a fairly thorough account of his life, but they do not tell the whole truth; unlike Rousseau, he withholds or palliates some of the items which would be discreditable to him. He portrays himself as he wants the world to see him.   Nevertheless, the *Memoirs* are a valuable document of French romanticism.

Estimate. Though egoistic, egotistic, and affected, Chateaubriand imparted a great deal of charm and magic to his writings. It is true that his religion "lacked the subtle intimacy of Faith"[12] and that his descriptions of nature are sometimes merely splendid rhetoric, but he inspired in many men a real religious faith and a sincere love for natural scenery. "It may be said that the French imagination had lost its source, and that Chateaubriand rediscovered and restored it."[13] "He thus leads the Romantic movement in these important novelties: medievalism, the revival of aesthetic Christianity; the impassioned description of exotic nature; and the enthronement of the melancholy ego therein."[14] His style "is concrete, imaginative, and rhythmical to such a marked degree that he is rightly regarded as the founder of modern French prose. . . ."[15] Finally, "his range of ideas is not extraordinary; but vision, imagination, and the passion which makes the imaginative power its instrument, were his in a superlative degree."[16]

✔ **GEORGE SAND** (pseudonym of Amandine Aurore Lucie Dupin, Baronne Dudevant, 1804–1876). "The embodiment of the spirit of Rousseau,"[17] she was born in Paris, but spent most of her childhood at Nohant in Berry. From 1817 to 1820 she was educated at a convent in Paris, where she became fervently religious. In 1820 she returned to Nohant and soon lost some of her fervor. Two years later she married Baron Dudevant, a coarse but well-meaning squire, whom she left in 1831 and whom she later divorced. She went to Paris again; there she associated with a great many philosophers, authors, and musicians, including Alfred de Musset, Frédéric Chopin, and Franz Liszt. She participated in several of the utopian reform movements — for the emancipation of women, republicanism, and Fourierism. In 1860 she retired to Nohant, where she lived and wrote during the remainder of her life.

Works. Miss Sand wrote more than a hundred novels plus six volumes of letters. The novels fall into four rather distinct categories:

NOVELS OF LOVE (*c.* 1831–1837). These illustrate Rousseau's theories about the beauties and the goodness of romantic love. Here Miss Sand follows the example of Madame de Staël (p. 93) in depicting the "misunderstood woman" (*femme incomprise*). She revolts against "loveless marriage, male tyranny, and the subjugation of women,"[18] and she pleads for feminine individualism and equality. In *Jacques* (1834), for example, a "magnanimous" husband commits suicide so that his wife and her lover may be happily united; and *Mauprat* (1837) might have been entitled *The Taming of a Boor.* Other novels in this group are *Indiana* (1831), *Valentine* (1832), and *Lelia* (1833).

NOVELS OF POLITICAL AND SOCIOLOGICAL RE-FORM (*c.* 1839–1849). The stories of this group reflect Sand's interest in the various movements of the 'thirties and 'forties which aimed at the regeneration of humanity. In *The Miller of Angibault* (*Le Meunier d'Angibault*, 1845) the pauper hero refuses to marry his wealthy sweetheart till she gets rid of her fortune, so that "they may follow together the new religion of brotherhood."[19] *The Sin of Monsieur Antoine* (*Le Péché de Monsieur Antoine*, 1847) advocates the communalism of Fourier. Some other noteworthy novels in this category are *Spiridion* (1839) and *Consuelo* (1842).

NOVELS OF COUNTRY LIFE (*c.* 1844–1858). This group contains what is probably Miss Sand's most enduring work, for here she is working without a "thesis." She draws many charming (though sometimes slightly idealized) pictures of the peasants and the rural scenery of France, especially of the Berry section. She is a superior psychologist and excels in depicting the artistic and sensitive temperament. The best novels of this category are *The Devil's Pool* (*La Mare au diable*, 1846), *Little Fadette* (*La Petite Fadette*, 1849), *François de Champi* (1850), and *The Master Bell-Ringers* (*Les Maîtres sonneurs*, 1852).

NOVELS OF MANNERS (*c.* 1858–1876). The novels of the last period resemble those of the first, except that the later ones are less violent, less exalted, and less propagandistic. Most of them are sentimental love stories. Like the works of the third period, they contain some penetrating psychological studies. The most memorable are *Jean de la Roche* (1860) and *Le Marquis de Villemer* (1861).

Estimate. George Sand's novels are seldom read today. Most of them are too topical. Nevertheless, although she founded no school, she was of considerable influence in her day. She did a great deal to spread the doctrines of social justice and the equality of women, and her novels had a profound effect on Russian thought of the last part of the nineteenth century. Although her ideas were generally borrowed, her style was her own — facile, clear, and fluid. It is true that she is sometimes overidealistic and sentimental and that she has been accused of condoning immorality, including free love and adultery. "But at her best she is widely sympathetic and interesting and conveys the sense of life in many ways,"[20] and she "represents what French critics ask of a novel, which should be half way between . . . precise and serious observation and pure imagination left to its own devices."[21]

The Historical Novel

One of the principal elements of romanticism is escapism, and one of the favorite havens for the escapist is the long ago. Consequently, the historical novel relating the dashing adventures of the heroes of the past appealed mightily to the French imagination in the early nineteenth century. Sir Walter Scott's novels were translated into French and became the models for virtually every historical novelist in France. Chateaubriand's *Martyrs* also helped set the trend. Perhaps the first full-fledged historical novel was Alfred de Vigny's *Cinq-Mars* (1826). Other famous writers of this literary type (all discussed under different headings below) were Mérimée, Hugo, and Alexandre Dumas the Elder.

POETRY

Since the mortal blasts of Malherbe (p. 63) lyricism had been dead in France. The romantic revival of emotionalism and subjectivism brought it back to life. *The Poetic Meditations* (1820) of Lamartine was the first book of lyric poetry since the days of Chénier.

ALPHONSE LOUIS–MARIE DE LAMARTINE (1790–1869). Lamartine was born at Mâcon in Burgundy of an old aristocratic family. After a happy childhood, he went to school at the Jesuit seminary in Belley. Then he spent four years of leisure and reading at Milly. In 1811 while traveling in Italy, he became infatuated with a little cigarette-maker of Naples, whom he later idealized in *Graziella*. Returning to France, he served first as a member of the royal guard of Louis XVIII and later as an attaché to the diplomatic corps at Naples.   In 1816 he fell in love with Madame Julie Charles, who died the following year; she inspired many of his poems.   The publication of *The Poetic Meditations* in 1820 made him famous immediately.   In 1829 he was elected a member of the Academy. After the fall of Charles X, he gave up his diplomatic career and sought a seat in the Assembly.   At first unsuccessful, he was eventually elected (1833) and from then till 1848 played an increasingly important role in politics.   He opposed the bourgeois government of Louis Philippe.   Directly after the revolution of 1848 he was the virtual dictator of France — for about three months.   Then the fickle and radical mob abandoned him for the glamorous Louis Napoleon, and Lamartine retired from politics forever.   Always extravagant and generous, he now fell into financial difficulties and spent the last years of his life writing continually, principally hackwork for periodicals.

Works.

POETRY.   The chief literary influences on Lamartine were the Bible, Rousseau, Saint-Pierre, Chateaubriand, Petrarch, Tasso, Milton, Ossian, and Young.   Whereas Chateaubriand wrote about religion, nature, and himself, Lamartine wrote about religion, nature, and woman; and, like Chateaubriand, he often associated two or perhaps all three of the topics in one work.   His religion is vaguer and less orthodox than that of Chateaubriand, but it is also deeper and more idealistic; sometimes it inclines toward pantheism. Lamartine's imagination is audial rather than visual; his descriptions are usually lacking in color — done principally in blacks and whites and grays.   He prefers to describe floating or soaring things — clouds, winds, and waves; "it is the essential quality of his genius to dematerialize everything that he touches."[22]   Much of his love poetry is idealistic and Platonic and, like that of Petrarch, tends to identify the physical with the spiritual; it often has a note of melancholy.

The technical characteristics of his poems are fluidity, diffuseness, facility, spontaneity, and "a suave harmony, continuing the tradition of Racine and of the eighteenth-century elegists."[23]

The most important volumes of his poetry are as follows: *The Poetic Meditations* (*Les Méditations poétiques*, 1820), *New Meditations* (*Nouvelles méditations*, 1823), *Poetic and Religious Harmonies* (*Harmonies poétiques et religieuses*, 1830), *Jocelyn* (1836), *The Fall of an Angel* (*La Chute d'un ange*, 1838), and *Poetic Recollections* (*Recueillements poétiques*,

1839). Some of his best individual lyrics are "The Lake" ("Le Lac"), which combines melancholy, love, and appreciation for nature; "The Crucifix" ("Le Crucifix"), in which he associates his love for Elvire (Julie Charles) with his religious beliefs; and "Song of Love" ("Chant d'amour"), a poem to his wife. *Jocelyn* is a long narrative poem which tells of the pure love of a priest for a young girl and of his renunciation. *The Fall of an Angel* is a long (11,000 lines) epic about an angel who, through love for a human woman, becomes human himself; it is not a success.

PROSE. Lamartine wrote several prose works. *Raphaël* (1849) and *Graziella* (1852) are semiautobiographical novels. The first is partially based on his love for Madame Charles; the other, on his affair with the Neapolitan cigarette-maker. *Confidences* (*Les Confidences*, 1849) and *New Confidences* (*Les Nouvelles confidences*, 1851) are autobiography proper. *The History of the Girondists* (*L'Histoire des Girondins*, 1847) is an inspirational but untrustworthy account of one portion of the French Revolution; the book helped to foment the revolution of 1848.

Estimate. Critical opinions of Lamartine have varied. He has been accused of diffuseness, flabbiness, vagueness, bombast, and insubstantiality; but he has been praised for intense emotion, spontaneity, tenderness, simplicity, melody, and harmony. Although Matthew Arnold thought him unimportant, Sainte-Beuve and Faguet disagreed and pointed out his historical significance. He brought lyricism back to France, and to his own age (as Gautier, his almost exact contemporary, says) "Lamartine was not only a poet; he was poetry itself."[24]

ALFRED VICTOR, COMTE DE VIGNY (1797–1863). Born at Loches in Touraine. After serving about fourteen years in the army and rising only from the rank of lieutenant to that of captain, he resigned (1827) and devoted his entire attention to literature. His first collection of poems had appeared in 1822 and had been brought out in an enlarged edition in 1826 under the title *Poems Ancient and Modern* (*Poèmes Antiques et modernes*). In the same year his novel *Cinq-Mars* was published. Thereafter he wrote some more poems, two plays, some stories, and a journal. In 1828 he married an Englishwoman, Lydia Bunbury, with whom he was never wholly compatible. Several years later he fell violently in love with an actress, Marie Dorval, whose infidelity and lack of honor embittered him. In 1845 he was received into the French

Academy. Twice he tried unsuccessfully to win an election to the National Assembly. About 1848 he retired to his château in Angoulême, where, after a protracted illness, he died.

Thought. Vigny, unlike most of the other French romantic poets, was a deep and original thinker. He was a pessimist, a solitary, and a stoic. He says that he was "born serious to the point of sadness," and his disappointments in the army, in love, and in politics did nothing toward cheering him up. Whatever the cause, "he was a disillusioned idealist who after reasoned reflection had come to the conclusion that in a world made up of good and evil the evil far outbalances the good, in fact that all is for the worst in the worst of all possible worlds."[25] Neither anybody nor anything is benevolent or trustworthy. The human throng is either stupid or dishonest; woman is always "more or less a Delilah"; nature is not a mother but a tomb; and even God is either malevolent or blind, deaf, and dumb. The poet, the man of genius, is therefore doomed to loneliness and sorrow. Vigny is, however, by no means a whiner. He believes that it is the obligation of each man "to suffer and die without speaking." This is a resignation made up of pride plus an awareness of the futility of resisting. There is one ray of hope breaking through the cloud of his pessimism: there is a true God, the God of the eternal realm of ideas, where noble souls may find impalpable and imperishable treasures.

Works.

POETRY. Vigny was perhaps "the least typical of the Romantics."[26] He shunned the effusion and display common to most of them; and, although he lived in melancholy, his gloom was less singular and less personal than the *mal de René*. His pity was not for himself individually but for mankind in general.

His method is first to choose a philosophic truth and then to express it symbolically or figuratively. In "Moses" ("Moïse"), for example, the great lawgiver "typifies the loneliness of genius."[27] Vigny's poems are concise, sober, and restrained.

Compared with most of the romantic poets, Vigny wrote little. He himself published only three small volumes of poetry: *Poèmes* (1822), *Eloa* (1824), and *Poems Antiques and Modern (Poèmes Antiques et modernes*, 1826). *The Destinies (Les Destinées)* was published posthumously in 1867.

NOVELS AND STORIES. In 1826 Vigny wrote *Cinq-Mars*, the first French historical novel. Following the example of Scott, he tried (rather successfully) to reproduce the local color of the time of Louis XIII, but unlike Scott, he took liberties with historical fact and with the character of Richelieu.   The plot consists of the struggle between the Cardinal and a young nobleman, Cinq-Mars, who wants to marry Marie de Gonzague.   *Stello* (1832) is a collection of three tales which relate the tragedies of three young poets who died ere their prime: Thomas Chatterton, André Chénier, and Nicolas Gilbert (a luckless French poet of the late eighteenth century).   *Military Servitude and Grandeur* (*Servitude et grandeur militaires*, 1835) is a group of tales about the life of soldiers, who are pitied for their sacrifices and praised for their stoicism and self-abnegation.

DRAMAS.   Besides adapting two Shakespearian plays (*Shylock*, 1828, and *The Moor of Venice* [*Le More de Venise*], 1829), Vigny wrote three original dramas.   *The Marshal of Ancre* (*Le Maréchal d'Ancre*, 1830) is a dramatization of an incident in the early seventeenth century "and is designed to illustrate the power of destiny."[28] *Quit for Fear* (*Quitte pour la peur*, 1833) is a *salon* comedy.   Vigny's best drama is the tragedy *Chatterton* (1835), which is a psychological study of the young English poet, who commits suicide when both his literary endeavors and his love affair with Kitty Bell meet with disappointment.   Chatterton typifies the poet-martyr who is doomed by his very genius to misunderstanding, loneliness, and failure.

Estimate.   As a novelist, storyteller, and dramatist, Vigny is barely remembered; and his poetry has never been widely popular. But he will never be forgotten by the few who refuse to be repelled by his austerity and his pessimism and who value classical restraint, vivid imagery, original thought, and intellectual honesty.

VICTOR–MARIE HUGO (1802–1885).   Hugo was born at Besançon.   His father, a general in the army of Napoleon, carried his family with him into Italy, and later his sons stayed with him in Spain.   After Waterloo Victor returned to Paris.   His formal education was neglected by both his parents, but he read a great deal (especially the works of Rousseau and Chateaubriand) and while in his early teens became enamoured of literature.   He wrote a tragedy when he was fourteen and three years later edited a newspaper, the *Literary Conservator*.   In 1822, the year in which he married Adèle Foucher, he published his first volume of poetry. In the early twenties he was a conservative and royalist, but by

1830 he had become an ardent liberal and democrat. His numerous novels, plays, and volumes of poetry published between 1822 and 1840, his self-confidence, and his vociferous advocacy of the romantic theories made him the recognized leader of the French romantics during the fourth decade. In 1841 he was admitted to membership in the Academy. Between 1843 and 1848 he forsook literature for politics; he soon became one of the leaders of the democratic party. His opposition to Napoleon III and the Second Empire led to his being exiled. He remained abroad from 1852 till 1870 — at Brussels, at Jersey, and (principally) at Guernsey. His last fifteen years were spent at Paris, where he enjoyed the role of grand old man of French letters.

Works. Abroad Hugo is best known as a novelist; in France he is considered first a poet. He also was celebrated in his own day as a dramatist, but as a group his plays are the least worthy of his works. In all three forms he is a thoroughgoing romanticist. While still a youth he said, "I wish to be Chateaubriand or nothing," and it was this predecessor who was the first great literary influence on Hugo.

POETRY. Believing that the poet sees truth more intuitively and more clearly than other men, and feeling that the poet's mission is to lead those other men to the light, Hugo often assumes the role of prophet. Many of his poems are on topical themes, especially political and sociological ones, such as the monarchy, democracy, and poverty; other favorite subjects are historical events, nature, domestic life, love, and childhood.

Two of his greatest poetic gifts are imagination and rhetorical dexterity. "His imagination declares itself in many ways: in the actual number and novelty of his images; in his power of sustained personification and vision; and particularly in his myth-making faculty, his evocation of immensity."[29] He is adept as a rhetorician. He has a tremendous vocabulary; he loves words, especially grandiose ones. The rhetorical devices which he uses repeatedly are "the double substantive [compound words], . . . the recurrent *motif*, . . . long enumerations, . . . parallel clauses, [and most particularly] . . . antithesis."[30]

Hugo's poems fill twenty-five volumes of his collected works. Some of the most significant volumes published during his lifetime are: *Odes and Ballades* (1826, 1828), which deal with political events, Hugo's admiration for Napoleon I, the poet's mission, and childhood; *The Orientals* (*Les Orientales*, 1829), a series of purely imaginary pictures of the East, where Hugo had never been (these were inspired by Byron and the Greek war for independence); *Autumn Leaves* (*Les Feuilles d'automne*, 1831), "verses of the interior of the soul," as the author calls them, about "nature, . . . man's destiny, . . . humanity, . . . [and] the graces and beauties of childhood";[31] *Songs of the Twilight* (*Les Chants du crépuscule*, 1835), concerned mainly with democracy, the Bourbons, and Napoleon; *The Punishments* (*Les Châtiments*, 1853), violent and satirical invectives against Napoleon III; *Contemplations* (1856), "perhaps the most personal [book] that Victor Hugo ever wrote,"[32] inspired by thoughts of the sea, of death, of social injustice, of his ideals and hopes, and of his own past experiences; and *Legend of the Centuries* (*Légende des siècles*, three series, 1859, 1877, and 1883), a sequence of poems "epic and dramatic in inspiration but lyric in form" which illustrate Hugo's belief in human progress as seen through the ages and which are often considered the "culmination of Hugo's poetry."

NOVELS. Hugo wrote romantic novels of adventure and also social novels; sometimes he combined the two types. He is a poor psychologist but a good painter of backgrounds. His novels, like his poems, show his love for color, for antithesis, and for the grand; and in his social novels he again assumes the role of prophet or priest.

Notre Dame de Paris (1831) and *The Wretches* (*Les Miserables*, 1862) are his two greatest novels. The former is a study of Paris in the fifteenth century. It abounds in colorful descriptions. The great cathedral — which has been called the protagonist of the book — dominates the scene. The plot revolves around Esmeralda, a young gipsy, for whom four men are striving: Pierre, a poet; Jehan, a villainous priest; Phoebus, a nobleman; and Quasimodo, a hunchback bell ringer. All except Phoebus meet a tragic death. *The Wretches* is a long (1970–page) investigation of the cruel effects of society on the proletariat. Jean Valjean, the hero, is a regenerated convict who rises to prosperity, saves an innocent man by offering himself as victim, is allowed to escape, and dies content, knowing that his efforts have assured the happiness of Cosette, his adopted daughter. Despite too superficial and too symbolic characterization and a highly improbable plot, the book is a powerful expression of Hugo's social views and has been a perennially popular novel.

The Strugglers of the Sea (*Les Travailleurs de la mer*, 1866) is a good story depicting man's eternal battle against nature. *The Man Who Laughs* (*L'Homme qui rit*, 1869) satirizes English life and manners in the days of the Stuarts. And *Ninety-Three* (*Quatre-Vingt-Treize*, 1872) is a historical novel dealing with an episode of the French Revolution.

DRAMAS. Hugo's preface to *Cromwell* (1827) was the French romantic dramatists' declaration of independence from the rules of the classicists. In the preface Hugo declares that a drama is to represent all sides of life — to show beauty and ugliness, happiness and sorrow, evil and goodness juxtaposed as they are in real life; that characters are to be individual and complex; that historical settings, costumes, customs, and local color are to be historically authentic; and that the unity of action is to be observed, but that the other two unities are artificial and should be ignored. Most of these ideas were borrowed from Shakespeare or Schlegel, but the preface served as a manifesto for the romantic dramatists.

Cromwell itself is a long, formless, completely unactable play in seventy-five scenes. Hugo ambitiously attempts to represent the whole Cromwellian epoch in England. The plot is concerned with the Protector's bid for the throne.

Hernani (1830), Hugo's best drama, contains many instances of *enjambement* (use of run-on lines and open couplets) and of shifting of the caesura in the alexandrine. The story is melodramatic, and the characters are all romantic types. The plot concerns the struggle of Hernani, the "gloomy bandit," against Don Ruy Gomez, guardian of Hernani's sweetheart. Gomez' vengeance brings disaster to all. The success of the play marked the triumph of the romantic drama.

Ruy Blas (1838), Hugo's second-best play, shows how a lackey rises to power and gains the love of the Queen of Spain; he is overthrown partly by the efforts of a villain and partly by his own short-comings. "The moral seems to be, once a lackey, always a lackey."[33]

Like most romantic drama, Hugo's plays are of minor importance today. They nearly always have a social or political thesis. The plots are fantastic, and the characters are rudimentarily drawn. Even the scenery and local color are superficial. They "contain neither enough human nor enough historical truth to please a cultured taste, and they depend for their interest entirely on their thrills and surprises and on the glamour of their style. In other words, they are the melodramas of a man of genius."[34] Their greatest merits are "the splendour and imaginative quality of their verse . . . vigour and . . . emotional intensity."[35]

Estimate. Victor Hugo "had the powers of a great genius and the soul of an ordinary man. . . . His faults as a man . . . cannot be dismissed as irrelevant and unimportant, for they are indissolubly bound up with the very substance of his work."[36] It is true that he was neither a clear nor an original thinker; that he had no sense of humor; and that he was inordinately vain (he felt that the city of Paris should be renamed for him!). It is true, too, that "all the worst tendencies of the Romantic Movement may be seen completely displayed in [his] dramas."[37] It is true, also, that his novels lack proportion, unity, probability, and convincing characterization. And, finally, it is true that his poetry is sometimes guilty of excess, exaggeration, shallowness, incoherence, topicality, and various lapses of taste.

Nevertheless, Professor Dowden (with perhaps too much enthusiasm) proclaims Hugo "the greatest lyric poet of France" and adds, "that he was the greatest poet of all literature might be urged."[38] Despite their faults and shortcomings, his poems at times show "an almost Classic beauty and restraint [and] unparalleled descriptive powers."[39] "His two supreme gifts as a poet are his extraordinary visual imagination and his feeling for the music and color of words. . . ."[40] "Words for him were living powers; . . . sensations created images and words, and images and words created ideas. He was a master of all harmonies of verse; now a solitary breather through pipe or flute; more often the conductor of an orchestra."[41] "No one who cares for poetry at all . . . can read any of his better works without gradually rising to a condition of enthusiasm in which the possible defects of the matter are altogether lost sight of. . . . This is the special test of poetry, and there is none other."[42]

ALFRED DE MUSSET (1810–1857). Musset was born in Paris. After making a brilliant record at the Lycée Henri IV, he became, at the age of eighteen, a member of the circle of Victor Hugo. In 1830 he published his first volume of poetry, *Tales of Spain and Italy*. Soon afterwards he, like Byron, began to poke fun at some of the absurdities of the romantics. In 1833 he fell violently in love with George Sand and accompanied her to Italy. The liaison ended two years later; their temperaments had become incompatible, and Miss Sand had begun an affair with a Venetian

doctor. Although the episode inspired some of Musset's best poetry, it eventually had tragic consequences for him: he "sank into despair and debauchery"[43] and died at the age of forty-seven.
Works.

POETRY. All Musset's poems are contained in two volumes, *First Poems* (*Premières poésies*, 1829–1835) and *New Poems* (*Poésies nouvelles*, 1836–1852). The *Tales of Spain and Italy* (*Contes d'Espagne et d'Italie*, 1830) are youthful effusions full of Byronic swagger and cynicism. The affair with George Sand sobered and matured Musset and transformed his swagger into despair. The four "Night" poems, perhaps his best efforts, reflect that despair. "May Night" ("La Nuit de mai," 1835) and "December Night" ("La Nuit de décembre," 1835) are cries of hopeless suffering. "August Night" ("La Nuit d'août," 1836) is a little more hopeful, and in "October Night") ("La Nuit d'octobre," 1837) the poet has found a measure of serenity. In "Memory" ("Souvenir," 1841) Musset finds consolation in the thought that beautiful memories can live on even after love itself is dead.

PROSE NARRATIVES. Musset composed several prose tales of varying length. The longest and most significant is his *Confession of a Child of the Century* (*Confession d'un enfant du siècle*, 1836), a fictionalized account of his affair with George Sand.

DRAMAS. After the complete failure of his *Venetian Night* (*Nuit Vénitienne*, 1831) Musset decided to write plays only for reading and not for production. Most of them were published between 1833 and 1837 in a periodical; they appeared in book form in 1840. In 1847, however, some of his comedies were discovered to be both actable and delightful, and since then they have been favorites on the stage.

His dramas are of three types: (a) *Idyllic comedies* "in the manner of Shakespeare." Two examples are *Fantasio* and *What Young Girls Dream About* (*À quoi rêvent les jeunes filles*). (b) *Drawing-room comedies* after the fashion of Marivaux. Most of these are "proverb-comedies," that is, comedies which illustrate a familiar proverb; examples are *A Door Must Be Either Open or Shut* (*Il faut qu'une porte soit ouverte ou fermée*) and *One Does Not Jest with Love* (*On ne badine pas avec l'amour*). In the latter the author again echoes his love affair with George Sand; it is hardly a comedy: the hero, rejected by the heroine, flirts with a village girl. The heroine becomes jealous, the village girl dies suddenly, and the hero and the heroine separate in sadness. (c) *Tragedies*. *Lorenzaccio* is the story of "a kind of Hamlet drawn against a Renaissance background."[44] The hero tries to reform a Florentine tyrant but is himself corrupted by the tyrant's vices.

Estimate. Musset is the only one of the French romantic poets with a sense of humor. Some of his earlier poems and many of his comedies contain lively wit. He is remembered most often, however, for his poetry. In this realm, it must be admitted, his range is narrow. Unlike most of the romantics, he is not at all interested in nature, progress, or humanity. With the possible exception of Vigny, he is the most introspective of the French romantic poets, and he is about the only one who gives us genuine and intimate descriptions of the joys and pains of love. It is true that he is not a careful technician, but his sincerity and depth of emotion make us forget minor flaws in workmanship. "Passion, the spirit of youth, sensibility, a love of beauty, intelligence, *esprit*, eloquence, graceful converse — these were Musset's gifts."[45]

DRAMA

Classical drama prevailed in France till after the fall of Napoleon I. The greatest influences on romantic drama were historical tragedies of other nations, especially the plays of Shakespeare and Schiller; earlier French melodrama; historical novels, particularly those of Scott; and the romantic revolt against all the classical rules. The dramatic theories of the romantics as set forth in Victor Hugo's preface to *Cromwell* have already been discussed. So also have the plays of three of the four major dramatists of the period: Hugo, Vigny, and Musset. The fourth was Dumas.

ALEXANDRE DUMAS THE ELDER (1802–1870). Son of a mulatto general in Napoleon's army, Dumas was born at Villers-Cotterets. When twenty years old, he went to Paris, served for a short time as secretary to the Duc d'Orléans, and then decided he would try to earn his living by writing. He found it necessary to do a great deal of miscellaneous reading, for he had had very little systematic education as a boy. His first successful play was *Henry III and His Court*, produced in 1829. From that date onward he wrote vast numbers of plays and novels; these earned for him enormous sums of money, which he squandered. He died poverty-stricken.

Works. Dumas was one of the most prolific writers in all world literature; his works fill three hundred sizeable volumes. Some portion of this output was written by his "factory," as he called a corps of hired collaborators. In America he is probably best known as a novelist, but most critics agree that his dramas are superior to his novels.

DRAMAS. Dumas' plays, chiefly in prose, are of two types: (1) spectacular history-dramas which abound in extravagant scenes and (2) personal dramas "of Romantic character and passion."[46] Of the first type one of the best known is *Henry III and His Court* (*Henri III et sa cour*, 1829), which is a meritorious tragic history involving jealousy and murder. An example of his personal drama of passion is *Antony* (1831), in which the hero kills the heroine so that he may restore her lost honor.

Dumas' best plays are "well-plotted and grimly powerful,"[47] but they "have the same melodramatic characteristics of Hugo's, and they are equally weak in psychological analysis."[48] "He [Dumas] possessed the dramatic sense, the instinct for strong situations, clearness, and a direct style in the development of plot, and dialogue of wonderful sharpness of outline. [But] he taught us nothing about the human soul. . . ."[49]

NOVELS. Dumas' novels are the best examples in French literature of the "cloak-and-sword" thriller. Their sources are usually history or memoirs, but Dumas "freely adapt[s]" these in order to make a good story. "His characters are of the simplest types and his style is poor; also he is fond of melodramatic incident and he boldly 'fakes' history when he cannot find it; consequently most of his work is below par from the standpoint of literature."[50] "Yet a better story-teller never existed. From the first page to the last he knows how to arouse and hold his readers' interests and to carry them along in the spirit of high adventure."[51]

The best known of his novels are as follows: the D'Artagnan trilogy — *The Three Musketeers* (*Les Trois mousquetaires*, eight volumes, 1844), *Twenty Years After* (*Vingt ans après*, 1845), and *The Viscount of Bragelonne* (*Le Vicomte de Bragelonne*, 1847); *The Count of Monte Cristo* (*Le Comte de Monte Cristo*, 1844–1845); and *The Black Tulip* (*La Tulipe noire*, 1845).

THE SHORT TALE

During the Middle Ages the fabliaux were the chief contributions to the field of the short narrative; these, of course, were in verse. During the Renaissance there were many short tales in prose, modeled on the Italian *novelle*. The seventeenth and eighteenth centuries frowned on such works, and except for the *Fables* of La Fontaine and the didactic contes of Voltaire, those eras stuck to poetry, drama, and long works in prose. At the beginning of the nineteenth century the short tale came back into French literature. Most often it was a tale of the supernatural, the fantastic, or the mysterious. XAVIER DE MAISTRE (1764–1852) wrote several "pathetic little tales of human misfortune" between 1794 and 1815. Vigny, Musset, Mérimée, and Balzac all wrote brief prose narratives. Three other famous story writers were CHARLES NODIER (1780–1844), GÉRARD DE NERVAL (1808–1855), and — by far the most important of the trio — Théophile Gautier.

THÉOPHILE GAUTIER (1811–1872). Born at Tarbes but brought at the age of three to Paris, Gautier first tried his hand at painting but soon deserted it for poetry. In 1830 he became a fervent supporter of Hugo's romantic theories — insofar as they were purely aesthetic. He always remained aloof from politics and reform movements. In 1840 he traveled through Italy, Algeria, the Near East, and Russia. During the latter half of his life financial difficulties compelled him to write continuously for magazines — short stories, novels, critical reviews, and accounts of travels. He died at Neuilly.

Works. Gautier's earliest works showed the worst faults of the romantic school, but by 1833 he had begun to recognize as faults many of his earlier practices. By 1835 he had clearly formulated a theory of "art for art's sake" — a theory which was later adopted by the French Parnassians and which influenced the English Aesthetic Movement of Walter Pater.

SHORT TALES. Like the tales of Nodier and Nerval, most of Gautier's shorter prose narratives deal with the macabre, the supernatural, or the fantastic. Most of these are to be found in two collections: *Stories* (*Nouvelles*, 1845) and *Novels and Tales* (*Romans et contes*, 1857). The best single tales are "The Amorous Corpse" ("La Morte amoureuse"), "A Night of Cleopatra" ("Une Nuit de Cléopâtre"), "Omphale," and "The Mummy's Foot" ("Le Pied de la momie"). These tales contain unusually vivid description and display an extraordinary sense of humor.

NOVELS. Gautier's novels show characteristics similar to those of his shorter prose narratives. His most famous novel is *Mademoiselle de Maupin* (1835), in which a young girl succeeds in captivating a man despite her disguise as a male. The preface to the book is Gautier's best expression of his theory of "art for art's sake."

POETRY. Gautier's early poems are similar to his early prose — too similar. *Albertus* (1832), for example, is a weird story of a witch and her transformations. By far the best poetry that Gautier ever wrote is found in *Enamels and Cameos* (*Émaux et camées*, 1852), a volume of short lyrics and descriptive pieces which bears testimony to the author's previous occupation of painting. The techniques of the artist's brush and the sculptor's chisel are transferred to the poet's pen; and — to shift the figure — each poem is a brilliant and carefully polished gem. Some of the best single poems in the volume are "The Castle of Memory" ("Le Château du souvenir"), "Study of Hands" ("Étude des mains"), "The Fantasies of Winter" ("Les Fantaisies d'hiver"), and "Variations on the Carnival of Venice" ("Variations sur le carneval de Venise").

Estimate. Gautier's niche in the French hall of literary fame is small but secure. His historical importance lies in his propounding of the theory of art for its own sake. This exclusion of all philosophical, social, and religious interests has, however, led some critics to condemn him for narrowness of scope and for "paucity of ideas." The intrinisic merits of his works are his purity of diction, his exquisite sense of color, and the perfection of his style. These merits have led M. Faguet to declare that Gautier "knew how to write as well as Victor Hugo, and better than all the other writers of the century."[52]

HISTORY

Although history does not ordinarily fall within the scope of an account of literature, some of the French historical writings of the nineteenth century are of such literary excellence as to deserve mention. The patriotism inspired by the Revolution and by the Napoleonic wars, the rise of political parties, and the romantic enthusiasm for the past all encouraged historical studies.

Professor Butler, taking a hint from Jules Michelet, divides the historians of the first half of the century into three groups:[53]

The "Romantic or Descriptive School." It aimed at making history a colorful and exciting narrative. The chief members of this school were JOSEPH FRANÇOIS MICHAUD (1767–1839), who wrote *The History of the Crusades* (*L'Histoire des Croisades*, 1811–1822); and AUGUSTIN THIERRY (1795–1856), "the father of modern French history,"[54] who wrote *History of the Conquest of England by the Normans* (*Histoire de la conquête de l'Angleterre par les Normands*, 1825) and *Accounts of Merovingian Times* (*Récits des temps Mérovingiens*, 1840).

The **"Philosophical and Political School."** It sought to analyze and dissect past events and discover causes and effects. The most important historians of this group were FRANÇOIS GUIZOT (1787–1874), who wrote many works of which the main ones were *History of Civilization in Europe* (*Histoire de la civilisation en Europe*, 1828–1830) and *History of Civilization in France* (*Histoire de la civilisation en France*, 1828–1830); FRANÇOIS MIGUET (1796–1884), who wrote a two-volume *History of the French Revolution* (*Histoire de la révolution française*, 1824); ADOLPHE THIERS (1797–1877), who wrote a ten-volume *History of the French Revolution* (*Histoire de la révolution française*, 1823–1827); and ALEXIS DE TOCQUEVILLE (1805–1859), who wrote *On Democracy in America* (*De la démocratie en Amérique*, 1836–1839) and *The Old Regime and the Revolution* (*L'Ancien régime et la révolution*, 1856).

[The] **"Resuscitation of the Buried Past" School.** JULES MICHELET (1798–1874), the greatest historian of the period, conceived of history as an "integral resurrection of life." His twenty-seven-volume *History of France* (*Histoire de France*, 1833–1867) shows his patriotism, his love for the people, and his sympathetic imagination.

LITERARY CRITICISM

From Renaissance days onward many great authors had expressed in writing their opinions of what literature should or should not be and had written evaluations of various literary works. It was not till the nineteenth century, however, that criticism became an art and a profession. Several methods of judging literature were suggested.

FRANÇOIS VILLEMAIN (1790–1870), like Herder in Germany, was interested in historical origins of forms and of motifs, and he was one of the first to perceive the values of a comparative study of the literatures of various nations.* SAINT-MARC GIRARDIN (1801–1873) was especially concerned with "the psychological and moral aspects of literature [and he was] the first to trace the evolution of a literary kind [genre]."[55]

---

* Herder in Germany was his forerunner.

Sainte-Beuve. Far greater than these men and perhaps the greatest of all French critics was Charles Augustin de Sainte-Beuve (1804–1869), who at first aspired to be a poet but later decided that his abilities were of another kind. For about three years (1827–1830) he was intimately acquainted with the circle of Victor Hugo and was himself an enthusiastic romanticist. Then, his romantic ardor beginning to cool, he delved into a study of religion, especially Calvinism, Jansenism, Methodism, and liberal Catholicism; the literary result of this study was a *History of Port-Royal* (*Histoire de Port-Royal*, 1840–1860). But meanwhile he did not renounce his interest in *belles lettres*. Between 1830 and 1848 he was writing numerous critical articles for literary periodicals; these articles were later collected under the titles *Contemporary Portraits* (*Portraits contemporains*, 1869–1871) and *Literary Portraits* (*Portraits littéraires*, 1862–1864). To these he added his famous series of weekly articles *Monday Chats* (*Causeries du lundi*, 1851–1862) and *New Mondays* (*Nouveaux lundis*, 1863–1870). His total critical writings fill forty-eight volumes. He also wrote some inferior poetry and a novel.

Sainte-Beuve's critical method is antithetical to that of his friend Matthew Arnold. Whereas Arnold's "touchstone" method advocates the use of an absolute norm (the best that has been thought and said) by which to measure a literary work, the Frenchman's milieu method aims at investigating the environmental, hereditary, and historical influences which contribute to the production of a piece of writing.

7

The Age of Realism, Naturalism, and Symbolism

(1842–1900)

Historical Background. When Louis Napoleon proclaimed the Second Empire in 1851, he had visions of restoring to France the glories she had enjoyed under Napoleon I. Yearning for international power and prestige, he led his country into three foreign wars: the Crimean War (1854–1856), the Italian struggle for independence (1859–1860), and the Mexican War (1863–1867); none of these were profitable for France. His domestic policy was more successful. He improved communications facilities, established a uniform postal rate, held two international expositions (1855 and 1867), and enlarged and modernized the city of Paris. Commerce and industry thrived, but eventually the factory system gave rise to the struggle between capital and labor.

The emphasis on material prosperity (to which an impetus was given by the Emperor), the various theories of evolution and determinism, and the enthusiasm for the scientific method all discouraged idealism and interest in spiritual matters.

The disastrous Franco-Prussian War put an end to the Second Empire in 1870, and the Third Republic was proclaimed. The French nation made a remarkably quick material recovery from the defeat; within three years it had rebuilt most of the bridges, roads, and buildings destroyed by the war and had also paid the huge indemnity, which the Prussians had hoped would cripple France for two or three decades.

The war had little effect on intellectual currents, save to deepen the pessimism which was already resulting from materialism, determinism, positivism, and loss of idealism. The negativistic philosophy of the German Schopenhauer was widely influential between 1875 and 1885. Then the pendulum began to swing in the other

114

direction. The optimism of Hegel, Fichte, and Bergson began to make itself felt, and Nietzsche's doctrine of salvation through forceful individuality gave men new hope.

The return to religion which almost inevitably follows a great war was retarded in France by the conflict between the liberal and democratic government and the conservative and traditionalistic Church. The Catholics feared that the new government would curtail the authority of the Church, and their fears were justified, for the liberals wanted to sever the relation between Church and state. After several rather indecisive attacks by both sides, matters were brought to a crisis by the famous Dreyfus Affair — an affair of such far-reaching and permanent consequences that it deserves special consideration.

An epidemic of anti-semitism had swept through Austria and Germany and was beginning to infect France. This prejudice was encouraged by reactionary Catholics and by materialistic merchants who resented Jewish commercial successes. In 1884 Alfred Dreyfus, a Jewish artillery captain, was convicted of treason — of divulging military secrets to Germany. After twelve years of argument and after two more trials, he was completely exonerated (1906).

This exoneration was a great victory not only for all those who believed in justice but also and especially for the liberals who had long urged the reduction of the power of the Catholic Church. Largely as a result of the Dreyfus Affair, the separation of Church and state had been effected in 1905, and after the acquittal of Dreyfus, the antireligious — especially anti-Catholic — sentiment was strong in France.

General View of the Literature. A survey of French literature of the last half of the nineteenth century consists in large measure of a discussion of four isms: realism, naturalism, Parnassianism,* and Symbolism.

By 1842 the old forms of romanticism that had been triumphant during the fourth decade were already on their way out, although Hugo and a few others continued to write some romantic verse for many years thereafter. Realism, of which there had been distinct traces since 1830, now received a powerful boost from several

---

* Although realism and Parnassianism are very similar, a distinction is made here between the techniques of Balzac and his followers (*c.* 1830–1860) and those of the school of Leconte de Lisle (below).

sources: first, the large number of eccentric — and usually indigent — writers and artists who led a "Bohemian" life in the Latin Quarter of Paris and who scoffed both at the ugly mediocrity of the bourgeoisie and at the egoistic pessimism of some of the romantics; and second, the caricaturists and the painters of the Barbizon school (especially Corot and Millet), who reacted against the violence and unreality of the romantic school of painting; the Barbizon artists turned to French landscapes and simple life for their subjects.

After 1850 two kinds of realism became discernible: first, "artistic realism championed by the school which took 'art for art's sake' as its device";[1] one member of this school was Gautier; Flaubert and the Parnassians may also be said to have fallen within this category. Second, there was "pseudo-scientific realism or naturalism,"[2] which Zola, leader of the naturalists, defined as "the formula of modern science applied to literature."   Naturalism went a step or so beyond earlier realism in seeking out the sordid and unsavory, which it described boldly and minutely.   As one wit put it: "A realist calls a spade a spade; a naturalist calls it a damned old shovel."

The military events of the half-century had surprisingly little effect on the literature.   Even the Franco-Prussian War was almost ignored, except for a few pieces by Maupassant, Zola, and Daudet. Philosophical trends, economic strife, and especially the Dreyfus Affair, all were treated at some length by the French writers.

The main kinds of writing during the era were history, literary criticism, the novel, the short story, poetry, and drama.

HISTORY

Ernest Renan (1823–1892).   The most illustrious historian of the age.   His most important works are (1) *The Origins of Christianity* (*Les Origines du Christianisme*, 1863–1881), in seven installments, of which the first installment, *The Life of Jesus* (*La Vie de Jésus*, 1863), rejects all supernatural and miraculous events and tries to give an authentic account of Christ as a man and (2) *History of the People of Israel* (*Histoire du peuple d'Israël*, 1888–1892), which traces the history of the Jewish race down to the birth of Christ. Not an orthodox Christian, Renan believed that all religions have some truth in them and should therefore be studied and tolerated. He is praiseworthy for his intellectual honesty and his excellent descriptive style.

LITERARY CRITICISM

Sainte-Beuve continued his writings almost till his death (see above). A second important critic was HIPPOLYTE TAINE (1828–1893). Taine adopted Sainte-Beuve's "milieu" method and made it a more exact and mechanical formula for judging a work. According to Taine, the critic must take into account the race; the environment; the immediate social, cultural, and philosophical pressures; and the "master faculty" (that is, the ruling characteristic) of each author.[3] Taine's *History of English Literature* (*Histoire de la littérature anglaise*, 1864, 1869), in five volumes, is still considered a standard and valuable work. Other writings of his deserving mention are *La Fontaine and His Fables* (*La Fontaine et ses fables*, 1860) and an unfinished book, *Origins of Contemporary France* (*Origines de la France contemporaine*, 1876–1894).

The critic ÉMILE FAGUET (1847–1916) thought "that it was the critic's duty to have a wide and sympathetic understanding of many things, and act as interpreter between the author and his public."[4]

THE NOVEL

By 1842 the novel was becoming the most important type of literature. The old romantic novel became decreasingly popular, and the realistic novel of contemporary life more and more significant till eventually it gave way to naturalism. Different tendencies are seen in the works of Daudet and Huysmans (below).

There are two main ways of responding to the problems and imponderables of life. One is to try to avoid them or forget them by allowing the imagination and the emotions to lead us elsewhere — to external nature, to the long ago, to the far away, or to the land of dreams. That way is romanticism. The other way is to face facts squarely, perhaps stoically, and to try to see all there is to be seen, even though some of it may be drab and ugly and painful. That way is realism.[5] By 1830 or 1835 some of the French writers had tired of what they considered an illusioned view of life as offered by the romantics. Revolting against the subjectivism, idealism, escapism, and occasional vagueness of romanticism, the realists strove for impersonality, objectivity, verisimilitude, and accuracy and minuteness of detail. In their attempt to find and depict the real, they turned to the present, to the commonplace, to science, to materialism, and sometimes to pessimism. They endorsed the romantics' championing of humanitarianism, social reform, and democracy.

Many of the French realists retained some romantic characteristics, and many of the predominantly romantic writers, e.g., George Sand, showed traces of realism.

The three most noteworthy of the early realists were Balzac, Stendhal, and Mérimée.*

HONORÉ DE BALZAC (1799–1850).[6] "The father of modern realism"[7] was born at Tours of a middle-class family. He went to school at the Collège de Vendôme in his native city, but showed more interest in spiritualism, Mesmerism, and Swedenborgism than in his assigned studies. From 1816 to 1819 he was an apprentice in law offices in Paris. Then he gave up law for literature. For most of the remainder of his life he was in debt, often changing his residence to escape persistent creditors. He tried many "get-rich-quick" schemes, but all were failures. After 1845, however, his financial condition was happier, as his books were bringing in substantial revenues. In 1850 he married a rich Polish countess, Madame Hanska, but died of a heart disease a few months after his wedding.

"By nature, Balzac offers a curious compound of the idealist and the materialist."[8] On the one hand, he had a powerful and romantic imagination, and he was deeply interested in the mystical and the occult. On the other hand, he was mightily concerned with material things, especially money; and he had a prodigious and photographic memory for details. His three chief desires were to be financially comfortable, to be famous, and to be loved. Toward those ends he labored indefatigably. He would write for weeks at a time with only the briefest intervals of sleep. "Exuberant and even titanic power is his special mark. No such industry and driving force had hitherto appeared in fiction."[9]

Works. During his early years as a writer Balzac turned out many pieces — including a drama — which were then deservedly ignored and which are now forgotten. The two works — or series of works — for which he is remembered are *The Droll Stories* and *The Human Comedy*.

---

* Since romanticism and realism overlapped, there is obviously no completely satisfactory way of separating the two chronologically. It has seemed preferable to discuss Balzac and his followers with the realists, despite the fact that many of Balzac's novels were published before 1842.

THE DROLL STORIES (*Les Contes drôlatiques*, 1833). A collection of short narratives written in a pseudo-Rabelaisian style. Many of them are filled with grossness and obscenity, but the humor, though broad, is often irresistible.

THE HUMAN COMEDY (*La Comédie Humaine*, 1829–1848).

Plan and Content. Although Balzac had written some successful novels before 1830, it was not till 1830–1834 that he clearly formulated his plan to write a comprehensive and detailed sketch of all French life. Just as Dante's *Divine Comedy* had portrayed the denizens of all the regions of hell, purgatory, and heaven, so *The Human Comedy* would depict every sort of person on the earth — or at any rate, in France. At first he planned to fit all his novels — those already written as well as those to come — into a great cycle, to be entitled *Studies of Customs* (*Études de Moeurs*). In 1835 he decided to add two more parts, *Philosophic Studies* (*Études philosophiques*) and *Analytic Studies* (*Études analytiques*). It was not till 1841 that he entitled the three parts, collectively, *The Human Comedy*.

Into this framework he poured about ninety-five titles and planned approximately fifty-five more, which he did not live to write. The amount he did write, however, was overwhelming — more than four million words, containing over two thousand characters, of whom about five hundred appear in more than one story. Some of the stories are merely short tales; some, novelettes; others, full-length novels.

The first part of the cycle, *Studies of Customs*, is subdivided into six kinds of "scenes," of which the contents overlap. These scenes are as follows: (1) *Of Private Life.* These deal with bourgeois people and especially with the emotions and passions of youth; under this heading come *Colonel Chabert* (1832) and *Father Goriot* (*Le Père Goriot*, 1834). (2) *Of Province Life.* These stories are concerned with innocent loves and hopes and violent passions, particularly of the people in the "provinces," i.e., in the sections of France fairly remote from Paris; the best novel in this group is *Eugénie Grandet* (1833). (3) *Of Parisian Life.* These attempt to do for Paris what the preceding group does for the provinces. Here are also some novels of business and intrigue. *Cousine Bette* (1846) and *Cousin Pons* (1847) fall within this group. (4) *Of Political Life* and (5) *Of Military Life.* Here, according to Balzac, is an attempt to interpret "the interests of the masses, the frightful movement of the social machine, and the contrasts produced by the particular interests which are entangled with the general interest."[10]   In (4) appears *A Mysterious Affair* (*Une Ténébreuse affaire*, 1844); and in (5) there are *The Chouans* (*Les Chouans*, 1829) and *A Passion in the Desert* (*Une Passion dans le désert*, 1830).   (6) *Of Country Life.*   In this group Balzac depicts calm, rural scenes in contrast with his other sketches of the turmoil of city life; but he tries to show that human nature, human interests, and human struggles are similar everywhere. This group contains *The Country Doctor* (*Le Médecin de campagne*, 1833), *The Village Priest* (*Le Curé du village*, 1839), and *The Peasants* (*Les Paysans*, 1844).

In Part II, *Philosophic Studies*, Balzac examines the causes which have produced contemporary society.   Under this heading are *The Skin of Affliction* (*La Peau de chagrin*, 1831) and *Séraphita* (1834–1835).

In Part III, *Analytic Studies*, Balzac attempts to analyze the principles which underlie the causes of society.   Here we find *The Physiology of Marriage* (*La Physiologie du mariage*, 1829), which is a treatise rather than a novel.

Method, Technique, and Style.   In an effort to reproduce the real, Balzac often begins his stories with long and tedious expositions — "topographical, socio-historical, biographical or generally descriptive."[11]   Sometimes he begins *in medias res* and then reverts to lengthy exposition.   Often he inserts digressions for the purpose of expounding his pet theories or of convincing his reader of the authenticity of his account.   Frequently his narration is in the first person.

In his novels dealing with social groups and milieus, he uses complex plots.   In the novels of character, however, his plots are simple, and the details of characterization are sometimes accumulated till a caricature results.   Often there is one trait which dominates a person and so drives him to destruction.   For example, Father Goriot's paternal devotion turns almost into criminal indulgence; Grandet's love for gold becomes a mania; and Cousin Bette's envy and jealousy are her undoing.

Balzac's all but incredible memory supplied him with an abundance — almost a superfluity — of detail.   He gives the minutest and most concrete descriptions not only of persons but also of things.   Though sometimes irrelevant, the details are usually directed toward one dominant impression.   Balzac is also skillful in making things and places help to explain his characters.   Combined with the technique of first-person narration, the details give the reader an illusion of reality scarcely surpassed in any other literature.

Though predominantly realistic, Balzac's works contain many romantic elements: melodramatic and violent events, sentimentality, mysterious and grotesque characters, individualism, exaltation of the passions and the imagination, exaggeration, and mysticism. His realistic characteristics include "truth-seeking, materialism of various kinds, the scientific viewpoint, careful documentation, encyclopedic breadth, democratic depiction, and the all-pervasive sociological interest."[12]

Summary of Criticisms. As an artist Balzac has many faults. His "style is bad; . . . his writing . . . is formless, clumsy, and quite without distinction; it is the writing of a man who was highly perspicacious, formidably powerful, and vulgar."[13] He is guilty of pedantry, obscenity, coarseness, prejudice, prolixity, tediousness, unnecessary digressions, and incongruous — even absurd — juxtapositions of realistic detail with fantastic events. He has a predilection for the squalid and the unhappy, and he is unable to depict or to understand the beautiful, the delicate, the subtle, the spiritual, and the refined.

Yet he is considered one of the greatest — perhaps *the* greatest — of all French novelists. His energy and power and breadth are fabulous. "The whole of France is crammed into his pages, and electrified there into intense vitality."[14] "All professions are represented: doctors, lawyers, priests, journalists, artists, business men, bankers, tradesmen, clerks, and servants are placed in their environments and viewed in their relationship to them."[15]

"The influence of Balzac has no limitations or end. He simply transformed fiction and made the modern novel the most comprehensive literary vehicle."[16] Not only in France but also in England, Germany, and America his influence has been immeasurable. Flaubert, Maupassant, Zoıa, George Moore, Howells, and Henry James are a few of those who have been most indebted to him.

STENDHAL (pseudonym of Henri Beyle, 1783–1842). He spent an unhappy childhood in his native city, Grenoble. Till 1812 he served in the army of Napoleon; subsequently he moved to Italy, where he lived from 1814–1821 and from 1830–1841, during the latter period serving as French consul. He died in Paris.

Works. Besides novels Stendhal wrote two works on music and composers, a history of Italian painting, a psychological essay on the nature of love, and a critical essay on Shakespeare and Racine. He is best known today, however, for the novels.

THE RED AND THE BLACK (*Le Rouge et le noir*, 1831). Stendhal's most famous novel. The hero, Julien Sorel (to some extent a self-portrait of the author), becomes disillusioned as a soldier after the restoration of the Bourbons and exchanges his red military garb for the black cloak of a priest. Sorel is a proud, cynical, self-willed, unprincipled young man. He makes love to two mistresses — to the second for purposes of furthering his ambitious plans. He attempts to murder the first mistress when she betrays him to the second. His life ends on the scaffold.

THE CHARTERHOUSE OF PARMA (*La Chartreuse de Parme*, 1839). A depiction of Fabrice del Dongo, "an Italian Julien Sorel,"[17] in the midst of an intrigue. A notable feature of this book is the description of the Battle of Waterloo.

Style. Stendhal is as much a romantic as he is a realist. He is romantic in his choice of subjects — colorful battles, crime, intrigue, and passion. Moreover, his plots are melodramatic, and his heroes are "exceptional men placed in exceptional circumstances . . . [who] have their dreams. . . ."[18] He is realistic, on the other hand, in his careful psychological analyses of characters, in his dry and impersonal style, and in his attention to detail.

PROSPER MÉRIMÉE (1803–1870). Mérimée was born in Paris of a French father and an English mother. For a while he attended the Collège Charlemagne and later studied law. He held several governmental positions, including those of senator and inspector of historical monuments. He was a friend of Stendhal and also of the Empress Eugénie. He became a member of the French Academy in 1843.

Mérimée wrote a drama, some poems, and some interesting self-revelatory *Letters to an Unknown* (*Lettres à une inconnue*, published 1873). He is best known, however, for his novels and tales. *The Chronicle of the Reign of Charles IX* (*La Chronique du règne de Charles IX*, 1829) is an excellent historical novel, indebted to Scott. The plot is fictitious, but the background is a faithful representation of the late sixteenth century. *Mateo Falcone* (1829) deals with violent passions of the Corsicans, and *Colomba* (1840) is a story of Corsican vengeance: the titular heroine encourages her brother in the murder of their hereditary enemy.

Like Stendhal (whom he admires and imitates) and like Balzac, Mérimée is a transitional figure between romanticism and realism. His interest in passion, violence, local color, and historical settings is romantic; but, as Dowden says, "The egoism of the romantic school appears in Mérimée inverted; it is the egoism not of effusion but of disdainful reserve."[19]   He abhors exaggeration and abstraction. His style is further characterized by complete objectivity, brevity, conciseness, and an excellent choice of words. He has been censured for his "cruel serenity" but praised for his "grasp of human character, reserved but masterly description of scenery, delicate analysis of motive, ability to represent the supernatural, pathos, grandeur, [and] simple narrative excellence."[20]

GUSTAVE FLAUBERT (1821–1880).   Flaubert was born in Rouen. His father was a doctor, and the medical environment in which Gustave was reared had a discernible effect on some of his works, especially *Madame Bovary*.   By the time he was ten years old, he was irrevocably devoted to literature; an attempt by his father to make a lawyer of him (1840–1845) was a failure.   After 1846, except for a trip to Egypt and the Orient in 1849, he lived at Croisset, near Rouen.   His later years were afflicted by a malady (either neurasthenia or epilepsy), aggravated, perhaps, by the labor of writing, to which he relentlessly drove himself.   He died suddenly of a stroke of apoplexy.

Theories, Methods, and Techniques.   By temperament Flaubert was a romantic.   He loathed everything that was bourgeois and ordinary, and he loved the violent, the unusual, and the colorful. Furthermore, his literary tastes preferred Chateaubriand, Hugo, and Gautier; he thought Balzac "second-rate" because of his careless style.   Yet Flaubert's literary theories and methods are predominantly realistic, and his subject matter often resembles that of the naturalists.

The three great literary principles that he invariably attempted to follow are these: (1) Accuracy of observation and documentation. It is said that, in order to describe a moonlit cabbage patch, he would wait — perhaps weeks — to observe one, and then while on the scene he would jot down details in a notebook.   One of the principal purposes of his journey to North Africa in 1849 was to authenticate his descriptions of ancient Carthage (in *Salammbô*). (2) Impersonality.   He disapproved romantic subjectivism, preferring to tell his stories objectively and dramatically.   (3) Exactness of diction. Flaubert was the proponent of the theory of "the exact word" (*le mot juste*). He claimed that in every instance there was only one word which precisely suited a writer's meaning; every other word was an approximation or a poor substitute. Consequently he was probably the most painstaking and self-critical novelist that has ever lived. It is said that he would spend several days on a single sentence — a remark borne out by the fact that he spent several years on each novel (six, for example, on *Salammbô*). His literary output was therefore very small.

Works.

MADAME BOVARY (1857). "The greatest novel of the century,"[21] is an almost purely realistic story exposing the romantic follies and sins of Emma Bovary. This sentimental and slightly vulgar heroine — with whom the reader does not sympathize — is a Norman bourgeoise, a type that Flaubert knew thoroughly. Emma's dreams of glamor and love lead her to boredom with her husband, a solid but prosaic rural doctor; to adultery; and finally to suicide. Professor Wright calls *Madame Bovary* "perhaps the greatest work of fiction that the nineteenth century has produced . . . and the most truthful picture ever made of mediocrity in France."[22]

SALAMMBÔ (1862). A "magnificent failure" in an attempt to reproduce realistically the scenes of ancient Carthage — of which city very little is actually known. Both the choice of subject and the colorful descriptions are romantic. The plot concerns the love of Salammbô, the daughter of King Hamilcar Barca and priestess of Tanit, for Mathos, a mercenary soldier of Libya. Historical details bury the story, and the setting seems more important than the events — or, as Flaubert himself puts it, "the pedestal is too large for the statue." The novel is a failure because "it is a monument of erudition rather than humanity."[23]

THE SENTIMENTAL EDUCATION (*L'Éducation sentimentale*, 1869). The story of Frédéric Moreau, a "male counterpart" of Emma Bovary. Moreau is a sentimental young man who unsuccessfully seeks romance in several amatory adventures; these end not in suicide but in "a flat mediocrity," which, in the eyes of Flaubert, was as tragic as death.

THE TEMPTATION OF SAINT ANTHONY (*Le Tentation de Saint-Antoine*, 1874). Like *Salammbô*, it is an attempt by Flaubert to let erudition plus imagination produce realism. The hero is the third- or fourth-century ascetic, who is tempted by the devil.

"A SIMPLE HEART" ("Un Coeur simple"), one of *Three Tales* (*Trois Contes*, 1877). This short narrative is an account of the "pathetic fidelity" of Félicité, a stupid Norman peasant, to the family whom she serves.

Criticism. Though lacking the breadth and energy of Balzac, Flaubert has a technical perfection to which the older novelist never aspired. Flaubert's shortcomings stem from his too great anxiety to follow his artistic principles. "His writing lacks fire; there is often a sense of effort in it; and, as one reads his careful, faultless, sculpturesque sentences, it is difficult not to long, at times, for some of the irregular vitality of Balzac."[24] Sometimes he is guilty of the same fault from which Balzac's work suffers — a superfluity of detail; and many of his passages would profit from excision. Finally, his field is narrow: he attempts only two kinds of stories — those dealing with contemporary Norman people of the lower strata, and those depicting ancient and foreign scenes. His merits are virtually perfect diction, a superb imagination, extraordinary descriptive power, incomparable characterization of the types of people whom he attempts to portray, and a gift of satirical criticism. "He is a writer repulsive to many, unintelligible to more, and never likely to be generally popular, but sure to retain his place in the admiration of those who judge literature as literature. . . . He ranks among the very greatest of prose writers."[25]

He influenced Maupassant, Zola, and Daudet.

ÉMILE ZOLA (1840–1902). Zola was born in Paris of poor parents; his father was an Italian engineer. What little education Émile received was scientific rather than literary. After working a while as a clerk in a publishing house and then as a journalist, he decided (about 1880) to spend all his time on literature. The same year he settled at Médan, where he lived in comparative seclusion till 1898. Then he came forth to take part in the Dreyfus Affair; his *I Accuse* (*J'Accuse*, 1898) caused his temporary exile to England. He died from accidental asphyxiation.

Theories and Methods. Zola is usually considered the founder and leader of French *naturalism*. The word is his own, chosen because his method is similar to that used in the natural sciences. This technique is a combination of minute and impersonal observation (derived from Balzac and Stendhal) and the experimental method used in science — "that is, he [the novelist] should expose his sensibility to life and he should work, as in a laboratory, upon the events and characters provided by experience."[26]　This method was suggested to Zola by his reading of Claude Bernard's *Introduction to Experimental Medicine* (*Introduction à la médicine expérimentale*, 1865). Zola explains his theories in *The Experimental Novel* (*Le Roman expérimental*, 1880).　His own usual procedure is to begin not with a plot or some character but with "a certain cross-section of life" which he wishes to portray.　Then he selects some suitable characters and endows each with a few simple traits.　His psychology is "of the most elementary kind.　It has been said that Zola gave a soul to things and withdrew the soul from man."[27]　The "cross-section" that he chooses to portray is almost invariably sordid, and the portrait is nearly always accompanied by the pessimism so characteristic of the realists and the naturalists.

Works.

THE ROUGON–MACQUARTS (*Les Rougon-Macquart*, 1871–1893).　A cycle of twenty novels, reminiscent of Balzac's great series.　It has been suggested that if Balzac's work is a "human comedy," Zola's cycle should be called a "bestial comedy."　"For Zola not only regarded man as an animal led by his appetites, but chose to chronicle the lives of a family of degenerates. . . ."[28]　The whole series is intended to give in general a picture of France during the Second Empire and in particular an account of the lives of the various members — "legitimate and illegitimate" — of the Rougon-Macquart family.　Each account attempts to show the character in relation to his special social and economic environment, with which he is frequently in conflict.　Many walks of life are depicted: *The Gin Palace* (*L'Assommoir*, 1877) is a picture of ordinary workmen who degenerate into drunkards; *Nana* (1880) is the story of a prostitute; *Germinal* (1885) tells of the hard life of the ill-treated miners and their strikes; *The Earth* (*La Terre*, 1888) deals with the rural peasant; and *The Debacle* (*La Débâcle*, 1892) — sometimes called Zola's masterpiece — is a story of the Franco-Prussian War.

OTHER NOVELS.　After the Rougon-Macquart series, Zola wrote a trilogy, *Three Cities* (*Trois villes*, 1894–1898) showing the influence of the Catholic priests in Lourdes, Rome, and Paris.　He planned a tetralogy: *The Four Gospels* (*Les Quatre Évangiles*, 1899–1903), but he lived to write only *Fecundity* (*Fécondité*), deploring race-suicide; *Travail*, urging improvement of the lot of the artist; and *Truth* (*Vérité*), based on the Dreyfus case.　*Justice* was to have been the fourth.

Estimate. Zola is a poor artist. His plots are too often merely series of loosely related tableaus. This construction makes for little suspense, and often, therefore, the novels are dull. This dullness is increased by the fact that many of the evils depicted are no longer current problems. The characters are too often types or mere representatives of a class; never do they become interesting, complex, human individuals. The descriptions, like those of Balzac, are too minute and consequently tedious. Zola is at his best when portraying the movements and emotions of crowds, and sometimes such portraits achieve grandeur. Most of the time, however, the reader feels that Zola has not digested his source material.

The question of the morality of Zola's writing has been debated for eighty years. There is no denial that he shows us a great deal of filth, but it is never made attractive; instead it is shown so that humanity will be sufficiently aroused to clean it up. Zola played a large part in clearing the way for the frank discussion of all problems, of which many had formerly been "banned" from "polite" conversation.

ALPHONSE DAUDET (1840–1897). Daudet was born at Nîmes in Provence. His early life was spent in penury. When he was eight, he moved with his family to Lyons; there he received his primary education. After teaching a year, he went to Paris (1857), where he became the secretary to the Duc de Morny in 1858. His first book (poetry) was published in the same year. After 1865 he devoted all his time to literature. Though he became famous with the publication of *Tartarin de Tarascon* (1872), he was never elected to the Academy.

Characteristics as a Writer. Daudet is often classed as a naturalist, and it is true that he follows the naturalists' impressionistic style and documentary method. But his warm, fun-loving, impulsive, sympathetic, generous, and kindly nature makes it impossible for him to adopt the objective and analytical attitudes of Zola. He resembles Dickens in his frequent combination of pathos and humor, and he is indebted to both Dickens and Thackeray for some of the techniques used in two or three of his later novels.

Works. It has been said that Daudet's imagination was only memory. His sources were his own observations and also people and situations of which he had read. As a result he has been accused of plagiarism (especially of the works of Dickens and

Thackeray) and of scandalously drawing only thinly veiled portraits of his friends (especially the Duc de Morny in *The Nabob*).

HUMOROUS AND PATHETIC TALES.   Many of these deal with humble and mistreated people, particularly those Daudet had known in Provence; and some of the tales are semiautobiographical. *The Little Thing* (*Le Petit chose*, 1868) — often compared with *David Copperfield* — is a touching reminiscence of the author's own boyhood.   *Tartarin de Tarascon* (1872) has as its hero a delightfully irrepressible Provençal braggart.   The sequel, *Tartarin over the Alps* (*Tartarin sur les Alpes*, 1885), shows the same hero as a mighty hunter, and this novel is as good as its predecessor.   *Letters of My Windmill* (*Lettres de mon moulin*, 1866) is a collection of charming and exquisite short stories about rural Provençal life.   Two of the best of the collection are "The Priest of Cucugnan" ("Le Curé de Cucugnan") and "The Mule of the Pope" ("La Mule du Pape").

NOVELS OF MANNERS.   Daudet wrote numerous novels of manners, usually set in Paris.   Some of these border on the naturalistic, and some cast aspersions at various personages.   All together they give an excellent picture of Paris during the years of the Second Empire and of the early decades of the Third Republic.   Some of the best known are *The Nabob* (*Le Nabab*, 1877), which contains pictures of the Duc de Morny, Sarah Bernhardt, and other notables; *Numa Roumestan* (1881), which shows a Provençal deputy struggling — and winning — against the "homicidal north"; *Sapho* (1884), which is a naturalistic but sympathetic portrait of a courtesan; and *The Immortal* (*L'Immortel*, 1888), which is an unbecoming satire on the Academy and specific Academicians.

Estimate.   If Daudet must be classed with the naturalists, let it be said that he is by all odds the most attractive one.   His diction is far simpler than that of the Goncourts, and his movement is faster and freer than that of Zola.   Furthermore, he has an exuberant sense of humor and — usually — a good sense of proportion. He has, in addition, a personal and human note lacking in all the others.   "He has neither the cold-bloodedness of Maupassant, nor the brutality of Zola, nor the incoherence of the Goncourts."[29] "Of them all, Daudet is on many accounts the most acceptable to an Anglo-Saxon public."[30]

THE SHORT STORY

GUY DE MAUPASSANT (1850–1893).   He was born at the Château de Miromesnil in Normandy of a family of the lower nobility. Much of his youth was spent at Rouen, where he was fond of sports, especially boating and fishing. After serving in the Franco-Prussian War, Guy secured a position in Paris in the Ministry of Marine. Between 1873 and 1880 he was a faithful disciple of Flaubert. His first work to attract attention was *Tallow Ball* (*Boule de suif*, 1880); its success persuaded its author to devote himself to fiction. Between 1880 and 1892 he turned out several novels and nearly three hundred shorter narratives. Incessant work plus dissipation ruined Maupassant's good health, and after 1885 he was obsessed by a fear of death. His mind became more and more unbalanced, and by 1892 he was almost insane. He died on the Riviera, in 1893, of general paralysis.

Technique, Style, and Tone. Maupassant formulated no artistic theory. He simply subscribed to Flaubert's realism without imitating his master's prolixity, occasional romantic tendencies, and hatred for what was bourgeois. He is the most purely realistic of the French writers, despite a few naturalistic elements in some of his later stories. His style is completely impersonal and dramatic.

Like Flaubert, he is a devout believer in *le mot juste*, and his diction is not only precise but also concise, natural, sober, and often sardonic.

"At its best, the structure of his works is marked by two things: an economy which gives only the essential elements of character, situation, and development; and an onward movement which combines logic with the maximum of simplicity. Hence a dramatic swiftness which is Maupassant's especial gift."[31]

Like the works of most of the realists and naturalists, his stories are pessimistic and morbid, and he is inclined to seek out the immoral. He does not, however, seek the bizarre or the sensational; he prides himself on describing and relating only what he himself has witnessed.

Works. Maupassant's stories and novels may be divided according to subject matter into six groups.[32]

ABOUT NORMANDY. About a fourth of his works deal with the life of the peasants and lower gentry of Normandy — its meanness, ignorance, shrewdness, narrowness, and pathos. "The Little Keg" ("Le Petit fût"), for example, tells how a petty financier encourages an old woman to drink wine so that she will shorten her life — so that she can no longer collect the annuity he is having to pay her. *One Life* (*Une Vie*, 1883) is a novel about Jeanne, a sensitive and idealistic Norman girl whose friends crush her by their betrayal. Her husband, Julien, proves to be a faithless mate, having an affair first with Jeanne's maid, Rosalie, and then with Jeanne's close and trusted friend. Jeanne is further disillusioned by discovering that both her father and mother have had extramarital affairs; and finally Jeanne's son, Paul, shows his lack of affection for her by leaving home to live with a prostitute, on whom he wastes the family fortunes. A remnant of happiness is restored to Jeanne by the loyalty of Rosalie and by Jeanne's adoption of Paul's baby girl.

Ernest Boyd says of *One Life* that "nominally it is the existence of one woman which is related, but the effect is to transcend the life of a woman and to show us the life of man, the futility of all human dreams."[33]

ABOUT THE FRANCO–PRUSSIAN WAR. Several stories depict the Prussians' treatment of the French. Some of the best tales of this group are *Tallow Ball* (*Boule de suif*, 1880), "The Prisoners" ("Les Prisonniers") and "Two Friends" ("Deux amis").

ABOUT BOURGEOIS LIFE IN PARIS. The best short story of this group (voted the most nearly perfect short story ever written) is "The Necklace" ("La Parure"), a tale full of the irony of fate: Madame Loisel loses a borrowed necklace; works for years to replace it, thereby ruining her appearance, health, and happiness; and then discovers that the borrowed jewels were paste!

ABOUT HIGH SOCIETY IN PARIS. Several of these are concerned with the wiles and ruses of women. *Fine Friend* (*Bel-Ami*, 1885) is the story of an upstart social climber.

ABOUT TRAVEL. Material for these tales was gathered in Maupassant's own journeys to Africa and Italy. Stories of some love affairs are included in this group. The scene of "Jules Romain" is the Riviera.

ABOUT INSANITY AND THE SUPERNATURAL. Here Maupassant has captured on paper the horrors of his own approaching madness. The best pieces are "Fear" ("La Peur"), "The Horla" ("Le Horla"), "A Madman" ("Un Fou"), and "The Corpse" ("La Morte").

Estimate. Although his field is narrow, within it Maupassant has never been surpassed. He has the careful artistry which Balzac lacks, and he has to an eminent degree Balzac's ability to reproduce reality. Maupassant's writing is "an almost fiendishly realistic treatment of modern life";[34] and, as G. Pellissier says, "He shows us the things themselves with perfect transparence, so well that, believing that we have them under our eyes, we are unaware of the writer."[35]

POETRY

After 1850 French poetry, like the prose, became less emotional, more objective, and more impersonal. Even the romantic poets, including Hugo, began to write more objectively. GAUTIER, having abandoned his wild, fantastic poetry, published the relatively restrained and descriptive *Enamels and Cameos* in 1852. His friend, THÉODORE DE BANVILLE (1823–1891) made many clever experiments in rhyme and rhythm, often employing words, as he said, for the mere music of their arrangement; his poems, though skillful and beautifully flawless, lack "spiritual and imaginative elements."[36]

Gautier and Banville serve as transitions between the Romantic and the Parnassian schools.

THE PARNASSIANS. In 1866 there appeared an anthology entitled *The Contemporary Parnassus, Collection of New Verses* (*Le Parnasse contemporain, recueil de vers nouveaux*).[37] The volume contained poems by Gautier, Banville, Charles Leconte de Lisle, François Coppée, Charles Baudelaire, Sully Prudhomme, Paul Verlaine, and Stéphane Mallarmé. The term *Parnassian*, at first applied to the poetry of any of the contributors, later was used with reference to only Leconte de Lisle, Coppée, Prudhomme, and José-Maria de Hérédia. These four poets stressed the intellectual rather than the emotional, and, like the naturalists, tried to adapt the methods of experimental science to poetry. All of them agreed that poetry should be impersonal, strive for the truth, and aim at perfection of form.

Charles Marie René Leconte de Lisle (1818–1894). Leconte de Lisle was the leader of the Parnassians, and it was the preface to his *Ancient Poems* (*Poèmes antiques*, 1852) which served as a manifesto for the group. He was a pessimist, who deplored the ugliness and stupidity of contemporary Europe. Much of his poetry, therefore, is escapist, finding its subjects in ancient Greece, the Orient, Finland, and the Far South. He is especially good at painting landscapes. His most prominent realistic traits, in contrast to these romantic ones, are "social imagination" and a confidence in modern science.

In addition to the *Ancient Poems*, his most famous volumes are *Poems and Poesies* (*Poèmes et poésies*, 1854), *Barbaric Poems* (*Poèmes barbares*, 1862), *Tragic Poems* (*Poèmes tragiques*, 1884), and *Last Poems* (*Derniers poèmes*, published posthumously, 1895). "Leconte de Lisle undoubtedly determined the direction of French poetry for some twenty years."[38]

José-Maria de Hérédia (1842–1905). A faithful disciple of Leconte de Lisle, he wrote only one volume of poetry, *The Trophies* (*Les Trophées*, collected 1893), a series of 118 sonnets, concentrated and impersonal poems dealing successively with ancient, medieval, and modern life.

Sully Prudhomme (1839–1907) and **François Coppée** (1842–1908). They "were merely artists in verse,"[39] and both eventually forsook the Parnassian creed.

CHARLES BAUDELAIRE (1821–1867). Born in Paris, he was always a "rebel against domestic restraint, against scholastic discipline, against any respectable career or behavior."[40] He soon spent a small fortune which he had inherited and then became involved in debt and in an unfortunate liaison. He earned some money as an art critic, journalist, and translator of Edgar A. Poe's short stories, which he popularized in Europe. After impairing his health by dissipation and debauchery, he went to Belgium to live, but was stricken with paralysis. He returned to Paris, where he died.

Baudelaire was a link between the Parnassians and the Symbolists. Like the former — to whose anthology he contributed *New Flowers of Evil* (*Nouvelles fleurs du mal*, 1866) — he emphasized truth-seeking and form rather than matter. Like the Symbolists, however, he was subjective; he delighted in suggesting the relationships among the stimuli of the various senses, and he found hidden spiritual meanings of which concrete things were the symbols. However, "the end which he pursued was not to interpret an idea but to provoke in the reader a state of mind."[41]

His one volume of verse, *The Flowers of Evil* (*Les Fleurs du mal*, 1857), is also reminiscent of Poe and Swinburne. It "depicts the successive soul-states of the author,"[42] and these are not at all consistent; some are abjectly repentant, others blasphemous and complacent toward evil. Many of the poems are filled with ennui, the macabre, depravity, perversity, introspection, violence, eccentricity, and a craving for strange and new sensations.

Baudelaire's poetry is exquisitely musical and rich in imagery.

Despite its sensuousness and subjectivity, it has a classical restraint and an artistic perfection of form.

"It has been said that contemporary French poetry proceeds almost entirely from Baudelaire. . . ."[43]

THE SYMBOLISTS. The French Symbolist movement of 1870–1900 was a reaction against the precise and prosaic realism of Flaubert and Maupassant. The movement takes its name from the fact that its leaders used symbols in a new way: not so much to make their writing clearer as to attempt to express the vague and mysterious thoughts, emotions, and sensations which are generally considered inexpressible. "To suggest," says Mallarmé, "there is the dream; it is the perfect usage of this mystery which constitutes the symbol."[44] Miss Butler says that the Symbolists' essential reform consisted in stripping poetry of everything but its purely musical and spiritual elements, and using these almost entirely for their suggestive value.[45] And Strachey adds: "Verlaine and his fellow-workers in verse attempted to make poetry more truly poetical than it had ever been before, to introduce into it the vagueness and dreaminess of individual moods and spiritual fluctuations, to turn it away from definite fact and bring it near to music."[46]* The characteristics of Symbolist poetry, then, are suggestiveness, "willful impressionism," subjectivity, disregard for grammatical construction, and dependence on the tonal qualities of words. Whereas the Parnassians had recognized a close kinship between poetry on one hand and painting and sculpture on the other, the Symbolists felt that music was the art which had most in common with poetry.

In addition to Verlaine, Rimbaud, and Mallarmé (discussed below), the principal Symbolists were the poets JEAN MORÉAS (1856–1910), JULES LAFORGUE (1860–1887), FRANÇOIS VIELÉ-GRIFFIN (1864–1937), and HENRI DE RÉGNIER (1864–1936); the novelist JORIS–KARL HUYSMANS (1848–1907); and the dramatist MAURICE MAETERLINCK (1862–1949, p. 137).

Paul Verlaine (1844–1896). Verlaine led a life of dissipation and debauchery. He was divorced by his wife, and he shot and wounded Rimbaud, his best friend and disciple. For this latter act

---

* Some historians call Verlaine and Rimbaud "Decadents" and make a distinction between them and the school of Mallarmé, whom they designate "Symbolists." The techniques of the two groups are so similar, however, that the distinction is often ignored.

he was imprisoned for about a year and a half at Mons (1873–1875). Thereafter he returned to Paris, where he spent the remainder of his life in squalor and poverty.

Verlaine's poetry is noted for its mystery, delicacy, music, passion, subjectivity, and melancholy. Some of his poems are lewd; others, full of remorse and religious devotion. His earliest volume, *Saturnine Poems* (*Les Poèmes Saturniens*, 1866), shows the influence of the Parnassians and of Baudelaire. Somewhat better are the *Elegant Festivals* (*Fêtes galantes*, 1869), delightful pictures of Versailles in the eighteenth century. *The Good Song* (*La Bonne chanson*, 1870) is a series of twenty-six poems celebrating his engagement to Matilde Mauté de Fleurville. *Romances without Words* (*Romances sans paroles*, 1874) is a collection of impressionistic views of Belgium and of lyrics of melancholy inspired by his alienation from Matilde (whom he had married in 1870). *Wisdom* (*Sagesse*, 1881), " 'one of the greatest books of religious verse in the world,' "[47] is a volume of poems occasioned by Verlaine's sincere but rather ineffective conversion to Roman Catholicism while he was in prison. Some of his best-known single poems are "Moonlight" ("Clair de lune"), "It Weeps in My Heart" ("Il pleure dans mon coeur"), "The Sky Is, over the Roof" ("Le Ciel est, par-dessus le toit"), and "Autumn Song" ("Chanson d'automne").

Arthur Rimbaud (1854–1891). The follower of Verlaine, he wrote all his poems while in his late teens. After the break with his master, Rimbaud "inflicted himself upon Paris and Europe for a few years,"[48] employing himself successively as a teacher, dockyard worker, soldier, interpreter, pressgang agent, cashier, and quarry overseer.[49] In 1880 he went to the east coast of Africa, where for eleven years he was engaged in commerce. He died in Marseilles.

Rimbaud's poetry has somewhat subtler music than that of Verlaine, but is equally suggestive. It is characterized by "tone-color, . . . deliberate naïveté, . . . fantastic eccentricity, . . . partial use of *vers libre* [free verse], . . . compressed syntax and wilful obscurity, . . . and [the] habit of coordinating closely images and suggestions around one main metaphor."[50]

His two best-known volumes are *The Illuminations* (*Les Illuminations*) and *A Season in Hell* (*Une Saison en enfer*); the latter is a "psychological autobiography." The most famous single poems are "The Drunken Boat" ("Le Bateau ivre") and "Sonnet of Vowels" ("Sonnet des voyelles").

Stéphane Mallarmé (1842–1898). Born in Paris, he taught French in England and English in France. Except for holding at his house the famous Tuesday meetings of those interested in Symbolism, he led a life of retirement. His attractive personality and ability as a conversationalist drew many to his "Tuesdays," and he was recognized as the leader of the Symbolists.

Mallarmé was deeply influenced by the works of the Pre-Raphaelites in England, of Baudelaire, of Verlaine, and of E. A. Poe (some of whose poems he translated into French). Not only did he have an "elliptical mind," but also he deliberately encouraged obscurity in writing, and he virtually ignored syntax. For him "a poem must be an enigma for the vulgar, chamber-music for the initiated."[51] His "desire to free poetry from matter and to suggest, by means of sounds and images, our subconscious thoughts and feelings, accounts for the obscurity of his prose and verse."[52] Almost every one of his poems is built around a single image or metaphor, around which is grouped a cluster of subordinate images which help to develop the central idea.

Several of Mallarmé's followers (especially Gustave Kahn and Jules Laforgue) employed vers libre, adapted in part from the free verse of Walt Whitman.

Mallarmé's most important volumes are *The Afternoon of a Faun* (*L'Après-midi d'un faune*, 1876); *Verse and Prose* (*Vers et prose*, 1893), a collection of some of his earlier pieces; and *Divagations* (1897), a book of prose containing many of his aesthetic theories. In *The Afternoon of a Faun* (to accompany which Debussy composed his tone poem of the same name), a faun gives voice to his amorous yearnings — "a dream of desire told at length"; and in "The Swan" Mallarmé symbolizes the "cold and sterile poet."

DRAMA

Romantic drama was short-lived, and even while it was alive, it was not popular with the bourgeoisie, the revolutionaries, or the democrats. Running concurrently, therefore, and continuing after 1850 was the comedy of manners, which had a far wider appeal. Later there were three more types: light comedy or *vaudeville*, naturalistic drama, and Symbolistic drama.

Comedy of Manners

Eugène Scribe (1791–1861). Scribe wrote about four hundred plays, many of them in collaboration with other dramatists. He began as a writer of farces and satiric songs, and then he turned to the more serious but still gay comedy of manners. His dramatic technique, especially in the construction of plots, is skillful; but "his plays are innocent of ideas or style, nor do they reveal more than very superficial powers of observation."[53] His most famous comedies are *The Silver Wedding* (*Le Mariage d'argent*, 1827) and *Comradeship* (*La Camaraderie*, 1836).

Émile Augier (1820–1889). Augier wrote some historical plays (e.g., *The Adventurer* [*L'Adventurière*, 1848] and *The Flute Player* [*Le Jouer de flûte*, 1850]). He is more famous, however, for his comedies of manners. *Gabrielle* (1849) attacks romantic sentimentality and false passion; and *The Son-in-Law of Monsieur Poirier* (*Le Gendre de Monsieur Poirier*, 1854) is a portrait of a bourgeois upstart. The action of most of his plots arises out of "the conflict between honour and money."

Alexandre Dumas the Younger (1824–1895). Son of the novelist, he has a "lesson" in almost every one of his dramas — a lesson voiced by a particular character recognized as the mouthpiece of the author. By far his most famous play is *The Lady of the Camellias* (*La Dame aux camélias*, 1852), on which the opera *La Traviata* was based. His plays became increasingly didactic and symbolical.

Victorien Sardou (1831–1908). Sardou wrote four kinds of drama: (1) comedy of intrigue, e.g., *The Fly Feet* (*Les Pattes de mouche*, 1861); (2) comedy of manners, e.g., *Our Intimates* (*Nos Intimes*, 1861) and *The Benoîton Family* (*La Famille Benoîton*, 1865); (3) political comedy, e.g., *Rabagas* (1872); and (4) historical drama, e.g., *Fatherland* (*Patrie*, 1869), *Hate* (*La Haine*, 1875), and *La Tosca* (1887). Sardou is a master of stagecraft and dramatic technique, and his comedies, though somewhat shallow, are lively and clever.

Light Comedy, or Vaudeville*

During the Second Empire light comedy was the most popular form of drama. The leading author of this form was EUGÈNE LABICHE (1815–1888), who (in collaboration with others) wrote *A Hat of Italian Straw* (*Un Chapeau de paille d'Italie*, 1851) and *The Journey of Monsieur Perrichon* (*Le Voyage de Monsieur Perrichon*, 1860),

---

* The term *vaudeville* is derived from *Vau de Vire* (Valley of the Vire [River]), the designation given to the satirical songs of the fifteenth-century poet Olivier Basselin. *Comédies avec vaudeville* soon came to be merely *vaudeville*.

his masterpiece. Other writers of light comedy were HENRI MEILHAC (1831–1897) and LUDOVIC HALÉVY (1834–1908), who collaborated in the composition of *Parisian Life* (*La Vie parisienne*, 1867), *Froufrou* (1869) and *The Little Marchioness* (*La Petite marquise*, 1874). Finally, there was EDOUARD PAILLERON (1834–1899), who became famous for *The World Where One Grows Weary* (*Le Monde où l'on s'ennuie*, 1881), a satire on female affectation.

Naturalistic Drama

Naturalism appeared in the novel before it reached the drama. In the latter form its popularity was brief. The only author whose naturalistic plays deserve mention is HENRI BECQUE (1837–1899). He knew little about stagecraft, his characterization is monotonous, and his dialogue is dull. The "slices of life" which he depicts objectively are sordid and drab. His best plays are *Michel Pauper* (1870), *The Ravens* (*Les Corbeaux*, 1882), and *The Parisian Woman* (*La Parisienne*, 1885).

Symbolistic Drama

In 1863 VILLIERS DE L'ISLE ADAM (1838–1889) became the precursor of Symbolism in the drama when he began to write plays which had "a spiritual and symbolical meaning above and beyond their real plot."[54] His best pieces are *Elën* (1863); *The Revolt* (*La Révolte*, 1870); and *The New World* (*Le Nouveau Monde*, 1880), which has as its background the American struggle for independence from England.

Maurice Maeterlinck (1862–1949). The leading Symbolist dramatist, Maeterlinck was born in Ghent. His most famous works are *Princess Maleine* (*La Princesse Maleine*, 1889); *The Sightless* (*Les Aveugles*, 1890); *Pélleas et Mélisande* (1892), set to music (an opera) by Debussy; *The Blue Bird* (*L'Oiseau bleu*, 1909), perhaps his best known play; *Death* (*La Mort*, 1813); and *The Miracle of Saint Anthony* (*Le Miracle de Saint-Antoine*, 1919). Most of these plays are based on history and legend, and they are noted for their delicacy, fantasy, dreamy melancholy, simplicity, and moral and psychological symbolism. Maeterlinck wrote also many essays on literature, nature, and death; some of these are *Life and Flowers* (*La Vie et les fleurs*, 1907), *Before the Great Silence* (*Avant le grand silence*, 1934), and *The Other World* (*L'Autre monde*, 1942).

8

The Twentieth Century

Historical Background. The "new idealism" and optimism which had begun about 1890 were strong during the first fourteen years of the new century. The philosophies of Bergson and Nietzsche were enjoying a great vogue. The period was one of colonial expansion, nationalism, and patriotism.

Intimations of trouble with Germany appeared as early as 1905, however, when the Kaiser insulted France at Tangiers; there was more friction at Agadir in 1911. Then, in 1914 came the storm which destroyed the German Empire and nearly devastated France.

The era between the first and second world wars was one of disillusionment, frustration, and cynicism. Conflicting political and economic beliefs made for instability in the government, and pacificism met opposition from those who feared the resurgence of German militarism, especially after Hitler's rise to power in 1933. The pragmatic philosophy of William James and the psychology of Sigmund Freud had a deep effect on French thought during this interim period.

Like the period following World War I, the years since the end of the last conflict have been filled with insecurity, disillusionment, and fear — especially the fear of Russia and of communism.

General View of the Literature. Many of the *fin du siècle* authors continued to produce in the twentieth century. Naturalism and Symbolism were already on the decline, but no new school of major significance took their place. Many minor schools, to be sure, had brief vogues — neoromanticism, Vitalism, Dynamism, Paroxysm, Futurism, and others; but there has been no group of sufficient importance to stamp its name on an epoch. Several general tendencies, however, may be noted. First, during the early years of the century the optimism, nationalism, patriotism, and activism of the era determined the course of much of the literature. At the same time some writers were turning to mysticism and religion. During each world war some good war literature was written, and after each conflict the literature reflected the pessimism and frustration of the nation. During the twentieth century there have been two other persistent trends: (1) increasing interest in the inner workings of the mind, including the subconscious; and (2) increasing social and political bias. One of the latest artistic schools is the surrealistic one, which (in painting as well as in literature) finds its material in the subconscious. A recent philosophical movement of importance to literature is existentialism, of which Jean-Paul Sartre is the leader. This movement emphasizes the meaninglessness of the universe, the complete freedom of the will, and man's ability to create his own destiny.

DRAMA

It has already been shown how Maeterlinck carried Symbolism in the drama well on into the twentieth century. Also beginning in the old century and continuing into the new were three other types of plays — the religious play, the "problem" play, and the neoromantic drama.

The Religious Play

Paul Claudel (1868–1955). Dramatist and diplomat (once ambassador to the United States), Claudel is a follower of Rimbaud and Mallarmé in his literary method, which is synthetic, associational, accumulative, and elliptical. His plays are written in rhythmical prose, divided into units of short lines or paragraphs. His poetic creed is that the poet alone can comprehend the universe and bring it into communion with the human mind. His theme is "the insufficiency of worldly success and 'the beauty and duty of self-mastery.' . . . Claudel's drama is, in fact, a glorification of activity and effort, as it is also a glorification of the Catholic religion. . . ."[1]

Some of his best plays are *Golden Head* (*Tête d'or*, 1891), *The Exchange* (*L'Échange*, 1894), *The Tidings Brought to Mary* (*L'Annonce faite à Marie*, 1912), *Agamemnon* (1912), and *The Hard Bread* (*Le Pain dur*, 1917).

He has also written some excellent religious poetry, especially *Verses of Exile* (*Vers d'exil*, 1895).

The "Problem" Play

The influence of the naturalists, of Dumas the Younger, of Augier, and of Ibsen can be seen in the so-called "problem" play, which flourished from 1890. Authors of this type of literature consider the stage a platform for the discussion of current questions and abuses. The problem dramas fall into two main categories: the psychological and the philosophical or sociological. The most outstanding authors of the psychological drama were GEORGES DE PORTO-RICHE (1849–1930), FRANÇOIS DE CUREL (1854–1928), and HENRI BATAILLE (1872–1922). The most eminent authors of the philosophical and sociological problem plays were CUREL (above), EUGÈNE BRIEUX (1858–1932) and CHARLES VILDRAC (1882–   ).

The Neoromantic Drama

Representing a reaction against naturalism and pessimism, the French neoromantic dramas of 1890–1915 were enthusiastically acclaimed by the theatergoers. Some of these dramas are comedies, some histories, some tragedies. Maeterlinck's Symbolistic plays might logically be placed in this group. Other important authors of the new romantic play were HENRI DE BORNIER (1825–1901), FRANÇOIS COPPÉE (1842–1908), and ROSTAND.

Edmond Rostand (1868–1918). Rostand is always a poet, and his best work is lyrical, heroic, and imaginative. His vocabulary is extraordinary. He excels in tense emotional situations and in "splendid climaxes." He handles "with equal deftness passages of historical description, emotional love scenes, passages of adroit exchange of wit, and scenes of tender pathos."[2] His two most famous plays are *Cyrano de Bergerac* (1897) and *The Eaglet* (*L'Aiglon*, 1900).

Cyrano de Bergerac is a romanticized account of the life of the seventeenth-century dramatist and novelist. Rostand's Cyrano is "a high-flown lover, a swaggerer and duellist, capable of everything from burlesque to rare self-sacrifice."[3] Because he has an ugly face (his enormous nose has become proverbial) and cannot hope to succeed in winning the heart of Roxane, he ghostwrites love letters to her for her accepted suitor Christian, who wins and marries her. Soon afterwards Christian is killed, but Cyrano keeps the secret of the wooing till near the end of his life. The revelation to Roxane as Cyrano approaches death provides a sentimental but effective conclusion.

The Eaglet, though somewhat weaker than *Cyrano,* is nevertheless an admirable play. It is the touching story of the son of Napoleon I — a son who himself aspires to power and fame. His attempt at conspiracy fails, and he dies miserably.

THE NOVEL

The novel is the richest field of twentieth-century French literature. The crop is so diversified that attempts at classification are difficult and perhaps meaningless. Six categories may, however, be established: psychological, exotic, satirical, idealistic, sociological and political, and biographical.

The Psychological Novel

The psychological novel was not, of course, a new phenomenon. Chateaubriand had essayed to analyze the minds of his characters, but only a few novelists (notably Stendhal and Sainte-Beuve) had followed his example. It remained for Bourget to revive the novel of analysis.

Paul Bourget (1852–1935). Bourget was born at Amiens. He studied medicine for a time, but about 1873 he decided to become an author rather than a physician. His scientific training contributed a great deal to his success as a psychological novelist.

His novels fall into two groups. The earlier group (1885–1889) consists of pessimistic books which probe into the "soul-states" of men, e.g., *Cruel Enigma* (*Cruelle Énigme,* 1885), *A Crime of Love* (*Un Crime d'amour,* 1886), and *André Cornélis* (1887). In 1889, with the publication of *The Disciple* (*Le Disciple*), Bourget underwent a profound change. He became greatly concerned about spiritual matters and (later) embraced the Catholic religion; thenceforth his novels were more moralistic and didactic, and they stressed the spiritual element in man. The preface to his *Promised Land* (*Terre Promise,* 1892) states his view that "the inquiry into the inner and moral life ought to be carried on parallel to the inquiry into the exterior and social life — the one clarifying, searching into, and correcting the other."[4] *The Halting-Place* (*L'Étape,* 1902), which follows his precept, is the story of a family who meet with inevitable disaster because they have wandered away from their national, social, and religious traditions.

MARCEL PROUST (1871–1922). Proust was born in Auteuil, a suburb of Paris. His father was a prominent physician and author; his mother was rich and cultivated. Although Marcel was a frail child and suffered from chronic asthma, he was able to finish the Lycée Condorcet and then to attend the Univeristy of Paris, from which he received a diploma. After a short period of military service, he lived in Paris, where he was very popular in the world of fashion; he devoted a great deal of his attention to "theatres, churches, and young girls."[5] After 1906 his asthma and his morbid sensitivity to dust, noise, and odors led him to shut himself up in an unheated and unventilated room. "He spent most of his last seventeen years in bed, bundled up in a long nightgown, sweaters, mufflers, stockings, gloves, and nightcap. When he arose, he usually wore a heavy fur-lined coat, indoors as well as out."[6] His rare visits to the outside world were usually made at two or three o'clock in the morning, at which time he would visit friends — if he could find any awake. All his important works were written after he became a recluse; on the day of his death (November 18, 1922) he was revising his *Cities of the Plain*.

Proust's work shows the influence of Stendhal, Balzac, Anatole France, Bergson, and Ruskin.

Remembrance of Things Past (*À la Recherche du temps perdu*),[7] upon which Proust's fame rests, is a tremendous *roman-fleuve* ("cycle-novel"; literally, "river-novel"), which runs to fifteen volumes in one edition. It consists of the following seven parts: *Swann's Way* (*Du Côté de chez Swann*, 1913), *Within a Budding Grove* (*À l'Ombre de jeunes filles en fleurs*, 1918), *The Guermantes Way* (*Le Côté de Guermantes*, 1920–1921), *Cities of the Plain* (*Sodome et Gomorrhe*, 1920–1921), *The Captive* (*La Prisonnière*, 1923), *The Sweet Cheat Gone* (*Albertine disparue*, 1926), and *The Past Recaptured* (*Le Temps retrouvé*, 1928).

Somewhat reminiscent of Balzac's *Human Comedy* and of Zola's Rougon-Macquart series, the cycle has as its theme the moral decadence of French society and the obliteration of class distinctions. Three strata of society are shown: the aristocracy (the Guermantes family), the "established bourgeoisie" (Swann and his coterie), and the *nouveaux riches* (the Verdurin family); these are interlinked by marriage. Proust achieves further artistic unity by allowing Marcel (the hero of the cycle and in many ways a self-portrait of the author) to attend the social gatherings of each of these groups. Considerable portions of the cycle are concerned with Marcel's love affairs and his tastes in painting, music, and literature. Episodes from the last three quarters of his life are recounted.

One of the most notable features of Proust's work is his psychological system. Like Bergson, he believes that "the immediate perception of reality . . . [is] the basis of all knowledge . . . [and that] our best instruments are neither the reason nor the conscious memory, but rather the spontaneous instinctive kind."[8] Proust's cycle relies, then, on introspection and subconsciously recaptured memories of his earlier life — memories which are often evoked by a name or a sensory stimulus; and one recaptured memory frequently suggests or recalls several others. Hence "vast correlations of sensations and ideas compose the texture of the novel, exteriorizing the network of the author's extraordinary brain."[9]

As might be expected, such a procedure produces a formless, profuse, and often tedious novel. Furthermore, Proust repels some readers by his amoral attitude and his unshrinking depiction of vice and perversion. His appeal, therefore, is to a restricted group who value his work for its psychological accuracy and its exceptional gallery of characters.

The Exotic Novel

Pierre Loti (pseudonym of Julien Viaud, 1850–1923). The exotic novel is best represented by the works of Pierre Loti. His voyages while he was a French naval officer furnished him with the material for many descriptive works. "He is gifted with intense power of reproducing feelings and the effect of scenery: an absolute emotionalist, he belongs to the lineage of Bernardin de Saint-Pierre and of Chateaubriand."[10] He is nearly always impressionistic and subjective. He ignores religion, morality, and philosophy; and he neglects plot and characterization. Since his main interest is in sensuous enjoyment and since he recognizes the transiency of the enjoyment, his works are pervaded by an air of melancholy. The scenes of some of his most famous novels are laid in many different lands: *The Marriage of Loti* (*Le Mariage de Loti*, 1880) in Tahiti; *My Brother Yves* (*Mon frère Yves*, 1883) and *Icelandic Fisherman* (*Pêcheur d'Islande*, 1886) in Brittany; and *The Disenchanted* (*Les Désenchantées*, 1906) in Turkey. During and after the First World War he wrote several attacks on Germany.

The Satirical Novel

ANATOLE FRANCE (pseudonym of Jacques Anatole Thibault, 1844–1924). Novelist, dramatist, satirist, critic, poet, and short-story writer. He was born in Paris, and there he attended the Catholic Collège Stanislas. In 1876 he was appointed Librarian to the Senate. Although he published some poetry and criticism before 1881, it was not till the publication of *The Crime of Sylvestre Bonnard* in that year that he became famous. He became a member of the French Academy in 1896. Two years later the Dreyfus Affair changed him from an aloof philosopher to a man of action. He wrote several works in defense of the liberal cause, and he became interested in socialism and communism. During World War I he was at first ardently patriotic but later inclined toward pacifism. After the war he retired to his estate near Tours.

Most literary historians are at a loss when they try to classify France as a novelist. He is a dilettante. "In his attitude toward life Anatole France combines the tolerance of Montaigne, the determinism of Taine, and the cynicism of the later Renan. . . . He ridicules all attempts, theological, metaphysical, or scientific, to arrive at absolute truth."[11] He frequently changes his point of view, and perhaps he is consistent only in his epicureanism and his devotion to beauty. His works are characterized by urbanity, sophistication, and a spirit of "universal raillery." Occasionally he is savagely sarcastic; more often he is amusedly ironical or reservedly sympathetic. He is fond of paradox and contradiction. In his style are combined "a musical rhythm, pictorial beauty, and a feeling for the genius of French syntax which can only be described as exquisite."[12]

France's most important works are as follows: (1) *The Crime of Sylvestre Bonnard* (*Le Crime de Sylvestre Bonnard*, 1881), in which Bonnard, a kindhearted old archeologist, commits the "crime" of kidnaping the orphaned daughter (in later editions, the granddaughter) of his old sweetheart. He takes her away from a school where she has been mistreated. When her legal guardian is discovered to be an embezzler, Bonnard is forgiven for the abduction, and the child is made his ward. (2) *Thaïs* (1890), in which the monk Paphnutius succeeds in converting the beautiful courtesan Thaïs, but he loses his own soul as a result of his physical passion for her. Massenet's opera *Thaïs* is based on this tale. (3) "The Procurator of Judaea" ("Le Procurateur de Judée," included in *The Mother-of-Pearl Box* [*L'Étui de Nacre*, 1892]), a short story in which France ironically depicts Pontius Pilate's obliviousness of his role in history. (4) The *Contemporary History* (*Histoire contemporaine*), a cycle of four novels:

The Elm of the Mall (*L'Orme du mail*, 1897), *The Osier Mannikin* (*Le Mannequin d'osier*, 1897), *The Amethyst Ring* (*L'Anneau d'améthyste*, 1899), and *Monsieur Bergeret in Paris* (*Monsieur Bergeret à Paris*, 1901). The last two deal with the Dreyfus Affair; all four are concerned with intrigue. France, through M. Bergeret, his mouthpiece, satirizes priests, soldiers, royalists, and scheming women. (5) *Penguin Island* (*L'Île des pingouins*, 1908), in which an old, half-blind monk discovers an island full of penguins, which he mistakes for human beings. The volume is a satire on the progress of mankind; about a fourth of it is concerned with the Dreyfus case. (6) *The Gods Are Athirst* (*Les Dieux ont soif*, 1912), in which France satirizes man's inhumanity as shown in the Reign of Terror during the French Revolution. (7) *The Revolt of the Angels* (*La Révolte des anges*, 1914), an anti-Christian satire in which a group of angels tire of heaven and descend to Paris.

The consensus of critical opinion is that France is the greatest French author of his era.

André Paul Guillaume Gide (1869–1951). Gide is remembered for three books of criticism — *Pretexts* (*Prétextes*, 1905), *New Pretexts* (1911), and *Incidences* (1925); and for his novels attacking the puritanical and intolerant attitude: *The Immoralist* (*L'Immoraliste*, 1902) is partially autobiographical and defends libertarianism; *Strait Is the Gate* (*La Porte étroite*, 1909) attacks the narrowness of Protestant beliefs; *The Counterfeiters* (*Les Faux-Monnayeurs*, 1925), Gide's masterpiece, is an indictment of those who teach false morals — those who "counterfeit" moral precepts. The novel tells the tale of Bernard Profitendieu, who leaves home because he believes himself illegitimately born.

Also important are Gide's *Journals*, which cover the years 1889–1939 and 1942–1949. The journal was for Gide a form for expressing "thoughts too fugitive, too homely and intimate, too pressing to be expressed appropriately or at all unless in jotting."[13] The *Journals* are thus especially valuable for giving us Gide's "off-the-record" observations, which, "in their cursiveness, have caught the feel of universal problems and the curve of their coming solution."[14]

In 1947 Gide was awarded the Nobel prize.

Gide's early approval of communism was withdrawn after a visit to Russia in 1935–1936, and he expressed his disillusionment in *Return from the U.S.S.R.* (*Retour de l'U.R.S.S.*, 1936) and *Afterthoughts on the U.S.S.R.* (*Retouches à mon retour de l'U.R.S.S.*, 1938).

Gide has long been famous as a stylist, and his influence on younger French writers has been very great.

The Idealistic Novel

Romain Rolland (1866–1944). Rolland was born at Clamecy in Burgundy. He attended the École Normale in Paris and for several years was a professor of music at the Sorbonne. During the First World War his pacificism and internationalism made him unpopular, and he retired to Switzerland. After the armistice he became interested in Russian communism. His last years were spent principally in writing about music, musicians, and socio-political matters.

Rolland is well known for his critical and biographical works on musicians, especially *Goethe and Beethoven* (1930) and *Beethoven: The Great Creative Epochs* (*Beethoven: Les Grandes époques créatrices,* 1928–1937).[15]

Jean Christophe (1904–1912), a ten-volume cycle novel, is, however, his most famous work. This is a spiritual biography of a German musician who goes first to Paris and then to Switzerland and Italy in an attempt to find happiness. *Dawn* (*L'Aube*), *The Adolescent* (*L'Adolescent*), and *The Revolt* (*La Révolte*) recount the hero's early life in Germany and his fleeing to Paris to escape German sentimentalism. *The Market on the Exchange* (*La Foire sur la Place*) tells of Jean's struggles in Paris and of the indifference of the Parisians — an account based partially on the experiences of Wagner. *Antoinette* deals with a love affair. *At Home* (*Dans la maison*) and *The Friends* (*Les Amies*) are concerned with various social and political experiences, wherein Jean finds some measure of satisfaction. In *The New Day* (*La Nouvelle journée*) the hero goes to Italy, where he finds serenity in a "twilight amour" with Grazia, an attractive Italian countess.

Jean Christophe has little plot, and its author has been censured for his disregard of form, diffuseness of language, didacticism, and lack of perspective and of sense of humor. The cycle has been admired, on the other hand, for its moral earnestness and its idealistic faith that conscientious struggle will eventually bring victory over materialism, meanness, and mediocrity. Furthermore, the cycle gives a wonderful panoramic view of life, and Christophe himself is a lovable and human character.

The Sociological and Political Novel

Georges Duhamel (pseudonym of Denis Thévenin, 1884–   ). Duhamel served as an army doctor during World War I; his experiences in the army helped to develop him into a mature novelist.

Duhamel's *Life of the Martyrs* (*Vie des Martyrs*, 1917) expresses his sympathy for the victims of war, and *Civilization* (1918) is an indignant attack on a "civilization" which would lead to a world massacre. A later tetralogy continues his sorrow over the "wreckage of society"; Salavin, the leading character, is a mean and irresponsible yet interesting and pitiable creature. The four Salavin novels are *Midnight Confession* (*Confession de minuit*, 1920), *The Abandoned Men* (*Les Hommes abandonnés*, 1923), *Two Men* (*Deux hommes*, 1925), and *Salavin's Journal* (*Journal de Salavin*, 1927). Another series of novels, *The Pasquier Chronicles* (*La Chronique des Pasquier*, 1933–1944) depicts life in France before the First World War. A lower middle-class family is the center of this life, and people of other spheres are shown occasionally. The canvas is large; many characters are drawn in some detail, but the series does not go so deeply into any one character as the Salavin novels do. The Pasquier series is somewhat inferior to the Salavin one.

"An intense identification of himself with others is considered the hall-mark of M. Duhamel,"[16] and he is noted for his "mystic fervor" — somewhat similar to that of the Russian novelists of the early part of the twentieth century. His first works have been censured for sentimentality and lack of clarity and of originality. At its best, however, his writing is clear and realistic, and his sensitivity and "spiritual insight" have made him one of the most important French novelists of this century.

Jules Romains (pseudonym of Louis Farigoule, 1885–   ). In 1908 Romains published *The Unanimistic Life* (*La Vie unanime*), in which he stated his theory of "unanimism" — the belief that the group is of the greatest importance and that the individual can attain significance only when merged with this group. Romains shared this belief with Duhamel.

Romains' novels are even more important than his philosophical work. *The Regenerated Town* (*Le Bourg régénéré*, 1906) tells how a socialistic idea transforms a stagnant little town into an alert and progressive community. In *The Death of Someone* (*Mort de quelqu'un*, 1911), Romains demonstrates how closely related to each other our lives are: the death of an aging engineer affects the lives of dozens of people. *Lucienne* (1922) is the study of an attractive woman who tries to break the hold which a bourgeois family (an "unfit group") has on the man she loves. In 1931 Romains began a series of novels to illustrate his unanimistic theories; these were published under the general title *Men of Good Will* (*Les Hommes de bonne volonté*). This is a tremendous series, consisting of twenty-seven novels, the last published in 1946. Here Romains gives prophecies and describes major world events from 1908 down into the 1920's. He draws portraits of many great historical figures of the age — for example, Poincaré, Lenin, Kaiser Wilhelm II, and Pétain. He gives a "juxtaposition of various worlds: the army, the Church, the political scene, the medical world, the French Academy; all the familiar themes of the novel: love, crime, pathos, worldliness, friendship, the greatness of obscure and humble characters, the selfishness and pride of the mighty."[17] So diverse is the subject matter (two volumes, for instance, are given to the battle of Verdun and two to a detective story) that Saurat remarks: "Every type of reader will find something in this extraordinary series."[18] The same commentator finds Romains (in *The Men of Good Will*) superior to Balzac in coherence and almost equal to that nineteenth-century novelist in the description of the "mentality and intrigues of professional literary men."[19]

Romains also wrote several plays. Perhaps the most noteworthy are *Knock, or the Triumph of Medicine* (*Knock, ou le Triomphe de la médecine*, 1923) and *The Dictator* (*Le Dictateur*, 1926).

Romains' works are distinguished by "sympathy in feeling, simplicity or a sort of scientific classicism in style, and originality in treatment."[20]

André Malraux (1901–   ). The son of prominent Parisians, Malraux studied Chinese and Sanskrit at the School of Oriental Languages. In 1923 he went to Indo-China, where he at first was engaged in archaeological research. Then he became interested in politics, joined the Young Annam League, which favored dominion status for Indo-China, and later took part in the Chinese National Liberation Movement.

All his novels are concerned with political and labor struggles. *The Conquerors* (*Les Vainqueurs*, 1928) has its scene laid in China during the late 1920's. *Man's Fate* (*La Condition humaine*, 1933) deals with the Chinese Revolution of 1924. *Days of Wrath* (*Le*

Temps du mépris, 1935), an attack on Nazism, depicts the concentration camps and the treatment of political prisoners in Germany. Finally, *Man's Hope (L'Espoir,* 1937) is concerned with the Spanish Civil War (1936–1939), in which Malraux served as a Loyalist aviator.

Malraux is skillful in describing the states of mind of his characters when they are in tense situations, and he is adept at catching and transmitting to the reader the danger and excitement of a great conflict between two political factions.

BIOGRAPHY

André Maurois (pseudonym of Émile Salomon Wilhelm Herzog, 1885–   ).   Maurois is well known for his amusing sketches of British character types of the First World War — especially *The Silence of Colonel Bramble (Le Silence de Colonel Bramble,* 1919).   More famous, perhaps, are his biographies.   In the first of these, *Ariel: The Life of Shelley (Ariel: La Vie de Shelley,* 1923), Maurois showed himself a disciple of Lytton Strachey.   A romanticized biography or a "psychological romance," *Ariel* established a vogue which was popular for twelve or fifteen years.   Maurois has also written novels and essays.

POETRY

As has been suggested above, French Symbolism continued well on into the twentieth century, especially in the drama and in poetry.   Some of the late Symbolists and also several other poets of the early 1900's were inspired by the optimism, idealism, and enthusiasm of the times.   After the war of 1914–1918 the tone became more somber, and — as in the other types of literature — disillusionment and pessimism began to take over.   Government, politics, social problems, and war became the themes of much French poetry.   Vers libre and "poetic prose" were widely used.

Once again, although exact categorization is difficult, four principal types of poets may be recognized: nature, religious, philosophical, and war.

Nature Poetry

Émile Verhaeren (1855–1916).   A Belgian poet who wrote in French, "This lover of the open air, of sunshine, wind and rain, is more akin to Wordsworth than any other French poet."[21]   He is particularly fond of Flemish landscapes and of the bright and beautiful in nature. But he has other loves, too. Like Whitman and Sandburg, he finds beauty and inspiration in the workaday world of men — the noise of their cities, the smoke of their factories, and the bustle of their commerce. He rejoices "in the vitality and violence of Nature, whether as triumphing in the marts of the world or as inextricably mingled with one's personal life and with the beauty of women."[22]

His vers libre is unusual, abounding in the alternation of short and long lines. His rhythm has a strongly marked cadence, and he makes frequent use of Symbolistic suggestion and onomatopoeia. His greatest fault, perhaps, is too much violence: "We grow weary of hearing the siren shriek."[23] Nevertheless, his genuine enthusiasm, his energy, his terseness, and his excellent vocabulary make him a significant poet.

The most important of his twenty-odd volumes are: *The Tumultuous Forces* (*Les Forces tumultueuses*, 1902), *The First Affections* (*Les Tendresses premières*, 1904), *The Multiple Splendor* (*La Multiple splendeur*, 1906), *The Sovereign Rhythms* (*Les Rhythmes souverains*, 1910), and *Moving Wheat* (*Les Blés mouvants*, 1913).

François Jammes (1868–1938). Jammes sees nature as a manifestation of God, and so he might be classed as a religious as well as a nature poet. He has often been compared with St. Francis of Assisi, and he has been described as "a Faun who has turned Franciscan Friar."[24] "He is essentially the poet of the countryside and of the beasts of the field, enjoying everything that a rural life can offer without ever seeking in nature a reflection of his own moods."[25]

His finest volumes are *From the Angelus of Dawn to the Angelus of Evening* (*De l'Angélus de l'aube à l'angélus du soir*, 1898) and *The Grief of the Primroses* (*Le Deuil des primevères*, 1901).

Paul Fort (1872–1960). The nature poet of the Île de France, the region of which Paris is the center. His love for nature is childlike, and like Verhaeren, he rejoices in all that is bright and strong and full of life. He has been called "the most curious example of the poet — at the same time spontaneous and subtle, natural and picturesque, ingenious and wise, opulent and neglected."[26]

Though his verses rhyme, he has the strange habit of printing each stanza as if it were a paragraph of prose.

His fame rests on his thirty-odd volumes of *French Ballads* (*Ballades françaises*) in several series, published after 1912.

Religious Poetry

Charles Péguy (1873–1914) must be added to those discussed above. Born at Orleans, he grew up in the midst of the cult of Joan of Arc, and to him she became the symbol of both France and Catholicism; he is medieval in his mysticism and devotion. His "mysteries" or quasi-epic poems about Joan are written in rhythmical prose, occasionally cut up into lines, and though repetitious, incoherent, and turgid in parts, have some passages of great sublimity.

Philosophical Poetry

Paul Valéry (1871–1945) was an apostle of Mallarmé and the Symbolists and after Mallarmé's death stopped writing poetry for nearly twenty years. Encouraged by André Gide and by now interested in the sciences, he began afresh about 1916. This poetry is guided by a "mathematical metaphysic" derived in part from Leonardo da Vinci. Valéry maintains that "pure poetry" "should 'eliminate life' in favor of a highly intellectualized conception and presentation. . . . Like Mallarmé, he wishes to give a 'sens plus pur' to the ordinary vocabulary and to symbolize abstruse themes." [27] His Symbolistic conventions and mannerisms—ellipsis, allegory, imperfect syntax—often lead to "unconquerable obscurity" but some "consider him one of the chief writers of contemporary French literature." [28] Besides his poetry he is well-known for philosophical and literary essays and lectures.

War Poetry

Louis Aragon (1897–   ) participated in the surrealistic movement and in communism. In World War II, after being evacuated at Dunkirk he became a leader of the underground resistance. His poetry on war, love, nature, and confidence in the future is memorable; his poems from the war years are collected in the volume *Aragon, Poet of the French Resistance*, 1945. But he was first known for novels, and later ones attempt to portray the whole of French society.

CAMUS AND SARTRE

Albert Camus (1913–1960). Born and educated in Algeria, Camus held jobs there and in Europe in journalism, the theater, teaching, and publishing.   He married and had two children. During World War II he was active in the Franch Resistance. Winner of the Nobel Prize in Literature for 1957, he was a novelist, playwright, and essayist, but above all a moralist.   In 1960 he was killed in an automobile crash in France.

The Stranger (*L'Étranger,* 1942) is a powerful novel which attests to Camus' abilities as a master of controlled art and deliberately simple narration. It reveals overwhelming emotional evidence of the absurdity of the attempt by the human mind to explain the inexplicable world in human terms.   *The Plague* (*La Peste,* 1947), a novel, is Camus' most anti-Christian work. It dwells on the injustice of Christianity, evidenced by the sacrifice of the innocent as exemplified by the death of a child, victim of the plague.   The chronicle testifies to the violence and injustice imposed on the city of Oran and to the belief that in times of tribulation man reveals more admirable than despicable traits. It is marked by constant understatement in descriptive style, the precise use of administrative terms and official language, the deliberate banality of words, and the use of irony to bring out the full horror of a situation. Camus' principal plays are *Caligula* (1938), *Cross-Purpose* (*Le Malentendu,* 1943), and *The Just* (*Les Justes,* 1950). *Caligula* represents Camus the young writer with its pathetic beauty, exuberant freshness, and vitality. *Cross-Purpose* is an improbable melodrama marked by economy of construction, terseness, simplicity, and gloom. Despite its sincerity and idealism, *The Just* is verbose, rhetorical and naïve, and exemplifies Camus' frequent over-simplification of ideas. His most significant non-fiction writings are *The Myth of Sisyphus* (*Le Mythe de Sisyphe,* 1942) and *The Rebel* (*L'Homme révolté,* 1951).

Jean-Paul Sartre (1905–   ), philosopher, essayist, novelist, dramatist, and writer of short stories. Born in Paris, Sartre was graduated in philosophy, taught in Laon and Le Havre and then studied in Berlin. In France he became a professor in the Lycée Pasteur at Neuilly. He was taken prisoner by the Germans in 1940 and repatriated in 1941. He abandoned teaching for journalism and in 1946 founded the "revue" *Les Temps modernes.*

His first novel, often considered his masterpiece, was *Nausea* (*La Nausée,* 1938), formed as the intimate journal of a young bachelor.   Perhaps more accurately designated a philosophical essay, it displays most of Sartre's interests except political ones—freedom, bad faith, the character of the bourgeoisie, the nature of thought, memory, art, and the phenomenology of perception. Sartre's most ambitous literary endeavor is a series of four novels (the last still incomplete) entitled *The Highroads of Liberty* (*Les Chemins de la liberté,* 1945). Dealing with, respectively, prewar Europe, the Munich crisis, and the fall of France in World War II, all of the first three books contain a study of people asserting or denying their freedom in order to achieve their fullness of *being.* Indecision and time are important factors in the creation of the individual's *essence. The Wall* (*Le Mur,* 1939), set against the Spanish civil war, is a collection of short stories in which "unauthentic" beings refuse to accept their liberty. Sartre's dramas are based on the same themes of liberty, responsibility, and heroism. *The Flies* (*Les Mouches,* 1943) is in the form of a Greek drama. *The Respectful Prostitute* (*La Putain respectueuse,* 1946) is set in the Deep South of the United States. *The Chips Are Down* (*Les Jeux sont faits,* 1947), written as a scenario, shows the futility of life.

Sartre is the exponent of an existentialism (inspired in part by the German philosopher Martin Heidegger) midway between Christian spiritualism and Marxist materialism. In his works he seeks to illustrate the propositions that: God does not exist; therefore man emerges in an absurd world which has no more reason or finality than man himself, and man is NOTHING—nothing more than a body indissolubly bound to a conscience which is perceptible only when something fills it. But man has one attribute: freedom of choice. He is free to construct his life as he will without benefit of a nonexistent deity or of a nonexistent *human* nature; we are what we make of ourselves, and the hero, for Sartre, chooses spontaneously outside of all conformity the act which truly expresses his nature. It is these tenets which underlie Sartre's formula: "Existence precedes essence."

Sartre shows exceptional power of observation, but has a deformed conception of existence and systematically downgrades human values. It is his artistic style which makes him acceptable; he is direct; his pages give the impression of being spoken rather than written; and he employs the language of the people, which is slang-filled, picturesque, strong, imperious, and teeming with images.

Bibliography for Modern French Literature

Ames, Van Meter. *André Gide*. Norfolk, Conn.: New Direction Books, 1947.

Bacourt, Pierre de, and J. W. Cunliffe. *French Literature During the Last Half-Century*. New York: Macmillan Co., 1923.

Boyd, Ernest. *Guy de Maupassant*. New York: A. A. Knopf, 1926.

Butler, Kathleen T. *A History of French Literature*. New York: E. P. Dutton and Co., 1923. 2 vols.

Dowden, Edward. *A History of French Literature*. New York: D. Appleton and Co., 1898.

Duclaux, Agnes Mary. *Twentieth Century French Writers*. London: W. Collins Sons and Co., 1919.

Faguet, Émile. *A Literary History of France*. New York: Charles Scribner's Sons, 1907.

Fowlie, Wallace. *Clowns and Angels: Studies in Modern French Literature*. New York: Sheed and Ward, 1943.

Nitze, William A., and E. Preston Dargan. *A History of French Literature*. 3rd ed. New York: H. Holt and Co., 1950.

Peyre, Henri, *The Contemporary French Novel*. New York: Oxford University Press, 1955.

Saintsbury, George. *French Literature and Its Masters*. Edited by Huntington Cairns. New York: A. A. Knopf, 1946.

——. *A Short History of French Literature*. 5th ed. Oxford: Clarendon Press, 1897.

Saurat, Denis. *Modern French Literature, 1870–1940*. New York: G. P. Putnam's Sons, 1946.

Schwarz, H. Stanley. *An Outline History of French Literature*. New York, A. A. Knopf, 1924.

Strachey, Giles Lytton. *Landmarks in French Literature*. New York: Oxford University Press, 1912.

Thody, Philip, *Albert Camus, A Study of His Work*. New York: Grove Press, 1959.

Thompson, Stith, and John Gassner. *Our Heritage of World Literature*. New York: Dryden Press, 1947.

Weatherly, Edward H., and Others. *The Heritage of European Literature*. Boston: Ginn and Co., 1948–1949. 2 vols.

Wright, Charles H. C. *A History of French Literature*. New York: Oxford University Press, 1925.

Part Three
Modern Spanish Literature

9

The Renaissance and the Golden Age

(1469–1681)[1]

Historical Background. The marriage of Ferdinand of Aragón to Isabella of Castile in 1469 was an event most fortunate for Spain. Under the joint reign of the two sovereigns (1479–1504),[2] the nation began its rise as a military and political power. Granada was won from the Moors in 1492 and Navarre from the French in 1515. The strength of the towns, of the legislature (Cortes), and of the nobility was steadily reduced. The discovery of America in 1492 led to the establishment of Spain's great colonial empire. And finally, the Inquisition (inaugurated on a nationwide scale in 1478) and the expulsion of the non-Christian Jews (1492) and of the non-Christian Moors (1502) made it clear that Spain was assuming the role of defender of Roman Catholicism. The policies of Ferdinand and Isabella are neatly summarized in the formula "one God, one King, one Law."[3]

These policies were, for the most part, continued and expanded during the reigns of the succeeding sovereigns (Charles I,[4] 1516–1555; Philip II, 1555–1598; Philip III, 1598–1621; Philip IV, 1621–1665; and Charles II, 1665–1700). The almost inexhaustible treasures of the New World made Spain rich, but caused her to neglect both the development of her own natural resources and the consolidation of her national unity. Furthermore, her kings felt it necessary to wage almost incessant war — against France and England for political reasons, against England and the Low Countries for religious reasons. In addition, Spain attacked the Mohammedans virtually all over the Mediterranean and its shores. Charles I (V) began this vast series of wars. Under Philip II Spain reached the height of its power and, upon the defeat of the Armada (1588), began its decline. That decline was rapid under the succeeding kings. Portugal, which had been made subject to Spain in 1580, became independent in 1640, and the Netherlands broke away from 1568 on.

157

The culture of the Italian Renaissance* began to enter Spain in the middle of the fifteenth century. The monarchs of Aragón had long ruled in Sicily and Sardinia, and in Naples since 1435; consequently Aragonese soldiers (and after 1469 Castilians, too) came into contact with the new learning. As early as 1429 there were two Spanish translations of the *Divine Comedy* and one of the *Decameron;* and by 1480 there were many admirers of Petrarch. Ferdinand and especially Isabella encouraged and patronized scholars and poets. Printing was introduced into Spain about 1474. Libraries were collected; new universities were founded;[5] and noblemen filled their palaces with paintings and other objects of art. Elio Antonio de Nebrija (or Lebrija) (1444–1532) was the leading Spanish humanist, and Luis Vives (1492–1540) was one of the greatest philosophers of the time.

Despite the considerable enthusiasm for the new learning, Renaissance culture was never so thoroughgoing in Spain as it was in Italy, France, and England. Its spread was retarded by (1) *españolismo* — the spirit of opposition to foreign influence; (2) innate Spanish resentment of rules; and (3) the Inquisition, which discouraged humanism and freedom of thought. The Inquisition prevented the Protestant Reformation from making any headway at all, but some reform was effected within the Church.

General View of the Literature. The course of Spanish letters ran rather closely parallel to that of the nation's political fortunes. The literature entered its most brilliant period at the beginning of the sixteenth century and reached its peak of glory in the works of Cervantes and Lope de Vega a hundred years later. Thereafter it suffered a decline, and, in the middle of the seventeenth century, affectation (Gongorism) began to vitiate the works of even the most capable writers.†

During the Golden Age the rather boisterous spirit of Renaissance humanism coexisted beside the sober spirit of medievalism. The same century that produced in France both Calvin and Rabelais produced in Spain Saint Teresa and the author of *Lazarillo de*

---

* For a discussion of the elements and characteristics of the Renaissance in general, see pp. 3–6.

† Cf. Marinism in Italy, *préciosité* in France, and euphuism in England. The name is derived from that of Luis de Argote y Góngora (1561–1627), a poet guilty of both *conceptismo* ("cultivated subtlety") and *culteranismo* ("cultivated obscurity"). All four terms apply to what is known as "Baroque" literature.

Tormes. Sometimes the two opposite spirits caused a conflict within one man — Cervantes, for example.

In Spain, as in Italy and France, the Renaissance inspired not only a reverence for ancient Greek and Latin but also an enthusiasm for the vernacular. The Castilian dialect soon was adopted as the official national language.

Unlike the Italians and the French, the Spanish authors generally refused to abandon the old literary genres in order to revert to classical types such as the epic and the ode; there were, of course, some exceptions. The most popular literary forms during the Golden Age were the ballad, the lyric, the prose romance, the novel, and the drama.

POETRY

The Ballad

A discussion of the origins, topics, and merits of the popular ballad (*romancero*) has already been given (Vol. I). Nevertheless, inasmuch as all of the major collections of ballads were made after the beginning of the Renaissance period, a few more words need to be said. Of the two thousand Spanish ballads now in existence, a handful were scattered through some fourteenth-century manuscripts. The first great compilation was the *Songbook of Ballads* (*Cancionero de romances*) published in Antwerp about 1550; new editions were brought out soon afterward. In the same year there was published at Saragossa the *Miscellany of Various Ballads* (*Silva de varios romances*). These two collections contain the majority of the genuine folk ballads of Spain. Later compilations[6] include some artistic or literary ballads (*romance artístico*, or *romance erudito*), at which a number of famous literary artists, including Cervantes and Lope de Vega, tried their hands.

The Lyric

Juan Boscán Almogáver (*d.* 1542). Boscán "initiated the poetic revolution of the Spanish Renaissance."[7] This aristocrat, at the suggestion of Navagero, the Venetian ambassador, began to try Italian (principally Petrarchian) meters in Castilian verse. His most important innovation was the use of the Italian eleven-syllable verse, and he also employed *ottava rima*, *terza rima*, and the sonnet form. In addition, he translated Castiglione's *Courtier* into good Spanish prose. Although Boscán's poetry (published by his widow in 1543) is of small intrinsic value, his introduction of Italian Renaissance meters and culture was of great and enduring value to Spanish poetry.

Garcilaso de la Vega (1503–1536). "The faultless poet" wrote only a small amount of verse, but what survives (thirty-eight sonnets, five odes, three eclogues, two elegies, and one epistle) is polished to perfection. Most of it is concerned with love, and usually it is pervaded by a "gentle melancholy." Although it is lacking in originality and content (it emulates the verse of Petrarch), its author "should be remembered as that Spanish poet most typical of the spirit of the Renaissance, and possessed of the most complete mastery of form."[8]

Fray Luis de León (1527–1591). Considered by some to be the greatest Spanish lyric poet of all time. As a priest and professor, he led an uneventful life (except for his trial for heresy, of which he was acquitted). He is a rarity among Renaissance figures: a scholar without pedantry and a writer without either vanity or affectation. A "Christianized Horace," he has the Latin poet's simplicity, artistry, serenity, love for nature, and hatred of vulgarity; but he loves nature as a means to an end — religious meditation. Two of his most famous lyrics are "Calm Night" ("Noche serena") and "The Secluded Life" ("Vida retirada").

Luis de León wrote also some excellent prose. "The Perfect Housewife" ("La perfecta casada") is an old-fashioned but wholesome portrait of the patient, subservient, humble, efficient married woman. "On the Names of Christ" ("De los nombres de Cristo") is a Platonic dialogue on the subject of the mystical meaning of the names by which Christ is called in the New Testament. Fray Luis' prose, like his poetry, is characterized by loftiness, simplicity, clarity, and precision.

San Juan de la Cruz (St. John of the Cross, 1542–1591). The greatest Spanish mystical poet. Inspired by the *Song of Solomon*, he employs unusually rich imagery and symbolism. "Poetic inspiration and religious ecstasy are fused in him; his soul is poetry. . . ."[9] By far his most famous poem is "The Dark Night of the Soul" ("Noche oscura del alma").

The Epic

No nation seriously affected by the Renaissance could resist attempting the epic. Several Spanish poets, including Lope de Vega, tried to write epics, but with little success. Most of them imitated Boiardo, Ariosto, and Tasso rather than Homer and Virgil. Only Camoëns* and Ercilla wrote epics worthy of consideration here.

Luis Vaz de Camoëns (*c.* 1524–1579). Born in Portugal, Camoëns was the son of a sea captain and grandson of a sailor who had accompanied Vasco da Gama on his voyage to India. Luis' life was a series of misfortunes: he was exiled for addressing his attentions to the king's favorite; he lost an eye in a naval engagement against the Moors; he amassed — and lost — a considerable fortune in India (where he lived from 1553 till 1569); he received little money and meager fame for his poetry; and he died in poverty.

THE LUSIADS† (*Os Lusiadas*, 1572). An epic (in ten books) which celebrates da Gama's voyage around the Cape of Good Hope to India (1496), the poem is marred by the incongruous — almost ludicrous — inclusion of much epic paraphernalia (inherited from Virgil), especially the participation of the Olympic gods in the action; for example, there is a continual conflict between Bacchus (who is opposed to da Gama's success in India) and Venus (who favors the Portuguese because they are the descendants of the Romans). Da Gama has various hardships along the east coast of Africa, but at length manages to reach Callicut. There he is treated hospitably till Bacchus, disguised as Mohammed, turns the prince against him. The big guns of da Gama's fleet persuade the prince to reconsider, however, and da Gama and his men are given presents and are allowed to depart. Venus rewards the voyagers by allowing them to touch at the Isle of Joy en route to Portugal.

The chief virtue of the poem is the fervent patriotism which, though it permeates the whole epic, is found in its most concentrated form in da Gama's review of Portuguese history (in Books III–V) to the King of Melinda in east Africa.‡

Alonso de Ercilla y Zúñiga (1533–1594). Ercilla is remembered for his *La Araucana* (1555–1590). The alleged subject of this

---

* Although Camoëns is a Portuguese poet and does not really belong in this chapter, it has seemed permissible to discuss him here inasmuch as no separate chapter is given to Portuguese literature. See also the discussion of Montemayor, below, under the Pastoral Romance.

† The title means "the Lusitanians," i.e., the Portuguese.

‡ This summary of history recalls both the monologue of Odysseus at the court of Alcinous and also Aeneas' account of his adventures, related at Dido's court. And the prophecies which Aeneas hears in Hades no doubt suggested the prophecies about the universe which da Gama hears on the Isle of Joy.

long poem (thrity-seven cantos) is the insurrection of the Araucanian Indians of Chile against their Spanish conquerors. Ercilla finds means, however, whereby to weave into the narrative many accounts of contemporary European events (such as the Battle of Lepanto, 1571) and of events drawn from mythology (such as the betrayal of Dido). Furthermore, the poem (like Camoëns' *Lusiads*) is weakened by the use of the old Virgilian and Homeric machinery. Although *La Araucana* is a strange work in which the many varied elements are insufficiently fused, the poet has achieved some excellent description of New World scenes and of battles; and his characterization of some of the main Spanish and Araucanian heroes (but not of the heroines) is unusually good. Ercilla anticipates Chateaubriand and Cooper in idealizing the American Indian.

PROSE FICTION
The Romance

The Romance of Chivalry. During the late Middle Ages the prose romance — a rather long narrative dealing idealistically with chivalry and the great deeds of heroes — was popular in Spain. Some of the romances, however, were mere translations, usually of French works. During the Renaissance many Spanish writers revived the form, and great numbers of romances were published during the sixteenth century.

Most of these works glorify the ideals of courtesy, constancy, bravery, and loyalty. The heroine is usually a young unmarried woman (rather than a matron, as in the French romances). The stereotyped plots are unreal and extravagant; they are made up of the hero's battles with other knights, beasts, giants, and magicians; and, of course, the hero always wins the battle and then claims the love of the maiden in whose behalf he has been fighting. Despite many absurdities, ridiculed in *Don Quixote*, the romances were entertaining to Renaissance readers and helped to prolong the existence of the ideals of chivalry.

The most famous romance is *Amadis of Gaul* (*Amadís de Gaula*), first printed by Montalvo in 1508; it went through many editions and had vast numbers of sequels. In addition to the Amadis cycle there is one about Palmerin, the greatest single romance of the cycle being *Palmerin of England* (*Palmerín de Ingalaterra*, 1547–1548). A third excellent romance is *Tirant the White* (*Tirant lo blanch*, 1490), by MOSSÉN JOHANOT MARTORELL and MOSSÉN MARTÍ JOHAN DE GALBA.

By 1700 the romances of chivalry had about expired. Their demise was hastened by the publication of *Lazarillo de Tormes* and *Don Quixote*.

The Pastoral Romance. In the middle of the sixteenth century the vogue of the pastoral romance, made popular by Sannazaro and Tasso, spread into Spain. The most famous and perhaps the best of the pastorals written on the Iberian peninsula is the *Diana* (1559) of JORGE DE MONTEMAYOR of Portugal (d. 1561); this is the most important source of Sir Philip Sidney's *Arcadia*. Other noteworthy pastoral romances are the *Diana in Love* (*Diana enamorada*, 1564) of GIL POLO (d. 1591), the *Galatea* (1585) of CERVANTES, and the *Arcadia* (1598) of LOPE DE VEGA.

The Novel

Exclusive of the romances (which some commentators designate as novels), there were two principal types of novel written in Spain during the Renaissance and the Golden Age — the idealistic and the realistic. *Don Quixote* is in a class by itself and is discussed separately at the end of this section.

THE REALISTIC NOVEL. Realistic fiction made its first appearance in Spain about the end of the fifteenth century and is of far greater importance than the idealistic fiction of the period.

The "Dramatized Novel."[10]

CELESTINA (published *c.* 1499[11]). Familiarly known as the *Celestina*,[12] this work is "the most authentic masterpiece written in Spanish prose up to that time."[13] In the longest (1526) edition it consists of twenty-two "acts," but it was never intended for the stage. In a manner that recalls Juan Ruiz' *Book of Good Love*, the author tells us that his purpose in writing the *Celestina* is to warn young people about the dangers of unrestrained love and of bad company. He then tells how Celestina, "half-witch, half-pander," encourages the guilty passion of Calisto and Melibea, a passion opposed by the parents of the girl. Calisto is killed by a fall from a ladder as he leaves Melibea's apartment in pursuit of men engaged to attack him. His beloved then commits suicide by leaping from a tower.

The plot, obviously, is not the chief attraction of the *Celestina*. It is in the delineation of characters that the author has earned immortality.   The crone from whom the work takes its name is a wonderful creation — "a satanic figure, heartless intelligence devoted to evil."[14]   Calisto is a conventional lover, and Melibea is a rather typical heroine.   More memorable are the low characters — panders, prostitutes, servants, soldiers, bullies, and the like.

The *Celestina* was immensely popular and also influential on later literature, especially on the works of the novelists and dramatists, including Cervantes, Lope de Vega, and many other authors in Italy, England, and Germany.   The great Spanish scholar Menéndez y Pelayo regards the *Celestina* as one of the three greatest works in Spanish literature (the other two being *Don Quixote* and Ruiz' *Book of Good Love*).

The Picaresque Novel.   Mérimée defines the picaresque novel as "a novel whose characters are drawn from that particular class of people, of low birth or fallen in station, who live at others' expense, deliberately place themselves beyond the pale of social convention and law, and keep themselves alive by sheer trickery, by the fertility of an unscrupulous imagination."[15]   Northup's definition is broader: "The picaresque novel is a realistic portrayal of criminal life in which criminals and their tricks constitute the chief source of interest."[16]   The typical picaresque novel is a biography of a wandering rogue (*picaro*); it is often told in the first person, and it usually is made up of a series of adventures loosely strung together. There is seldom a love affair.   The novel is most often humorous, satirical, and cynical.

Some important forerunners of the genre are Petronius' *Satyricon*, Apuleius' *Golden Ass*, the medieval animal epic (especially the *Roman de Renart*), Pulci's *Morgante Maggiore*, and Brant's *Ship of Fools*.

Its successors are even more illustrious.   The Spanish picaresque novel flourished for more than a hundred years, and its influence soon spread to Italy, France, Germany, and England.   In the last named country, some of the authors most indebted are Nashe (*The Unfortunate Traveler*), Fielding, Smollett, Dickens, and Thackeray.

*LAZARILLO DE TORMES.**   The first really important picaresque novel.   It appeared anonymously in Alcalá, Burgos, and Antwerp in 1554;[17] its author is still unidentified.   Lazarillo, the "antihero" (as the main character has been called) is a proverbial picaro, drawn partly from folklore.   The book tells of Lazarillo's

* The whole title is *The Life of Lazarillo de Tormes and His Fortunes and Adversities* (*La vida de Lazarillo de Tormes y de sus fortunas y adversidades*).

ancestry and birth (a parody of the genealogies of the knights in idealistic fiction); his life of starvation, cunning, and crime; the tricks he plays on people; and his ultimate settling down as the husband of a canon's mistress. There is much satire directed against the vices of the clergy, especially the performance of "miracles."

Immediately and widely popular, the work was placed on the Catholic Index, and an expurgated edition was published in 1573. Two sequels (in which Lazarillo lives in the sea and becomes a leader of tunny) appeared in 1555 and 1620. Many imitations were written between 1590 and 1660.

MATEO ALEMÁN (1547–1610). Alemán wrote *Guzmán de Alfarache* (Part I, 1599; Part II, 1605). This work purports to be the memoirs of a Sevillan picaro, who wanders through many adventures. He is, successively, a kitchenboy, a porter, a gallant, a soldier, a beggar, a page, a buffoon, a procurer, a thief, a merchant, a student, and the husband of an heiress; his adventures and escapades carry him to Toledo, Florence, Rome, Milan, Genoa, Saragossa, Madrid, Alcalá, and back to Sevilla. He is at last sentenced to the galleys, where he writes his memoirs.

Alemán employs the device of placing a long moral at the end of each adventure — probably so that his book will not offend authorities. Though a bit dull for most modern readers, the moralistic passages added to the popularity of the work in the seventeenth century. Alemán has a wide knowledge of life (he himself was something of a picaro); his style is easy and popular; and his vocabulary is abundant. Some critics consider *Guzmán* the greatest of the Spanish picaresque novels.

ALONSO JERÓNIMO DE SALAS BARBADILLO (1581–1635). He wrote *The Daughter of Celestina, or the Ingenious Elena* (*La hija de Celestina, o la ingeniosa Elena* (1612, 1614), a tale about a female rogue, or picara, who plays tricks on her lovers instead of on various masters.

LUIS VÉLEZ DE GUEVARA (1579–1644). He is famous for *The Lame Devil* (*El diablo cojuelo*, 1641), a satirical picaresque novel about a student who releases a devil from a flask and is rewarded by being taken on a flight through the air, during the course of which he is allowed to see various scenes of life in the slums and in castles (the devil makes the roofs transparent). Le Sage (in *Le Diable boiteux*) improved upon Guevara's version, which is ingenious in conception but which is poorly sustained as a narrative. Vélez de Guevara is also famous for his dramas; he wrote about four hundred, of which eighty are extant. Most of these are on historical themes.

FRANCISCO DE QUEVEDO Y VILLEGAS (1580–1645). One of the greatest of the picaresque novelists is Quevedo. He is best remembered for his *History of the Life of Buscón* (*Historia de la vida del Buscón*, 1626). This is the story of Pablo, a rascal who follows his wealthy schoolmate to Alcalá, where Pablo engages in various sorts of mischief. He joins a gang of thieves, poses as a cripple, becomes an actor, and eventually emigrates to America. Quevedo makes no attempt to moralize or to create an original, verisimilar character. The novel is a clever but brutal, cynical, and coarse tale of villainy.

MIGUEL DE CERVANTES SAAVEDRA (1547–1616). The greatest figure in Spanish literature and one of the greatest men of world literature. He was born in Alcalá; his father was an unsuccessful physician, who moved about from city to city to try to improve his fortunes. Of Miguel's education little is known. He probably had scant formal schooling, but undoubtedly read widely though perhaps desultorily. In 1569 he went to Italy, where he first was employed in the household of Cardinal Acquaviva at Rome. The following year he became a soldier and performed garrison duty. He distinguished himself for gallantry in the Battle of Lepanto (1571), in which he received three wounds; one of them left his hand crippled for life. In 1575 he sailed for Spain, but his ship was captured by pirates, and he and his brother were sold into slavery in Algiers. He was not ransomed till 1580. Then he returned to Madrid, married (1584), and tried to earn a living by writing dramas and a pastoral novel (*Galatea*). Meeting with little success, he took a position as a purchasing agent in 1587, a position which he held for about six years; and from about 1594 till 1598 he served as a tax collector. During these eleven years he was incarcerated several times for illegal seizures of property and for irregularities in his accounts.[18] It was probably while in prison in 1602 or 1603 that he began *Don Quixote*. From 1606 till his death in 1616 he lived in Madrid, where he spent most of his time writing.

Works.

DON QUIXOTE or *DON QUIJOTE** (Part I, 1605; Part II, 1615).

* *Quixote* is the old spelling; *Quijote* is modern Castilian.

Composition and Publication. When Cervantes first began his greatest work is not known. In the Prologue he says that the Don is the sort of person who "might be begotten in a prison," and consequently tradition has held that the novel was begun about 1602 or 1603 during one of Cervantes' many incarcerations. Be that as it may, Part I was finished in 1603 or 1604 and published in 1605. The popularity of this part induced a person who called himself Alonso Fernández de Avellaneda[19] to write a second part (1614). The appearance of Avellaneda's work spurred Cervantes on to finishing his own Part II, which was published the next year.

Purpose and Meaning. Virtually all commentators are agreed that Cervantes' original purpose in writing *Don Quixote* was principally to burlesque the romances of chivalry and that, as the narrative progressed, it somehow took on a deeper and broader meaning than the author had at first intended. There is violent disagreement, however, as to what that deeper and broader meaning is. Some critics have thought the novel an attack on some specific individual (Charles I, Philip II, Loyola). Another has suggested that it is merely an attempt to expound the nature of madness. Another has believed it to be Cervantes' confession of his own disillusionment. Several have tried to interpret it as some sort of allegory; one in particular has suggested that it is a mystical allegory concerning the nature of divine love and that Dulcinea (Quixote's beloved) is an anagram for *Divina Luce* (Divine Light). Some commentators have thought that Cervantes agrees with Sancho and is ridiculing idealism in the person of Quixote, whereas some others have believed that the author identifies himself with the knight and is praising "faith and character rising above the ills of sense."

Perhaps Coleridge was near the truth when he said that Cervantes' design is "to present personified the two elements of human nature: soul and sense, poetry and prose." Surely Cervantes, even while laughing at Sancho and Quixote, is in sympathy with *both* of them and identifies himself to some extent with each. It seems doubtful that he deliberately set about to personify anything. What apparently happened is this: Desiring to satirize the absurdities of the chivalric romances, Cervantes drew a portrait of a poor man who had lost his wits by reading such romances and who imagined himself a knight errant. Then Cervantes drew Sancho — a down-to-earth peasant — as a foil. As the story progressed, the author found himself somewhat in sympathy with both the realistic Sancho and the idealistic Quixote; the two had become complementary rather than antagonistic to each other. They had "come to represent the two types of human wisdom — that which knows how things really are and that which knows how they ought to be."[20]

The Story. Having lost his reason from too much reading of the romances of chivalry, the middle-aged Quixote imagines himself an aspirant to knighthood, equips himself with rusty armor and a decrepit horse (Rozinante), and sets out to earn his spurs. He chooses a peasant girl (Dulcinea del Toboso) as "the mistress of his heart" and immediately believes her to be a fine lady, for whose sake he will do his great deeds. After several adventures (including being knighted by an innkeeper, whom he believes to be the lord of a castle), the Don meets the earthy Sancho Panza, who becomes his squire. The two engage in many other exploits; the most famous are Quixote's battle with a windmill, which he believes to be a giant; a fight with a Biscayner; and Sancho's service as governor of the Isle of Baratraria. Finally Carrasco, one of Quixote's friends, disguises himself as a knight and, for Quixote's own good, overcomes him in combat. He requires Quixote to promise to abstain from knightly practices for a year; but the humiliated and brokenhearted Don returns to his own village, becomes ill, and dies a few days later.

Style and Technique. As Northup says, "Cervantes possessed not one style but several. He was a master at suiting his diction to his narrative."[21] The style of most of the novel is "simple, realistic, racy." But when he wishes to ridicule the old romances, he makes his language stilted and archaic. He can also be bombastically rhetorical or straightforward.

Some of the slovenliness of *Don Quixote* has been found to be the fault of its printer. But Cervantes himself is guilty of many contradictions, lapses of memory, incongruities, and anachronisms.

The plot, somewhat similar to that of the picaresque novel, is little more than a string of adventures; and it seems almost certain that Cervantes had planned only a few episodes before he began to write. Several extraneous short tales are intercalated into the main narrative.

The two principal characters are superbly drawn: Don Quixote, the epitome of unselfish but misdirected devotion to an ideal; and Sancho Panza, the shrewd though ignorant realist. The minor characters, too, are deftly drawn; many are mere types, but there is an infinite variety — priests, students, wenches, shepherds, inn-keepers, nobles, and dozens of others that inhabited sixteenth-century Spain.

Evaluation. Regardless of Cervantes' intended interpretation, nearly everybody has found not only entertainment but also a personal "message" in *Don Quixote.* Like Shakespeare, Cervantes has given not only an incomparable picture of his own countrymen but also a picture of human nature everywhere, and consequently *Don Quixote* approaches the ideal of pleasing all and always. "Cervantes ranks with Shakespeare and with Homer as a citizen of the world, a man of all times and countries, and *Don Quixote*, with *Hamlet* and the *Iliad*, belongs to universal literature, and is become an eternal pleasaunce of the mind for all the nations."[22]

The influence of *Don Quixote*, of course, has been inestimable. Critics agree that few other works have contributed so much to the development of prose fiction. Translated into nearly all languages, the novel has had an effect not only on literature but also on politics, sociology, and ethics. "Its influence can never be traced even approximately, but one can confidently say that no other novel has so served to make the world better."[23]

MINOR WORKS. *Don Quixote* has so overshadowed Cervantes' other writings that the average reader hears little of them. There are, however, a rather large number of lesser works. Cervantes wrote some poetry; most of it is poor, but a few of his sonnets are commendable. He aspired to be a great dramatist, but none of his thirty-odd plays has ever been a success on the boards. He wrote a dull pastoral romance (*Galatea*, 1585) and an almost equally dull idealistic novel of love and adventure (*Pérsiles y Sigismunda*, published posthumously, 1617). His *Trip to Parnassus* (*Viaje del Parnaso*, 1614) is a monotonous critical enumeration (in verse) of about a hundred and fifty poets. Finally, there is the collection of twelve short narratives *Exemplary Tales* (*Novelas exemplares*, 1613), which, according to some critics, would perpetuate their author's name if he had written nothing else. These tales exhibit a variety of tones and techniques. Some are crude and realistic; others are delicate, romantic, and fanciful. Several of them show Cervantes' originality and his powers of observation and description. One of them, "The Colloquy of the Dogs" ("Coloquio de los Perros"), is the tale of Monipodio, the master of a school for thieves; his jackal, Ganchuelo, "who never steals on Friday"; Pipota, a female sot; and

Berganza, a witty dog.   Other excellent tales from the group are "Rinconete and Cortadillo" and "The Deceitful Marriage" ("El Casamiento Engañoso").

THE DRAMA

There is evidence that between 1100 and 1400 a great deal of dramatic writing was done in Spain.   There must have been miracles, mysteries, and moralities such as existed in the other countries of western Europe; and in addition there were probably pageants, mimes, mummeries, and the like.[24]   None of these, however, has survived.   In the middle of the fifteenth century GÓMEZ MANRIQUE (*c.* 1415–1490) composed some short dramatic pieces for certain social and religious occasions; but these can hardly be called dramas.   It was not till nearly a hundred years later that Spanish drama really began.

Juan del Encina (*c.* 1469–1529).   "The father of the Spanish drama" was also a lyricist and musician.   As early as 1492 he wrote an *égloga*, or short dramatic sketch modeled on Virgil's *Eclogues*.   Thereafter he wrote many other dramatic pieces, some on religious subjects, others on secular ones.   The best known are the *Eclogue of Plácida and Vitoriano* (*Égloga de Plácida y Vitoriano*), *Eclogue of Three Shepherds* (*Égloga de tres pastores*), *Eclogue of Cristino and Febea* (*Égloga de Cristino y Febea*), and *Brawl Scene* (*Auto del repelón*).[25]

Although Virgil and Poliziano were his models, Encina made a step toward realism in allowing his peasants to speak their own rustic dialect; and the *Brawl Scene* is a realistic farce in which students play tricks on peasants coming to market and then engage them in a scuffle.

"Encina did not bring drama to the people, but secularized it and made it popular with the aristocracy."[26]

Bartolomé de Torres Naharro (d. *c.* 1531).   Torres Naharro was a more powerful and more original dramatist than Encina. Following the theories of Horace, he divided the drama into five acts (*jornadas*), and he made a distinction between realistic comedy (*comedia a noticia*) and romantic or idealistic comedy (*comedia a fantasía*).   Of the former sort he wrote *Kitchen Comedy* (*Comedia tinellaria*),[27] a satire on the waste and corruption in a cardinal's household, and *Military Comedy* (*Comedia soldadesca*), a play on the unhappy predicament of an Italy ravaged by soldiery.   Some of his best "comedies of fantasy" are *Swanskin* (*Serafina*), a "romantic love intrigue," and *The Wedding Play* (*La Ymenea*), "the first cape-and-sword play in Spanish literature, with window love-making and a compromised lady."[28]

Other Predecessors of Lope de Vega. GIL VICENTE (*c.* 1470–1536) wrote pageants, farces, comedies, and tragicomedies. He is remembered for his "lyric grace," his satire against social evils, and his religious liberalism. His best play is *Ignez Pereira*, the story of a peasant girl who marries twice — first a glamorous but improvident knight, and second a plain but honest man of her own station.

LOPE DE RUEDA (*c.* 1510–1565) "democratized the drama." Leader of the first barnstorming troupe, he took drama to the provinces. He is remembered for his short skits or farces (*pasos*), which generally had slight plots but which were enlivened by many delightful stock characters, e.g., the rustic, the barber, the negro, and the Biscayan. Rueda's diction is brisk, racy, and popular.

JUAN DE LA CUEVA (*c.* 1550–1620) reduced the comedy to four acts, deliberately rejected the unities, and wrote the first Spanish national drama, employing themes of the old chronicles and ballads.

LOPE FÉLIX DE VEGA CARPIO (1562–1635). The second greatest figure in Spanish literature. Of humble origin, he had little formal education, but learned some Latin, music, dancing, and fencing. His precocity (he wrote a drama when he was twelve) soon earned him various patrons. About 1585 he was actively engaged in writing plays for the company of Jerónimo Velázquez, and two years later he was banished from Castile for lampooning the Velázquez family. Moving to Valencia, he continued to write dramas. And, while there, he eloped with a highborn maiden and incurred her family's wrath. In 1588 he sailed with the Armada. Surviving the disaster, he accepted the patronage of the Duke of Alba and served as the entertainer for the family of that nobleman till 1595. Then he returned to Madrid, bought a house, married a butcher's daughter (his first wife had died), and engaged in a scandalous series of amours. Except for a six-year residence in Toledo (1604–1610), he lived in Madrid the remainder of his life. In 1614 he became a priest, but that fact did not put an end to his "gallant intrigues." The last forty years of his life were spent in incessant writing.

Almost everybody agrees that Lope de Vega was "the world's most prolific playwright," and one scholar claims that "no other writer in the world's history even remotely approaches his record for productivity."[29]   In addition to twenty-one volumes of non-dramatic works, he wrote an incredible number of plays.   His contemporary biographer Montalbán says that Lope wrote 1,800 *comedias** plus 400 *auto sacramentales* (religious dramatic pieces descended from the medieval mystery), and these do not include short skits, interludes, and the like.   Perhaps these numbers are too large, but 426 *comedias* and 42 *autos* have survived.   Lope himself boasts that he wrote "more than a hundred *comedias* in twenty-four hours each."   Such fertility led his contemporaries to call him "the prodigy of nature."

Nondramatic Works.   Although Lope is remembered chiefly for his plays, he tried his hand at almost all the types of literature that were popular during his time — the epic, the romance, the novel, the lyric, and the critical poetic essay.

THE EPIC.   Lope wrote historical, religious, romantic, and mock epics.

Among the historical epics are: *Dragontea* (1598), a review of contemporary events, perhaps more an invective against Sir Francis Drake (whence the title) and against England than it is an epic; *Jerusalem Conquered* (*Jerusalem conquistada*, 1609), an account of Richard the Lion-Hearted's unsuccessful attempt to take the Holy Land from Saladin (it is too full of love affairs and legendary matter, but it tells of many interesting episodes, and it has some clever characterization); and *Tragic Crown* (*Corona trágica*, 1627), the story of Mary Stuart (like *Dragontea*, it is characterized by violent tirades against the English).

His best religious epics are *Isidro* (1599), a long narrative about San Isidro Labrador, the patron saint of Madrid, and *The Shepherds of Bethlehem* (*Los pastores de Belén*, 1612), the story of Mary, Joseph, and Jesus up to the time of their flight into Egypt.

Lope wrote the romantic epic *The Beauty of Angelica* (*La hermosura de Angélica*, 1602), a sequel to Ariosto's *Orlando Furioso*.   The plot is weak, and the poem is too heavily laden with "episodes, digressions, and allusions to local events."[30]

His mock epic *The Battle of the Cats* (*Gatomaquia*, 1634) is delightfully humorous, full of clever irony and parody.   It is concerned with the affairs of Zapaquilda and her two lovers Marramaquiz and Micifuf.

* For Lope the word *comedia* meant merely "play" — comedy, tragedy, or tragicomedy.

THE ROMANCE. In 1598 Lope followed the literary fashion and wrote a pastoral romance. In *Arcadia* he recounts some of the adventures of himself and his friends, who, of course, become shepherds and shepherdesses. The Duke of Alba is Anfriso, and Lope himself is Belardo. The plot drags, and the whole work has the usual faults of the pastoral — artificiality, sentimentality, too many classical and mythological allusions, and improbability.

THE NOVEL. *Dorotea* (1632) is a semiautobiographical novel of romantic adventure, into which Lope weaves many details of his affair with the actress Elena Osorio. This work is far better than the *Arcadia*. The incidents are entertaining, the dialogue is effective, and a great deal of genuine passion is well described.

THE LYRIC. Lope "will always rank as one of the greatest of Spanish lyricists."[31] He composed virtually every kind of lyric then in vogue — sonnets, eclogues, songs, odes, elegies, and others. Some were serious, others light; some were religious, others secular. He wrote also many epistles and ballads as well as lyrics. He is best in his sonnets, ballads, and short lyrics. These usually have the virtues of spontaneity, simplicity, and directness; they are less affected than the poetry of most of Lope's contemporaries.

THE CRITICAL POETIC ESSAY. In 1609 Lope published a poem of nearly four hundred lines of unrhymed hendecasyllabic verse entitled *The New Art of Making Comedies in This Time* (*El arte nuevo de hacer comedias en este tiempo*). Here he exhibits his acquaintance with the classical rules for writing plays, proclaims his approval of them — and then refuses to abide by them. The new kind of play (*comedia nueva*) which most pleases the mob has rules of its own: mixture of comic and tragic elements, violation of the unities, suiting the diction to the speaker, division into three acts with the denouement beginning about the middle of the last act, suspense, intrigue, and the use of a variety of metrical forms in each play (sonnets for soliloquies, ballad meter for narration, quatrains for love poetry, and so on).

Dramatic Works.

CLASSIFICATION. Mérimée[32] divides Lope's plays into two main classes: (1) *comedias,* or three-act dramas, and (2) one-act dramas. In the first group are historical, romantic, mythological, pastoral, and biblical plays; saints' lives; and cloak-and-sword dramas ("intrigue plays of contemporary middle-class or aristocratic manners"). The one-act plays include *autos*, *loas* (witty prologues), and *entremés* (short farces).

CHARACTERISTICS. The characteristics of Lope's plays are those which he defends in the *New Art of Making Comedies*. In addition, he makes much use of the "point of honor," that is, the threat to a man's honor or a woman's virtue. His historical plays are generally based on Spanish topics taken from the chronicles and ballads. The cloak-and-sword plays are romanticized stories with very complex plots, involving mistaken identities, disguises, misunderstandings, and the like.

HISTORICAL PLAYS. Some typical historical plays are *Rome in Ashes*[33] (*Roma abrasada*, 1629), which retells the story of Nero's reign (incidentally, Lucan and Seneca [both claimed as Spaniards] and Christianity are praised), and *The New World* (*El nuevo mundo*, 1614), which tells about Columbus' discovery of America and his return to Spain (much of the action takes place in the New World).

ROMANTIC OR "NOVELESQUE" PLAYS. An example of the romantic drama is *Punishment without Vengeance* (*El castigo sin venganza*, 1631), the story of a young man's love affair with his stepmother. His father metes out punishment by having his son kill the stepmother without knowing who his victim is, and then the father incites bystanders to kill the son for having murdered the stepmother. More significant is *Sheep's Well* (*Fuente Ovejuna*), a play revolving around the "point of honor." A nobleman, who is the governor (*comendador*) of the small town of Sheep's Well, seduces one of the young peasant girls of the community. Outraged, the men and women of the town kill the nobleman by impaling him on lances and pitchforks. The king sends a prosecutor to try to discover the identity of the murderer, but the people of Sheep's Well stick together and refuse to disclose which one or ones have participated in the crime. The prosecutor reports the matter to the king, who forgives the whole town and agrees that its citizens were right in defending their honor. The philosophical point of the play is not so much that the people are right as that the king will be just when he knows the facts and that the king may control a man's wealth and even his life but not his honor: that belongs to the man's own soul.[34]

CLOAK–AND–SWORD PLAYS. Two of Lope's best cloak-and-sword dramas are *The Steel of Madrid* (*El acero de Madrid*, 1603), in which a girl deceives her father by pretending to take ferric concoctions from a fake doctor (really the friend of her lover) and by meeting her lover while engaging in walks prescribed by the "doctor"; and *St. John's Eve* (*La noche de San Juan*, 1631), in which two ladies finally succeed in marrying their chosen lovers in spite of brothers' oppositions and a series of misunderstandings which lead each of the four principals to doubt the loyalty of his or her beloved.

Evaluation. "No one of his plays is wholly bad, no one a finished masterpiece."[35] Lope's eagerness to please the populace and to keep them supplied with new plays leads him into the sins of carelessness, repetitiousness, and failure to get the most out of a given situation. Furthermore, since his paramount purpose is simply to entertain, he makes "all other interests subordinate to the interest of the story."[36] Consequently, he slights characterization, and he rarely wrestles with the deep and eternal problems of the human soul.

His merits, obviously, are amazing fertility, versatility, and variety. His excellent "theater-sense" makes everything he touches take "on life, motion and illusion of reality, with all its complexity, diverting or disturbing. There is never a suspicion of fatigue, effort or exhaustion."[37] And his style, despite his hastiness, is nearly always graceful, charming, facile, and appropriate.

Lope de Vega's fecundity is equalled only by his contemporary popularity. "For a long time nobody else was willingly heard on the stage,"[38] and his plays were soon presented in Italy, France, and even Turkey.

Although he invented no new dramatic practices or tendencies, he had the genius to perceive which ones were the most effective, and his brilliance and his productivity enabled him to establish, almost singlehandedly, the Spanish national drama. "Historically he is important as the dramatist who found the formula which prevailed in Spain until the neo-Classic reaction of the eighteenth century."[39]

TIRSO DE MOLINA (pseudonym of Gabriel Téllez, *c.* 1571–1648). One of the greatest of the followers of Lope de Vega. He was born in Madrid and educated at Alcalá de Henares. He became a priest in 1601. Except for much traveling in the performance of his priestly duties, he lived an uneventful life. Like Cervantes and Lope de Vega, Tirso tried several types of literature.

Nondramatic Work. *The Villas of Toledo* (*Los cigarrales de Toledo*, 1624) is a framework miscellany (imitative of Boccaccio's

Decameron) in which several aristocrats visit each other in their villas and tell stories, act out dramas, recite poems, and engage in philosophical discussion. Included is a critical defense of the "new comedy" as written by Lope de Vega.

Dramatic Works. The most important of Tirso's works are dramas, of which he is said to have written more than four hundred; eighty-six survive. The majority of these are published in seven collections: three appear in the *Cigarrales* (1624); twelve in *Twelve New Comedies of Master Tirso de Molina*, Part I (*Doce comedias nuevas del Maestro Tirso de Molina, primera parte*, 1627); four in Part II (1635); twelve in Part III (1634); twelve in Part IV (1635); four in Part V (1636); and three *autos* in *Sugared Instruction* (*Deleitar aprovechando*, 1635), another miscellany similar to the *Cigarrales*. The other twenty-nine plays are scattered through various other collections.

Again like Lope, Tirso wrote historical, religious, and cloak-and-sword plays.

HISTORICAL PLAYS. *Woman's Prudence* (*La prudencia en la mujer*) shows how the dowager queen, Doña Maria, by prudence and tact saves the throne for her young son, Fernando IV. Some critics consider this the best historical play in Spanish literature.

RELIGIOUS PLAYS. *The Doubter Damned*[40] (*El condenado por desconfiado*) treats the theological problems of free will versus predestination and of faith versus good works. Paulo is persuaded by the devil to leave his hermitage and seek Enrico, whom he discovers to be a bully. Disillusioned, Paulo becomes a bandit. Meanwhile Enrico shows some virtue by refusing to kill an old man who resembles his (Enrico's) father, but he kills another man in anger. Enrico repents, dies, and goes to heaven. Paulo, again duped by the devil, refuses to believe in Enrico's salvation and therefore is damned for his lack of faith.

CLOAK–AND–SWORD PLAYS.

DON GIL OF THE GREEN BREECHES (*Don Gil de las calzas verdes*). *Don Gil* has an exceedingly complicated plot. Juana, deserted by her lover, disguises herself as a man and makes the lover's new sweetheart fall in love with her. She uses other disguises, too, and completely confuses her family, her servant, and her lover.

THE DECEIVER OF SEVILLA (*El burlador de Sevilla*). By far Tirso's most famous and influential play. In it the dramatist

created the character Don Juan as the world has since known him.[41]
This "deceiver," rake, gambler, and blasphemer, after leaving a
string of broken hearts and broken homes, kills in a duel Don Gonzalo, the father of one of his ladyloves. Later Juan tweaks the
beard of the stone effigy of Gonzalo and invites the figure to dinner.
The statue accepts, attends, and then returns the hospitality by
inviting Juan to an entertainment at the tomb. Though warned
by his friends, Juan courageously goes to the church and is strangled
by the statue; his soul is carried off to hell.

The most readily discernible trait of Tirso's Don Juan is his
profligacy. A second — and one often overlooked, as Northup
points out[42] — is his bravery. His complete fearlessness of both
human and supernatural powers is admirable in spite of his lack of
conscience.

Tirso's play has, of course, been most influential all over Europe.
Authors and musicians from Iceland to Italy have been inspired
by the theme. A few of the most famous to treat it are Molière,
P. Mérimée, Rostand, Zorilla, Shadwell, Byron, Shaw, and
Mozart.

Estimate. Menéndez y Pelayo thinks that "Tirso stands closer
to Shakespeare than any other Spanish dramatist in his power of
creating characters and in the intensity of his poetic life."[43] Although this may be rather excessive praise, certainly Tirso surpasses Lope de Vega in those respects singled out by Menéndez.
Mérimée ranks Tirso between Lope and Calderón.[44] Despite
Tirso's occasional immorality, his "intensity," character portrayal,
"humanity, wit, and lightness of touch"[45] make him one of the four
greatest Spanish dramatists of the seventeenth century.*

JUAN RUIZ DE ALARCÓN Y MENDOZA (*c.* 1580–1639).
Born in Mexico, Alarcón was a hunchback. Far less prolific than
Lope and Tirso, he wrote only twenty plays;[46] these were published
in two parts, 1628 and 1634.

Alarcón is important for introducing a moral element and a
seriousness of purpose into Spanish drama. Thereby he became a
great influence on French authors of comedy, especially Corneille
and Molière.

Walls Have Ears (*Las paredes oyen*) is an attack on slander. Doña
Ana, suspecting her suitor (Mendo) of infidelity, arranges an eaves-

---

* The other three are Lope de Vega, Alarcón and Calderón.

dropping party, to the utter undoing of the slanderous and faithless Mendo. In *The Suspicious Truth* (*La verdad sospechosa*) each fabrication leads an otherwise attractive young aristocrat ever deeper into difficulty, so that he at length loses his beloved and falls into disgrace. Corneille's *Menteur* is a free translation of this play.

Alarcón's "obvious concern for ethics, the philosophical bearing of his themes, the regular structure of his plots, his moderate use of exciting incidents, and lastly his regard for style, all make him the most classic, in the French sense, of the dramatic writers of the century."[47]

PEDRO CALDERÓN DE LA BARCA (1600–1681). Born in Madrid of an aristocratic family, he attended the Universities of Alcalá and Salamanca (1614–1620). After some traveling he devoted himself to writing plays, and his success persuaded Philip IV to reward him with the Order of Santiago (1636). For a time he served the Duke of Infantado (1637–1640) and later the Duke of Alba (1645–*c.* 1649). Between those periods he was in the army (1640–1642) and fought in a campaign against Catalan rebels. In 1651 he became a priest and ceased writing plays for the public, but he continued to compose *comedias* and *autos* for the Court.

Types of Works. Calderón wrote some nondramatic works, but they are of no importance. His 180 plays,[48] however, make him one of Spain's four greatest dramatists. Professor Ford says that these plays may be divided according to the three distinctive seventeenth-century Spanish ideas that they reflect: "(1) intense devotion to the Christian religion, to the Catholic faith with all its beliefs and practices; (2) absolute and unquestioning loyalty to the Spanish sovereign; and (3) a highly developed, even grossly and abhorrently exaggerated, feeling for the point of honor."[49] Sometimes these categories overlap, as, for example, in *The Mayor of Zalamea* (below).

RELIGIOUS AND PHILOSOPHICAL DRAMAS. Most of Calderón's religious and philosophical plays may be subdivided into (1) dramatizations of saints' lives, (2) treatment of theological problems, and (3) *autos sacramentales* (usually dramatized allegories). The best example of the first subdivision is *The Constant Prince* (*El príncipe constante*, 1629), a glorification of Prince Fernando, the son of John I of Portugal. Fernando is captured by the Berbers and put to death (1443). *Life Is a Dream* (*La vida es sueño, c.* 1636), Calderón's most famous drama, defends the freedom of man's will and teaches that if this life is only a dream, what we do in the dream determines our place in the reality to which we awaken at death; man is a doer and a maker in the dream. By using his powers of reason, the hero, Sigismondo, saves himself from bestiality, has a successful life on this earth, and earns himself a place in heaven.

MONARCHICAL AND HISTORICAL PLAYS. The masterpiece in this category is *The Mayor of Zalamea* (*El alcalde de Zalamea, c.* 1644). Pedro Crespo, peasant-farmer and mayor of his town, condemns an army captain to death for seducing his (Pedro's) daughter and then refusing to marry her. When the military powers threaten the town, Pedro is upheld by the king, who makes him perpetual mayor.

"POINT OF HONOR" PLAYS. Popular in the seventeenth century but somewhat repugnant now are Calderón's plays which carry to an illogical and sometimes morbid extreme the "point of honor." By *honor* Calderón means "a very touchy sentiment of conjugal honor, which is tarnished by the least breath of suspicion. . . . Honor is therefore in this case synonymous with reputation."[50] In such plays the author assumes "that a husband has the right to slay, not only a more or less culpable lover, but even an absolutely innocent wife, whose fair fame chance has beclouded with a suspicion of frailty or sin."[51] The brother of a maiden is bound by much the same code. *The Mayor of Zalamea* borders on this theme. Other plays in this group are *The Doctor of His Honor* (*El médico de su honra*) and *The Painter of His Dishonor* (*El pintor de su deshonra*).

Estimate. Calderón, like Lope de Vega, was almost forgotten during the eighteenth century, but his fame was catapulted by some romantic critics (especially the Schlegels), who, in their enthusiasm, mentioned him along with Sophocles and Shakespeare. Saner judgment considers him a great dramatist but too national and topical to "achieve universality." Too often his Gongorisms and his adherence to the "barbarous honor code" offend twentieth-century tastes. His greatest merits are a sound knowledge of stage technique, a fertile invention, genuine and fervent religious convictions, and great lyrical power.

RELIGIOUS AND PHILOSOPHICAL PROSE

The two conflicting attitudes of medievalistic devotion and world-liness which were present in Renaissance Spain are manifest, respectively, in the works of Santa Teresa and Gracián.

Santa Teresa de Jesús (*Teresa de Cepeda y Ahumada*, 1515–1582). "The greatest female writer in Spanish literature"[52] and one of the greatest of all religious mystics, was born in Ávila. At the age of seven Santa Teresa ran away from home "to seek martyrdom," and at nineteen she became a member of the Order of Discalced Carmelites, of which she later became the mother superior. She was canonized in 1622.

The most important of her preserved writings are four hundred letters (written 1561–1582), an autobiography (*Libro de su vida*, written 1562–1566), and *The Inner Castle, or the Apartments* (*El castillo interior, o las moradas*, written 1577, published 1588). She wrote also a few mediocre poems and some mystical prose (in addition to *The Inner Castle*).

The autobiography, which was written at the suggestion of her confessor, is remarkable for its colloquial, friendly, and confidential style.

More important is *The Inner Castle*. Each of its seven "apart-ments" or "abodes" represents a stage of prayer of increasing ecstasy, the seventh being "annihilation in the bosom of Divine Love."[53] The work shows Teresa's exceptional ability to translate into words the intensely personal and subjective emotions of the mystic. Of her style Luis de León, her contemporary and the editor of her works, said: "In form of diction, in purity and ease of style, in grace and admirable arrangement of words, and in an untaught elegance that is wholly delightful, I doubt if any writing in our language is equal to this."[54]

Baltasar Gracián (1601–1658). In almost every respect the antithesis of Santa Teresa. Though a Jesuit, he is pessimistic, prag-matic, and humanistic. His *Prudent Man* (*Discreto*, 1646) is a sort of Spanish *Courtier* which discusses in detail the twenty-five "adorn-ments" or qualities which the perfect, educated gentleman should have. His *Handy Oracle, or the Art of Prudence* (*Oraculo manual o arte de prudencia*, 1653), is a collection of three hundred epigrams of worldly wisdom. Gracián's masterpiece is *The Would-Be Critic* (*El criticón*, 1651, 1653, 1657), an allegorical and philosophical narrative of the "travels" of one Critilo through the regions of adolescence, adulthood, and old age. There is little action, much philosophizing. Andrenio, "the man of nature," anticipates Rousseau's "noble savage."

Gracián has a shrewd and quick mind, but he lacks moral depth. His style is often spoiled by his inevitable, almost perverse *conceptismo* ("cultivated subtlety"), and the superfluity of epigrams becomes tiresome.

10

Since 1700

Historical Background. The history of Spain since 1700 holds little of interest for the student of world literature and so may be passed over rapidly. The nation has remained "economically prostrate and politically impotent" during most of the time, and it has been continually torn by foreign wars and internal disturbances. Charles II died in 1700 and was succeeded by Philip V of the French House of Bourbon; this dynasty remained on the throne till 1931, except for six years during the Napoleonic era (1808–1814), six more years of interregnum (1868–1870), rule by Amadeus of Savoy (1870–1873), and republican government (1873–1874). The Spanish-American War of 1898 deprived Spain of her last American and Pacific possessions. In 1931 Alfonso XIII went into exile, and the Second Republic was declared. Five years later General Francisco Franco led a successful Fascist revolution (1936–1939); since then he has been dictator of the country. Spain did not participate in either World War.

General View of the Literature. When Calderón died in 1681, the production of great Spanish literature also came to an end.

The early Bourbon rulers, endeavoring to gallicize Spain, introduced many cultural and educational improvements: the National Library was founded in 1712, the Royal Spanish Academy in 1714, and the Academy of History in 1735.

By 1725 French neoclassicism was beginning to influence Spanish writers, and now instead of aping former Spanish authors, they began to reverence Boileau and to imitate La Fontaine, Molière, and Racine. It should be emphasized, however, that the neoclassic movement never was as effective in Spain and England as it was in France; once again Spanish individualism and the ingrained resentment of things foreign caused several writers to reject neoclassic theories and practices. Altogether the eighteenth century was a rather barren one for great Spanish literature.

As in most of the other countries of western Europe, anticipation

182

of romanticism became noticeable in the latter part of the eighteenth century. Since neoclassicism had never taken very firm root in Spain and since Spaniards were naturally inclined more toward emotionalism than toward rationalism, the romantic triumph was less sensational in Spain than elsewhere. In 1833 many men of letters who had been in voluntary exile in France and England during the oppressive reign of Ferdinand VII came back to Spain and brought with them romantic ideas. Their return marks the beginning of Spanish romanticism "as a full-fledged, self-conscious movement."[1] This movement was at its height between 1833 and 1845.

About the middle of the century, materialism and the loss of religious faith led to pessimism, which was reflected in the literature.

After the Spanish-American War a spiritual and cultural renaissance began in Spain. The so-called "generation of 1898" undertook to improve education and literature, and they opposed narrow nationalism, conservatism, and religious intolerance. Many competent poets, novelists, dramatists, and scholars participated. They formed no school, but all opposed the traditional Spanish literary vices of carelessness, improvisation, and wordiness. Two conflicting tendencies were discernible, one toward *préciosité* and obscurity, the other toward simplicity and clarity.

The few noteworthy literary productions of the last two and a half centuries have been in the fields of the novel, the drama, and poetry.

THE NOVEL

The only important novelist of the eighteenth century was José Francisco de Isla y Rojo (1703–1781), whose *History of the Famous Preacher Brother Gerundio de Campazas, alias Zotes* (*Historia del famoso predicador Fray Gerundio*, etc., 1758) is a burlesque of the sensational and rococo pulpit oratory of the preceding generations.

During the romantic period Spanish novelists translated and imitated Scott, Chateaubriand, Cooper, and Manzoni. Hundreds of historical novels were produced, but none were of the top rank.

After romanticism began to wane, the novelists turned to a humorous but realistic novel of manners, most often depicting life in a particular region of the nation. Some of the more important regional novelists were Cecilia Böhl von Faber (Fernán Caballero,

1796–1877), who is credited with beginning the genre in Spain; JUAN VALERA Y ALCALÁ GALIANO (1824–1905), whose novels are about Andalusian life; ANTONIO DE ALARCÓN Y ARIZA (1833–1891), who is remembered especially for his humor; JOSÉ MARÍA DE PEREDA (1833–1906), whose novels are about the Montaña region and who "is in many respects the greatest of the modern Spanish realists";[2] LA CONDESA EMILIA PARDO BAZÁN (1852–1921), who was not only a regional novelist but also a disciple of French Naturalism; ARMANDO PALACIO VALDÉS (1853–1938), who wrote about Asturias; and finally VICENTE BLASCO IBÁÑEZ (1867–1928), who wrote regional novels about Valencia, sociological novels about South America, and a novel about the First World War. BENITO PÉREZ GALDÓS (1843–1920) wrote a series of historical romances and also several novels of social reform.

In the twentieth century RAMÓN MARÍA DEL VALLE-INCLÁN (1870–1936) has written erotic novels; and PÍO BAROJA (1872–1956) has written historical novels, regional novels, and novels on political themes.

THE DRAMA

In the eighteenth century there were many Molièresque comedies of some merit; the tragedies were artificial, awkward, and insipid. RAMÓN DE LA CRUZ CANO Y OLMEDILLA (1731–1794), reacting against neoclassicism, wrote some good realistic comedies. LEANDRO FERNÁNDEZ DE MORATÍN (1760–1828) was the best Spanish disciple of Molière.

FRANCISCO MARTÍNEZ DE LA ROSA (1789–1862) wrote the first successful romantic play — *The Venetian Conspiracy* (*La conjuración de Venecia*, 1830) — a melodrama filled with love-making, mystery, and intrigue. ÁNGEL DE SAAVEDRA, Duke of Rivas (1791–1865), wrote *Don Álvaro, or the Force of Destiny* (*Don Álvaro, o la fuerza del sino*, 1831, 1835), a sensational tragedy about a superhuman hero pursued by fate; this play was used as the libretto for Verdi's opera *La Forza del Destino*.

BRETÓN DE LOS HERREROS (1796–1873) returned to realism; his light and witty plays satirize middle-class society. JOAQUÍN DICENTA (1863–1917) created Spanish proletarian drama.

In the twentieth century the first outstanding dramatist was JACINTO BENAVENTE Y MARTINEZ (1866–1954), who wrote children's plays and plays of social satire. More famous is FEDERICO GARCÍA

Lorca (1899–1936), who wrote both comedies and tragedies. Among his most famous plays are *Blood Wedding* (*Bodas de sangre*, 1933), the story of a feud and the murder of eloping lovers; *Yerma* (1934), the tragedy of a woman whose childlessness and yearning for children become an obsession; and *The House of Bernarda Alba* (*La casa de Bernarda Alba*, 1936), a devastating play about a tyrannical and hypocritical woman whose harsh treatment breaks the spirit of her daughters and drives them to insanity and suicide.

POETRY

Most Spanish poetry of the eighteenth century is narrative, satirical, or didactic. Tomás de Iriarte (1750–1791) is best known for his moralistic fables in verse. Gaspar Melchor de Jovellanos (1744–1811) was a statesman and reformer as well as a poet. He wrote didactic pieces, satires, and poetic epistles. Juan Meléndez Valdés (1754–1817) was influenced by Gessner, Young, Thomson, and Rousseau; his poetry is famous for its sweetness and formal perfection. He wrote eclogues, ballads, and some didactic works. Manuel José Quintana (1772–1857) is remembered for his patriotic and humanitarian odes. Though primarily a neoclassicist, he is preromantic in his emotionalism.

José de Espronceda y Delgado (1808–1842) was the greatest Spanish romantic poet. An admirer of Byron and Goethe, he was pessimistic, disillusioned, and patriotic. He excelled in the *leyenda*, or poetic romance, and in the short lyric. José Zorrilla y Moral (1817–1893) wrote many excellent *leyendas* (e.g. "Granada"), famous for their atmosphere and mood; Zorrilla is equally well known for his colorful dramas, especially his version of the Don Juan legend, *Don Juan Tenorio* (1844). Gustavo Adolfo Bécquer (1836–1870), "a belated romanticist," is famous for his simple, dreamy, melancholy *Rimes* (*Rimas*, 1871) and for his prose legends which abound in the magical, the fantastic, and the supernatural.

Ramón de Campoamor (1817–1901) broke with romanticism and wrote epigrams and other poems which he called *doloras* — narratives "in which eternal verities are symbolized, characterized by brevity, delicacy, pathos, and philosophical teaching hidden beneath irony."[3] His sentimentality and willingness to tell a story made him popular with his contemporaries. Gaspar Núñez de Arce (1832–1903) also wrote sentimental narratives. He was a poet of the despair and pessimism which resulted from religious doubts and disillusionment in politics.

The so-called Modernist movement in Spanish poetry began about 1900. The Modernists, led by the Nicaraguan poet RUBÉN DARÍO (1867–1916), aimed at a synthesis of the theories of the French Parnassian and Symbolistic schools. They tried to appeal to the eye as well as the ear, and they stressed individualism, subjectivism, attention to form, and the enrichment of the poet's vocabulary. The most important Modernist poets in Spain were MANUEL MACHADO (1874–1947), ANTONIO MACHADO (1875–1939), and EDUARDO MARQUINA (1879–1946). JUAN RAMÓN JIMÉNEZ (1881–1958) was at first identified with the Modernists, but later reacted against their vagueness and *préciosité*. He is noted for his simplicity, exquisite artistry, and intensity of emotion. Many of his poems are melancholy and elegiac. RAMÓN PÉREZ DE AYALA (1880–   ) is a novelist and a nature poet. GABRIELA MISTRAL (1889–1957) the Chilean poet, whose real name was Lucila Godoy Alcayaga, received the 1945 Nobel Prize in Literature. Her poetry, noted for its fluent lyricism, reflects her passionate desire for even-handed justice.

Bibliography for Modern Spanish Literature

Bell, Aubrey F. G. *Contemporary Spanish Literature*. New York: A. A. Knopf, 1925.

Campbell, Roy. *Lorca: An Appreciation of His Poetry*. New Haven: Yale University Press, 1952.

Fitzmaurice-Kelly, James. *Chapters on Spanish Literature*. London: A. Constable and Co., 1908.

————. *A History of Spanish Literature*. New York: D. Appleton and Co., 1898.

Ford, Jeremiah D. M. *Main Currents of Spanish Literature*. New York: H. Holt and Co., 1919.

Kane, Elisha K. *Gongorism and the Golden Age*. Chapel Hill, N. C.: University of North Carolina Press, 1928.

Krutch, Joseph Wood. *Five Masters*. New York: J. Cape and H. Smith, 1930.

Mérimée, Ernest. *A History of Spanish Literature*. Translated and revised by S. Griswold Morley. New York: H. Holt and Co., 1930.

Northup, George Tyler. *An Introduction to Spanish Literature*. Chicago: University of Chicago Press, 1925.

Peers, E. Allison. *A History of the Romantic Movement in Spain*. Cambridge, England: Cambridge University Press, 1940.

———— (ed.). *Spain: A Companion to Spanish Studies*. 3rd ed. London: Methuen and Co., 1938.

Ticknor, George. *History of Spanish Literature*. 4th ed. Boston: Houghton, Osgood and Co., 1879. 3 vols.

Part Four
Modern Germanic Literature

The Sixteenth Century: Renaissance and Reformation

Historical Background. The political chaos which had existed throughout Germanic lands during the latter part of the Middle Ages continued into the sixteenth century and beyond. Charles V, Emperor of the Holy Roman Empire from 1519 till 1556, was too busy with foreign wars to devote much attention to the unification of Germany; and his immediate successors did little more than he toward that end.

The historical events which are of particular importance to a student of literature lie in the intellectual and religious fields. Renaissance ideas* began to seep into Germany about the middle of the fourteenth century. From the very first, however, the humanistic movement took a unique direction in north-central Europe. The reasons are not hard to discover. In the first place, the revival of classical literature, especially Latin, was for Italy — and to some extent for France and Spain — a revival of its own past glories; for Germany "the Renaissance was exotic."[1] Closely related to that reason is the fact that humanism appealed primarily to the aristocratic and intellectual elite in Germany who could speak Greek and Latin, whereas it appealed to a far wider audience in the countries where the languages were derived from Latin. Probably the main reason why the Germanic lands turned toward religious reform while the Italians were embracing humanism is that the temperaments of the two races are so different. The Germans have always been comparatively Hebraistic (in Arnold's sense); the Italians and French, Hellenistic.

It should not be assumed, however, that humanism made no headway at all in Germany. On the contrary, Johann Reuchlin (1455–1522), Desiderius Erasmus of Rotterdam (see below), and many others became great scholars in the classical languages. Interest in the humanities and the invention of printing gave con-

* See above, p. 3.

siderable impetus to learning in general; at least fifteen schools and universities were founded between 1348 and 1555; and Luther himself was friendly toward the New Learning except where it conflicted with his religion.

As early as the latter part of the fourteenth century John Wyclif in England, Johann Huss (or Hus) in Bohemia, and others had attacked the corruption within the Catholic Church. Individualism, the spread of learning, and the questioning attitude of the Renaissance led many to doubt the infallibility of the Church and to seek out and examine the documents on which Christian doctrines were founded. In 1517 Martin Luther posted on the door of Wittenberg Cathedral his famous ninety-five theses condemning the pope-sanctioned practice of selling indulgences and three years later publicly burned the papal bull of excommunication. Many followers flocked to his standard, and his *Augsburg Confession of Faith* in 1530 may be considered the "beginning of organized Protestantism." Charles V tried in vain to stamp out the new heresy, but was forced in 1555 to grant freedom of worship to Catholics and Protestants alike (decision of the Diet of Augsburg).

General View of the Literature. It was inevitable that the German literature of the sixteenth century should be deeply influenced by the religious disturbances. Erasmus' *Praise of Folly* (see below) and other works (all in Latin) satirized the corrupt Churchmen, attacked the vices of the Church, and upheld simple Christian virtues. The most important Protestant writers* were LUTHER, ULRICH VON HUTTEN (1488–1523), and JOHANN FISCHART (*c.* 1546–1590).

Older literary traditions, such as the drama and the Mastersong, were continued by Hans Sachs, but even he was affected by the Protestant reforms (see below).

Many interesting tales and romances, chiefly anonymous, were published as chapbooks; the most famous is *Dr. Faustus* (1587), which was translated into English almost immediately and which furnished Marlowe with the theme for his drama. JÖRG WICKRAM (d. *c.* 1560) wrote the first German novels; one of these is *The Gold Thread* (*Der Goldfaden*, 1557).

Minor genres were collections of anecdotes, geography, history, and proverbs.

---

* Erasmus was a critic of the Church but not a Protestant.

⩗ ERASMUS

Desiderius Erasmus (Gerhard Gerhards, or Geert Geerts; *c.* 1466–1536) was born in Rotterdam. Orphaned, he was placed by his guardians in an Augustinian monastery, where he soon learned to despise the coarseness and corruption of the monks. Through the intercession of the Bishop of Cambray (whose secretary he became), he was allowed to leave the cloister, and subsequently he traveled over most of Europe, including England. He lectured at Cambridge from 1511 to 1514 and associated with More, Colet, Grocyn, and the other great English scholars of the time. He died at Basle.

Erasmus spent most of his long life teaching humanism and simple Christian piety. As he traversed Europe, he continually attacked violence, cruelty, hypocrisy, and corruption of all sorts. He was especially critical of corruption within the Church. Although his various works helped to foment the Reformation, he at first stood aloof from Luther's rebellion and later actually opposed it — because of its revolutionary nature.

Works. Virtually all Erasmus' works are in Latin. He translated the New Testament into Latin and included with the translation a scathing commentary on the abuses of the Church; he compiled a large number of Greek and Latin proverbs; he wrote several moral and instructional treatises; he wrote some letters of great autobiographical value; and — most important of all — he composed the *Praise of Folly* and the *Colloquies.*

THE PRAISE OF FOLLY (*Encomium Moriae,* 1509). This is a satire, suggested by Sir Thomas More and probably inspired by Brant's *Ship of Fools* (Vol. I). The work purports to be an "oration" delivered by Folly herself; actually it is a rather formless monologue, in which Folly exposes the vices of the time. Wittily sarcastic, Erasmus "praises" fools of all ranks and professions — "old crabbed philosophers," wanton maidens, magistrates, naturalists, astrologers, physicians, poets, rhetoricians, lawyers, courtiers, kings, and many others. He especially singles out the Churchmen, from the pope down to the monks and pardoners. The "praise," of course, is put into the mouth of Folly herself and so is a blistering indictment of the greed, violence, hypocrisy, superstition, dishonesty, and selfishness of all of Folly's brood. That brood, says Erasmus, includes all of us, for only God is truly wise: "And indeed the whole proceedings of the world are nothing but one continued scene of Folly, all the actors being equally fools and madmen. . . ."[2]

THE COLLOQUIES (Colloquia, 1526). These are sixty-three conversations originally written for the diversion and encouragement of Erasmus' students. They are on such varied topics and overlap so inseparably that a precise classification is impossible. They can, however, be divided rather arbitrarily into six groups: (1) exposure of ritualistic fallacies, (2) invective against corruption within the Church, (3) divulgence of popular imposture, (4) deploring of contemporary personal sins, (5) practical advice for laymen, and (6) miscellaneous discussion of amusing topics — not didactic. A few examples will suffice to demonstrate his attitudes: "The Religious Pilgrimage" and "Rash Vows" condemn the useless and oftentimes vicious trips made to shrines, for saints should not be worshipped. A variety of tricks and frauds are exposed in "The Horse Cheat," "The Apparition," and "The Beggars' Dialogue." In "The Young Man and the Harlot" the object is to "implant chastity in the minds of young men." Manners becoming to a youth are outlined in "The Schoolmaster's Admonition" and "The Youth's Piety." Several conversations are devoted to the praise of true scholarship and to the scorning of pedantry, e.g., "Echo," "Thalia and the Barbarian," and "The Assembly of Grammarians."

The total import of the *Colloquies* is very great. There is little doubt that they helped speed the Reformation in Germany and England. In addition, they are important for the sketches of student life and for the autobiographical bits we find in them.

MARTIN LUTHER

Martin Luther (1483–1546) was born at Eisleben. In 1505 he became an Augustinian monk at Erfurt, and in 1508 he accepted a professorship at the University of Wittenberg. Three years later he visited Rome, where he was shocked by the corruption of the clergy. It was not till 1517, however, that the promiscuous sale of indulgences caused him to nail his theses to the door of the cathedral. After he had burned the bull of excommunication, he was ordered to defend his actions before the Imperial Diet at Worms (1521). His defense was rejected; he refused to recant; and he was outlawed. Friends hid him in Wartburg Castle in Thuringia, and there (later assisted by his close friend Philip Melanchthon [1497–1560]) he began his translation of the Bible. In 1525 he renounced

his monasticism and married a former nun, Katharina von Bora.
Five years later he and his followers issued the *Augsburg Confession*,
and in 1537 they held a conference, at which they agreed to break
all ties with the Roman Catholic Church. Luther died in his
native town.

Luther's nature was a combination of strength and tenderness.
Sometimes he was violent and passionate; at other times, mild and
sympathetic. He was always courageous, sincere, and confident
of the righteousness of his cause.

Translation of the Bible (New Testament, 1522; complete
Bible, 1534). Luther's was not the first German translation of the
Bible, but all its predecessors had been based on the Latin Vulgate.
Luther went back to the original Hebrew and Greek, as edited by
Reuchlin and Erasmus. He wrote the translation in the High
Saxon dialect of the chancellery at Meissen, which he considered
the most common German tongue. But he freed that official
dialect of its stiffness; he studiously avoided pedantry and deliberately sought out and employed the idiom of the common people.
The translation "is admirably true to the original, and unsurpassed
in pregnancy of meaning, in vigor and clearness, and in use of the
right word in the right place."[3] This translation was soon used
throughout all Germany. "For untold generations of Germans
his Bible remained the only book which was read in the home. . . .
The language of his Bible became the language of the entire German
nation. And so Luther may rightfully be called the founder of
the New High German literary language."[4] "The influence of
Luther's Bible on subsequent German literature has been similar
in kind, and perhaps even greater in degree, to that of the King
James Bible in English literature."[5]

Original Prose. In addition to the translation of the Bible,
Luther wrote a great many pieces of original prose. Most of these
are polemical tracts, epistles, sermons, and letters. His letters and
Table Talks (*Tischreden*) show amiability, gentleness, and humor.
Three of his greatest and most historically important theological
treatises (all written in 1520) are *To the Christian Noblemen of the
German Nation* (*An den christlichen Adel deutscher Nation*), *On the Babylonian Captivity of the Church* (*Von der babylonischen Gefangenschaft der
Kirche*), and *On the Freedom of a Christian* (*Von der Freiheit eines Christen-
menschen*). He advocates nationwide compulsory education in *To
the Councilmen of All Cities in Germany, that They Should Establish and*

Maintain Christian Schools (*An die Ratsherren aller Städte deutschen Landes, dass sie christliche Schulen aufrichten und halten sollen,* 1524).

Hymns. One of Luther's most important contributions to literature as well as to the Protestant cause was his collection of thirty-seven hymns. Some were original; others, free rendering of Latin hymns and some of the Psalms. Some of the best known are "A Mighty Fortress" ("Ein' feste Burg"), "the battle hymn of the Reformation"; "Come, Holy Ghost" ("Komm, heil'ger Geist"); "Praise Be to Thee, O Jesus Christ" ("Gelobet seist Du, Jesu Christ"); and "In the Midst of Life Are We" ("Mitten wir im Leben sind").

HANS SACHS

Hans Sachs (1494–1576), the son of a tailor, was born in Nürnberg (Nuremberg). As a child he attended a Latin school, and then in 1509 he was apprenticed to a shoemaker. About the same time he began to study the art of Mastersong. From 1512 to 1517 he traveled all over Germany as a journeyman cobbler. Returning to Nürnberg, he married Kunigunde Kreutzer, became a successful shoemaker, and settled down to a long, uneventful, and happy life, saddened only in his old age by the death of his wife and all seven of their children. He is famous for his joviality, kindliness, and manliness.

Works. Sachs was a very prolific writer. He composed more than six thousand poems and more than two hundred dramas.

POEMS. Nearly all of Sachs' poems are in short (four-beat) rhyming couplets. Over four thousand of his poems are Mastersongs (see Vol. I) and are therefore artificial and of little value. Of more importance are his other poems. These are on a variety of subjects. In some he stoutly defends the Reformation; the most famous in this group is "The Wittenberg Nightingale" ("Die Wittenbergische Nachtigall"), an allegory in which a nightingale (symbolizing Luther) leads back to the pleasant meadows some sheep which have been lost in the desert. Other poems, many of them gnomic or aphoristic, contain much genial humor, common sense, tenderness, and "moral soundness."

DRAMAS. Sachs is most widely renowned for his dramas, of which some are still acted. He tried biblical plays, history plays, and tragedies with little success. The following types were better:

Skits. Some of his dramatic works are little more than short, witty dialogues with almost no plot. A good example is *St. Peter with the Goat* (*St. Peter mit der Geiss*), in which the apostle, seeing injustice rampant on earth, asks God to allow him to come down and run things. Granted permission, he begins by trying to control an unruly goat, which task is so arduous that he gives up the whole project.

Shrovetide Plays.* Sachs followed the examples of his predecessors in writing short sketches on secular topics. Though somewhat coarse, his are less indecent than most of the other Shrovetide plays. They have witty and lively dialogue, realistic characterization, and rather simple plots. One of the best is *The Hot Iron* (*Das heisse Eisen*), in which a wife tests her husband's fidelity by the old ordeal of carrying a hot piece of iron. He secretly insulates his hands and then embarrasses her by subjecting her to the same test.

Estimate. Though popular in his own day, Sachs was almost forgotten during the seventeenth and eighteenth centuries. He was "rediscovered" by Goethe, who called him to the attention of the world in "Hans Sachs' Poetical Mission" ("Hans Sachsens poetische Sendung"); and Wagner celebrated him in the opera *Die Meistersinger von Nürnberg*. He is now admired not so much for his artistry, which is admittedly lacking, but for his common sense, unfailing good humor, wit, and invaluable depiction of sixteenth-century German life.

* This genre is discussed in detail in Vol. I.

12

The Seventeenth Century

Historical Background. The only German historical event of importance during the seventeenth century was the Thirty Years' War (1618–1648). This was brought on by the Hapsburgs' renewed attempts to stamp out Protestantism. The Protestants were aided by Denmark, Sweden, and France, and once again they won freedom of worship. Such freedom, however, was dearly bought. Germany was so utterly devastated and so nearly depopulated (about two-thirds of the population perished) that she was unable to recover for almost a century.

General View of the Literature. The confusion, uncertainty, and moral and spiritual degeneracy which accompanied and followed the war had, naturally enough, an adverse effect on the literature. In the early years of the century many writers tended to embellish their works with words borrowed from other languages, especially French. In order to combat this tendency, several clubs sprang up whose aim was to purge the German language of foreign words. This process of purification was undertaken by many of the poets, but it was followed by both reactions and counterreactions (see *Poetry*, below).

The century was for the most part literarily barren, but there was a little religious poetry, drama, and prose fiction; and Jakob Böhme (1575–1624) wrote some mystical prose which was influential on Milton and Blake.

POETRY

One of the most influential of the language purifiers was MARTIN OPITZ (1597–1639), who, paradoxically, inveighed against gallicisms and championed the vernacular at the same time that he urged writers to imitate the Renaissance authors of Italy and France,* thereby inaugurating what is known as the Pseudo-

---

* The Pleiad in France had endorsed a similarly paradoxical course. See p. 55.

Renaissance. In his book entitled *Book On German Poetry* (*Buch von der deutschen Poeterei*, 1624), Opitz advocates "verbal correctness," the use of classical and historical allusions, the "regular alternation of accented and unaccented syllables" in poetry, and the use of French alexandrine verse. As was to be expected, Opitz' works and those of most of his followers (notably FRIEDRICH VON LOGAU [1604–1655] and PAUL FLEMING [1609–1640]) are formally "correct" but artificial and generally lacking in feeling.

A reaction to Opitz' colorlessness and sterile regularity led such poets as HOFMANN VON HOFMANNSWALDAU (1617–1679) and CASPAR VON LOHENSTEIN (1635–1683) to write "baroque" literature, that is, to imitate Italian Marinism — extravagant figures of speech, bombast, *préciosité*, and pedantry. This reaction drove CHRISTIAN WEISE (1642–1708) and others into a neoclassical counterreaction, which aimed at simplicity and wit.

Perhaps the greatest contribution to German poetry during the seventeenth century was made outside these movements and countermovements. PAUL GERHARDT (1607–1676), second only to Luther in religious poetry, wrote a large number of beautiful hymns. Some of the best known are "How Shall I Receive Thee" ("Wie soll ich dich empfangen"), "O Bloody and Wounded Head" ("O Haupt voll Blut und Wunden"), "Awake, My Heart, and Sing" ("Wach auf, mein Herz, und singe"), and "Now All the Woods Are Peaceful" ("Nun ruhen all Wälder").

DRAMA

Andreas Gryphius (1616–1664). Gryphius wrote lyrics, tragedies, and comedies. Some of his lyrics are in the style of Opitz, but others are deeper, more personal, and more thoughtful. Most of the latter group are bitter and pessimistic, despairing of this world and finding hope only in the afterlife.

Gryphius' tragedies, which are written in stilted alexandrines, show little familiarity with stagecraft. There is almost no action or suspense, and often horror is substituted for real tragedy. *Leo Arminius* (1646) is the story of a conspiracy which succeeds in deposing and murdering a great emperor. *Cardenio und Celinde* (1647) is perhaps the first "bourgeois tragedy"; it is the story of a student of Bologna who threatens to murder the husband of his beloved, but supernatural powers prevent the crime. *Katharina von Georgien* (*c.* 1647) is the tragedy of a heroic queen who prefers death to apostasy. *Carolus Stuardus* (1649) is a condemnation of the English for the execution of Charles I. And *Papianus* (1659) is another tragedy of a martyr.

Gryphius' comedies are better. *Horribilicribrifax* (*c.* 1650) ridicules not only the cowardly braggart soldier (such as the author saw during the Thirty Years' War) but also linguistic pedantry. *Herr Peter Squenz* (1663) is a version of the Pyramus and Thisbe story, drawn from a Dutch and English version of Shakespeare's *Midsummer Night's Dream.* The Beloved Rose-among-Thorns (*Die geliebte Dornrose*, 1660), an amusing play about love among peasants, has been called "the best comedy before Lessing."[1]

THE NOVEL

Hans Jakob Christoffel von Grimmelshausen (*c.* 1625–1676). Grimmelshausen wrote "the one prose classic of the century."[2] That classic is *Simplicissimus* (1669), a picaresque story about Sternfels von Fuchshaim, the adopted child of a peasant. Sternfels is driven from the peasant's farm by a band of soldiers; hides in a cave, where he learns religion from a hermit; becomes a page and then a robber; finds a treasure; marries; deserts his wife; plays the *beau* in Paris; and, after other adventures, returns to the cave of the hermit (now discovered to be his own father) and settles down to a life of study and contemplation.

Despite some long, dull passages, the *Simplicissimus* is generally an entertaining tale, and it depicts realistically and vividly the "atrocities of the war, the humors of vagabondage, the coarseness of a dissolute society, the manners and customs and superstitions of the people."[3]

13

The Eighteenth Century

Historical Background. The eighteenth century was for Germany a period of great political and cultural significance. Although the country was still a hodgepodge of more or less independent states bound together in a loose confederation, Prussia began to emerge as the dominant power, and glimmerings of a national consciousness began to appear. In the Seven Years' War (1756–1763) the brilliant leadership of Frederick II (the Great, ruled 1740–1786) enabled Prussia, assisted by troops from Hanover and subsidies from England, to withstand the armies of France, Austria, and Russia.

In Germany, as in most of the other western European countries, rationalism and deism attracted many adherents. These systems of belief were opposed first by pietism (a "revival of simple piety" plus religious emotionalism*) and later by Rousseauism. The theories of Diderot and Rousseau about democracy, the rights of man, and individual liberty, which played so large a part in bringing about the French and American revolutions, led to no political upheaval in Germany — probably because there was no central authority to revolt against and because Joseph II and Frederick II, popular heroes who had done a great deal to improve the lot of the average man, strengthened the people's faith in monarchy.

In the social and intellectual realms, Rousseauism superimposed on rationalism helped to foster the powerful indigenous movement known as the "Storm and Stress" (*Sturm und Drang*), which "had as its objectives a reform of political and social life and the regeneration of literature."[1] "Political liberty, social equality, the exaltation of primeval nature, of genius, of poetic creation without any regard whatsoever for the traditional laws of art — in short, the perfect freedom of the individual, was the ideal and goal of the new generation."[2]

The subjectivism and lack of restraint of the Storm and Stress were opposed by Immanuel Kant (1724–1804), one of the world's

---

* Cf. the Evangelical movement in eighteenth-century England.

greatest philosophers. He held that it was reasonable and necessary to postulate free will, immortality, and the existence of God as
the source of goodness and beauty; and his famous "categorical
imperative" emphasized obedience to the feeling of moral obligation.

General View of the Literature. Little German literature worthy of
consideration was written between 1700 and 1750. The influence
of French literature was still strong, but the works of English
authors, particularly of Shakespeare, Milton, Defoe, Addison,
Thomson, Sterne, and Macpherson, had more and more effect on
German letters as the century advanced.

About 1725 JOHANN CHRISTOPH GOTTSCHED (1700–1766), perceiving the low state of German literature, undertook a reform.
He urged the adoption of all the rules of French neoclassicism and
the following of French and English neoclassic models. He stressed
"moral edification," common sense, and clarity. Like almost all
other neoclassicists, he rejected imagination and emotionalism.

Perhaps Gottsched's reforms came too late, or perhaps the temperament of the German people was inimical to neoclassicism.
Whatever the cause, neoclassicism never obtained the foothold in
Germany that it had in France. JOHANN JAKOB BODMER (1698–
1783) and JOHANN JAKOB BREITINGER (1701–1776) of Zürich attacked the theories of Gottsched and defended the return to emotion
and fancy. The Swiss won the battle about 1750.

The only authors of the first half of the century who must be mentioned are ALBRECHT VON HALLER (1708–1777), who wrote some
didactic poems and some lyrics; FRIEDRICH VON HAGEDORN (1708–
1754), who wrote fables and some jovial songs full of the *carpe diem*
philosophy of Horace and Anacreon; and CHRISTIAN FÜRCHTEGOTT
GELLERT (1715–1769), who wrote some religious poetry of deep
and sincere feeling, some fables in the vein of La Fontaine, many
hymns, some sentimental comedies, and what one historian has
called "the first emotional novel of family life in Germany,"[3] *The
Swedish Countess* (*Die schwedische Gräfin*, 1747–1748).

Inspired by the deeds of Frederick II, by pietism, and by Rousseauism, German literature began to revive in the middle of the
century. The Storm and Stress, which began about 1748, was
a powerful stimulant. For a hundred years literary activity flourished as it had not done since the Middle Ages.

One of the most potent literary influences of the Storm and Stress and on German romantic literature was Johann Gottfried Herder (below), who, as a champion of the "natural" emotions, attacked rationalism, conventions, abstract rules, and the artificiality of neoclassicism.

The earliest literature of the Storm and Stress was excessively violent and unrestrained, but it was soon succeeded by the so-called "classical" writing of such men as Lessing, Goethe, and Schiller. From about 1780 to 1830 the greatest German masterpieces were produced. These were principally in the fields of the novel, the drama, and lyric and epic poetry.

THE NOVEL*

Before 1700 several long prose narratives which might be termed novels had been written in Germany. Wickram (Ch. 11), PHILLIP VON ZESEN (1619–1689), and others had turned out romantic stories about knights, the Orient, and heroes; Zesen had composed *Adriatic Rosamund* (*Die Adriatische Rosamund*, 1645), a "psychological novel of seventeenth-century family life . . ., but [it was] dull and untrue to life"[4]; CHRISTIAN REUTER (b. 1665) and others had written several parodies of novels of travels and adventures; and Grimmelshausen had produced *Simplicissimus* (Ch. 12). It remained, however, for Wieland to write the first "modern" novel.

CHRISTOPH MARTIN WIELAND (1733–1813). He was the son of a poor preacher of Württemberg. After spending his youth as a pietistic Christian, he went (at the invitation of Johann Jakob Bodmer) to Zürich in 1752. There he remained for about seven years, gradually losing his pietism and inclining more and more toward worldly and hedonistic pursuits. In 1769 he became a professor at the University of Erfurt. Three years later he accepted the position of tutor to Prince Karl August of Saxe-Weimar. Pensioned in 1775, he spent the remainder of his life at Weimar and Ossmannstedt.

Novels. "Wieland . . . strengthened and elevated the German novel. He turned it away from pedantry and merely ephemeral content to the treatment of deep psychological questions and to a more finished presentation of the themes involved."[5] He also brought rhyme back into German poetry.

* The novels of Goethe are discussed below under another heading.

AGATHON (1766–1767).   According to Professor Priest, *Agathon* "is the first important psychological novel in German; its convincing description of inner change and growth of character set a new, commanding standard in German novel-writing."[6]   And Lessing called it "the first and only novel for the thinking head."[7]   It is a semi-autobiographical novel about an Athenian youth, who, somewhat like Wieland himself, falls from the purity and piety of his early days into sensuality; finally he finds peace and wisdom in a life of moderation in which pleasures and virtues, tempered by reason, both have their place.   The titular hero is exiled, associates for a while with some bacchantic maidens, and is captured by pirates and sold into slavery in Smyrna.   There he falls in love with Danae, whom he rejects when he discovers her to be wanton. Escaping, he engages in political and governmental enterprises in Athens and then in Sicily in an attempt to give his life meaning, but he finds only disillusionment.   Finally he goes to Tarentum, where Archytas, a Pythagorean philosopher, teaches him to seek perfection and moderation.   Danae, having reformed, comes to Tarentum, and it appears that she and Agathon will be happily married, but she renounces the pleasures of the flesh and devotes herself to purity and to a quest for the beautiful.

GERON THE NOBLE (*Geron der Adlige*, 1777).   This is another psychological novel; here loyalty and honor struggle against the temptations of passion.   The setting is the court of King Arthur.

THE PEOPLE OF ABDERA (*Die Abderiten*, 1780).   This novel is a satire on the stupidity of German provincial life.   The scene is ancient Greece.

Poetry.   Though probably better known today as a novelist, Wieland was more famous in his own day as a poet, and even some twentieth-century critics consider *Oberon* his masterpiece.

MUSARION (1768).   This didactic epic seeks to prove that "sexual love . . . must be saved from animalism by the sense of beauty."[8]   Musarion, a beautiful and voluptuous woman, persuades Phanias that the sage, like the "other sons of earth," is moved by bodily beauty but that the wise man is able to see the ideal Beauty reflected in the substantial.

OBERON (1780).   This is a semi-ironical epic which harmoniously blends the Old-French romance *Huon of Bordeaux* with the Titania-Oberon story from Shakespeare's *Midsummer Night's Dream.* Forced by Charlemagne to go to Bagdad on a perilous quest, Huon is successful and brings back Rezia, the Caliph's daughter, as his betrothed. On their return journey they succumb to their passion but expiate their sins by courageously facing many hardships. In the meantime, Oberon and Titania, the king and the queen of the elves, have quarreled and can be reconciled only by the demonstration of bravery and fidelity in a pair of mortals. Oberon selects Huon and Rezia as the pair; it is through his aid that the mortal lovers overcome their trials, and it is their faithfulness that brings about Oberon's reconciliation with Titania. Goethe thought the poem so excellent that he sent Wieland a laurel wreath.

Translations. Between 1762 and 1766 Wieland translated twenty-two of Shakespeare's plays into German. These were among the most widely read German versions of the English dramatist's works till A. W. Schlegel began his translations in 1797.

LITERARY CRITICISM

GOTTHOLD EPHRAIM LESSING (1729–1781). Lessing was born at Kamenz. He earned a reputation for brilliance at the school of St. Afra at Meissen; then, like Klopstock, he decided to study theology. Enrolling at the University of Leipzig (1746), he studied not only theology but also medicine, philology, and literature. In addition, he began to write poetry and drama. His acquaintance with theatrical people, including the actress Karoline Neuber, shocked his pious pastor father but taught young Lessing a great deal about the world in general and dramaturgy in particular. In 1748 he forsook Leipzig for Berlin, where he continued to study for three years; he supported himself by writing comedies, translating, and doing some journalistic work. From December, 1751, till December, 1752, he attended the University of Wittenberg, receiving his Master's degree at the end of the year. Thereafter he lived a few years at a time in various places: Berlin, 1752–1755; Leipzig, 1755–1758; Berlin, 1758–1760; Breslau, 1760–1765; Berlin, 1765–1767; Hamburg, 1767–1770; and Wolfenbüttel, 1770–1781. These sojourns were interrupted by many visits elsewhere, including a trip through Austria and Italy (1775–1776). During all these years Lessing earned his livelihood as a dramatist, secretary to a Prussian general, critic of the national theater (Hamburg), and librarian of Wolfenbüttel. In 1776 he was married to Eva König, who died about fifteen months later. He himself was fatally stricken with apoplexy while in Brunswick.

Works.   Lessing is almost equally famous as a dramatist and as a critic.   He also composed some relatively unimportant prose fables, some lyrics, and some epigrams.

LITERARY CRITICISM.   In addition to those mentioned here, other literary theories of Lessing will be indicated in the discussion of his dramas.

LETTERS CONCERNING THE NEWEST LITERATURE, or *LITERATURE LETTERS* (*Briefe die neueste Litteratur betreffend,* or *Litteraturbriefe,* 1759–1765).   Written in collaboration with Moses Mendelssohn (1729–1786) and Friedrich Christoph Nicolai (1733–1811), these "letters" make a sweeping criticism of contemporary German literature.   They expose poetasters, incompetent translators, "warped pedagogues," and false moralists.   Of far greater importance is the direction which the *Letters* helped to give to German literary theory and practice in general: Gottsched's theories are censured; the French classical tragedy is shown to be not so thoroughly Greek as had formerly been believed; and Sophocles and Shakespeare instead of Racine are held up as models for imitation.

LAOCOÖN, OR THE BOUNDARIES OF PAINTING AND POETRY (*Laokoön, oder über die Grenzen der Malerei und Poesie,* 1766).   In 1764 Johann Joachim Winckelmann (1717–1768) had published a work entitled *History of Ancient Art* (*Geschichte der Kunst des Altertums*).   Contrasting an ancient Greek statue of Laocoön with Virgil's description of the same man, he had illustrated his thesis that "noble simplicity and quiet grandeur" are the essential characteristics of Greek art.   He had praised the Greek statue, because in it he had found artistic restraint — a restraint lacking in Virgil's poetic account of the Trojan sufferer (*Aeneid,* II).   The implication of Winckelmann's "discovery" was that the provinces of poetry and those of the plastic arts are identical.   In *Laocoön* Lessing refutes this belief and establishes beauty and not ethics as the aim of the painter and the sculptor.   He demonstrates that those arts are static — limited in time and space — and are therefore primarily descriptive, whereas poetry is dynamic — dependent on the succession of things in time — and is therefore largely narrative.   The great significance of this thesis is that it helped to put an end to the eighteenth-century tendency to make poetry descriptive.

HAMBURG DRAMATURGY (*Hamburgische Dramaturgie,* 1767–1769).   This work enlarges upon the theories contained in the *Letters Concerning the Newest Literature*. Lessing shows that the neoclassical theories of drama are a misinterpretation of Aristotle. He upholds the unity of action and the Aristotelian requisite of arousing fear and pity, but he disagrees with the Greek critic, who considers common people unsuitable protagonists in tragedy.

DRAMA. The state of the German drama in 1750 was worse than deplorable. It was artificial and servilely imitative of the French neoclassic drama of Corneille and Voltaire. It blindly accepted the false Italian and French interpretation of the three unities. Except for the works of Sachs, Gryphius, and Lohenstein, no drama worth mentioning had been written in Germany since the Middle Ages, and there had never been any great dramatic masterpiece. Lessing now came to do for the drama what Klopstock was doing for non-dramatic poetry. But Lessing did far more. He, Goethe, and Schiller gave Germany for the first time dramas worthy to be placed beside the dramatic masterworks of other nations.

Lessing's early comedies are to be distinguished from those of his contemporaries only by their "lively dialogue in easy, natural prose." His first was *The Young Scholar* (*Der junge Gelehrte*, 1748), which reveals some of his own experiences as a student. It was not till 1755 that Lessing made a clear break with the old tradition.

MISS SARA SAMPSON (1755). "The first tragedy of middle-class life on the German stage."[9] Rejecting the views of the French and Gottsched that tragedy should be concerned only with exalted personages, that it should be written in alexandrines, and that it should observe the unities, Lessing follows English dramatists and writes in prose about ordinary people. The names of the characters are drawn from Lillo, Congreve, and Richardson. The story, too, recalls the plays of Lillo and Shadwell and the novels of Richardson: Mellefont lures Sara away from home; they are discovered at an inn by Marwood, Mellefont's former mistress, who unsuccessfully tries to win Mellefont back. When Marwood learns that Mr. Sampson is willing to forgive his daughter, she poisons Sara, and Mellefont commits suicide.

PHILOTAS (1759). A one-act tragedy pervaded by the patriotism aroused by Frederick II. Philotas, a Macedonian prince, has been captured by the enemy. When he hears that his father is about to make a disadvantageous peace in order to save him, he commits suicide. Here Lessing strives for classical simplicity and again uses prose.

MINNA VON BARNHELM (1767). "The first masterpiece of German comedy"[10] is, according to Goethe, "the most direct outgrowth of the Seven Years' War, of perfect north German national content, the first theatrical production based on important events in contemporary life."[11] The plot is rather intricate: Tellheim, a Prussian major, is in disgrace with the military authorities, who unjustly accuse him of accepting bribes from the enemy Saxons during the Seven Years' War. Fearing lest he besmirch the fair name of his fiancée, the Saxon heiress Minna von Barnhelm, Tellheim breaks off relations with her. Minna follows and tells him that she has been disinherited. Overjoyed, he resumes his suit, but now she refuses to be a burden to him. A letter from the king exonerates Tellheim, Minna confesses that her story about being disowned was a falsehood, and all ends well. Although the plot is not especially original, the action is in "close touch with the events and the ideas of the time . . . [and] the characters . . . are themselves living and actual."[12] The play reflects Lessing's eagerness for concord among the various German states.

EMILIA GALOTTI (1772). Lessing's version of the old story of Appius and Virginia. Emilia, engaged to Count Appiani, is desired by the Prince of Guastalla, who hires bandits to kill the Count. The Prince "rescues" Emilia and takes her to his villa. Orsina, the former mistress of the Prince, discloses the plot to Odoardo, Emilia's father, who then goes to the villa and stabs Emilia to save her from disgrace. Though the scene is in Italy, Lessing portrays the cruel and insolent practices of the German nobility.

NATHAN THE WISE (*Nathan der Weise*, 1779). Lessing's greatest fictional work. Hardly a drama (Lessing calls it a "dramatic poem"), it has a meager and improbable plot. It is primarily an exposition of its author's deism. It teaches religious tolerance, brotherly love, and simple piety. Nathan, a good and wise Jew, has adopted and reared a Christian girl. He finds himself in difficulty when a Knight Templar, who has come to fight Saladin for the Holy Sepulchre, wishes to marry the adopted daughter. All problems are solved when daughter and Templar discover that they are brother and sister, and both are revealed as the children of Saladin's lost brother, who had married a German wife. Saladin then asks Nathan which of the three religions — Christian, Mohammedan, and Jewish — is the true one. Nathan answers with the parable of the three rings (adapted from Boc-caccio's *Decameron*, I, 3); he hints that perhaps all religions are fakes. But the main message is that *each* religion is true provided it leads men to virtue, and therefore there should be no contention among the adherents to the different beliefs. But Lessing does not overlook the element of faith; he adds that it is better for God alone to know ultimate truth.

Evaluation. Lessing was the greatest purely literary figure in Germany before Goethe. As a dramatist he "was able to utilize his minute knowledge of men in the creation of characters who are true to life, and he could experience within himself their psychological changes; this twofold gift made him a genuine dramatist. We may therefore reckon him among the leading original authors of his country. . . ."[13] Despite his prejudices and his blindness to the greatness of Corneille and Racine, Macaulay thought him the greatest critic of Europe, and Priest adds that his criticism "laid the foundation of a new German drama."[14] "From whatever angle Lessing's activity is regarded, it sums up all that was best in the movement of his time. . . . In his criticism of literature and art he expressed the ripest judgments of the eighteenth century; while as a creative artist he laid, single-handed, the foundations of the modern German drama."[15]

JOHANN GOTTFRIED HERDER (1744–1803). "While Lessing may be considered as the culmination of the German eighteenth century, Herder ushers in our modern world."[16] Herder was the son of a poor preacher of Mohrungen, East Prussia. His youth was one of strict discipline and wide reading. In 1762 he enrolled at the University of Königsberg with the intention of studying medicine, but he soon changed his mind and devoted himself to theology and philosophy; he was especially impressed by the lectures of Immanuel Kant. His friend Johann Georg Hamann (1730–1788) inspired in him an enthusiasm for Shakespeare and taught him English, using *Hamlet* as a textbook. And the writings of Rousseau became one of the most lasting influences on his thought. In 1764 he became a teacher and curate in Riga; after five years there he resigned his position and made a "grand tour" by sea to Nantes and thence to Paris, where he met Diderot and d'Alembert. He returned to Hamburg and there made the ac-quaintance of Lessing. For a few months he was the tutor of the heir-apparent of Holstein-Eutin, but in September 1770 trouble with his eyes forced him to resign and go to Strasburg for an operation. There he entered into a close friendship with Goethe, a friendship which was an important element in Goethe's literary development. In 1771 Herder became chaplain at the court of Bückeberg, and there he remained till 1776, when through Goethe's influence he received an appointment as President of the Lutheran Consistory at Weimar. Association with Wieland, Goethe, Jean Paul, and others was at first stimulating and pleasant; but as Herder grew older, he became increasingly irritable and perhaps resentful of the successes of Goethe and Schiller. He remained in Weimar till his death in 1803.

Influence. Herder has been called the "founder of the literary movement of the 'Sturm and Drang.' "[17] As a follower of Rousseau and Hamann, he, perhaps more than anybody else in Germany, helped to banish the neoclassic dependence on reason and on the ancients and to encourage reliance on natural human impulses and emotions. The "unperverted soul of the people," he proclaimed, was the source of all true poetry, which must be spontaneous and unpremeditated. The folk song, the Bible, Homer, and Shakespeare he cited as examples of "natural" and therefore great literature. He conceived of poetry "as the universal language of mankind . . . and prepared the way for that new conception of 'world literature' which Goethe, and especially the Romanticists, did much to propagate, while at the same time . . . [he] laid the foundations of the modern study of comparative literature."[18]

Works. Like his master Rousseau, Herder was important more for his power of inspiration than for the intrinsic merit of his writings. Several of his literary productions, however, were so influential as to deserve individual attention.

PAPERS ON RECENT GERMAN LITERATURE[19] (*Fragmente über die neuere deutsche Literatur*, 1766–1767). This work is a defense of the emotions and an attack on the neoclassic dependence on "cold common-sense" and "spirit of imitation." Here Herder also offers a "new conception of literature as the reflection of a definite, national civilization, to be judged not from any preconceived standard, but entirely in the light of historical development. . . . Herder thus became the founder of the scientific study of literature."[20]

SHAKESPEARE (an essay in *On German Ways and Art* [*Von deutscher Art und Kunst*, 1773] by several authors). Here he depicts the English dramatist as a "product of his time and environment"[21] and as a great "natural" poet, equal to the ancient Greeks in imagination and feeling.

FOLK SONGS (*Volkslieder*, 1778–1779; later renamed by an editor *Voices of the Nations* [*Stimmen der Völker*]). This is a collection of 182 folk songs of many lands; forty are German in origin, and the others are excellent translations by Herder of songs from the Scandinavian countries, England, France, Spain, Italy, Lapland, Greenland, Peru, and elsewhere. The entire collection did a great deal to revive German interest in the ballad and the folk song. Along with Bishop Thomas Percy's *Reliques* (1765), Herder's volume was a significant contribution to the growth of the attitudes which led to romanticism.

IDEAS ON THE PHILOSOPHY OF THE HISTORY OF MAN-KIND (*Ideen zur Philosophie der Geschichte der Menschheit*, 1784–1791). This is probably Herder's masterpiece. It contains most of his literary and philosophical ideas, and it sets forth his beliefs about the cultural evolution of man. "He conceived humanity as a great whole, and . . . tried to demonstrate a divine progression of the human race leading to the highest culture, to true religion, to 'humanity.' "[22] Diversities in the progress of different nations are to be explained by variations in individual people and in their natural environments; and each nation has contributed to the growth of human culture.

POETRY

FRIEDRICH GOTTLIEB KLOPSTOCK (1724–1803). "The greatest lyric poet between Walther von der Vogelweide and Goethe,"[23] was born in Quedlinburg. In 1739 he was sent to school at Schulpforta, where he was inspired by the study of Homer, the Bible, and Bodmer's translation of Milton. In 1745 he began the study of theology at Jena; there he wrote in prose the first three cantos of the *Messias*. After spending some time as a tutor, he accepted an invitation from Bodmer, the Swiss translator of Milton, to visit him in Zürich. Klopstock's interest in worldly pleasures caused a coolness between host and guest, and when Frederick V of Denmark invited Klopstock to come to live in Copenhagen, Klopstock joyfully accepted. In 1754 he married Margaret Möller, with whom he lived happily till her death four years later. In 1770 the death of Frederick V, which was followed by some political changes, induced Klopstock to retire to Hamburg; but he was

allowed to keep his Danish pension. Except for short visits elsewhere, he remained in Hamburg till he died.

Works.

MESSIAS. From childhood Klopstock aspired to do for Germany what Milton had done for England — write a great Christian
epic. When he was twenty-one, he began the *Messias* in prose, and
(perhaps following a hint from Gottsched) he converted into
hexameters the three cantos he had written; the poetic version was
published in 1748. In 1751 Cantos I–V appeared; in 1756,
Cantos VI–X; in 1769, Cantos XI–XV; and in 1773, Cantos XVI–
XX. The total runs to nearly 20,000 lines.

The theme of the long poem is Christ's redemption of mankind.
The story begins with Christ's ascent of the Mount of Olives and
ends with his taking his place beside God in heaven. Obviously,
there are not enough events in the New Testament narrative between these two limits to provide action for so long a poem. Klopstock strains — unsuccessfully — to give significance to every trivial
incident, and he tries to make up for the dearth of action by calling
before us numbers of angels, devils, and even the Trinity. He fails,
furthermore, to humanize his characters. The result of all these
shortcomings is that "of all the religious poems of the world, the
Messias is unquestionably the most monotonous and difficult to
read."[24] The best parts of the epic are the imaginative descriptions
in the first few cantos.

LYRICS. Klopstock's poetic genius was lyric rather than epic.
In 1771 he published a volume entitled *Odes* — by which he meant
simply "poems." Except for a few hymns, all of these are in a
form which approximates free verse — no rhyme and what their
author calls "free rhythm." Klopstock pours his own powerful
emotions into these lyrics, which celebrate friendship, love, nature,
liberty, poetry, and patriotism. In almost all of them there is a
deep religious fervor. Some of the best known are "To Fanny"
("An Fanny"), "The Lake of Zürich" ("Der Zürcher See"), "My
Fatherland" ("Mein Vaterland"), "The Festival of Spring" ("Die
Frühlingsfeier"), and "The Summer Night" ("Die Sommernacht").

DRAMAS. Klopstock wrote six dramas. Three are on Biblical
themes: *The Death of Adam* (*Der Tod Adams*, 1757), *Salomo* (1764),
and *David* (1772). The other three form a trilogy on Hermann
(Arminius), a national hero: *Hermann's Battle* (*Hermannsschlacht*,
1769); *Hermann and the Princes* (*Hermann und die Fürsten*, 1784), and

Hermann's Death (*Hermanns Tod*, 1787). These plays have no "dramatic life," but contain some good lyrical passages. Perhaps their chief merit lies in their reflection of Germany's renewal of interest in its own past.

Estimate. Klopstock's greatest contribution to the growth of German literature was — despite sentimentality — the revival of feeling and imagination. Moreover, he refined and enlarged the poetic vocabulary, and he introduced some ancient meters and some new rhythms. Although Herder's remark that one ode by Klopstock "outweighed the whole lyric literature of Britain" is ridiculous, the remark suggests the influence which Klopstock had on his contemporaries.

DRAMA

Lessing (above) was the first great German dramatist of the eighteenth century. It was his innovations and his new dramatic theories which to a large extent freed German drama from its French neoclassic tendencies and so paved the way for the achievements of Goethe and Schiller.

JOHANN WOLFGANG VON GOETHE (1749–1832). Goethe was born at Frankfurt-am-Main. His father, who had become a lawyer and had risen to a position of civic importance, was reserved, austere, strict, opinionated, and pedantic. His mother, only eighteen years older than her son, was of a cheery, equable, serene disposition. Perennially young, she had an excellent imagination and loved storytelling. Young Wolfgang went to school first in Frankfurt and later (1765–1768) in Leipzig, where he studied law. Illness forced him to return home in 1768, but two years later he was able to finish his legal studies at the University of Strassburg. There he met Herder, who "unloosed all the Storm and Stress elements which were slumbering in the young poet, by teaching him that his own heart is each man's most precious possession and its expression his first duty."[25]

In 1770 Goethe formed a liaison with Friederike Brion, the unspoiled daughter of a pastor of Sesenheim. This liaison lasted almost a year and inspired a great deal of Goethe's poetry; it was broken off in 1771, with great remorse on the part of the poet.[26]

Again in Frankfurt, he spent most of the next four years practicing law and writing. In 1773 he achieved literary fame by writing the drama, *Götz von Berlichingen,* and the following year *The Sorrows of Young Werther* caused a still greater sensation.

In 1775 Karl August, the eighteen-year-old Duke of Saxe-Weimar, invited Goethe to visit in the capital Weimar. The invitation was accepted, and from that date till his death in 1832 (except for a visit to Italy) Goethe made Weimar his home. Between 1778 and 1786 he held various positions under the Duke, including that of prime minister. In 1782 he was made a nobleman.

Burdened by official duties and distressed by a hopeless passion for a married woman, Charlotte von Stein, Goethe fled to Italy in September, 1786. There he eagerly drank in Italian art, culture, and scenery for about a year and a half.

Goethe's relations with three people require comment. The first of these is Charlotte von Stein, wife of one of the Duke's officials. This pure and high-minded woman had a salutary effect on Goethe's character and poetry from 1775 till 1786. Then, becoming aware that he could no longer "be satisfied with mere friendship," Goethe made his Italian journey.

The second person to be mentioned is Christiane Vulpius, the pretty but uneducated daughter of a minor Weimar official. In July, 1788, she became Goethe's mistress and housekeeper, and she bore him a son. Goethe married her in 1806.

The third acquaintance — and the most influential on Goethe's poetry — is Friedrich Schiller. The two poets met in 1788, but it was not till 1794 that they became intimate. From that date till Schiller's death in 1805 each was the inspirer and critic of the other's works. Goethe, whose creative ability seemed to be drying up from 1790 till 1794, received new inspiration from the younger man and confessed to him: "You have given me a second youth and have again made me a poet, which I had virtually ceased to be."[27]

Opinions about Goethe's character differ. Priest thinks that "he was straightforward and kind, sincere and warm-hearted; he was most earnest in his search and admiration for truth and beauty. . . . Serious work was his life."[28] Wilkinson, on the other hand, doubts Goethe's sincerity and accuses him of egoism, egotism, and a shockingly selfish disregard of others.[29] Whatever the truth may be, it is certain that Goethe was handsome, personable, spirited, witty, ambitious, and industrious. His greatest aim in life was "self-culture"; he himself said: "I wish to act like the greatest men. I wish in nothing to act like the merely greater. This desire — to make the Pyramid of my Being . . . soar as high as can be in air — outweighs all else and permits hardly a momentary forgetting."[30]

Works. Nearly all Goethe's works are autobiographical in greater or lesser degree. From his most intimate lyrics to his dramas we can detect some incident, some love affair, or some phase of his development.

Like his elder contemporary Voltaire, Goethe was exceptionally versatile as well as prolific. From his teens till a few months before his death at the age of eighty-two, he wrote almost continuously; the results fill 120 volumes. The types of literature for which he is most famous are the lyric, the epic, the novel, and the drama; in addition he wrote ballads, operettas, scientific articles, literary criticism, and an autobiography.

LYRICS AND BALLADS. The steady development of Goethe's genius can be traced in his short poems. The earliest lyrics are full of passion and show clearly the effects of the Storm and Stress. Those written at Weimar between 1775 and 1786 are somewhat calmer and more objective, but they still are filled with an intense yearning for spiritual and intellectual tranquility. The lyrics written soon after the poet's return from Italy are sensuous and humanistic. And those of his old age are pensive, aphoristic, and philosophical. A large number of his ballads and lyrics, especially the earlier ones, are on the subjects of love and nature. "The Heather-Rose" ("Das Heidenröslein"), for instance, is a ballad which gives a symbolic account of Goethe's affair with Friederike Brion, and the lyrics "Found" ("Gefunden") and "Springtime All Year" ("Frühling übers Jahr") are tributes to his wife Christiane. A perennially favorite ballad (set to music by Schubert) is "The Erlking" ("Der Erlkönig"), a tragic story of a dying boy whose father is taking him on horseback to see the doctor; the child has hallucinations of being tempted by the king of the elves to come to fairyland; the boy dies in his father's arms when the Erlking threatens to use force. Other favorites are "Wanderer's Night Song" ("Wandrers Nachtlied"), "Welcome and Departure" ("Willkommen und Abschied"), "The Godlike" ("Das Göttliche"), "Mignon," "Harper's Song" ("Lied des Harfners"), and "Song of the Spirit over the Waters" ("Gesang der Geister über den Wassern").

AN EPIC: *HERMANN UND DOROTHEA* (1797). Written in dactylic hexameter, it is an attempt to "bring back the spirit of

Homer into the modern epic."³¹   Goethe succeeds in giving an "objective and classic" atmosphere to the poem.   Based on an incident alleged to have happened in Bavaria to a Protestant exile from Salzburg in 1732, the tale is changed by Goethe to an account of a Palatinate refugee in 1796.   Hermann, son of an innkeeper, falls in love with the fugitive Dorothea and eventually persuades his father to agree to the match despite the girl's lack of a dowry. There is much philosophizing about patriotism, parental authority, and individual freedom.   With the exception of *Faust*, the epic is Goethe's most popular long work.

NOVELS.

THE SORROWS OF YOUNG WERTHER (*Die Leiden des jungen Werthers*, 1774).   A sentimental epistolary novel modeled on Rousseau's *New Heloïse*.   Much of the emotional content is drawn from Goethe's love affair with Charlotte Buff; and the catastrophe is based on the suicide of Goethe's friend Karl Jerusalem.   The novel is an excellent mirror of the pains and passions of the Storm and Stress period.   The plot tells how the young daydreamer Werther sees Lotte at a social gathering, conceives an overwhelming passion for her, departs when he hears that she is engaged to another, returns to find her married, and commits suicide.   Though too sentimental for twentieth-century tastes, the novel has some excellent characterization (especially of Lotte), some moving descriptions of nature, and "an unsurpassed presentation of a soul in travail."

WILHELM MEISTER'S APPRENTICESHIP (*Wilhelm Meisters Lehrjahre*, 1796) and its sequel *WILHELM MEISTER'S TRAVELS, OR THE RESIGNED* (*Wilhelm Meisters Wanderjahre, oder die Entsagenden*, 1821–1829).   Novels on the education and the maturing of a merchant's son.   They reflect Goethe's own life, errors, and growth.   In the *Apprenticeship* the hero sets out to learn about life and its meaning.   He tries first in the theater, where he has a love affair with Marianne and where he becomes acquainted with the works of Shakespeare (here Goethe inserts a valuable interpretation of *Hamlet*).   Wilhelm renounces the theater and undertakes as his life's work the rearing of the son which Marianne has borne him.   He becomes entangled simultaneously with Therese and Natalie and at length marries the latter.   After witnessing the death of Mignon, a young girl whom he has rescued from maltreatment, he feels his "apprenticeship" at an end.   The lesson he has learned is to work hard and take life and its duties seriously. The sequel is a dull but not unsuccessful attempt to show the mature Wilhelm in relation to society.

Both novels are poorly constructed, the second being little more than a collection of unconnected stories which are irrelevant to the main narrative.

Opinions of the morality of the two books vary. Some critics have thought them an authentic and instructive account of human searching for the answer to the riddle of life. Wilkinson disagrees and thinks them "a reek of animalism, open, contented, cheerful, unashamed animalism, only to be likened to the fable of Circe's sty."[32]

DRAMAS.

GÖTZ VON BERLICHINGEN (1773). An excellent expression of the spirit of the Storm and Stress, despite the fact that the scene is laid in the sixteenth century. Götz is a German Robin Hood — a robber who defends the poor, harasses the noble and the priest, and is the champion of liberty. Weislingen, his friend and the sweetheart of his sister Maria, wavers between allegiance to Götz and to the court party. Götz, leading a peasants' revolt, is wounded, captured, and condemned to die by Weislingen's hand. Weislingen destroys the decree of death but is himself poisoned by a court beauty. Götz' wounds prove fatal, but he dies crying, "Freedom! Freedom!" The romantic spirit, the excellent character portrayal, and the terse diction made the drama a great success in 1773.

EGMONT (1787–1788). Another semihistorical drama. It depicts the struggle of the Dutch against the Spanish in the sixteenth century. The hero unwisely trusts the treacherous Spaniards and becomes a martyr to the cause of Dutch liberty.

IPHIGENIA AT TAURIS (*Iphigenie auf Tauris*, 1787). An adaptation of Euripides' play of the same name. Goethe changes the denouement. Instead of allowing Athene to appear *ex machina* to order King Thoas to free Iphigenia and Orestes, Goethe allows the king to be overcome by the goodness and purity of the heroine and the repentance of Orestes. In this drama a classic simplicity and restraint have replaced the Storm and Stress elements of Goethe's earlier plays.

TORQUATO TASSO (1790). A romanticized version of the last years of the great Italian poet. Goethe himself says that the theme of the drama is "the disproportion between talent and life" — that is, the turmoil in the soul of the artist when his artistic temperament comes into conflict with the hard realities of life. Like Racine's tragedies, *Tasso* is centered on a moment of emotional crisis. When the action begins, the poet has just completed *Jerusalem Delivered*, and the Princess Leonora, with whom he is in love, crowns him with a wreath of laurel; excited by the events of the moment, Tasso forgets the gulf between himself and the princess, and he is rebuked by the duke's minister Antonio, a practical man of the world. A breach widens between Antonio and Tasso until the latter challenges the minister to a duel. The duke intervenes and confines Tasso. Outraged — especially as he feels himself to be a great poet — Tasso requests and receives permission to leave Ferrara. When Leonora comes to tell him goodbye, his emotions get the better of him, and he makes love to her. Despite the gentleness with which she rejects him, Tasso is plunged into despair. At length he "finds himself" by accepting the friendship of the practical Antonio, whom he considers complementary to himself, a dreamer. Tasso's inner struggles recall Goethe's own vicissitudes not only in his official capacity at the court of Duke Karl August but also in his relations with Frau von Stein.

FAUST, A TRAGEDY (*Faust, eine Tragödie*, begun 1769, completed and published 1832).

Sources. German legend tells of a Johann (or Johannes) Faustus, "professor of magic and black arts," who lived in Frankfurt about 1525. The chapbook of 1587 (p. 192) relates how the same Dr. Faust engaged in some trickery, entered into a compact with the devil, and received his punishment. Marlowe's drama on the subject was written about 1590. And finally, there were many oral accounts still current in the eighteenth century. Goethe was familiar with all these sources.

Form and Technique. Faust is written in many different verse forms, and parts of it are in prose. The word *drama* is almost a misnomer; actually the work is a long dramatic poem in two parts (about 16,000 lines). To present both parts on the stage in Goethe's form would be impossible.

Story. Like the biblical book of Job, Part I of *Faust* opens with a prologue in heaven, in which God gives the devil Mephistopheles permission to tempt Faust. Mephistopheles then goes to Faust and offers him wealth, women, honor — anything he wishes; in return Faust must surrender his soul to the devil when Mephistopheles has succeeded in blotting out Faust's ambition and his yearning for higher things — whenever Faust finds one moment so fair that he asks it to linger. Faust agrees to the terms, and they sign the pact in blood. Mephistopheles first tries Faust with the sensual pleasures of drinking and carousing. This failing, he decides to tempt Faust with love and so takes him to the Witches' Kitchen and gives him a potion which restores Faust's youth. Then follows the famous Margaret (or Gretchen) episode. With Mephistopheles' help, Faust seduces the young girl. Her brother Valentin is killed in a duel with Faust, who is forced to flee the city. Gretchen gives birth to a child, which she kills in a frenzy of despair, and then she is thrown in prison to await execution. Faust and Mephistopheles try to release her, but she refuses to escape because she has repented her sins and wishes to atone with her death. As she dies, Mephistopheles cries out that she is damned, but heavenly voices proclaim her saved. So ends Part I.

In Part II[33] Faust and Mephistopheles go to the court of the German emperor, whom they aid in his financial difficulties by introducing paper money, and they are told to call up Helen of Troy. Faust himself yearns for Helen, but she disappears at his touch — the allegorical expression of Goethe's belief that perfection can not be obtained suddenly and without real striving. Next Faust is transported to Greece, where with Mephistopheles' aid he succeeds in winning Helen. Their marriage symbolizes Goethe's own poetic ambition — the union of "Northern art and poetry with the Greek ideal of beauty."[34] The offspring of the pair, Euphorion, soars too high in the air and falls dead; this is Goethe's representation of Byron. Helen again vanishes. After aiding the emperor in battle, Faust settles down to the governing of a land, where he devotes himself to the welfare of others. Anticipating the accomplishment of his aims, he experiences a moment of bliss to which he might say, "Tarry." Then he dies. Mephistopheles, believing that the contract has been fulfilled, claims Faust's soul, but angels maintain that the "moment" has been attained not through the devil's help but through Faust's own spiritual growth — *in spite of* Mephistopheles. They bear Faust's soul to heaven, where it is welcomed by Gretchen and Mary.

Meaning and Philosophy. Goethe's *Faust* is more than an allegory of man's selling his soul for power, pleasure, knowledge, and wealth.

It is a study of the struggle against the "impulses of negation and evil which reside in every normal man. . . . Briefly, its lesson is that so long as man strives toward a worthy goal, he is deserving and sure of redemption in the broadest sense."[35] Or as John Macy states the meaning: "The road itself is the goal, life is its own end and must justify itself from within; perfection is beyond our reach. . . . Thus our highest achievement is a noble striving, a tireless creative living."[36]

As has often been pointed out, Faust in many ways resembles Goethe himself. Both yearned for — and attained — power and wordly pleasure; both contemplated and rejected suicide; both saw the right but often consciously and deliberately chose the wrong; and both were egocentric. The Gretchen story is in some respects parallel to Goethe's affair with Friederike Brion.

Criticisms. Faust has been censured for its formlessness and heterogeneity. Many commentators consider the second part dull and obscure. Sometimes the characterization is inconsistent — for example, when Gretchen sings of her hard home life.

Admitting that the work has some dull and some obscure passages, most critics have agreed that *Faust* is not only Goethe's greatest work but the greatest piece of literature written since the death of Shakespeare or Dante. Thomas says that it contains "some of the noblest imaginative poetry, the profoundest criticism of life, the most engaging realism, the most exquisite humor, and the most pathetic tragedy of woman's love, that had ever found expression in the German language."[37] Benjamin W. Wells says that it "is by the unanimous consent of German critics the greatest work of their literature, the most characteristical product of the German mind."[38] And Priest calls it "the profoundest and richest poetry of all the products of modern literature."[39]

Its greatness lies in its broad understanding of humanity and human frailty; its passages of great beauty and power, such as the scene of the death of Gretchen; and its endorsement of the struggle toward higher values.

Estimates. A few commentators have refused to concede Goethe a place among the giants of literature, because, they contend, his works are too autobiographical and do not reflect any greatness of soul in the author — one of Longinus' requirements for literary excellence. The majority of critics, however, disagree. Heine, for instance, says of him: "Nature wanted to see how she looked and she created Goethe."[40] Matthew Arnold calls him "Europe's sagest head, . . . Physician of the iron age."[41] Scherer labels him "the greatest poet of the eighteenth and nineteenth centuries."[42] Robertson remarks: "That Goethe was the most universally gifted of men of letters has long been recognised. . . ."[43] And Hermann Grimm pulls out all the stops in designating Goethe "the greatest poet of all nations and all times."[44] Some of these estimates are perhaps a bit too enthusiastic, but for more than a century most men have agreed that Goethe is one of the world's four or five greatest literary figures.

JOHANN CHRISTOPH FRIEDRICH VON SCHILLER (1759–1805). Schiller was born at Marbach in Württemberg. After a rather unhappy childhood, he was forced to attend a military school (1773–1779) and study law; later he changed to medicine. In 1779 he settled in Stuttgart as an army surgeon. Three years later he fled to Mannheim to escape the tyranny of the Duke of Württemberg. For several years he wandered from place to place, including Leipzig (1785–1786), Dresden (1786–1787), and Weimar (1787–1788). During much of this period he was poverty-stricken. A professorship at the University of Jena which Goethe secured for him (1789) and an annuity from the Duke of Holstein-Augustenburg beginning in 1791 helped to relieve his suffering. Three years later he was paid a considerable sum to edit an "aesthetic" monthly magazine, *The Hours* (*Die Horen*), to which he asked Goethe to contribute. Thus began their correspondence and close friendship, which lasted till Schiller died. In 1799 the friendship was made even more intimate by Schiller's moving to Weimar. There he died in 1805.

Works. The ever-recurrent theme in Schiller's works is the love for liberty. In his early dramas there is a violent passion for individual liberty — political and social. In later works the desire is more for general and spiritual freedom. His last plays show the influence of Kant's ethics and aesthetics.

In addition to dramas Schiller wrote a history of the Thirty Years' War, several essays on aesthetics (below), some good epigrams, and a fairly large number of philosophical lyrics and ballads. His lyrics are reflective and "achieve their effect less by the direct expression of feeling than by the artistic expression of philosophic thought."[45] His ballads, too, generally illustrate some ethical ideas. Some of his best-known "philosophical lyrics" are "The Walk" ("Der Spaziergang"), "The Eleusinian Festival" ("Das eleusische Fest"), "To Joy" ("An die Freude"), "The Artists" ("Die Künstler"), and "The Song of the Bell" ("Das Lied von der Glocke"). Some famous ballads are "The Battle with the Dragon" ("Der Kampf mit dem Drachen"), "The Diver" ("Der Taucher"), and "The Pledge" ("Die Bürgschaft").

ESSAYS. Deeply impressed by Kant's philosophical and aesthetic works (especially the *Critique of Practical Reason* [*Kritik der praktischen Vernunft*, 1788] and the *Critique of Judgment* [*Kritik der Urteilskraft*, 1790]), Schiller himself felt a compulsion to write on the relationship between art and morality. He agreed with Kant in opposing lax and false rationalism, epicureanism, and the subjectivity, self-indulgence, and "agressive individualism" of the leaders of the Storm and Stress movement. He agreed with Kant, too, in believing in freedom of the will and the necessity for obeying the voice of duty or conscience. In aesthetics, however, which Schiller adopted as his special field for inquiry, he broke with Kant. In his *Philosophical Letters* (*Philosophische Briefe*, 1786–1788), he holds that there is an inherent quality in an object that determines whether that object is beautiful; Kant says that there is no objective criterion. Schiller believes that "freedom in appearance" (*Freiheit in der Erscheinung*) is such a criterion; his meaning is that a work of art is beautiful when it follows all the laws of technique without *appearing* to be constrained or restricted. (This theory is closely related to Schiller's belief that the aim of education is to train a man in such a fashion that he will *will* to do the right.) In *On Grace and Dignity* (*Über Anmuth und Würde*, 1793) he again disagrees with Kant in asserting that beauty and the human form are not incompatible; he tries to demonstrate "that there [is], apart from what he calls 'architectonic' beauty, another beauty in man which has its basis in the personality: this is 'Anmut' or Grace and is the expression of a beautiful personality or of the 'schöne Seele', whereas dignity is the expression of a lofty mind."[46] The same ideas are continued in *Letters on the Aesthetic Education of Men* (*Briefe über die äesthetische Erziehung des Menschen*, 1795), perhaps his most important treatise on aesthetics; here he argues that beauty and morality are inseparable and that the finest and greatest culture is the result of a union of "Anmuth" and "Würde." The treatise entitled *On Naive and Sentimental Poetry* (*Über naive und sentimentalische Dichtung*, 1795–1796) divides poets into two classes: the "naive" or "natural" poets (found principally but not exclusively in ancient times), who are superior because they reproduce nature itself spontaneously, objectively, and unreflectingly; and the "sentimental" or "reflective" poets, from whom civilization has taken away the union of receptivity and spontaneity; these poets (and most moderns, Schiller says, are "sentimental") are inferior because they deal with nature only at second hand, as it were; they deal with ideas; but they, too, have their role — reflecting, deducing, seeking "after the ideal . . . the approximation to the infinite."[47] Robertson thinks this essay an apologia for its author's own poetry, for Schiller was aware that he was reflective rather than "naive."

DRAMAS.

THE ROBBERS (*Die Räuber*, 1781). A play (in prose) of violence and intrigue. Victim of the machinations of his brother Franz, Karl Moor has been estranged from his father and has become leader of a band of robbers, but, like Götz von Berlichingen, is a "noble robber," who punishes the wicked and helps the needy. Hearing that Franz has imprisoned their father and is trying to force Amalia, Karl's sweetheart, to marry him, Karl attacks with his robber band. Franz commits suicide, the father dies on beholding Karl as a robber, Amalia asks to be killed when she hears that Karl's oath to the robbers will prevent him from marrying her, Karl obliges by killing her with his sword, and then he gives himself up to the officers of the law because he has perceived that his premises have been false — that lawbreaking is not the way to right wrongs.

INTRIGUE AND LOVE (*Kabale und Liebe*, 1784). A prose "tragedy of middle-class life." Ferdinand, son of an unscrupulous minister who has gained control of a small state, loves Luise, a musician's daughter. In order to prevent the match, the minister forces Luise to pretend that she is involved in an intrigue. Before she can explain to Ferdinand, she and he drink poison which he has prepared. Ferdinand's father repents and confesses his crime to the guardians of the law. The play is an exposé of the hidden infamies of which the nobility was often guilty, and it is also a demonstration of how mistreatment of the bourgeoisie by the nobility can bring tragedy to both social groups.

DON CARLOS, PRINCE OF SPAIN (*Don Carlos, Infant von Spanien*, 1787). Schiller's first drama in blank verse. The plot is simple: Don Carlos, son of Philip II, is in love with his stepmother

Elizabeth. Their attachment is discovered by the king, who delivers Don Carlos to the Grand Inquisitor. The first three acts (written 1785) were at first primarily a domestic tragedy; the last two (and the revision of the first three) are more concerned with matters of state, in which Don Carlos' friend and adviser, the Marquis Posa, is the leading figure. Posa is "the ambassador of humanity" — a stout defender of liberty, through whom Schiller voices his own political idealism and his enthusiasm for wise and benevolent government. Schiller's shift in emphasis from love to political theorizing left the plot construction weak: there are two tragedies — Posa's and Don Carlos'. The merits of the drama lie "in the abundance of deep thought and in the dignified and yet impasioned language."[48]

WALLENSTEIN (1798–1799). A play in three parts. *Wallenstein's Camp* (*Wallensteins Lager*, 1798) is a one-act *vorspiel*, or prologue; *The Piccolomini* (*Die Piccolomini*, 1799) and *The Death of Wallenstein* (*Wallensteins Tod*, 1799) have five acts each. The protagonist is the historical Wallenstein, Duke of Friedland, the commander-in-chief of the imperial forces in the Thirty Years' War. Ambitious for power, he turns traitor and conspires with Sweden against his emperor. He is betrayed by his former friend, Octavio Piccolomini; and he is deserted by most of his soldiers. He falls before Buttler, another "friend" whom he has formerly trusted. Here for the first time Schiller has created a great tragic figure. A subplot is concerned with the love affair of Wallenstein's daughter Thekla and Piccolomini's son Max, who is dramatically useful as an idealistic foil to the power-hungry Wallenstein.

MARIA STUART (1800). A historical tragedy as well as a psychological one, but the emphasis is on psychology. There is little action. When the play opens, Mary (or Maria) has already been condemned to die; most of the drama is taken up with Mary's accusations against Queen Elizabeth, who is made to appear morally culpable. Though admirably courageous, Mary is perhaps too innocent to be a really tragic heroine. But she is guilty as an accessory in an attempt on the life of Elizabeth, and she accepts her approaching execution as punishment by God for her past sins.

THE MAID OF ORLEANS (*Die Jungfrau von Orleans*, 1801). A "romantic tragedy" (as Schiller himself calls it) in which Joan of Arc appears as the embodiment of patriotism and devotion to God. Real tragic conflict results from her momentary forgetting of her mission in the sparing of the young Englishman Lionel. She atones with her subsequent renunciation of Lionel and also with her death.

THE BRIDE OF MESSINA (*Die Braut von Messina*, 1803). A "tragedy of fate" on a variation of the old Oedipus theme. The Prince of Messina is forewarned that a daughter yet unborn will bring death to both his sons. When Beatrice is born, he orders her thrown into the sea, but her mother saves her and hides her away till she is a young woman. Both Caesar and Manuel, her brothers, fall in love with her without, of course, knowing her identity. In jealousy Caesar stabs Manuel and then, upon learning that Beatrice is his sister, commits suicide. The mother is a majestically tragic figure. Schiller's enthusiasm for the dramas of Sophocles is evi-denced by his use of a chorus (which does not sing, but whose leaders speak), by the role played by fate, and by inclusion of the theme of inherited guilt.

WILLIAM TELL (*Wilhelm Tell*, 1804). An epical drama on the liberation of Switzerland from Austria. It tells the familiar story of Tell's successful struggle against the tyrant Gessler. It has always been a favorite with the Swiss and German people and an inspiration to patriotism.

Estimate. Although most modern critics consider Schiller in-ferior to Goethe and claim that he lacks Goethe's breadth and realism, a few consider him — at least in the drama — greater than Goethe. James K. Hosmer thinks that Schiller is "Göthe's peer" in the drama and that he "can best stand as the most representative German poet. No other is more thoroughly noble. . . ."[49] Wil-kinson agrees, especially concerning the nobility, and believes *Wallenstein* "the greatest poem in German literature."[50] And Robertson says: "Schiller is a great example of what Carlyle called 'the poet as hero.' . . . His writings are inspired with a noble idealism and a lofty aspiration, but they have less message for the modern world than the impartial realism of Goethe. . . . But he remains Germany's greatest dramatist."[51]

14

The Nineteenth Century

Historical Background. The conquests of Napoleon Bonaparte dealt a severe blow to the hopes of the German patriots and those who were beginning to make Germany aware of herself as a nation. French domination lasted from 1803 till 1813. As usually is the case, military setbacks did not extinguish the patriotic zeal, but instead fanned the flames higher; and uniting against the common enemy helped to bring the loosely confederated states closer together. Some of the dramas and lyrics of the great poets — especially Lessing's *Minna von Barnhelm*, Schiller's *William Tell*, and Goethe's *Faust*, Part I (published 1808) — gave the German-speaking states an illustrious common heritage and emphasized the idea of a common fatherland.

The German armies that helped defeat Napoleon in 1813 had been promised various reforms, including more political liberty and a constitutional government. Their expectations were disappointed. A policy of reaction, inaugurated by Metternich in Austria, was adopted by most of the states; and participation in the government and freedom of the press and of speech were denied the people. The period of reaction and absolutism continued for several decades, but popular discontent grew so strong that it became open rebellion in 1848. Then some steps toward constitutional government were taken, and some of the absolutist policies were abolished. In 1871 the German people were given "exemplary social legislation."

In the meantime tremendous progress in the direction of national unity was made. In 1815 Austria allied itself with some of the other states in the German Confederation; in 1834 the formation of the Zollverein began real unification; and in 1866 the North German Confederation was formed. Finally, Germany defeated France in the Franco-Prussian War (1870), and William I was declared emperor of the German Empire in 1871.

Much the same economic, industrial, social, and philosophical problems that confronted nineteenth-century France also faced

Germany. The increase in the number of factories, the growth of urban centers, the rise of a powerful mercantile social class, the conflicts between capital and labor, the discoveries in science — all these led toward materialism and pessimism.

Several important German philosophers helped to determine intellectual, political, social, and aesthetic trends, not only in Germany but in all the other parts of the world, too.

Johann Gottlieb Fichte (1762–1814) "defended the rights of the individual against the abstract moral laws of Kant, . . ."[1] and so helped to encourage the German romantic movement in literature.

Friedrich Ernst Daniel Schleiermacher (1768–1834) tried to reconcile life and religion and to make religion every man's personal concern; for him religion was "only another name for all higher feelings and aspirations; religion was the poetry of the soul."[2]

Georg Wilhelm Friedrich Hegel (1770–1831) tried to bridge the gap between Kantian ontological dualism and Platonic doctrines about the spirit or soul, and he tried to reconcile both with Christian self-abnegation. His "absolute idealism" holds that the universe is and ever since its creation has been in a continuous process of evolution, of self-realization. Both mind and matter (which are hardly distinguishable from each other) have existed since the beginning; and mind, interacting with matter, has evolved spirit. This process will continue to evolve a finer and nobler universe. This optimistic theory, which Hegel attempted to apply to history, religion, ethics, art, literature, and virtually all other realms, was a potent tonic to the thinkers of Europe between the years 1830 and 1870.

Friedrich Wilhelm Joseph von Schelling (1775–1854), a mystic, contributed to the romantic movement by proclaiming the emotions and the imagination safe guides. Nature and spirit, he said, are but different aspects of the "world soul," and in art the two aspects are blended.

Opposed to Hegelianism was Arthur Schopenhauer (1788–1860), a complete pessimist. He held that the will is the only reality, that the world is malignant, that the act of willing leads men into misery, and that therefore the negation of the will — including the will to live — is the final good. Schopenhauer denied the existence of God, freedom of the will, and immortality of the soul.

Karl Marx (1818–1883) has, of course, been one of the most influential political philosophers who have ever lived. *The Communist Manifesto* (1848) by Marx and Friedrich Engels (1820–1895) and *Capital* (*Das Kapital*)[3] propound the theories that the entire price of a commodity should remunerate the labor required to produce it, that capital should not share in profits, and that labor therefore should rise in a class war and seize and redistribute all property and all means of production.

Finally, Friedrich Wilhelm Nietzsche (1844–1900) attacked the asceticism of Schopenhauer and exalted the will. He had only contempt for Christianity, morality, conscience, and altruism. All of these he considered mere weakness, and he deplored weakness of any sort. The "will to power," he claimed, is the highest good; and he advocated the cultivation of a race of "supermen" — creatures physically powerful, unscrupulous, and pitiless. Nietzsche's philosophy is essentially optimistic — an affirmation of individualism, hope, and activity. His most famous work embodying the philosophy of the superman is *Thus Spake Zarathustra* (*Also sprach Zarathustra*, 1883–1885).

General View of the Literature. German literature of the nineteenth century followed much the same course as that taken by French literature — romanticism, realism, and naturalism.

It has already been shown that many romantic elements were present in the Storm and Stress of the 1780's and that Goethe and Schiller tried to blend their native romanticism with a classicism derived from the ancients. It was not till the end of the eighteenth century, however, that the romantic movement in German literature was recognized as such.

In 1797 several young men banded together for the purpose of encouraging and propagating a number of principles which have since become known as romanticism: "return to the popular and native, opposition to mediocrity and false rules, to extreme forms of eighteenth-century enlightenment, and to dogmatism, complete freedom of the life of the spirit and of the imagination."[4] These young men were August Wilhelm Schlegel (1767–1845), poet and translator of Shakespeare and Calderón; his brother Friedrich Schlegel (1772–1829), poet, novelist, essayist, and critic, who "laid the foundations for 'romantic poesy' ";[5] Novalis (pseudonym of Friedrich von Hardenberg [1772–1801]), mystical poet and novelist; Wilhelm Heinrich Wackenroder (1773–1798), essayist; and Johann Ludwig Tieck (1773–1853), dramatist, poet, and short-story writer. The first issue of the critical organ of the group, the *Athenäum,* in

1798 (the same year in which Wordsworth and Coleridge published their *Lyrical Ballads*) marks the beginning of the German romantic movement. The group chose Shakespeare, Herder, Goethe, and Schiller as its models, and it was also influenced by Klopstock and Richter. The philosophers Fichte and Schelling were closely associated with the movement. This group was ten years ahead of the Italian romanticists and twenty years ahead of the French.

About 1804 a second wave of romantics set up headquarters in Heidelberg. They were Friedrich de La Motte-Fouqué (1777–1843), poet, novelist, and dramatist; Clemens Brentano (1778–1842), poet; Achim von Arnim (1781–1831), dramatist and — with Brentano — collector of a famous volume of folk songs, *The Boy's Magic Horn* (*Des Knaben Wunderhorn*, 1805–1808); Jakob (1785–1863) and Wilhelm (1786–1859) Grimm, philologists, folklorists, and collectors of fairy tales; and Joseph von Eichendorff (1788–1857), poet and novelist.

Other important romanticists were Ernst Theodor Amadeus Hoffmann (1776–1822), novelist; Heinrich von Kleist (1777–1811), dramatist and novelist; Adalbert von Chamisso (1781–1838), poet; Johann Ludwig Uhland (1787–1862), poet and philologist; Franz Grillparzer (1791–1872), dramatist and novelist; and Heinrich Heine (1797–1856), poet and essayist.

By 1830 romanticism was definitely on the way out, and by 1848 social, political, and economic trends had effected the triumph of realism. Literature became more politically and socially conscious. Lyricism waned, and the principal literary forms were the drama, the novel, and the novelette (*Novelle*). The chief realistic dramatists were Friedrich Hebbel (1813–1863) and Otto Ludwig (1813–1865). The main novelists were Karl Lebrecht Immermann (1796–1840) and Fritz Reuter (1810–1874). Among the best writers of short prose narratives were Theodor Storm (1817–1888), Gottfried Keller (1819–1890), and Konrad Ferdinand Meyer (1825–1898).

Under the influence of Zola, Maupassant, Schopenhauer, Nietzsche, Tolstoy, and Dostoevsky, German literature evolved from realism into naturalism, which found its chief expression in the drama and in the novel. The leading German dramatist of this school was Gerhart Hauptmann (1862–1946). The most effective criticism of society came not in Germany proper but in Scandinavia. Henrik Ibsen (1828–1906) and Björnstjerne Björnson (1832–1910) in Norway and August Strindberg (1849–1912) in Sweden were

closely related to the French and German realists and naturalists.
At the very end of the century Symbolism began to supersede
naturalism, but the discussion of this trend falls more logically under
the heading of the twentieth century.

ROMANTICISM (1798–1830)

Poetry

Friedrich Hölderlin (1770–1843).   At the very beginning of
the romantic period stands the lyricist Hölderlin — passionate in
his adoration of ancient Greece yet deeply influenced by the Storm
and Stress and by such subjective works as Goethe's *Werther*.   His
admiration for Greece and his "pantheistic faith in the oneness of
God and nature, formed the two poles of Hölderlin's nature; and
through all his writings runs a passionate craving for a harmony he
never succeeded in attaining, and a subtle pessimism of disillusionment."[6]   Such a pessimism appears in "Song of Fate" ("Schick-
salslied") from *Hyperion* (1797–1799), which is a long (two-volume)
romance about Hyperion, a Greek youth who helps his nation fight
against the Turks in 1770; the romance has little plot and is full of
Hyperion's own emotions.   Other good short poems by Hölderlin
are "To the Germans" ("An die Deutschen") and "To the Ether"
("An den Äether").

Novalis (pseudonym of Friedrich von Hardenberg, 1772–1801).
Novalis wrote lyrics remarkable for their deep, mystical, religious
devotion and their idealization of love.   The best are "If I Have
Only Him" ("Wenn ich ihn nur habe"), "He Is the Lord of the
Earth" ("Das ist der Herr der Erde"), "Song of the Dead" ("Gesang
der Toten"), and "Hymn to the Night" ("Hymnen an die Nacht").
Novalis began but did not finish a romantic novel, *Heinrich von Ofter-
dingen;* the scene is laid in the Middle Ages, and the hero is a poetical
knight who, after the death of his sweetheart, finds consolation in the
quest for the "blue flower" symbolizing romanticism.

Joseph von Eichendorff (1788–1857).   The greatest German
nature poet of the later romantic period.   In addition to poems
about nature, he wrote lyrics about love and lyrics about home.
Most of his best poetry is collected in the volume entitled simply
Poems (*Gedichte*, 1837).   Though his range is narrow, Robertson says
of him that "in the long history of German song no other poet has

written so many lyrics that still justify the adjective flawless."[7] Some of his best lyrics are "In a Cool Hollow" ("In einem kühlen Grunde"), "O Valleys Wide, O Heights!" ("O Täler weit, O Höhen"), and "It Was as if the Heaven" ("Es war, als hätte der Himmel"). Besides poetry Eichendorff wrote several dramas, literary criticism and history, novels, and short tales. Of the last named, "From the Life of a Good-for-Nothing" ("Aus dem Leben eines Taugenichts," 1826) is an amusing little masterpiece about the wanderings of a young musician.

Wilhelm Müller (1794–1827). An admirer and disciple of Lord Byron, Müller won his first fame as a champion of the Greeks in their war for independence from Turkey; his *Songs of the Greeks* (*Lieder der Griechen,* 1821–1824) are enthusiastically patriotic, but somewhat sentimental. Müller also wrote some ballads (e.g., "The Casting of the Bell at Breslau" ["Der Glockenguss zu Breslau"]); some love poetry (e.g., *The Beautiful Maid of the Mill* [*Die schöne Müllerin*]); and some nature poetry (e.g., *Winter Journey* [*Winterreise*]). The last two titles refer to cycles of poems — both set to music by Franz Schubert.

HEINRICH HEINE (1797–1856). Heine was born of Jewish parents in Düsseldorf. After an unsuccessful attempt in business, he began the study of law in 1819 and took his degree at the University of Göttingen in 1825. In the same year he was baptized in the Christian faith. He spent most of the next six years traveling at his uncle's expense — in Germany, Italy, and England. During this time he published two volumes which earned him fame: *Travel in the Harz* (1826) and *Book of Songs* (1827). His sarcastic attacks, however, on various individuals and on several governments in Germany made him unpopular. This unpopularity, his disgust with social and political conditions in Germany, and visions of political justice in France induced him to move to Paris in 1831; there he lived the remainder of his life. In the early 'thirties he became a member of "Young Germany," an organization of youthful writers who had as their main purposes the opposing of the reactionism of the era and the establishing of a liberal German government. In 1848 he began to suffer from a malady of the spine; his last eight years were spent in agony on his "mattress-grave," as he called it.

Three love affairs influenced his poems. From about 1819 till 1823 he was in love with Amalie, the daughter of his uncle Salomon

Heine; the love was unrequited. In the winter of 1834–1835 he met Eugénie Mirat, whom he married six years later. And finally, he had a great passion for Elise von Krienitz (alias Camille Selden), his faithful nurse during his last years of illness.

Commentators have always found Heine a mass of puzzling — and sometimes irritating — ambiguities and inconsistencies. Born a Jew, he embraced Christianity; and yet he was at times bitterly scornful of the best in both Judaism and the Christian religion. Born a German, he fled to Paris; and yet he censured both Germany and France. He had a superb gift of tender and delicate lyricism; and yet he was endowed with "an Aristophanic power of satire and cynicism."[8] A romantic poet, he poured ridicule on romanticism. Perhaps the explanation of these inconsistencies is that he was a prophet born out of his time — possessed of the reforming zeal, but without a great cause to endorse.

Works. Most of Heine's works are "Young German" rather than strictly romantic. Heine's fame rests chiefly on his short lyrics and ballads, but he wrote also several volumes of prose which were widely read in his own day. Most of the short poems were published in the following volumes: *Poems* (*Gedichte*, 1822), *The Book of Songs* (*Das Buch der Lieder*, 1827), *New Poems* (*Neue Gedichte*, 1844), *Romancero* (*Romanzero*, 1851), and *Last Poems* (*Letzte Gedichte*, 1853, 1855).

LYRICS. Heine's lyrics differ from most German lyrical poetry in that he dispenses with "the delicate spiritual reticence and subtle twilight effects . . . [and employs] a bold concrete imagery, which seems to drag the most fleeting emotions into the unequivocal glare of daylight."[9] Many of his lyrics — from the earliest through the last — are intensely personal. They express many moods and emotions — sorrow, gaiety, humor, passion, pain, and regret. One of his favorite themes is unrequited love. "Of this he has sung more poignantly than any poet before him or after."[10] He is also a nature poet, and he better than any other German poet has captured the beauty and romance of the sea. A few of his best-known lyrics are "A Pine Tree Stands Alone" ("Ein Fichtenbaum steht einsam"), "Say, Where Is Thy Fair Beloved" ("Sag', wo ist dein schönes Liebchen"), "When I Look into Thine Eyes" ("Wenn ich in deine Augen seh' "), "Thou Fair Fisher-Maiden" ("Du schönes Fischermädchen"), "Thou Art Like a Blossom" ("Du bist wie eine Blume"), "On the Wings of Song" ("Auf Flügeln des Gesanges"), "In the Lovely Month of May" ("Im wunderschönen Monat Mai"), "I

Shall Not Be Angry" ("Ich grolle nicht"), and "Thou Hast Diamonds and Pearls" ("Du hast Diamanten und Perlen").

BALLADS. Though less numerous than his lyrics, Heine's ballads are only slightly less popular. Here he captures the spirit of the folk song. "The Loreley" ("Die Lorelei"), for example, is a sad little legend about a beautiful maiden on a mountain top beside the Rhine who lures sailors to destruction on the rocks. "The Two Grenadiers" ("Die Grenadiere") is a story about the patriotism of two soldiers of Napoleon who have been captured in Russia but are now making their way back to France. "Belshazzar" ("Belsazer") is a terse but powerful version of the famous feast in which the Babylonian king's fate is foretold by a hand which writes on the wall (see Dan. 5).

PROSE. Heine's prose shows him to be an excellent though uneven stylist. "Within the same paragraph the purest poetic feeling may clash with the bitterest satire and cynicism."[11] But he is always clear, smooth, and light of touch. *Pictures of Travel* (*Reisebilder*, 1826–1831), in four volumes, tells of his journeys through Germany, Italy, and England. The best part is Book I, *Travel in the Harz* [*Mountains*] (*Harzreise*). "Nothing so wicked, and at the same time so brilliant and amusing, had before been written in the German language."[12] The work is marred, however, by unwarranted attacks on individual men, institutions, and religion.

Heine called himself "a soldier in the Liberation War of Humanity." While in Paris he wrote many articles for German newspapers in which he assailed the antidemocratic forces in Germany and urged the establishment of a liberal government. He had warm praise (along with some censure) for France, and he retained his affection for Germany even while attacking her institutions. These articles were published in three volumes: *French Affairs* (*Französische Zustände*, 1833), *The Salon* (*Der Salon*, 1835–1840), and *Lutetia* (1854).

Finally, *The Romantic School* (*Die Romantische Schule*, 1836), a book which intends to enlighten Frenchmen on the subject of German romanticism and which contains many acute observations. Unfortunately, it shows some bad taste in ridiculing certain people, and some of its statements are inaccurate.

Estimate. Heine's attacks on Germany and his venomous jibes at particular German people probably account for the fact that his native land has often underrated him as a poet. In other lands his lyrics have been more popular and influential than those of any other

German poet.   It is not too much to say that, if we except Goethe, Heine is the greatest lyricist that Germany has ever produced.

Nikolaus Lenau (Nikolaus Franz Niembsch von Strehlenau, 1802–1850).   Lenau was one of the most pessimistic and tragically unhappy of German poets; in many ways he was comparable to Giacomo Leopardi (Ch. 2).   He was influenced by Goethe, Eichendorff, and Byron; and he was in sympathy with the Young German movement.   His first volume, entitled simply *Poems* (*Gedichte*, 1832), consists principally of little pieces about peasant life in Germany and Hungary (Lenau was born at Csatád in Hungary); even these early poems were filled with sadness, melancholy, and religious doubt. He spent a short while in America, where he hoped to find freedom and happiness; he wrote some poems in praise of America and especially the American Indian, e.g., "The Blockhouse" ("Das Blockhaus") and "Niagara."   *Faust* (1836) is a lyrical drama expressive of the author's own bitterness and sorrow.   *Savonarola* (1837) and *The Albigenses* (*Die Albigenser*, 1842) are long and pessimistic epics which glorify freedom of conscience.   Even into the epics and the drama Lenau pours his own feeling, for his gift is essentially lyric. "No poet of Northern Europe expresses as intensely as Lenau the feeling of 'eternal autumn,' of unrelieved despair. . . . He gave the most poignant expression to that pessimism which formed the dominant note in German literature between 1850 and 1880."[13]

Eduard Mörike (1804–1875).   The exquisite delicacy, simplicity, spontaneity, tenderness, suggestiveness, and sense of humor of Mörike's lyrics entitle him to a place second only to that of Heine among German romantic poets.   His first volume, *Poems* (*Gedichte*, 1838), contains many gems, such as "The Forsaken Maiden" ("Das verlassene Mädchen"), "Agnes," and "Soldier's Betrothed" ("Soldatenbraut").   His ballads are perhaps a bit less successful, e.g., "The Lovely Rohtraut" ("Schön-Rohtraut"), "The Fire-Rider" ("Der Feuerreiter"), and "The Shadow" ("Die Schatten"). Mörike also wrote some excellent fairy tales (*Märchen vom sichern Mann*, 1838).   And he left unfinished a novel, *Nolten the Painter* (*Maler Nolten*, 1832), which recalls *Wilhelm Meister* in both its contents and its formlessness; although the plot is poorly constructed, the novel is valuable for its excellent characterization and for the short poems which the author scattered through it.

Drama

The genius of romanticism is lyrical and introspective rather than dramatic. It is entirely natural, therefore, that the romantic age in Germany produced few figures who attained great stature in drama. LUDWIG TIECK (1773–1853), one of the leaders of the early romantic school, wrote the witty and satirical *Puss-in-Boots*[14] (*Der gestiefelte Kater*, 1797) to ridicule the sentimental drama; and he wrote several plays which glorified medieval times. Other minor dramatists were Fouqué and Arnim. The two playwrights who have the greatest significance for world literature are Kleist and Grillparzer.

Heinrich von Kleist (1777–1811). A Prussian nobleman whose whole life was a series of misfortunes. He gave up a military career in order to further his education but soon abandoned his university pursuits. Depressed by Germany's disgraceful defeats at the hands of Napoleon and by the failure of his own plays, and beset by poverty after the death of his patroness Queen Luise, Kleist shot himself.

Romantic in the turbulence of their passion, in their subjectivity, and in the eccentricity of some of the characters, Kleist's dramas have also the classical characteristics of clarity of purpose and of outline. His depiction of characters is realistic: "his men and women live, and each is a distinct individuality."[15] His uncompromising search for truth sometimes leads him so close to naturalism (in the French sense) that he fails to distinguish between the terrible and the horrible.

His first work, *The Schroffenstein Family* (*Die Familie Schroffenstein*, 1803), is a fatalistic tragedy — representative of Kleist's own Storm and Stress — in which a feud between two families brings death to a pair of lovers. *Penthesilea* (1808) "is a reproduction of the Homeric age in the lurid light of a distraught Romanticism."[16] The Amazonian queen kills Achilles because she thinks he has scorned her love; then she gnaws his body and finally commits suicide. *Kitty from Heilbronn* (*Das Käthchen von Heilbronn*, 1808) is a romantic comedy of chivalry. Kitty, who is supposed to be the daughter of an armorer, loves the knight Wetter von Strahl and faithfully follows him around, despite his rude treatment of her. When she is discovered to be the illegitimate daughter of the emperor, the knight marries her. Although the plot — particularly the denouement — is fantastic, "the dreamy indomitable Käthchen is a delightful creation, and the play is full of romantic charm."[17]   *Hermann's Battle* (*Die Hermannsschlacht*, written 1808, published 1821) is a patriotic drama on the ancient Arminius story, previously dramatized by Klopstock.   For Kleist, Rome is equivalent to France and the land of the Cheruskans to Germany.   His last and best drama is *The Prince of Homburg* (*Der Prinz von Homburg*, written 1810, published 1821).   It is a semihistorical drama with its scene in the seventeenth century.   Prince Friedrich wins a great victory at Fehrbellin by disobeying the command of his superior officer.   Condemned to be executed, he at first shows a cowardly fear of death, but soon regains control of himself and admits the justice of the sentence.   He is pardoned by the Elector of Brandenburg.   The Prince is Kleist's greatest piece of characterization.

Among Kleist's many short stories one is of importance.   "Michael Kohlhaas" (1810) is the account of a "law-abiding horse-dealer" whose horses are wrongfully taken by a nobleman.   Failing to receive justice by legal means, he takes the law into his own hands, regains his horses, and starts civil war à la Götz and Karl Moor. Knowing that he has exposed tyranny and injustice, he submits to his own execution.   The story "is a masterpiece of straightforward, realistic narrative."[18]

Franz Grillparzer (1791–1872).   Grillparzer, "the greatest Austrian," was born in Vienna, and there he lived virtually all his long, timid, uneventful life as a petty government official.

His first notable work is *The Ancestress* (*Die Ahnfrau*, 1817), a "spook-tragedy," in which the spirit of a woman is fated to watch over a family till its crimes are atoned for.   Far superior is *Sappho* (1819), a somewhat romanticized account of the love and suicide of the great Greek lyricist.   With deep sympathy Grillparzer depicts the conflict between Sappho's love for Phaon and her devotion to art. This play and several later ones show Grillparzer's romanticism as well as his great interest in the ancient classics.   *The Golden Fleece* (*Das goldene Vlies*, 1820), made up of *The Guest* (*Der Gastfreund*), *The Argonauts* (*Die Argonauten*), and *Medea*, is a powerful psychological study of the guilt of Jason and of the famous sorceress.   The Fleece itself, like the Rhinegold, is the symbol of a curse hanging over all its possessors.   *King Ottokar's Weal and Woe*[19] (*König Ottokars Glück und Ende*, 1825) is another psychological portrait.   The tragedy recounts the Bohemian king's struggle against Rudolf of Hapsburg. The theme of *A Faithful Servant to His Master* (*Ein treuer Diener seines*

Herrn, 1830) is a subject's loyalty to his sovereign. Bancban risks his life to save the queen although her brother has persecuted Bancban's wife to the point of suicide. *Waves of the Sea and of Love* (*Des Meeres und der Liebe Wellen*, 1831) is Grillparzer's finest play; it is a dramatic version of the Hero and Leander story; his Hero is a charming and innocent young heroine "who belongs in the select company of Shakespeare's Juliet and Goethe's Margaret."[20] *Life Is a Dream* (*Der Traum, ein Leben*, 1834) tells how a dream saves Rustan from the tragic consequences to which his worldly ambitions threaten to lead him. Finally, *Woe to Him Who Lies* (*Weh' dem, der lügt*, 1838) is Grillparzer's only comedy. The hero, Leon, Bishop Gregory's cook, sets out to rescue the bishop's nephew from Barbarians. His promise always to tell the truth not only leads to many comic situations but also outwits the Barbarians. The play was not a success when it was first presented but is now recognized as a comic master-piece.

Grillparzer was the greatest dramatist of the period who wrote in the German language. His plays will survive because of their "deep feeling for poetic truth, . . . sincerity, . . . fine psychological analysis of human character and action, [and] the dignity and the deep but restrained passion of his men and women. . . ."[21]

The Novel

It is, of course, impossible to say at what moment the German novel ceased to be "classical" and became "romantic." The influence of Rousseau, Sterne, and other sentimentalists was still powerful at the turn of the century.

Many of the earliest German novels which may be called romantic were attempts to emulate Sir Walter Scott. ACHIM VON ARNIM, WILHELM HAUFF (1802–1827), and WILLIBALD ALEXIS (pseudonym of Wilhelm Häring, 1798–1871), all wrote romantic historical novels, but none had sufficient knowledge or historical insight to produce works of real value.

Another romantic element — love for the fantastic and the supernatural — is shown in the works of E. T. A. Hoffmann.

Jean Paul (Friedrich Richter) (1763–1825). Sentimentalist and humorist, Jean Paul was influenced by Sterne, Rousseau, and Wieland, but succeeded in writing original and charming short stories, novels, and character sketches. "The Contented Little Schoolmaster Maria Wuz" ("Das vergnügte Schulmeisterlein Maria

Wuz") and "Quintus Fixlein" are short tales about rural life. His longer works, though somewhat too intricate in style, too sentimental, and too allusive for twentieth-century readers, are, nevertheless, remarkable for their "semi-ironical humor and delicate feeling."[22] *Titan* (1800–1803) is the story of a prince who is reared in ignorance of his parentage. After an "apprenticeship" and sentimental education reminiscent of that of Wilhelm Meister, he succeeds to the throne.

"No writer of the time enriched German literature with so many striking and illuminating images, so many passages of high imaginative beauty."[23] His pictures of simple life still make pleasant reading.

Ernst Theodor Amadeus Hoffmann (1776–1822). Hoffmann is remembered as the author of fantastic tales and tales of terror. Balzac called him the creator "of that which lacks the appearance of existing but which, nevertheless, has life."[24] *Fantastic Pieces in the Manner of Callot** (*Fantasiestücke in Callots Manier*, 1814–1815), a four-volume collection of essays and tales, made Hoffmann famous; best known in the collection are "The Golden Pot" ("Der goldne Topf") and "Musical Sorrows of Johann Kreisler, the Bandmaster" ("Johannes Kreislers des Kapellmeisters musikalische Leiden"). *The Devil's Elixir* (*Die Elixiere des Teufels*, 1815–1816) is a Gothic novel of horror suggested by Matthew G. Lewis' *Monk* (1796); in Hoffmann's novel a Capuchin monk embarks on a series of gruesome crimes as the result of tasting an old and mysterious brew which he finds in the monastery; he is redeemed by love and repents. *The Brothers of Serapion* (*Die Serapions Brüder*, 1819–1821) is another four-volume collection of tales — some morbid and full of terror, others milder.

Hoffmann is remembered, too, as the inspirer of Jacques Offenbach's opera *The Tales of Hoffmann.*

REALISM AND NATURALISM (1830–1900)

Drama

Christian Friedrich Hebbel (1813–1863). Hebbel brought the realistic drama to Germany. Born of poor parents at Wesselburen in Holstein, he had great financial difficulty in securing an educa-

---

* A seventeenth-century French artist, noted for his "grotesque style."

tion, but eventually succeeded in attending the universities of Heidelberg and Munich. He began writing drama in 1839 and achieved some success with his first tragedy, *Judith* (1840). From 1843 to 1845 he traveled in France and Italy on a stipend from King Christian VIII of Denmark. Settling in Vienna, he married the actress Christine Enghaus (1845). Henceforth his plays were comparatively well received, and he was in relatively easy circumstances. He died soon after the production of one of his most ambitious dramatic efforts, *The Nibelungs*.

Hebbel "created a type of drama which anticipates Ibsen in its keen dialectic of passion, and suggests Nietzsche in its predilection for characters that live themselves out in a spirit of reckless and vehement self-assertion — supermen and superwomen."[25] Most of his tragedies present violent emotional conflicts or abnormal situations. He does not hesitate to probe relentlessly into human motives and human character. Sometimes this probing and this penchant for the violent and the abnormal alienate some readers.

Judith (1840) is a version of the story from the Apocrypha. The titular character saves her country by yielding herself to the enemy Holofernes and then murdering him. *Genevieve* (*Genoveva*, 1843) and *Herod and Mariamne* (*Herodes und Mariamne*, 1850) are both on the theme of a wife outraged by a loathsome husband. *Agnes Bernauer* (1852) deals with the conflict between rights of the individual and the demands of the state. Feeling that the Duke has been allowing love to interfere with his official duties, his father drowns the Duke's beautiful wife Agnes in the Danube. *Gyges and His Ring* (*Gyges und sein Ring*, 1854) is based on a story from Herodotus. King Kandaules of Lydia permits Gyges, made invisible by means of a magic ring, to see Queen Rhodope "in her naked beauty." Learning of the insult and desiring to remove the stain on her honor, Rhodope persuades Gyges to kill Kandaules and marry her. Then she commits suicide. The last work Hebbel wrote is a trilogy: *The Nibelungs* (*Die Nibelungen*, 1862), which consists of *The Horny-Skinned Siegfried* (*Der gehörnte Siegfried*), a one-act prologue; *Siegfried's Death* (*Siegfrieds Tod*), in five acts; and *Kriemhild's Revenge* (*Kriemhilds Rache*), also in five acts. The trilogy is a rather faithful rendering of the *Nibelungenlied*, but Hebbel softens and modernizes some incidents which would offend a nineteenth-century audience.

"Whatever may be the ultimate judgment of his dramatic work, . . . there can be no question of . . . the success he achieved in filling dramatic poetry with a new psychological significance. The whole subsequent development of the European drama stands in his debt."[26]

Otto Ludwig (1813–1865). He and Hebbel were born in the same year, and both suffered from poverty.

A careful artist and an ardent admirer of Shakespeare, Ludwig spent a great deal of time revising his works to make them conform to the standard set by the English master. Consequently his output is small.

His forte lies in the delineation of character and in creation of atmosphere. He is adept at handling details of observation, and he has a predilection for the very small. He is inferior to Hebbel in the presentation of an emotional conflict.

The Hereditary Forester (*Der Erbförster*, 1850) is an exceptionally gloomy tragedy about a forester who claims that, since his grandfather and father formerly held the same position which he now holds, he cannot legally be discharged. When the new owner of the forest dismisses him, he seeks revenge by shooting who he thinks is the owner's son, but the victim is discovered to be his own daughter. *The Maccabees* (*Die Makkabäer*, 1854) is the story (derived from the Apocrypha) of Leah's noble sacrifice of her seven sons for the causes of patriotism and religion. Although the dramatic structure is loose, there are many scenes of great beauty and power.

In addition to tragedies Ludwig wrote some fairly good comedies (e.g., *Hans Frei* [1842–1843] and *Madame de Scudéry* [*Das Fräulein von Scuderi*, 1848]) and some good stories about village life (e.g., "Out of the Frying Pan into the Fire"[27] ["Aus dem Regen in die Traufe," 1857] and "Between Heaven and Earth" ["Zwischen Himmel und Erde," 1856]).

HENRIK IBSEN (1828–1906). Ibsen was born at Skien, the capital of Telemark Province, Norway. In 1836 his father, formerly a prosperous merchant, went bankrupt, and the family was plunged into poverty. From 1844 to 1850 Henrik worked in an apothecary shop in Grimstad. There he studied Latin in preparation for university examinations; his first drama, *Catiline* (written 1848–1849) was the result of his reading Sallust. In 1850 he went to Oslo, where he received a "conditional standing" on the entrance examinations at the university. He continued to write plays and poetry. In the fall of 1851 he was hired as assistant director and playwright for the National Stage in Bergen. He continued in this capacity for about six years. In 1857 he became director of the Norwegian Theater in Oslo. The following year he was married to Susannah Thoresen, who was thenceforth a great aid and inspiration to him. In 1862 his theater had to close because of financial difficulties, and Ibsen was given a temporary position with the Christiana theater. A grant-in-aid enabled him to study Norwegian folklore, and a traveling fellowship made it possible for him to visit Paris and Rome (1864). He remained in Italy till 1868. In the meantime he had become famous in Norway with the publication of *Brand* (1866) and *Peer Gynt* (1867). After this he was able to support himself by writing. From 1868 till 1876 he lived in Dresden, and from 1876 till 1891 in Munich — except for short sojourns elsewhere and a long stay in Rome (1880–1885). In 1891 he returned to Oslo, where he lived the remainder of his days.

Technique. Ibsen was a great innovator. He wrote a new kind of drama, different from the traditional types not only in theme and subject matter but also in technique.

In the first place, most of his plays are "problem" plays; he is more interested in presenting a social or individual problem than in solving it. Clearly perceiving the maladies of modern society, he refrains from offering a panacea and is content merely to diagnose. "For him it suffices to show up, by a set of striking illustrations from life, the extant maladjustments, and the generally unconfessed impotence of our long-existent and somewhat worn religious, political, and social ideals."[28]

In order to present the "striking illustrations" Ibsen finds that a new sort of plot is necessary. Now, dramas with little physical action on the stage date from the days of Aeschylus, and Racine wrote plays in which the interest is principally psychological. Ibsen's innovation is the presentation of a character as he begins to awaken to the maladjustment between himself and another person or between himself and society in general. Like Racine, Ibsen usually allows the action to begin only slightly before the catastrophe, and then he employs the so-called "analytic" method of revealing crucial events which have led up to that catastrophe.[29] The employment of this method causes many of Ibsen's plays to observe one or more of the three unities, but, unlike Racine, he felt no compulsion to follow any pre-established dogma, as is shown in his complete disregard of the unities of time and place in *Peer Gynt* and *When We Dead Awaken* and in his use of a subplot in *A Doll's House*,

Since the action is chiefly psychological, it is obvious that Ibsen's interest is more in characters than in plot. But his purpose is not primarily to show us character development. "The object of the play is, then, to show them [the characters] for what they are, in action and reaction, and to explain them, in a way, by gradually lifting the curtain from over their past history."[30] He often gains suspense, through the analytical method, by allowing us at first to misjudge a character and then to discover his true nature.

Although his characters frequently have some typical characteristics, they are not mere types. They are individual human beings with unique personalities. In *A Doll's House*, for instance, Helmer is a typical complacent, self-satisfied husband, but his cowardice, his essential dishonesty, and — most of all — his inability to see his own hypocrisy and egocentricity make him the one and only Torvald Helmer who has ever existed. Perhaps it is the *combination* of typical traits that makes Ibsen's characters unique — and universal.

Ibsen is extraordinarily skillful in the use of minor characters as foils or analogues to the main ones. In *Hedda Gabler*, for example, Juliana Tesman exists only for the sake of others, in contrast with the titular protagonist, who thrives on the destruction of the happiness and the lives of others.

A few critics have denied that Ibsen employs symbolism. The great majority of them, however, agree that he uses symbols in some of his major plays. The very titles of some of them seem to prove this beyond dispute — e.g., *A Doll's House* and *The Wild Duck*. Can there by any doubt that the pieces of sculpture in *When We Dead Awaken* symbolize Ibsen's own former literary productions? There is often critical disagreement about what a person or thing symbolizes, but that he or it symbolizes something is ordinarily a matter of unanimous opinion.[31]

Closely related to Ibsen's use of symbolism is his employment of key phrases. The frequent recurrence of the symbol and of such expressions as "miracle," "lark," and "squirrel" in *A Doll's House;* "joy of living" in *Ghosts;* and "ideal demand" in *The Wild Duck* serves to drive home the ethical, social, or psychological point that the dramatist is eager to make. The cue-words and symbols are used in a way somewhat similar to Wagner's employment of the *leitmotif* in his "music dramas."[32]

Brand and *Peer Gynt* (two early "romantic" plays) are written in verse. Most of Ibsen's works are in prose — a simple, concise, and natural prose, which he considers appropriate for realism. He uses few adjectives, and he avoids declamation, ornamentation, and long speeches, especially long expository or narrative speeches for the purpose of enlightening the audience on anterior actions.

Thought. As has been suggested above, Ibsen was an innovator in thought as well as in technique. He perceived with unusual clarity the hypocrisy, the selfishness, the folly, the supineness, the shallowness, and the cowardice of modern society and its conventions, and he dared to expose them ruthlessly. He dared to discuss openly the problem of venereal disease, conjugal fidelity, and the right of a wife to leave her husband because of incompatibility; such topics were taboo in Ibsen's day, and his treatment of them brought a world-wide storm of abuse down on his head. His intention, of course, was to present a problem with such clearness and force that people would be spurred into finding a solution. "He sought not beauty but absolute truth and fidelity to one's ideals; he strove not to elevate the reader but to arrest him, even if it be through ugliness and squalor."[33]

One of the specific problems he was most concerned about was the emancipation, education, and dignity of woman. Her rights and capabilities as compared with those of man are dealt with in *Ghosts, A Doll's House, The Lady from the Sea,* and *Rosmersholm;* and in nearly every one of his plays a woman is the necessary complement or inspiration to man.

Somewhat closely related to this topic is Ibsen's interest in a person's self-realization, whether that person be male or female. Influenced by Goethe and Nietzsche, the dramatist preaches the development of all a person's possibilities — the discovery and expression of one's true self, "the enthronement of the Individual, the apotheosis of the Egotist, the cult of the Superman."[34] He points out the tyrannies which society perpetrates on the individual and the falsities to which it drives him. Yet time after time he also warns against excessive egoism that leads to the detriment of others.

Such warnings indicate that Ibsen was a firm believer in freedom of the will; and so he was. But he was also greatly concerned with the roles that heredity and environment play in shaping a man's destiny. The discoveries of Darwin and some of the other scientists made a profound impression on him, and in many of his plays he emphasizes the large extent to which his characters' natures and actions are determined by their early rearing and by heredity.   In some of his plays (notably *A Doll's House* and *Ghosts*) these determinants become a new sort of tragic fate.

The discussion of fate suggests a question to which the answer is still in dispute.   Is Ibsen an idealistic optimist or a realistic pessimist?   Some commentators hold that he renounces idealism and is a pessimist about the future.   Others have claimed that, despite his realistic portrayal of the sad predicament of society, he puts his faith in idealism and looks forward hopefully.[35]

Specific Plays. Ibsen's plays fall into three main periods.   In the first (*c.* 1850–1867) he wrote chiefly romantic "dramas of ideas in the grand style."   In the second period (1877–1890) come the realistic plays dealing with social problems.   In this period fall most of his important works.   In the last period (1891–1899) Ibsen turned more to the consideration of individual problems.   These last plays are often mystical and allegorical.

FIRST PERIOD.

BRAND (1866).   The story of an idealistic preacher who advocates carrying out God's will with an utter disregard of private and selfish interests.   Practice of his principle costs him his wife and child; and eventually his own congregation, for whom he has sacrificed everything, turn against him and drive him out into the snow, because — being human and sinful — they cannot follow the arduous path in which he wishes to lead them.   Brand is overwhelmed by an avalanche, but dies retaining his faith.

PEER GYNT (1867).   The account of a dissipated dreamer and braggart who yearns for the virtuous maiden Solveig, but lacks the perseverance necessary to win her.   He becomes a profligate and outlaw, and neither Solveig's efforts to reclaim him nor the death of his mother Ase change his ways.   He has many adventures, including elopement with Ingrid, a sojourn with trolls, participation in African slave trade, and flirtation with the Arab Anitra.   Aged and disillusioned, he returns to Norway, where the Buttonmolder (Death or Fate) convinces him of his uselessness.   He is finally redeemed by the pure love of Solveig.   There are distinct similarities between Peer and Faust and between Solveig and Gretchen.

SECOND PERIOD.

THE PILLARS OF SOCIETY (*Samfundets Stötter*, 1877).   As the name suggests, this is a satire on the hypocrisy of society.   Karsten Bernick, a "first citizen" of the town, is regarded as a pious member of the church, an exemplary family man, and a respectable leader of the community; but his whole life has been built on hypocrisy, selfishness, and falsehood, which he has been clever enough to conceal. At length, threatened with exposure, he becomes contrite; and even though the danger of exposure is removed, he makes a complete confession and is morally regenerated.

A DOLL'S HOUSE (*Et Dukkehjem*, 1879). Ibsen's plea for the recognition of woman as a being entitled to consideration as an intellectual and spiritual companion to man. Nora Helmer commits forgery in order to save the life of her sick husband Torvald. Danger of exposure reveals that Torvald is a moral coward and hypocrite and that Nora has lived a life of sham with him as his plaything, his doll. Nora deserts him in order to "find herself."

GHOSTS (*Gjengangere*, 1881). An indictment of the "double standard" of morality and of religious hypocrisy. Oswald Alving inherits his father's immoral tendencies and is also a victim of his father's venereal disease, which at the end of the play brings on Oswald's insanity. His mother, who revolts against a society where such conditions can exist, is the real protagonist of the tragedy.

AN ENEMY OF THE PEOPLE (*En Folkefiende*, 1882). Perhaps Ibsen's retort to the people who objected to his exposure (as in *Ghosts*) of the ills of society. The "enemy" is Dr. Stockmann, who ruins the economic prosperity of a health resort by revealing that its supposedly beneficial waters are in reality germ-polluted.

THE WILD DUCK (*Vildanden*, 1884). A protest against half-truths and perhaps a defense of pragmatism. In it Ibsen seems to be saying that sometimes the absolute truth is not the highest good and that we need some illusions in order to be happy. The fourteen-year-old Hedvig commits suicide upon being told that she is an illegitimate child.

*ROSMERSHOLM** (1886). One of Ibsen's strongest condemnations of uncontrolled individualism. Rebecca West has such an ardent desire for the married Rosmer that his wife, Beate, commits suicide to prevent a family disgrace. Rosmer is somewhat affected by Rebecca's free-thinking, and she, in turn, is improved by his high ideals. When he discovers that Rebecca caused Beate's death, he and Rebecca kill themselves.

HEDDA GABLER (1890). Another story of a selfish and willful woman whose unbridled desire to dominate and destroy others

* A place-name.

brings death to herself and to an author and misery to almost every-body else who is closely associated with her.   Lövborg, Hedda's castoff lover, is inspired by the gentle and noble Thea to pull himself out of the dissipation into which he has fallen and to write a book. He becomes famous.   Hedda, now married to a boring pedant, leads Lövborg back to dissipation, secretly burns the manuscript of his second book, and then lends him a pistol with which to shoot himself; he dies, however, in a brawl.   Threatened with exposure, Hedda kills herself.

THIRD PERIOD.

THE MASTER BUILDER (*Bygmester Solness,* 1892).   This has been variously interpreted as a study of senescence, a study of sexual aberrations, a condemnation of romanticism and idealism, and a defense of romanticism and idealism.[36]   Most commentators see in it some autobiographical hints, especially of Ibsen's "extraordinary attachment" for the eighteen-year-old Emilie Bardach in 1889. Halvard Solness, an architect, has ceased to build churches and has grown rich and famous by building dwelling houses.*   On his last house he places a great steeple.   Hilda Wangel, aged twenty-three, appears on the scene, reminds Solness that ten years previously he promised her a "kingdom," and challenges him to hang a wreath on the steeple as he did on that of his last church.   He accepts the challenge, is seized with vertigo, and plunges to his death.

WHEN WE DEAD AWAKEN (*Naar vi doede vaagner,* 1899).   Ad-mitted by nearly all critics to be autobiographical, but few can agree on the interpretation of its symbolism.   Is it a reaffirmation of idealism and a condemnation of Ibsen's realistic period?   Is it a glorification of the union of love and art?   Or is it an admission of the destruction to which idealism leads?[37]   Rubek, a sculptor, has created a great work of art under the influence of Irene, a beautiful young girl who served as his model for the figure.   When he shows that he is not physically in love with her, she leaves him, and he turns to the carving of creatures who resemble animals.   He marries Maia for companionship but tires of her.   Irene returns, Maia willingly goes away with a brutish huntsman, and Rubek and Irene together climb a high mountain, from which there is no returning.

Criticism and Evaluation.   Ibsen has been censured for admit-ting many small improbabilities into his plays.   His psychological

---

* Possibly a reference to Ibsen's turning from romantic, idealistic drama to the realistic drama of social criticism.

accuracy has been questioned in such matters as the permanence of Bernick's sudden rehabilitation (in *The Pillars of Society*). More damaging are the charges of obscurity and topicality. As for the former, it must be admitted that for the average theatergoer or reader some of the symbolism is virtually meaningless and that even Ibsen's most devoted admirers disagree about its interpretation. But much of the symbology is transparent, and most of the time the main point or message of the play is entirely clear and indisputable. As for the accusation that Ibsen's plays are "dated," it is true that many of the social problems which he discusses (e.g., feminism) have been largely solved; but the psychological and spiritual predicaments in which his characters find themselves are as current as they ever were.

His characters are universally interesting people — typical as well as individual. His plots, though sometimes a bit sensational, are always exciting, to say the least; and despite the fact that little happens on the stage, the action never drags. There is always a conflict which creates suspense (even though the conflict is psychological), and this conflict is always handled by Ibsen with supreme craftsmanship.

Historically, Ibsen is important as a castigator of the false and shallow morality of the late nineteenth century and as the most influential innovator in the drama since the days of Racine and Molière. Among the authors most indebted to him are Hauptmann in Germany, Shaw and Joyce in Great Britain, Strindberg in Sweden, and O'Neill in America.

HERMANN SUDERMANN (1857–1928). This dramatist, novelist, and short-story writer was born in East Prussia, attended school in Königsberg, and then went to Berlin; there he continued his education and settled down. About 1889 he became interested in the theater, and soon his plays made him famous and rich. He remained in the capital the rest of his life.

Though exceedingly popular as a dramatist between 1890 and 1905, Sudermann is not now considered a first-rate artist. His dramas, in addition to being somewhat "dated," lack "the psychological depth and truth of great art";[38] and they are too sensational and theatrical.

DAME CARE (*Frau Sorge*, 1887). Sudermann won his first fame with a somber, semiautobiographical novel, *Dame Care*, which deals with the tribulations of a shy, unattractive man whose father becomes bankrupt, whose mother dies, and whose sisters are disgraced by being seduced. He himself is sent to the penitentiary for arson, but is at last redeemed by a woman who waits for him at the prison doors.

HONOR (*Die Ehre*, performed 1889, published 1890). This is Sudermann's first play. Its theme is the contrast between the conception of honor held by the family of a factory owner and that held by the family of his poor employee. The philosophical conclusion is that "conventional honor [is] one of the conventional lies."[39] The son of the employee is outraged by the willingness of his parents and his sister to accept a large check which the factory owner sends to the sister, who has been seduced by the factory owner's son. The employee's son has a higher sense of honor, turns his back on his vulgar family, delivers a scathing denunciation to the factory owner, and then runs away with the owner's daughter. The denouement is poorly motivated, but the setting is effective, and the frank treatment of the moral problem was enthusiastically received by the German public of Sudermann's day.

HOME, or *MAGDA* (*Die Heimat*, or *Magda*, 1889). This is another attack by Sudermann on false conceptions of honor. Magda, the heroine, leaves home to escape the tyranny of her father, an old army officer. She is seduced and then deserted by a young lawyer. After becoming a famous actress, she returns to her home town for a visit and patches things up with her father. When he learns of her seduction, however, he insists that the family honor be saved by her marrying her seducer. Under coercion the lawyer agrees to marry her if she will give up her career as an actress. Magda agrees to this condition for the sake of her old father; but she balks when the lawyer insists that she give up her child. In a rage, the father draws a pistol to shoot her, but falls dead with a stroke of apoplexy. Thus Magda regains her freedom, but her conscience suffers for her share in her father's death.

OTHER PLAYS. In addition to these plays, Sudermann wrote many others which contributed to his fame and fortune. *Sodom's End* (*Sodoms Ende*, 1891) is a satirical tragedy about the sinfulness of Berlin. *Happiness in a Nook* (*Das Glück im Winkel*, 1896) is the story of a virtuous young matron who resists the blandishments of a would-be lover and thereby finds a new sort of happiness with her elderly husband.

GERHART JOHANN HAUPTMANN (1862–1946). Hauptmann was born at Salzbrunn in Silesia. After trying his hand at sculpture, painting, and natural science, he traveled a while in Spain and Italy and then settled in Berlin. Soon he came under the influence of the French naturalists and of Ibsen, and he began writing plays. For most of his long life he turned out both naturalistic and romantic dramas, and sometimes he combined the two techniques. In 1912 he received the Nobel prize for literature. By the time of his death in 1946 he was recognized as "the patriarch of modern German literature."

Works. In his earliest dramas Hauptmann was one of the most extreme of the naturalists. Employing the so-called scientific method, he did not hesitate to deal with tabooed subjects — sexuality, disease, alcoholism, and violence. His *dramatis personae* are nearly always of the working class.

BEFORE SUNRISE (*Vor Sonnenaufgang*, 1889). A sordid tragedy about the alcoholic family of a farmer who becomes rich upon discovering coal on his premises. His first wife and his elder daughter are sots like himself, and his second wife is a "vulgar adulteress." His younger daughter Helene, however, is a decent and attractive girl, who has been away at school. She becomes engaged to a young scholar, but he runs away when he learns of the family weakness for drink. Helene commits suicide.

THE WEAVERS (*Die Weber*, 1892). Considered by some to be Hauptmann's masterpiece, it is a depressing picture of the mistreatment of poor peasants. The play is based on a historical rebellion of some Silesian weavers in 1844. The uprising leads to much destruction of property and to murder, but the poor weavers (who, incidentally, are the joint protagonists) are no better off at the end.

HANNELE'S HEAVEN-JOURNEY (*Hanneles Himmelfahrt*, 1893). Here we can discern some Symbolism, or Modern Romanticism, beginning to mingle with Hauptmann's naturalism. Hannele, the poor daughter of a drunken mason, is sexually mistreated by some brutal men. She tries to drown herself, but is rescued and carried to an almshouse. There she has heavenly visions of her teacher, in the shape of Christ, raising her from the dead. When the vision vanishes, she dies.

THE BEAVER COAT (*Der Biberpelz*, 1893). This is a naturalistic comedy — a rare phenomenon, for most naturalistic literature is inclined to be pessimistic or tragic. The play is a satire on Prussian law courts and their dispensing of justice. When a beaver coat is stolen, Judge Wehrhahn is too stupid and too much interested in other matters to convict the obviously guilty culprits.

FLORIAN GEYER (1895).   A return to pure naturalism, it is an unsuccessful attempt to dramatize the Peasants' War of the sixteenth century.

THE SUNKEN BELL (*Die versunkene Glocke,* 1896).   This is another swing in the direction of romanticism, but it has a few naturalistic elements.   It is a study of a man torn between a yearning for a carefree, unproductive life and his sense of obligation to his wife and his community.   Heinrich, a bell founder, has produced his masterpiece, a bell for a church.   As he hauls it to its intended destination, a faun overturns the wagon and dumps the bell into the lake; Heinrich barely escapes drowning.   The nymph Rautendelein lures him away from home and work and leads him to a mountain retreat, where for some time Heinrich lives with her, worships nature, and makes pagan bells.   Besought by his wife and by the village priest to return to his old home, Heinrich is not persuaded till he hears the sound of the sunken bell — a sound produced by the hand of his wife, who has committed suicide by drowning.   He comes back to the village, but now it refuses to receive him.   When an attempt to return to Rautendelein is equally unsuccessful, he gives up hope and dies.

OTHER WORKS.   Additional dramas by Hauptmann are *Poor Henry* (*Der Arme Heinrich,* 1902), a romantic play derived from Hartmann von Aue and *Before Sunset* (*Vor Sonnenuntergang,* 1932), a "symbolic counterpart" to *Before Sunrise.*

Though best known as a dramatist, Hauptmann was also a novelist, a short story writer, and a poet.   Two novels deserve to be mentioned: *The Fool in Christo Emanuel Quint* (*Der Narr in Christo Emanuel Quint,* 1910), a work which reflects the then current trend toward mysticism; and *The Island of the Great Mother* (*Die Insel der grossen Mutter,* 1925), a "satiric idyl."

The Novel and the Short Story

The novel and the short story showed the same realistic and naturalistic tendencies that we have noted in the drama.   All three forms were written by many of the great authors of the century. Some of the most important prose narrators were Immermann, Freytag, Storm, Keller, and Meyer.

Karl Lebrecht Immermann (1796–1840). One of the earliest realistic novelists was Immermann. In 1836 he wrote *The Epigoni** (*Die Epigonen*), a semiautobiographical novel concerning life in the second and third decades of the nineteenth century. Indebted to Goethe's *Wilhelm Meister*, the novel deals "with the conflict between the rising middle class and the old aristocracy . . . [and thereby inaugurates] the social novel of the next generation."[40] Immermann's *Münchhausen* (1838–1839) is a satirical contrast of the evils and absurdities of high society with the simple virtues of peasant life. The short story "The Upper Court" ("Der Oberhof"), imbedded within the novel, is an exquisite village romance which has become Immermann's most popular work. In addition to novels, Immerman wrote many comedies and tragedies.

Gustav Freytag (1816–1895). Dramatist, critic, and novelist. *Debit and Credit*[41] (*Soll und Haben*, 1855) is a humorous and sympathetic account of how Fritz von Fink, a young merchant, comes to the rescue of the noble house of Rothsattel and eventually marries the baron's daughter. The realism of the novel lies in its pictures of German commercial life. *The Lost Manuscript* (*Die verlorene Handschrift*, 1864) is even more romantic and more conventional. While searching for a lost manuscript of Tacitus, a professor neglects his young wife, with whom a prince then falls in love. The birth of a child makes the professor forget about the manuscript. Freytag's most famous work is a series of eight novels collectively entitled *The Ancestors* (*Die Ahnen*, 1872–1880), in which he traces the historical development of the German people from the fourth century down through 1848.

Theodor Storm (1817–1888). Almost equally famous as a writer of short stories and as a lyricist, Storm made his first mark in the world of literature with the publication of his volume *Poems* (*Gedichte*) in 1853; most of the pieces deal with the still life and quiet natural scenes of his native Schleswig-Holstein. His earliest stories (Novellen) are romantic rather than realistic; the most famous is "Immensee" (1852). As he grew older, his stories became more realistic and subtler in psychology; "Viola Tricolor" (1873), "Paul the Puppet-Player" ("Pole Poppenspäler," 1874), and "Psyche" (1875) show this change in technique. During the 'seventies he turned to the historical story; "Submerged in the Waters" ("Aquis

---

* An *epigone* is an "aftercomer," one "late-born," or (as Priest defines it, p. 283), "a weak descendant of a strong creative race."

Submersus," 1877) is his best of this type.   In his last years he wrote his realistic masterpieces: "The Sons of the Senator" ("Die Söhne des Senators," 1881), "Hans und Heinz Kirsch" (1883), and "The Rider of the White Horse" ("Der Schimmelreiter, 1888); these are principally psychological portraits.

Gottfried Keller (1819–1890).   Virtually all commentators agree in recognizing Gottfried Keller as one of the greatest authors of German stories and novels.   Robertson calls him "the greatest writer of short stories"[42] in German literature; and Thomas adds that Keller's "books are on the whole the very best reading to be found in the whole range of nineteenth-century German fiction."[43] Keller was also a good poet.

He was born in Zürich, Switzerland, and a large percentage of his works have a Swiss setting.   As a youth he wrote some poetry, but devoted himself principally to painting; discovering that he had missed his calling, he began anew in 1848, attended the University of Heidelberg for two years, and then went to the University of Berlin for five years.   He had published his first volume *Poems* (*Gedichte*) in 1846, but it had attracted little notice.   In 1851 a second collection, *New Poems* (*Neuere Gedichte*) contained some fine pieces.   While in Berlin, he turned to prose fiction, and there his true genius made itself manifest.   He returned to Zürich in 1855 and remained there till he died.

GREEN HENRY (*Der grüne Heinrich*, 1854–1855).   This is a four-volume, autobiographical novel somewhat reminiscent of *Wilhelm Meister*.   Though rather formless and slow in movement, it is an appealing story of Henry Lee's attempt to find himself and his vocation.   Like Keller himself, the hero, a native of Zürich, aspires to be an artist, goes abroad to study, abandons art, and returns to his native land reconciled to obscurity.

THE PEOPLE OF SELDWYLA (*Die Leute von Seldwyla*, 1856; revised 1874).   This is a collection of stories about the people of the towns and villages of Switzerland.   Some of the stories are romantic, some realistic; some are funny, some sad.   "Romeo and Juliet of the Village" ("Romeo und Juliet auf dem Dorfe"), for example, is a tragic tale of two young lovers whose families are feuding over the boundary line between their farms; the boy and the girl dance at a festival and then drown themselves.   Other well-known stories from *The People* are "The Three Just Comb Makers" ("Die drei gerechten Kammmacher") and "Dietegen" (added in the 1874 edition).

ZÜRICH TALES (*Züricher Novellen*, 1878). This is another collection of superior short narratives. Among the best in the collection is "The Banner of Seven Upright Men" ("Das Fähnlein der sieben Aufrechten"), a story about Swiss political affairs in the early part of the century; it is especially famous for its genial humor. Another fine tale is "Hadlaub," which is concerned with the collecting of minnesongs.

MARTIN SALANDER (1886). This is a comparatively dull novel of modern Swiss life and politics.

OTHER COLLECTIONS OF NOVELLEN. Some additional collections of Keller's stories are *Seven Legends* (*Sieben Legenden*, 1872) and *The Epigram* (*Das Sinnegedicht*, 1882).

Keller's stories do not have especially exciting or ingeniously constructed plots. They have no great "message." Their charm lies in their irresistible humor and in their revelation of the author's own engaging, spontaneous, and robust personality.

Konrad Ferdinand Meyer (1825–1898). Like Keller, Meyer was born in Zürich. In his earlier years he wrote alternately in French and German, but after the Franco-Prussian War all his works were in German. Also like Keller, he wrote short stories, poetry (lyrics, ballads, an epic, and an idyl), but he is best known for his novels.

Jürg Jenatsch (1876) is a semihistorical novel about the Thirty Years' War. *The Saint* (*Der Heilige*, 1880) tells the story of Thomas à Becket. In 1883 Meyer published five novels: *The Amulet* (*Das Amulet*), *The Shot from the Pulpit* (*Der Schuss von der Kangel*), *Plautus in the Nunnery* (*Plautus im Nonnenkloster*), *The Page of Gustavus Adolphus* (*Gustav Adolfs Page*), and *A Boy's Sorrows* (*Die Leiden eines Knaben*). *The Monk's Marriage* (*Die Hochzeit des Mönchs*) appeared in 1884; *The Woman Judge* (*Die Richterin*) in 1885; *The Temptation of Pescara* (*Die Versuchung des Pescara*) in 1887; and *Angela Borgia* in 1890.

As many of the titles indicate, Meyer was interested most in the Renaissance. Although he lacks the infectious humor and the warmth of Keller, he is a more careful artist; his novels have finer polish and better balance and proportion.

15

The Twentieth Century

Historical Background. The political and military history of Germany during the first half of the twentieth century is so well known that only the briefest outline will suffice. Under Kaiser Wilhelm II Germany began World War I in 1914. Decisively defeated by the Allies in 1918, she lost all her colonies, Alsace-Lorraine, and some frontier territory. The Republic of Germany (Weimar Republic) was proclaimed in 1919. For fourteen years the nation remained in a deplorable condition; her economy was severely damaged, the government was highly unstable, and the people were under a cloud of war guilt. As early as 1923 Adolf Hitler made a bid for power in the famous "Beer Hall Putsch" in Munich; although this attempt proved abortive, Hitler continued to gain power, and by 1933 he was able to seize complete control of the country. He abolished the Weimar Republic, set up the so-called Third Reich with himself as dictator, repudiated the Versailles Treaty which had ended World War I, carried out a campaign of racial purification (pro-Aryan, anti-Semitic), annexed Austria (1937) and part of Czechoslovakia (1938), and began World War II by attacking Poland in 1939. Germany was defeated again in 1945. Since then the eastern portion (proclaimed the German Democratic Republic, 1949) has remained under Russian influence; and the western section (proclaimed the Federal Republic of Germany, 1949) has been under French, British, and American supervision.

General View of the Literature. As in the nineteenth century, so in the twentieth: German literature has followed the same trends as French literature. The extreme forms of naturalism have pretty well disappeared, but realism has continued to exist side by side with neoromanticism.

World War I inspired some patriotic poetry and some realistic plays and novels. Most of this literature was ephemeral though historically interesting.

Hitler's totalitarian regime virtually put an end to all genuine aesthetic and philosophical activity in Germany. Many scientists, authors, and philosophers found refuge in other parts of the world. Franz Werfel, Erich Remarque (or Krämer), Thomas Mann, and Albert Einstein are among the most eminent of those who escaped to America, where they continued their intellectual endeavors.

The lyric, the drama, and the novel have been the most significant literary types since 1900.

POETRY

In the early years of the century there was a great revival of lyricism. The pendulum swung away from naturalism and materialistic impressionism and toward Symbolism and the sentimental form of romanticism known as "Expressionism." After the First World War the lyric became soberer, deeper, and more spiritual. The principal lyricists of the century are Dehmel, George, Hofmannsthal, Rilke, and Werfel (all discussed below).

Richard Dehmel (1863–1920). A disciple of Nietzsche. His poetry is a combination of the realistic and the romantic, the mystical and the rational. It "seethes with the confused and unsettled ethical ideals of its time; it is often crass and sensual, even morbid and cruel."[1] His three favorite themes are sex, the "relationship of the individual to cosmic life, and man's duty to his fellow."[2] His principal volumes of verse are *But Love* (*Aber die Liebe*, 1893), *Woman and World* (*Weib und Welt*, 1896), and *Two Human Beings* (*Zwei Menschen*, 1903). Some of his best single lyrics are "The Silent City" ("Der stille Stadt"), "Many a Night" ("Manche Nacht"), and "The Goldfinch" ("Der Stieglitz").

Stefan George (1868–1933). George was the antithesis of Dehmel and led a reaction against the chaos and effusiveness of Dehmel's poetry. "An aristocrat of the spirit,"[3] George was bitterly opposed to realism and naturalism. His poetry is cool, restrained, esoteric, aloof, and neoclassic. Directed at a small but select circle, it comes near achieving the Symbolistic aim of expressing the inexpressible. He preaches the gospel of "ethical idealism, . . . beauty, absolute truth, light, and clarity."[4] George published his lyrics in a number of small volumes; some of the most significant are *Hymns* (*Hymnen*, 1890), *The Calendar of the Soul*[5] (*Das Jahr der Seele*, 1897), *Tapestry of Life* (*Teppich des Lebens*, 1899), *The Seventh Ring* (*Der siebente Ring*, 1907), and *The Star of the League* (*Der Stern des Bundes*, 1914). Several of his short poems are "Leo XIII,"

"Day-Song" ("Tag-Gesang"), "The Monastery" ("Das Kloster"), and "Ripening" ("Reifefreuden").

Hugo von Hofmannsthal (1874–1929). An Austrian, Hofmannsthal was one of the leaders in the German Symbolic movement. Though indebted to the works of Stefan George, his poems are warmer and more readily understandable. He is perhaps more famous as a librettist for Richard Strauss; he wrote the words for *Salome* (1905), *The Cavalier of the Rose* (*Der Rosenkavalier*, 1911); and *Ariadne on Naxos* (*Ariadne auf Naxos*, 1911). He wrote some other original dramas: *The Fool and Death* (*Der Tor und der Tod*, 1893) and *The Marriage of Sobeide* (*Die Hochzeit der Sobeide*, 1899). Finally, he adapted some old plays: Sophocles' *Electra* (*Elektra*, 1903), Otway's *Venice Preserved* (*Das gerettete Venedig*, 1905), and the morality *Everyman* (*Das Spiel von Jedermann*, 1912).

Rainer Maria Rilke (1875–1926). Rilke was born in Prague. A disciple of Stefan George, Baudelaire, and the Russian novelists, Rilke combined Symbolism with a deep emotionalism. He was far more concerned than George was with humble people and spiritual matters. "His poetry, it has been well said, is a seeking after God. . . ."[6] Many of his poems are mystical. His main collections of lyrics are *The Book of Pictures* (*Das Buch der Bilder*, 1902), *The Book of Hours* (*Das Stundenbuch*, 1905), and *New Poems* (*Neue Gedichte*, 1907, 1919). Some of his best-known pieces are "The Angels" ("Die Engel"), "The Solitary" ("Der Einsame"), "Lament" ("Klage"), and "Autumn Day" ("Herbsttag").

THE DRAMA

REALISM OR NATURALISM. Although Symbolism and Expressionism were becoming more and more the vogue in the early years of the twentieth century, Sudermann, Hauptmann, and some others who had written dramas prior to 1900 continued to turn out plays of varying degrees of realism or naturalism. Most significant of these other authors who have not previously been discussed are Schnitzler and Wedekind.

Arthur Schnitzler (1862–1931). An Austrian who used Vienna as a setting, he wrote many plays and short stories depicting the decadence of the early part of the century. His dramas have relatively little action but are noted for their clever dialogue. Lange says that these dramas are "symptomatic of a listless age."[7] Some of the best known are *Flirtation* (*Liebelei*, 1895), *The Legacy* (*Da*

Vermächtnis, 1898), *The Green Cockatoo* (*Der Grüne Kakadu*, 1899), *The Veil of Beatrice* (*Der Schleier der Beatrice*, 1900), *Young Medardus* (*Der junge Medardus*, 1910), and *Professor Bernhardi* (1912).

Frank Wedekind (1864–1918). Wedekind's plays combined realism with the grotesque and the bizarre. Although some critics find his works indecent to the point of being repellent, at least one has praised him for his courage in depicting "the boldest and the most fascinating world of demoniacally dislocated bourgeois characters."[8] Wedekind's dramas are expressive of the despair, cynicism, and skepticism prevalent among many of the literary figures of the early 1900's. His *Springtime Awakening* (*Frühlings Erwachen*, 1891) is an unusual treatment of the problems of the adolescent. *The Earth-Spirit* (*Der Erdgeist*, 1895), *Pandora's Box* (*Die Büchse der Pandora*, 1903), *Hidalla* (1904), and *The Grisly Suitor* (*Der greise Freier*, 1905) all are "decadent" and grotesque plays about sinners and criminals. Some later and more palatable dramas are *Music* (*Musik*, 1907) and *Francisca* (*Franziska*, 1911).

EXPRESSIONISM. The Expressionistic movement was especially strong in the drama during the first quarter of the twentieth century. Although the movement was not thoroughly unified and although certain factions within it disagreed on some matters, virtually all emphasized the need for more emotionalism, for social and spiritual reform, and for more faith in God and immortality. There were two especially important factions. The first, led by GEORG KAISER (1878–1945), KURT HILLER (1885–   ), JOHANNES ROBERT BECHER (1891–1958), and ERNST TOLLER (1893–1939), was the so-called Activist branch; this group tempered its emotionalism with rationalism and was especially concerned with political and social reform. Another faction, led by FRANZ KAFKA (1883–1924), FRITZ VON UNRUH (1885–   ), PAUL KORNFIELD (1889–194?), FRANZ WERFEL* (1890–1945), and REINHARD JOHANNES SORGE (1892–1916), was particularly interested in the relations between man and God—in "the liberation of the soul [rather] than in the reforms of society."[9] This group is less rationalistic than the first one.

The method of the Expressionists was to express the author's inner life — dreams, hopes, fears, and the like — by means of external, unrelated objects. "The essence of [Expressionistic] drama . . . consists in the depicting of sorrow and suffering rather

---

* Werfel's works, including his plays, are discussed below under the heading of the novel — the form which made him most famous.

than in action; but this suffering implies an ethical victory over apparent worldly successes. The typical Expressionistic drama ends with the discovery of positive values in life even if the hero succumbs."[10]   And it holds out bright hope for the future.

Georg Kaiser (1878–1945). His early plays are satiric comedies, such as *The Jewish Widow* (*Die jüdische Witwe*, 1911) and *King Mark* (*König Hahnrei*, 1913).   *The Citizens of Calais* (*Die Bürger von Calais*, 1914) is not only Kaiser's first Expressionistic drama but also one of the opening guns of the Expressionistic movement.   It is the story of Eustache de Saint-Pierre, who commits suicide in order to prevent any one of a group of six other citizens from having to decide whether to offer himself to the King of England for execution. Thus, in keeping with Expressionistic ideals, the hero wins a moral victory although he meets death.   *Gas*, Part I (1918) is the account of a rich man's son who, after an explosion of his father's gas works, wants to close the plant and provide farmland for the workers so that they will be safe and happy.   A capitalist group succeeds in persuading the workers that such a change will be disadvantageous, and so in order to prevent a riot and possible bloodshed, the son gives up his altruistic dream — but only for the present, for his daughter promises to make the dream come true in the future.

Other Expressionistic plays of importance by Kaiser are *From Morning till Midnight* (*Von Morgens bis Mitternachts*, 1916), *The Centaur* (*Der Zentaur*, 1916), *The Coral* (*Die Koralle*, 1917), and *Colportage* (*Kolportage*, 1924).

Ernst Toller (1893–1939).   Like Kaiser, Toller assails the ills of contemporary civilization and suggests solutions — solutions which he cannot effect but which he envisions for the future.   *The Transformation* (*Die Wandlung*, 1919) is about a young sculptor, turned soldier, who is at first proud of his part in World War I but whose pride turns to revulsion when he becomes aware that ten thousand men have been killed in a battle.   He breaks up his statue "Victory of the Fatherland," is filled with love for humanity, becomes a politician, and leads a crusade against materialism. The play is unique in its alternation of realistic scenes with fantastic or visionary ones.   *The Machine-Breakers* (*Die Machinestürmer*, 1922) suggests a different solution of industrial problems from that offered by Kaiser in *Gas*.   Toller holds that the answer is not the destruction of machines or gas plants but the reforming of the society that mans them.

THE NOVEL

The same trends that we have noticed in the twentieth-century drama are discernible in the novel, too. Realism, naturalism, neoromanticism, and Expressionism are all present. Before World War I most of the significant novels were concerned with diagnosing social and political ills. They exposed the falsity of many of the nineteenth-century values and warned of the impending collapse of the bourgeois culture. Between 1914 and 1939 the novelists were seeking some meaning for the individual and for the nation in a world which had lost its meaning. The hopes, attitudes, and objectives of the Expressionists were recognized to be of paramount importance. Virtually every novelist who wrote between the two great wars was to some degree an Expressionist. In addition to the three major novelists of the century — Wassermann, Thomas Mann, and Werfel — there were numerous good novelists of lesser magnitude.

Ricarda Huch (1864–1947). She wrote a historical trilogy on the Thirty Years' War, *The Great War in Germany* (*Der grosse Krieg in Deutschland,* 1912–1914).

Hermann Stehr (1864–1940). By turns a naturalist, a neoromanticist, an Expressionist, and a surrealist. In his later and more important novels he dropped the deterministic attitude of the naturalists and became an adherent of the Expressionistic "belief in the absolute and creative power of the human resolve."[11] Some of his best-known works are *Three Nights* (*Drei Nächte,* 1909), *Peter Brindeisener* (1924), *Nathaniel Maechler* (1929), and *The Descendants* (*Die Nachkommen,* 1933).

Heinrich Mann (1871–1950). This elder brother of Thomas Mann wrote satirical novels, exposing and attacking Germany's ills before 1914. In *The Land of Cockayne* (*Im Schlaraffenland,* 1900) he criticizes bourgeois life for its sensuality and superficiality. *Professor Rubbish* (*Professor Unrat,* 1905) employs caricature in the style of Wedekind. *The Subject* (*Der Untertan,* 1917) is an attack on Germany's spirit prior to World War I. *The Head* (*Der Kopf,* 1925) is a satirical study of the Wilhelmian era. And finally, two late works, *The Youth of King Henry IV* (*Die Jugend des Königs Henri Quatre,* 1935) and *The Completion of King Henry IV* (*Die Vollendung des Königs Henri Quatre,* 1938) are biographical novels with didactic implications.

Hans Grimm (1875–1959). This novelist is most famous for *Folk without Room* (*Volk ohne Raum*, 1926), a semihistorical novel about adventures of some Germans in southwest Africa; it is perhaps too serious a book, but it has some excellent human characterization. Grimm is well known for his Novellen, too: *South African Tales* (*Südafrikanische Novellen*, 1913), *Passage through Sand* (*Der Gang durch den Sand*, 1916), and *The Judge in the Karu* (*Der Richter in der Karu*, 1930).

Hermann Hesse (1877–   ). Before the end of the First World War this poet and novelist wrote "a series of subdued and musical novels of private, provincial, and melancholy lyricism:"[12] *Peter Camenzind* (1904), *Gertrud* (1910), and *Demian* (1919). After the war his thinking became deeper and more serious. *The Wolf of the Steppes* (*Der Steppen Wolf*, 1927) is a rather shocking portrait of a generation torn between lawlessness and bourgeois timidity. His two last novels suggest as the solution to world problems the Expressionistic ideals of self-sacrificial devotion; these novels are *Narcissus and Goldmund* (*Narziss und Goldmund*, 1930) and *Glass Bead Play* (*Glasperlenspiel*, 1943).

Erwin Guido Kolbenheyer (1878–   ). He is the author of several important historical novels: *The Love of God* (*Amor Dei*, 1908), *Master Joachim Pausewang* (*Meister Joachim Pausewang*, 1910), and the trilogy *Paracelsus* (1917–1925).

Franz Kafka (1883–1924). A neoromanticist, Expressionist, and surrealist, Kafka wrote short stories, journals, letters, parables, and novels. His reputation rests principally on works published posthumously, edited by his friend Max Brod. *Collected Writings* (*Gesammelte Schriften*, 1935–1937) contains most of the shorter pieces. The three novels (all unfinished) appeared earlier. *The Lawsuit* (*Der Prozess*, 1925), *The Castle* (*Das Schloss*, 1926), and *America* (*Amerika*, 1927) form, according to Brod, "a trilogy of loneliness." And, according to Lange, "Like every other work of Kafka's, they reflect, in a seriously religious sense, the experience of human isolation and the pathos of exclusion. Man, forever aware of 'guilt,' is compelled to face the 'trial' of life in a universe whose pattern and coherence are fundamentally uncertain and incomprehensible."[13] Kafka's main beliefs are that man can never understand God's purposes but that he is obligated to seek with all his might those purposes insofar as they pertain to man's actions here on earth, and man must submit and obey. Kafka's works give an excellent picture of Europe and especially Germany during the decades immediately preceding and following the First World War. His style is characterized by an extensive use of religious symbolism; compactness; intensity; minute analysis of religious and philosophical problems; and numerous grotesque, fantastic, nightmarish scenes which may be termed surrealistic — scenes which Lange thinks resemble those of Charlie Chaplin, Walt Disney, Poe, and Dickens.

Ernst Wiechert (1887–1950). This novelist belongs to a group of writers who, disillusioned by Germany's defeat in 1918, launched a "back-to-nature" movement; by "returning to nature" this group meant a rather stoical acceptance of life and its obligations. Like so many other novelists of the period, Wiechert and his associates attacked what they considered to be the falsities of the prewar bourgeois civilization. Wiechert's best-known novel is *The Baroness* (*Die Marjorin*, 1934).

Erich Maria Remarque (or Krämer, 1897–). He wrote several novels on World War I and the subsequent period of depression in Germany. The best known are *All Quiet on the Western Front* (*Im Westen nichts Neues*,[14] 1929) and *The Road Back* (*Der Weg zurück*, 1931).

JAKOB WASSERMANN (1873–1934). One of the earliest Expressionists, Wassermann used the psychoanalytic method to explore human emotions and the human soul. His principal thesis is "man's individual responsibility for the whole of mankind."[15] In *The Jews of Zirndorff* (*Die Juden von Zirndorff*, 1897) he treats the still-current problem of the hardships of the Jewish people scattered throughout Protestant lands. *Caspar Hauser* (1908) is a novel about a sensitive foundling whose soul is made greater by a series of sufferings which it endures. Two later novels are *Christian Wahnschaffe* (1919) and *The Maurizius Case* (*Der Fall Maurizius*, 1928).

There is much scholarly disagreement about Wassermann's merits as a novelist. Lange calls his works "minor fiction" and says that he "has not achieved a single novel of major importance."[16] This same critic believes that Wassermann's style is "flamboyant" and "mannered" and that the novels are superficial and artificial. Robertson concurs and doubts "whether any of his work has more than a transient value."[17] W. R. Benét, however, thinks that Wassermann's work has "depth of feeling and insight into the human soul."[18] And W. P. Friedrich considers Wassermann one of the three major German novelists of this century (the other two being Werfel and Thomas Mann).[19]

THOMAS MANN (1875–1955). Mann was born in Lübeck. When he was fifteen, his father died, and three years later the family moved to Munich. Thomas worked for a while as a clerk in an insurance office, but, upon the publication of two stories, devoted his time to writing. His first important literary work was *Buddenbrooks* (1901), which went through fifty printings in ten years and won him an international fame. In 1933 the Nazis condemned his books, and Mann took up his abode in Switzerland. Later he, his six children, and his brother Heinrich came to the United States.

Influenced by Nietzsche, Schopenhauer, and Freud, Mann is interested in the psychological and philosophical problems arising out of the individual's relations with twentieth-century society, which he regards as decadent. He is especially concerned with the role of aesthetics in the modern world.

Mann is a very careful literary artist, taking almost infinite pains with each narrative. His "style is always highly artistic and has much in common with musical composition. We find recurrent leitmotifs, contrapuntal devices, striking antitheses, lyrico-philosophic intermezzi, and similar artistic features. . . . His works may aptly be styled symphonies in words."[20] Some critics have thought him occasionally verbose and guilty of irrelevancies.

BUDDENBROOKS (1901). Based partially on the history of Mann's ancestors, *Buddenbrooks* is a long novel about the decline of a prosperous family of German merchants during the eighteenth and nineteenth centuries. As the financial fortunes of the Buddenbrooks deteriorate, the members of the family become increasingly interested in art, learning, and music. Hanno Buddenbrook, the last of the clan, is a sickly youth, whose effete aestheticism is symbolic of the material decay of the family.

TONIO KRÖGER (1903). A novelette about an artist's inner conflict. "No problem," says Tonio, "none in the world, is more tormenting than that of artistry and its effect on humanity."[21] Tonio feels a great gulf to exist between himself and the general run of people because he is a writer, but he is also aware of a gulf between himself and the pure artists who seek beauty alone because he has a deep love for plain, happy, active people. His inner conflict is resolved when he realizes that the poet's duty is to seek out and transmit to others not abstract beauty but the beauty and happiness of everyday life. *Tonio Kröger* contains many long philosophical speeches, but some critics consider it Mann's masterpiece because it is comparatively concise.

THE MAGIC MOUNTAIN (*Der Zauberberg*, 1924). A long symbolic novel. Hans Castorp visits his cousin at a tuberculosis sanatorium in the Swiss Alps (representing the realm of pure aestheticism). Feeling that he himself may be infected, Hans remains several weeks, during which time he has many deep philosophical discussions with Settembrini (representing humanism and liberalism), Peeperkorn (representing animal sensuality), and others. Hans breaks away from the spell of the mountain to become a soldier in World War I. Somewhat like Tonio Kröger, he finally learns to maintain "a balance between the aesthetic and the practical tendencies of his nature."[22] *The Magic Mountain* is by far Mann's most famous novel and, according to many critics, his best.

OTHER WORKS. Other important works by Mann are *Mario and the Magician* (*Mario und der Zauberer*, 1930), an allegorical novelette on the effects of Fascism in Italy; *Joseph* (1933–1943), a four-part novel in which the titular character "represents the artist who redeems society by his own vicarious suffering";[23] and *The Beloved Returns* (English title for *Lotte in Weimar*, 1940), still another philosophical novel concerning the role of the artist; it tells of an imaginary visit with Goethe in his old age.

Mann was awarded the Nobel Prize for literature in 1929. He is considered the greatest living German author and, along with Proust and Joyce, one of the greatest novelists of this century.

FRANZ WERFEL (1890–1945). Poet, dramatist, and novelist. He was born in Prague of Jewish parents. Like so many other writers and thinkers, he escaped Nazidom by fleeing first to France and thence to America.

Like Rilke and Wasserman, he was firmly convinced of the importance of spiritual values, and he had a mystical belief in the brotherhood of man and in the existence of some power immanent in all the world. Soon after World War I he assailed the attitudes which had led to the war and proclaimed universal brotherhood as the only condition which would save mankind.

POEMS. Like the poetry of Dehmel, Werfel's lyrics are largely concerned with the relation between the individual ego and the outside world. His most important volumes of verse are *The Friend of the World* (*Der Weltfreund*, 1911), *We Are* (*Wir sind*, 1913), *One Another* (*Einander*, 1915), and *The Day of Reckoning* (*Der Gerichtstag*, 1919).

NOVELS.   It is as a novelist that Werfel has won his largest group of readers.   *The Forty Days of Musa Dagh* (*Die vierzig Tage des Musa Dagh*, 1934) is a best seller concerning an Armenian siege of the First World War.   *The Song of Bernadette* (*Das Lied von Bernadette*, 1942) was also highly successful and was made into a moving picture. It is the life of a French saint in whose church Werfel is said to have taken refuge during the invasion of France in 1940.   *Star of the Unborn* (*Stern der Ungeborenen*, 1945) is an imaginative narrative of the distant future when world brotherhood will really exist and when Judaism and Roman Catholicism will be the only two religions.

Lange says that in the novels of Werfel (and some others) "the real purpose of the expressionistic attitude becomes clear: it is a radical attempt to maintain the force and validity of metaphysical aspirations in a fundamentally antispiritual world, the debilitated forms of which require re-examination."[24]

PLAYS.   Almost equally important are Werfel's plays.   In them he voices, of course, the same Expressionistic ideas that are found in his lyrics and novels.   In the foreword to his *Trojan Women* (*Die Troerinnen*, 1915) — an adaptation of Euripides' play of the same name, Werfel sums up the "inner purpose of tragedy" in answer to the question why Hecuba must die: "The poet does not give Man the right to die.   The DUTY of Man is to live.   For Man's life is a duty.   Duty means resistance to the inhuman world, to Nature, belief in the intermediary rôle of mankind, which exists in order to give meaning to the world."[25]   *The Mirror-Man* (*Der Spiegelmensch*, 1920) is a drama which presents once more the "Faust-problem of the two souls within our breast."[26]   In the drama the Mirror-Man's soul leaves his body, goes through various experiences which purify and strengthen it, and then returns to the body.   *Juarez und Maximilian* (1924) is a historical tragedy; *Paul among the Jews* (*Paulus unter den Juden*, 1926) reasserts Werfel's fervent belief in the importance and the obligation of the individual and also in the existence of a spiritual God.

Bibliography for Modern Germanic Literature

Bertaux, Félix. *A Panorama of German Literature from 1871 to 1931.* Translated by John J. Trounstine. New York: McGraw-Hill Book Co., 1935.

Bruford, Walter Horace. *Germany in the Eighteenth Century.* Cambridge, England: Cambridge University Press, 1935.

Erasmus, Desiderius. *The Praise of Folly* New York: Peter Smith, 1941.

Francke, Kuno. *German After-War Problems.* Cambridge, Mass.: Harvard University Press, 1927.

Friederich, Werner P. *History of German Literature.* New York: Barnes & Noble, Inc., 1948.

Heller, Otto. *Henrik Ibsen: Plays and Problems.* Boston: Houghton, Mifflin Co., 1912.

——. *Studies in Modern German Literature.* Boston: Ginn & Co., 1905.

Hewett-Thayer, Harvey Waterman. *The Modern German Novel.* Boston: Marshall Jones Co., 1924.

Hosmer, James K. *A Short History of German Literature.* Revised ed. New York: Charles Scribner's Sons, 1910.

Jorgenson, Theodore. *Henrik Ibsen: A Study in Art and Personality.* Northfield, Minn.: St. Olaf College Press, 1945.

Klenze, Camillo von. *From Goethe to Hauptmann.* New York: Viking Press, 1926.

Lange, Victor. *Modern German Literature, 1870–1940.* Ithaca, N. Y.: Cornell University Press, 1945.

Lee, Jennette. *The Ibsen Secret.* New York: G. P. Putnam's Sons, 1907.

Liptzin, Sol. *Historical Survey of German Literature.* New York: Prentice-Hall, 1936.

Moses, Montrose J. *Henrik Ibsen: The Man and His Plays.* New York: M. Kennerley, 1908.

Priest, George Madison. *A Brief History of German Literature.* New York: Charles Scribner's Sons, 1932.

Robertson, John G. *A History of German Literature.* Revised ed. London: Blackwood, 1949.

Rose, William. *Men, Myths, and Movements in German Literature.* New York: Macmillan Co., 1931.

Samuel, Richard, and R. Hinton Thomas. *Expressionism in German Life, Literature and the Theatre (1910–1924)*. Cambridge, England: W. Heffer and Sons, 1939.

Scherer, Wilhelm. *A History of German Literature*. Translated by Mrs. F. C. Conybeare. 3rd ed. New York: Charles Scribner's Sons, 1899. 2 vols.

Shaw, George Bernard. *The Quintessence of Ibsenism*. New York: Brentano's, 1913.

Silz, Walter. *Early German Romanticism*. Cambridge, Mass.: Harvard University Press, 1929.

Thomas, Calvin. *Goethe*. Revised ed. New York: A. A. Knopf, 1929.

——. *A History of German Literature*. New York: D. Appleton and Co., 1909.

Thompson, Stith, and John Gassner. *Our Heritage of World Literature*. New York: Dryden Press, 1942.

Viëtor, Karl. *Goethe: The Poet*. Translated by Moses Hadas. Cambridge, Mass.: Harvard University Press, 1949.

——. *Goethe: The Thinker*. Translated by Bayard Q. Morgan. Cambridge, Mass.: Harvard University Press, 1950.

Weatherly, Edward H., and Others. *The Heritage of European Literature*. Boston: Ginn and Co., 1948–1949. 2 vols.

Weigand, Hermann J. *The Modern Ibsen: A Reconsideration*. New York: H. Holt and Co., 1925.

Wells, Benjamin W. *Modern German Literature*. Boston: Roberts Brothers, 1897.

Wilkinson, William Cleaver. *German Classics in English*. New York: Funk and Wagnalls Co., 1900.

Willoughby, L. A. *The Classical Age of German Literature, 1748–1805*. Oxford: Oxford University Press, 1926.

——. *The Romantic Movement in Germany*. Oxford: Oxford University Press, 1930.

Zucker, Adolf Eduard. *Ibsen, the Master Builder*. New York: H. Holt and Co., 1929.

Part Five
Modern Russian Literature

16

The Golden Age

(*1820–1883*)

Historical Background. The earliest known inhabitants of Russia were the Eastern Slavs (or Slavonians), a branch of the Indo-European race, who, at some unknown date, probably came from the region around the Danube River. By the ninth century there was a semblance of political organization; Novgorod and Kiev were the two chief centers of civilization. The primitive religion of the Eastern Slavs was a worship of ancestral spirits and of the forces of nature.

Probably as early as the beginning of the tenth century, Christianity had begun to infiltrate into Russia from the Byzantine Empire. In 988 Prince Vladimir of Kiev accepted Greek Orthodox Christianity and "baptized Russia wholesale."[1] Missionaries from Byzantium brought with them various religious books written in the South Slavonic (or Old Church Slavonic) dialect (somewhat different from the East Slavonic, but still intelligible to the Russians) and in the South Slavonic alphabet, which, according to tradition, was invented in 855 by Cyril out of Hebrew, Armenian, and Coptic characters, plus a few of his own origination. So far as is known, this was Russia's first alphabet, and the dialect went a long way toward determining both the literary and the spoken languages.

Vladimir and his successors encouraged learning by sponsoring the copying of manuscripts and by establishing schools; the latter, however, had as their main object the training of ecclesiastics, and most manuscripts were of a religious nature.

Between 1238 and 1240 the Tatars (or Tartars) overran nearly all of Russia. Their destruction of Kiev had the effect of driving many cultivated people farther north, especially to Moscow, which now began to assume importance as the center of Russian civilization.

Tatar dominion lasted nearly two and a half centuries. Prince Ivan III of Moscow threw off the last vestiges of Tatar supremacy in 1480 and succeeded in creating for the first time a unified nation, with autocratic power concentrated in his own hands. The economy under the Muscovite regime was founded on slave labor. For almost exactly two hundred years Russia remained isolated from the rest of the world; neither the Renaissance nor the Reformation touched her till the end of the seventeenth century.

In 1682, however, when Peter the Great came to the throne, he opened the doors to the West and encouraged the importation of Western civilization, especially that of Germany and France. Russian students were sent abroad, and foreign tutors were brought in. These policies were continued under the Empresses Elizabeth and Catherine II.

Despite the enlightened and progressive attitudes of Peter and some of his successors toward culture, these monarchs maintained autocratic and oppressive rule of the people. The new intellectual currents affected only the upper classes, and there was no such thing as education for the masses, who remained in serfdom.

The liberal and democratic ideas of eighteenth-century France found their way into Russia and sometimes — in spite of censorship — into print. Alexander Radischev dared to write a book condemning autocracy and the institution of serfdom, and he was exiled to Siberia for his daring; he is considered the first Rusian martyr to the cause of political and social reform.

The defeat of Napoleon in 1812 helped to awaken national consciousness and also to spread liberal doctrines. Dissatisfaction with the autocratic policies was strong enough in December, 1825, to bring on a revolt of some army officers in favor of a constitutional government. The occasion was the accession of Nicholas I upon the death of Alexander I. The Decembrists (as the revolutionists were called) were quickly subdued, and the reign of Nicholas I (1825–1855) was unusually oppressive. Alexander II (reigned 1855–1881), however, granted many liberal reforms, including emancipation of the serfs in 1861.

General View of the Literature. It was not till the nineteenth century that Russia produced a literature worthy of becoming part of the world's cultural heritage. A rapid survey of all literary activity before 1800 will therefore be sufficient.

The earliest Russian books were manuscript copies of sermons, saints' lives, accounts of religious pilgrimages, parts of the Bible, and the like. The oldest extant manuscript is a copy of the Gospels made by Deacon Gregory for Ostromir of Novgorod about 1056–1057. About five hundred manuscripts dating from the eleventh to the thirteenth century have survived. Many religious ballads and hymns were handed down orally.

At the same time — and presumably much earlier — there was a considerable amount of secular composition, of which a large percentage was transmitted orally till later times. This secular writing may be divided into three large classes: (1) folklore, consisting of ballads, harvest songs, betrothal songs, funeral songs, incantations, riddles, and the like; (2) quasi-historical narratives, in which fact is often blended with legend (the most celebrated of these narratives is the chronicle of Nestor [b. *c.* 1056], a monk of Kiev, who traces the history of the Slavonians from Noah's Flood down to 1110); and (3) rhythmical prose romances, probably sung or recited by court poets or professional bards (these are similar to the French *chansons de geste*). Some of the prose romances are of national and some of Byzantine origin. Only one has been preserved, *The Tale of the Band of Igor** (written *c.* 1190–1200), concerning the disastrous raid made by Prince Igor of Novgorod on the Polovtsy in 1185. Igor's band is defeated, and he himself is captured but escapes from prison and finally makes his way back to Kiev.

From the beginning of the Tatar period (1240) to the beginning of the reign of Peter the Great (1682), literature of only very minor significance was produced. More sermons, books of moral instruction, saints' lives, chronicles, letters, and memoirs were written. The most noteworthy are (1) the six epistles which passed between Ivan IV (the Terrible) and the alleged traitor Kurbsky (1563–1579) and (2) an autobiography (1672–1673) by the Archpriest Avvakum, who was burned at the stake for heresy in 1681.

There was no original drama or prose fiction before 1682, but there were some translations of both types. Seeds of the drama were present in church rituals as early as the sixteenth century, but they did not germinate into full-fledged plays. The later Russian

---

* The difficulties of transliteration of the Russian alphabet, general lack of familiarity with the Russian language, and the fact that nearly all anthologies and literary histories have found it preferable to give only English titles — all these considerations have led to the abandonment in this chapter of giving both the foreign and the English titles.

drama is an imitation or an outgrowth of the Latin drama (brought in through the schools) and the German secular drama (brought in by strolling players). About 1677 a group of romances of chivalry, translated from Polish, became a landmark in the development of the prose narrative.

The reforms of Peter the Great effected Russia's own Renaissance.[2] Knowledge of the Greek and Roman classics and of the French neoclassics invited imitation, and soon dramas modeled after the works of Corneille and Racine, and "epics and tragedies, elegies and idyls, fables and light verse, and particularly Horatian odes and satires, all according to the rules of Boileau"[3] were turned out in profusion. Glorification of Peter and his successors followed much the same pattern as the French works extolling Louis XIV. None of these works had much literary merit.

"Modern Russian literature dates from the establishment of a continuous tradition of secular imaginative literature in the second quarter of the eighteenth century."[4] During most of that century the majority of literary work was still imitative, pretentious, and awkward. There were a few men, however, who deserve to be mentioned.

PRINCE ANTIOCH CANTEMIR (1708–1744) wrote several vigorous satires against the old prejudices, the new foppishness, and the opposition to the era of enlightenment.

VASILY TREDIAKOVSKY (1703–1769) wrote some poor poetry and made numerous translations of French works, but he is best remembered for his formulation in Russian of the neoclassical theories of poetry and for his works on Russian prosody.

MIKHAIL LOMONOSOV (*c.* 1711–1765) was the "real founder of modern Russian literature."[5] He wrote stately odes in a new verse form, "based on equi-syllabic and accentual feet," and he enriched the Russian language by insisting on the use of Church Slavonic for the "high" style and of colloquial expressions for the "low."

ALEXANDER SUMAROKOV (1718–1777) wrote satires, fables, and literary criticism. He is most famous as the author of the first regular Russian drama, the tragedy *Khorev* (1747). He was also the director of the first Russian theater (1756), built in St. Petersburg (Leningrad).

GAVRIIL DERZHAVIN (1743–1816), deist and epicurean, was the greatest poet of the period. His fame rests on his lyrics, cantatas, and ballads. He loved the great, the magnificent, the sublime, the joyous. His language was powerful and vigorous though often barbaric and lacking in formal correctness.

DENIS FONVIZIN (1745–1792) owes his reputation to two prose comedies of social satire in the classical style: *The Brigadier-General* (1766) and *The Minor* (1782). Fonvizin excels in comic dialogue and in characterization, especially of the crude, the brutish, the uneducated or half-educated, and the hypocritical.

Opposed to the neoclassical tendencies of these writers were three authors, who, in their fondness for simplicity and for matters of the heart, were forerunners of romanticism. These three were NIKOLAY KARAMZIN (1766–1826), the author of prose narratives and of a twelve-volume *History of the Russian State* (1818–1826); VASILY ZHUKOVSKY (1783–1852), an almost inspired translator of Uhland, Schiller, Dryden, Thomson, Gray, Southey, Scott, Moore, Campbell, and Byron; and IVAN KRYLOV (1768–1844), a translator of La Fontaine's fables and an excellent fabulist in his own right.

The period from 1820 (the date of Pushkin's first publication) to 1883 (the date of the death of Turgenev) was the Golden Age of Russian literature.[6] The first two decades might be described as the era of romanticism, for during those years Pushkin and Lermontov, the two great romantic poets, wrote their poems.

Realism began to displace romanticism in the early 'forties. As a matter of fact, some of Pushkin's later works (e.g., *Eugene Onegin*, 1833) showed some realistic characteristics. The publication of Gogol's *Dead Souls* in 1842 marked the beginning of Russia's great age of realistic fiction. Between that date and 1883 Gogol, Turgenev, Dostoevsky, and Leo Tolstoy in their masterpieces brought something new to world literature — something enigmatically termed "the Russian soul," which in literature "means a unique combination of the most vigorous and candid realism with extreme sensitiveness, awareness of the pangs of the human heart, and aspiration toward the highest ideals."[7] This sympathy for human sufferings helps to distinguish Russian realism and naturalism from French, which was more objective. Turgenev probably came nearest to the French objectivity, but even he was intentionally didactic at times.

The greatest literature of the Golden Age was its novels and its lyric poetry, but there were also some good short stories, memoirs, and dramas.

POETRY

Except for the work of Pushkin and Lermontov, Russian poetry of the nineteenth century was mediocre. ALEXEY KOLTSOV (1808–1842) wrote some poems in emulation of Pushkin and some philosophical pieces, but is best remembered for his "artificial folk-songs"; he has been called the Russian Burns. FYODOR TYUTCHEV (1803–1873) wrote philosophical and nature lyrics in a style which combines classical and romantic elements. ALEXEY K. TOLSTOY (1817–1875) is the greatest Russian author of humorous and satirical verse. He wrote, in addition, some dainty lyrics; two volumes of narrative poetry; *The Vampire* (1840), a tale; *Prince Serebryany* (1863), a novel; and a trilogy of historical dramas: *The Death of Ivan the Terrible* (1866), *Czar Theodore* (1868), and *Czar Boris* (1870). AFANASY FET (1820–1892) was an "uncompromising champion of the rights of pure poetry."[8] His early poems are similar to French Parnassian poetry and are devoted to art for art's sake. He also wrote some nature lyrics and, later, some reflective and philosophical pieces. NIKOLAY NEKRASOV (1821–1877) wrote folk-song poetry and objective poems about the sufferings of the people; unfortunately, he was deficient in craftsmanship and artistic taste.

ALEXANDER PUSHKIN (1799–1837). "The Byron of Russia" was born in Moscow of an old, aristocratic family; his great-grandfather was a Negro, a favorite of Peter the Great. Alexander's early childhood was spent under the instruction of French tutors. From 1811 to 1817 he attended the lyceum at Tsarskoye Selo, a few miles from Moscow. After graduation he secured a clerkship in the Foreign Office at St. Petersburg, which he held till 1820; then some of his scurrilous and "revolutionary" epigrams induced the Czar to transfer him to a position in southern Russia. In the same year his first poetic volume appeared; this was *Ruslan and Lyudmila*. Pushkin's "exile" (spent chiefly in the Crimea and the Caucasus) lasted four years; in 1824 he was dismissed from the service and ordered to retire to his mother's estate in the Province of Pskov, where for two years he learned much folklore from his old nurse Arina Rodyonovna. During the six years away from St. Petersburg Pushkin engaged in several love affairs and wrote many lyrical and narrative poems and a drama. In 1826 he was restored to favor and returned to the capital, where he resumed the wild life he had indulged in before his exile. In 1831 he married Natalie Goncharova, a beautiful but frivolous girl of eighteen, whose extravagant habits (well matched with his own) plunged him ever deeper in debt. Appointment as "gentleman of the chamber" proved irksome, and so did the condescension of the great courtiers. Rumors of his wife's intimacy with her brother-in-law at length forced Pushkin into a duel, in which he was killed.

Works.

NARRATIVE. Pushkin first became famous as the author of rather long narrative poems. *Ruslan and Lyudmila* (1820) is a fantastic fairy tale about a young bride who is kidnaped in a storm by a sorcerer; after many adventures the miserable husband rescues her, and they live together happily ever after. The poem has been set to music in the form of an opera by Glinka. Byronic influence is manifest in the romantic narratives *The Robber Brothers* (1821), *The Captive of the Caucasus* (1822), and *The Fountain of Bakhchisaray* (1824). The latter two have dark, beautiful heroines, passionate and disillusioned heroes, and Oriental settings; they are two of Pushkin's most popular works. *The Gipsies* (1827), laid in Bessarabia, is a tragic poem dealing with a man's inability to discard his "convention-bred feelings and passions, especially the feeling of ownership of his mate."[9] *Poltava* (1829) is a romantically heroic poem which celebrates Peter the Great's famous victory over Charles XII of Sweden in 1709.

Pushkin's most famous — and perhaps most characteristic — work is the "novel in verse" *Eugene Onegin* (1833). The hero, a young man of society, is drawn from the dissipations of the city by the death of his father. He settles on his country estate, where soon he becomes friendly with Lensky, a young poet, who introduces him to the Larin sisters, Olga and Tatyana; Olga is Lensky's fiancée. Tatyana falls in love with Eugene, but he politely snubs her as a provincial rustic. Annoyed by her parents' attentions, he flirts with Olga, who succumbs to his charms. Lensky challenges him to a duel and is killed. Later, after Tatyana has moved to the city, married a rich nobleman, and become sophisticated, Eugene sees her and falls in love. She confesses her love for him, but remains faithful to her husband. According to one critic, *Eugene Onegin* "is thoroughly Russian, and contains perhaps the best description of Russian life, both in the capitals and on the smaller estates of noblemen in the country, that has ever been written in Russian literature."[10] Tchaikovsky made an opera of the poem.

LYRIC. Pushkin wrote some lyrics in behalf of liberty and liberalism, but his best songs are about nature and love. His early lyrics (1816–1819) are graceful and gay; those of the period 1820–1823 are somewhat more personal, more passionate, more nearly perfect technically. Those of his last period (1824–1837) are far more serious and form "a body of lyric verse unapproached in Russian and unsurpassed in any poetry."[11] Many of these later poems are based on personal experiences but are general in tone. Their beauty is classical in simplicity and restraint. Some of his best lyrics are "The Storm," "Napoleon," "Foreboding," "For the Shores of Thy Distant Fatherland," "The Winter Morning," "Winter Evening," "Prophet," "A Nereid," and "Portrait."

DRAMATIC. Pushkin wrote four "little dramas" or dramatic sketches; these are not real plays but comparatively short studies of character and dramatic situation. They are *Mozart and Salieri* (1831), *The Feast during the Plague* (1831), *The Covetous Knight* (1836), and *The Stone Guest* or *Don Juan* (1840). By far his most important dramatic effort is *Boris Godunov* (1831), a historical tragedy in blank verse. It is the first Russian attempt at romantic (as opposed to French classical) tragedy. There is a tendency toward narration rather than dramatic action, the diction is stilted, and the blank verse is monotonous; but the characters are admirably portrayed. It is a tragedy of expiation: Godunov, Czar of Russia (*c.* 1551–1605), is accused by a pretender of having murdered the rightful heir to the throne. The people support the pretender and massacre all the extant Godunovs. Moussorgsky made an opera out of the drama.

Estimate. Pushkin is regarded as a great poet not for the depth or nobility of his ideas nor for the grandeur of the personality which his poetry mirrors. "The beauty of form, the happy ways of expression, the incomparable command of verse and rhyme are his main points. . . ."[12] Waliszewski lists his greatest merits as an "exceptionally perfect harmony between his subject and his form, a miraculous appropriateness of expression, a singularly happy mingling of grace and vigour, and an almost infallible feeling for rhythm."[13] By means of this verbal felicity "Pushkin created the modern Russian poetic language. He freed it from dead hyperbolism and false solemnity; he brought it closer to the living language of the people, and gave it sincerity, dignity, flexibility, and vigor."[14] According to Ivar Spector, "Pushkin has done more for the Russian language than Shakespeare for the English."[15]

He is primarily a national bard rather than a universal one, but in Russia "Pushkin's name leads all the rest."[16]

MIKHAIL LERMONTOV (1814–1841). Lermontov was the descendant of a Scottish captain, George Learmont, himself the descendant (according to tradition) of Thomas the Rhymer. Mikhail's mother died when the boy was three years old, and he was reared by his maternal grandmother, part of his youth being spent in the Caucasus. Expelled from the University of Moscow for a minor offense (1832), he entered a military school and in 1834 was given a commission in the Hussars of the Guards. A violent poem attacking the courtiers who permitted Pushkin to be killed (1837) caused Lermontov's first exile to the Caucasus for about a year, and a duel with the French ambassador's son caused a second exile to the same region (1840). The following year he himself fell in a duel caused by an insult to a fellow officer.

Influenced by Schiller, Byron, and Shelley, Lermontov is the poet of a soul in revolt against despotism, against any sort of restrictions of individual freedom, against the ugliness and shallowness and emptiness of life. In his poetry we find a new note — a note of indignation about things as they are.

The Demon (completed *c.* 1840*) is a "fantastic poem," possibly suggested by Byron's *Heaven and Earth,* about a lonely, embittered Spirit of Evil who is transformed by his love for the mortal Tamar, a nun. *Mtzyri* (1840) is a poem about a Circassian boy who, brought up in a monastery, yearns for freedom and at last escapes, only to be mortally wounded by a leopard.

Lermontov's short lyrics breathe the same spirit. Many show a love for natural beauty — especially the still and majestic beauty of the Caucasus. Some of the best are "The Angel," which has been called "perhaps the most wonderful *romantic* lyric in the Russian language";[17] "The Prayer"; "The Snail"; "Testament"; and "A Sail."

Lermontov wrote one novel in prose. *The Hero of Our Times* (published serially 1839–1840), partially autobiographical, is a story about a cynical and disillusioned but clever young man who kidnaps a beautiful Circassian girl, tires of her, seems relieved to see her killed by his rival, and then proceeds to other adventures, including a duel. Lermontov himself called the novel "the portrait of the

---

* Lermontov published few of his poems. The dates given here will therefore be those of completion rather than of publication.

vices of our generation."[18] The portraiture clearly tends toward satirical realism.

Lermontov is far deeper, more pessimistic, and more egocentric than Pushkin. "And if Pushkin is fundamentally national, acquiring international significance through his closeness to his native land, Lermontov is of universal value in himself as expressing those doubts and moods and gropings which are common to cultivated man."[19]

THE DRAMA

In addition to Pushkin and the great novelists Gogol, Turgenev, and Leo Tolstoy (below), ALEXANDER GRIBOEDOV (1795–1829) wrote some famous dramas. *Woe from Wit* (1825), his best-known work, is a Molièresque comedy full of wit and amusing characterization. ALEXANDER OSTROVSKY (1823–1886) employed the "slice-of-life" technique in many of his forty-eight plays; the most famous of his dramas are *The Bankrupt* (1850), *The Poor Bride* (1852), *Poverty Is No Crime* (1854), *The Profitable Post* (1857), *The Thunderstorm* (1860), and *The Forest* (1871).

THE NOVEL

Gogol, Turgenev, Dostoevsky, and Leo Tolstoy were, of course, the greatest novelists of Russia's Golden Age. There were other important ones, however. SERGEY AKSAKOV (1791–1859) wrote earthy but comparatively objective and peaceful books, of which the best known are *A Family Chronicle* (1856) and *Years of Childhood of Bagrov Grandson* (1858). ALEXANDER GONCHAROV (1812–1891) is famous for *Oblomov* (1858), an excellent character study of the laziness and ineffectiveness of the Russian nobility. ALEXEY PISEMSKY (1820–1881) wrote pessimistic and skeptical novels, the most popular of which is *A Thousand Souls* (1858). MIKHAIL SALTYKOV–SHCHEDRIN (1826–1889), like Goncharov and Chekhov, wrote about the decay of the nobility; *The Golovlev Family* (1872–1876) is a satirical novel. Finally, NIKOLAY LESKOV (1831–1895) wrote reactionary novels (*Nowhere*, 1864; *At Knives' Points*, 1870–1871) and a somewhat sympathetic picture of the life of the clergy (*The Churchmen*, 1872).

NIKOLAY GOGOL (1809–1852). Gogol was born in Sorochintsy of an aristocratic Ukrainian family. After a halfhearted education at the lyceum of Nezhin (1821–1828), he went to St.

Petersburg with great ambitions. A long narrative poem which he brought with him was a total failure. He worked for some time as a government clerk and then as a teacher. His two-volume collection of short stories about Ukrainian life (1831–1832) was enthusiastically received, and after an unsuccessful year as a professor of history, he decided to make literature his profession. In 1835 he published some more stories and some essays. The following year the production of his play *The Inspector-General* was acclaimed by the public, who saw in it an attack on the autocratic and inefficient governmental system — a meaning which the author did not intend. A similar meaning, plus a condemnation of serfdom, was also read into the first part of *Dead Souls*, which appeared in 1842. Most of the time after 1836 Gogol lived abroad, chiefly at Rome. He continued to write, but was dissatisfied with the results. *Selected Passages from a Correspondence with Friends* (1847), a purely imaginary set of epistles, met with universal disapproval. In despair, Gogol turned to religion, and in a fit of melancholia, burned all but a few fragments of a second version of Part II of *Dead Souls*. His health, already bad, was further impaired by ascetic practices, and he died in a state of gloom in February, 1852.

Style and Technique. Gogol's best works are a strange and wonderful combination of profoundest sympathy, photographic realism, and hilarious humor. His satire is nearly always subjective; that is, his objects of attack are projections of his own self. Perhaps this explains his extraordinary ability to show pity for his characters while he is laughing at them.

The most persistent characteristics of his style, according to Mirsky, are "high-pitched, poetic rhetoric, . . . grotesque farce, . . . [and] extraordinary intensity and vividness of *sight*."[20] Everything he saw was romantically transformed or exaggerated, and his characters, though convincing, are caricatures. "He is considered the first realist, . . . yet he constantly oversteps the boundaries of realism. He is supposed to picture Russia as it actually is, yet he is always exaggerating in the direction of the grotesque, or of the romantic, or of the symbolic."[21]

His creative imagination is miraculous. "If mere creative force is to be the standard of valuation, Gogol is the greatest of Russian writers."[22]

As has been intimated above, Gogol is a reformer but not a revolutionist. He meant to suggest not the overthrow of the old order, but the self-reformation of each individual. His works (especially *The Inspector-General* and *Dead Souls*) have, however, been hailed both by his contemporaries and by later generations as an indictment of the autocratic and bureaucratic regime.

Works. Gogol's principal volumes are: *Evenings on a Farm near Dikanka* (Volume I, 1831; Volume II, 1832), eight short stories about nature and people in the Ukraine; *Mirgorod* (1835), another collection of stories; *Arabesques* (1835), a volume of miscellaneous prose, including essays and stories; *The Inspector-General* (1836), a comedy; *Dead Souls* (1842), an unfinished novel; *The Cloak* (1842), a novelette; and *Selected Passages from a Correspondence with Friends* (1847).

THE INSPECTOR–GENERAL (or *The Rivizor*). It "is generally held to be the greatest piece of dramatic writing in the language."[23] It is so funny that when it first reached the printing shop, "the typesetters could not work for laughter. . . ."[24] The corrupt mayor and other officials of a provincial town have learned that an inspector-general is coming from St. Petersburg to have a look at the governmental functioning, and he is coming incognito! The frantic local officials mistake a penniless gambler for the inspector, load him down with bribes and the promise of the mayor's daughter, and discover their error just as the real inspector's arrival is announced.

DEAD SOULS. Considered Gogol's magnum opus. The author intended, apparently, to write three parts, to correspond to the three books of Dante's *Divine Comedy*, the first representing damnation, the second purgation, and the third salvation. Only Part I and fragments of Part II were ever published. There is only the beginning of a plot: Chichikov, the incarnation of "self-satisfied inferiority," is a rogue who hits on the get-rich-quick scheme of buying up "dead souls" (that is, serfs who have died since the last census and on whom the owners are required to pay poll tax) and of mortgaging them; then with the money thus obtained, he will buy some live serfs and an estate. His plan works well till some of the sellers of the "dead souls" begin to divulge his secret. The virtue of the novel lies in its depiction of the social and economic conditions of the country and in its characterization of Russian types: the strong, silent businessman, the widow, the bully, the miser, and so on.

THE CLOAK. Akaky Akakyevich, a timid and unambitious government clerk, spends his whole life copying manuscripts verbatim and earns the equivalent of two hundred dollars a year. He finds it necessary to buy a new cloak or overcoat, for which he has to economize a long time. When robbers stop him and steal the cherished cloak, he seeks aid in the police courts, but is "brushed off" by the pompous official. When he is returning home, the exposure to the weather gives him a quinsy, and he dies. His ghost haunts a section of the city till it catches the pompous official and takes his cloak. Then it is seen no more.

IVAN TURGENEV (1818–1883). Turgenev was born at Orel; his mother was an heiress; his father, a retired colonel. In 1827 the family moved to Moscow. After attending the Universities of Moscow, St. Petersburg, and Berlin, Ivan accepted a governmental position in the capital (1843), but gave it up two years later in order to spend all his time on literature. In the meanwhile he had become a close friend of the singer Madame Viardot (Pauline Garcia), whom he followed abroad in 1847; he returned to Russia when his mother died in 1850. *A Sportsman's Sketches* (published serially 1847–1851) established his fame as an author. For eighteen months (1852–1853) he was banished from St. Petersburg because he had written too eulogistic an obituary of Gogol. From 1853 till about 1861 he was the dictator of Russian literature. The liberals' hostile reception of *Fathers and Sons* (1862) induced him to absent himself from Russia most of the last twenty years of his life. He continued to seek the company of Madame Viardot, first at Baden-Baden and later (1871) at Paris, where he died.

Style and Technique. In his stories and novels Turgenev often interlards realistic (in the Russian sense) accounts of people with lyrical descriptions of nature. His attitude toward his characters is almost entirely objective; he rarely pulls the covers from their souls. But he delicately and masterfully reveals their natures by relating their actions and their effects on other people. He is better at depicting women than men, and most of his men are shown as inferior to or dependent on women. In his earlier narratives he portrays the serfs as sturdy, intelligent people with a dignity of their own; frequently they are shown in contrast with their stupid or cruel or frivolous owners. In some of his later works he places his hopes on the middle class as the potential saviors of the country. In the shorter narratives the social message is usually implied rather than being stated; in the novels the message is emphasized by the inclusion of many conversations about current problems; often the

conversations are inartistically forced into the texture of the narrative. He is more Westernized in his attitudes than Dostoevsky.

Works. Turgenev wrote poetry, drama, short stories (or novelettes), and novels. Nearly all his poetry was written between 1843
and 1847, and it is of no importance. His plays come mainly in the
period 1843–1852. *A Month in the Country* (1850) is a psychological
play about a young woman and an older one in love with the same
man; and *The Provincial Lady* (1851) is a light comedy. It is on his
stories and his novels that his reputation rests.

A SPORTSMAN'S SKETCHES (1847–1851). A collection of
stories and vignettes of rural life against a background of nature.
They are actually abolitionist tracts — more effective as propa-
ganda, probably, because they seem at first glance to have no social
or political axe to grind. Two of the best single sketches are "The
Singers" and "Bezhin Meadow."

FATHERS AND SONS (1862). A novel about Bazarov, a young
naturalist and Nihilist, who is shown in contrast with his mild and
conservative parents and friends. He puts his entire faith in
natural science as the solution to all problems. He accompanies a
friend, Arkady, home from school and becomes his rival for the
hand of Madame Odintsov, a young widow. Arkady transfers his
affections to the widow's sister, but Madame Odintsov never accepts
Bazarov's suit. While dissecting the body of a man who has died
of typhus, Bazarov is infected and dies — a victim of the science he
had regarded as the savior of mankind. The work is the first great
elaboration on Nihilism.

SMOKE (1867). A story about Litvinov, a young man whose
affections vacillate between Irina, a selfish but cowardly pleasure
seeker, and Tatyana, a less glamorous but far nobler creature.
When Irina reneges on a plan to desert her husband, Litvinov
returns to Tatyana (after a two-year interim) and is accepted. The
title is symbolic of the chaos and meaninglessness of "everything
human, especially everything Russian,"[25] as it appears to Litvinov
after Irina's defection — and as it must have appeared to Turgenev
in Paris.

NEW EARTH (or *Virgin Soil*, 1876). Turgenev's attempt[26] to
present the revolutionary activities of the 1870's and to show the
inability of the idealists and "intellectuals" to put their schemes
into action. Nezhdanov, a young radical, falls in love with Marianne, niece of a rich gentleman. Marianne, too, is a revolutionary,

and she and Nezhdanov go away together to live at the home of Solomin, a factory-manager, who believes in peaceful rather than violent change. When governmental authorities threaten to arrest Nezhdanov, he recognizes that he can never accomplish his aims of reform, and consequently he commits suicide. Solomin flees with Marianne and marries her in order to avoid appearances of immorality. According to Spector, Solomin is Turgenev's representative of the solid and saving middle class.

OTHER NOVELS AND STORIES. Other important works by Turgenev are the novels *Rudin* (1856), *A Nest of Nobles* (1859), and *Spring Freshets* (1872). Two excellent novelettes are *A Quiet Backwater* (1854) and *First Love* (1860).

FYODOR DOSTOEVSKY (1821–1881). Dostoevsky was born in Moscow, where his father was a resident physician in a large public hospital. The boy received his earliest education from his father, his mother, and tutors. He also read widely — the Bible, Schiller, Shakespeare, Scott, Dickens, Sand, Hugo, Pushkin, Zhukovsky, and others. In 1834 he was sent to a private boarding school in his native city; and then in 1837, when his mother died, he enrolled in the Military Engineers' School in St. Petersburg. He was graduated as an ensign in 1841 but remained three more years, one as a student and two as an officer in the drafting department. In 1844 his father was murdered by his own serfs, and Fyodor resigned his commission in order to devote himself to literature. His first volume, *Poor Folk*, sent the critics into raptures; but its successors were disappointing. In 1849 he was arrested with several other young men for holding secret meetings for the discussion of socialism and reforms. He was convicted and sentenced to death. As he and some others stood before the firing squad, the sentence was commuted to hard labor; one of the convicts had already gone insane. Dostoevsky's next four years were spent in a Siberian prison, and for six years after his release he was forced to serve in the army. During this time (1857) he married Marya Isayeva. He returned to St. Petersburg in 1859, where for several years he published some journals and continued his own writing. In 1864 his wife and brother died, and his second journal (*The Epoch*) failed. Dostoevsky now was bankrupt and in addition had to support his brother's family. In 1866 he sold the copyright to all his works for $1500. The following year his fortunes began to mend. He married his stenographer, Anna Grigorievna, who thenceforth was a capable and faithful helper. The two traveled in western Europe for four years — partly to elude his creditors. By 1871 he had paid some of his debts and returned to Russia. The last ten years of his life were relatively happy and prosperous ones, except for recurrent attacks of epilepsy, which, along with poverty, had plagued him nearly all his life.

Works. Dostoevsky's works fall into three periods. In the first (1846–1849) his writings show the influence of Gogol. He has Gogol's combination of sympathy and grotesque naturalism (actually he is far more intensely sympathetic), but he lacks Gogol's sense of humor. *Poor Folk* (1846) is filled with passionate pity "for the downtrodden, half-dehumanized, ridiculous, and still noble human being."[27] This short novel is the story of the love of the poor copyist Makar Dievushkin for Barbara Dobroselova, a destitute seamstress. Although they love each other, the girl despairs of their ever having enough money to live comfortably and so marries the rich Bwikov. *The Double* (1846) is the painful tale of a clerk who is driven insane by the obsession that another clerk has "usurped his identity." *Mr. Prokharchin* (1847) tells about the death of a miser who has collected a fortune but who has lived in squalor. Other stories in Dostoevsky's first period are *The Landlady* (1848) and *Netochka Nezvanova* (1849).

The fiction of his middle period (1857–1863) is similar to that of the first but is less indebted to Gogol. *The Manor of Stepanchikov and Its Inhabitants** (1859) relates how Foma Opiskin, a parasite, bullies and humiliates his host's family. *The Insulted and Injured* (1861), which shows the influence of Dickens, is an inferior novel about a foolish youth in love with two girls at the same time. *Memoirs of a House of the Dead* (1861–1862), based to a large extent on the author's experiences in the Siberian prison, is a morbid account of the lives of convicts.

The novels of Dostoevsky's last period (1863–1881) are more psychologically profound and more emotionally intense than the earlier ones, and most of his greatest writing was done after 1863. *Memoirs of the Underground* (*Letters from the Underworld*) (1864) is an exception; one of his poorest stories, it is made up of the adventures of a "weak-willed Russian" when he comes into contact with some criminal types. It is important, however, as a semiautobiographical

---

* Entitled *The Friend of the Family* in Constance Garnett's translation.

document. *The Gambler* (1866) is based on Dostoevsky's own attack of gambling fever which he suffered while in western Europe.

CRIME AND PUNISHMENT (1866). Though diffuse and full of irrelevancies, it is one of his most powerful books. It is the study of a man, Raskolnikov, who believes himself justified in murdering an old woman for her money. He is forced to commit a second murder to escape detection, but he suffers terrible remorse, confesses his crimes, and is redeemed by the pure love of Sonya, who has engaged in prostitution in order to support her family. She accompanies Raskolnikov when he is sentenced to seven years of imprisonment in Siberia, and they eagerly anticipate the time when they can return to Russia and begin a new life.

THE IDIOT (1869). A narrative about Prince Myshkin, who is really not an idiot at all, but is considered a fool by his companions because he is so gentle, self-sacrificial, and altogether saintly. Both Agila, a general's daughter, and Mastasya, the former mistress of a rich merchant, fall in love with Myshkin. Out of pity he agrees to marry the latter, who refuses to accept his sacrifice and marries Rogozhin. Knowing that she still loves the Prince, Rogozhin kills her in a fit of jealousy and is exiled to Siberia. Agila marries a criminal, who deserts her. Myshkin, formerly subject to attacks of epilepsy, "leaves for Switzerland in a state of disability and mental derangement."[28]

THE POSSESSED (or *The Devils*, 1871). This work contains brilliant portraits of Stagrovin, an unscrupulous and conscienceless "hero"; Kirilov, an insane atheist who offers his life for the sake of the revolutionary cause; and Verkhovensky, a "plotter, flatterer, idolator, and murderer."[29] Stagrovin leads his group of Nihilists into many crimes, including murder and arson. Kirilov assumes the guilt of one of the murders and commits suicide "for the good of the cause"; Verkhovensky flees from the country; and Stagrovin, perceiving that his life is a failure, kills himself.

THE BROTHERS KARAMAZOV (1879–1880). Considered Dostoevsky's best novel. The plot revolves about Fyodor Karamazov; his three legitimate sons Dimitri, Ivan, and Alyosha; and his illegitimate son Smerdyakov. Fyodor is a cruel, violent, sensual, and selfish man, who has wasted his dead wife's money on alcohol and women. Dimitri, like his father, is impulsive and passionate, but, unlike Fyodor, is lovable. Ivan is a skeptic with a conscience.

Alyosha is a priestly and upright person, as gentle and innocent as a child. Smerdyakov is a vicious imbecile and epileptic. Dimitri quarrels with his father over a woman and threatens to kill him. Smerdyakov actually does kill the old man, but the blame falls on Dimitri, who is convicted and sent to Siberia. Ivan's remorse at not staying at home to protect his father when he knew of the danger drives him insane, and Smerdyakov hangs himself.

Criticism. Dostoevsky's faults are readily discernible. For many tastes his novels are too morbid, too full of pain, suffering, crime, insanity, and abnormality. Nikolay Mikhaylovsky says that the most characteristic feature of his novels is cruelty. As a stylist he has many shortcomings. "The besetting sin of Dostoevski is endless garrulity with its accompanying demon of incoherence. . . ."[30] His novels abound in extraneous and entirely irrelevant events, and they are almost entirely formless.

These defects are offset by his many great virtues. His fervent compassion, his profound thought, his love for all living creatures, his intense religious devotion, and his invariable willingness to forgive rather than condemn — all these make his novels great human and Christian documents. "Probably no man ever lived who had a bigger or warmer heart than Dostoevski. . . . [He] has been surpassed in many things by other novelists. . . . But of all the masters of fiction, both in Russia and elsewhere, he is the most truly spiritual."[31]

LEV (LEO) TOLSTOY (1828–1910). Tolstoy was born at the family estate of Yasnaya Polyana. His father was a count, his mother a princess. His mother died when he was two years old, and his father died seven years later. In 1843 he enrolled at the University of Kazan, where he studied Oriental languages and law. In 1847 he left without taking a degree. For four years he tried managing his large estate in Samara, but, apparently both bored and discouraged, went to the Caucasus, where his brother was stationed, and enlisted in the army. For several years he lived the typically licentious life of a soldier of the time, indulging in wine, women, and gambling. He participated in some border expeditions and later in the defense of Sevastopol (1854–1855) in the Crimean War. In the meantime he had written the semiautobiographical *Childhood* (1852), which Nekrasov published in *The Contemporary* and which earned him some fame. Between 1857 and 1861 Tolstoy made three visits to western Europe — Germany,

England, Italy, and Switzerland — to study methods of education; upon returning he opened a school on his estate. In 1862 he married Sophya Andreyevna Behrs, who was a perfect wife, mother, and helpmeet. She bore him thirteen children, managed his household efficiently, and aided him in his literary efforts (for example, she copied the whole manuscript of *War and Peace* seven times in handwriting). Tolstoy continued to write rather steadily. In 1879 he underwent a spiritual transformation. He renounced and denounced the Russian Orthodox Church and embraced "Christianity without Churchianity." That is, he discarded all dogma and ritual and adhered to the ethical precepts and examples of Christ. He foreswore profane literature and art and tried to dispose of his property. He attempted to put his principles into practice by working side by side with the peasants in the field and by displaying the simple Christian virtues. Many disciples listened to his teachings and accepted the new creed of Tolstoyism. He was excommunicated by the Church in 1901. The major portion of his writing after 1879 consisted of polemical tracts, theological treatises, and other works aimed at spiritual and moral edification. His last few years were rendered unhappy by his wife's estrangement, which was brought on by her failure to remold her own views in accordance with Tolstoyism. When he was eighty-two years old, he decided to leave home secretly and go into seclusion. Ten days later he became ill on the train and died at Astapovo.

Thought. Tolstoy always had a very active conscience. Even in his youthful days his profligacy seems to have been the result of boredom plus a frantic but hopeless search for meaning in life. After the Crimean War he found a goal to strive for — the education of the peasants. As a rich aristocrat he always had a sense of *noblesse oblige*, and as a disciple of Rousseau he believed firmly in the goodness of the common man, especially the rural peasant. Repeatedly he decried the shallowness and hypocrisy of modern civilization. He repudiated Western civilization especially, and particularly its materialism. In his later years he identified "Reason with God and with Knowledge, [but] the Reason he described emanated from the heart rather than the head."[32] Reason became almost the same thing as conscience. His later thought, as Phelps points out, is not so much a change as it is a development of his earlier beliefs. "Tolstoyism teaches that there is no God, other than the moral law inside man. Instead of being motivated by outward inducement, that moral law moves in obedience to an inward spontaneity. The inner life underlies the universe. The end or the goal of inner action is inner peace (happiness)."[33]

Style and Technique. In many ways Tolstoy's novels and stories (as well as his life) are a contrast to those of Dostoevsky. The works of the former are all carefully written and have undergone the most painstaking revision. His tone is one of authority. He prefers to write about the nobility and the peasants instead of the poor middle class, and his characters are usually normal, ordinary, and simple. "His style is deliberately prosaic — purged to chemical purity of all 'poetry' and rhetoric — sternly puritanical prose. . . . This combination of a very pure colloquial vocabulary with a very complicated and logical syntax makes the peculiar individuality of Tolstóy's Russian."[34]

His method is to subject his material to the most minute analysis; "hence it is that the details he offers are not complex cultural facts, but, as it were, *atoms* of experience, the indivisible units of immediate perception."[35] But he uses so many of these details, and each one is so clearly the result of his own observation of humanity that the reality of the person or thing described strikes home to the reader with great force. Where Turgenev is objective, Tolstoy is subjective and allows us to follow the inner mental and emotional processes of his men and women.

Works. Tolstoy wrote a great deal; the Centenary Edition of his works (1929–1937), in English, runs to twenty-one volumes. Spector divides these works into three distinct periods: the first, from 1852 till 1862 (the date of his marriage); the second, from 1862 till 1879 (the date of his conversion); and the third, from 1879 till 1910. He wrote little of importance after 1899.

FIRST PERIOD.

CHILDHOOD, BOYHOOD, YOUTH (1852–1856). Three sketches based on his own life. They are introspective and fairly conventional, but the last two show increasing signs of his later analytical method.

SEVASTOPOL (1855). In three parts — *Sevastopol in December, Sevastopol in May,* and *Sevastopol in August* — comprising a series of sketches of the Crimean War. Tolstoy deglamorizes warfare and indicts civilization for allowing it. He emphasizes the bravery of the common soldier rather than that of the officers, and he praises the enemy as well as Russians.

THE COSSACKS (written 1853–1854, published 1862).   A philosophical narrative in which the everyday life of the Caucasians is described in detail.   The author begins here to show his belief in simple life close to nature.   Olenin, the hero, has much of Tolstoy's early restlessness.   This hero, a fashionable youth of Moscow, has become disillusioned and weary with the dissolute life of the city and seeks meaning in the simplicity of Cossack life. He falls in love with Marianna, a Cossack girl, whose affection wavers between him and a suitor of her own people.   When the latter is wounded, Olenin watches Marianna nurse him and sees that it is the Cossack that she really loves.   He returns to Moscow.

SECOND PERIOD.

WAR AND PEACE (1865–1869).[36]   "The national novel of Russia"[37] is a tremendous (four-volume) account of Russian life in the early part of the nineteenth century.

In order to understand the novel thoroughly, one must comprehend both Tolstoy's attitude toward history and also his motives and designs in writing the book.   His diaries of the 1840's and some statements he made in the 1860's indicate clearly that for him history was a science of only secondary importance — a study which might lead to philosophical or moral conclusions.   In effect, he denies that there can be such a thing as a "philosophy of history" or that history has any real "meaning."   His theory of history, as expressed in Part Two of the Epilogue of *War and Peace*, is almost fatalistic: human will and human effort affect history almost none at all; this is especially true of the wills and efforts of the so-called makers of history — the great generals, emperors, and the like. History is a combination of purely material, elemental forces and of Divine Providence; the accidental is of great importance.   Tolstoy's two "real realities" (according to Karpovich) are the life of the spirit and the everyday lives of ordinary human beings and their eternal cyclical development through birth, life, procreation, and death.

Holding this view of history and of the realities of life, Tolstoy intended *War and Peace* as a "family" novel with the historical events of the Napoleonic era to be used only as a background.   His treatment of the wars is similar to that of Thackeray in *Vanity Fair*. As the book advances, the "war" portions increase in importance, and Tolstoy tries — not entirely successfully — to blend the "war" theme with the "peace" one; and he uses his comments on historical events as a sort of cement between the two themes.

The story revolves around four families: the Volkonskys, the Rostovs, the Kuragins, and the Bezukhovs. Tolstoy deals first with one family and then with another, as events dictate; and he succeeds admirably in tying the four threads together.

Story. Pierre Bezukhov, who is probably more of a protagonist than anybody else in the novel, is generous and idealistic, but physically unattractive and sometimes guilty of social faux pas and violent outbursts of rage. At the first of the book he is an idler and a gambler, and he is shunned by most society groups as a bore. When his father dies, however, and he inherits not only a title but also an immense fortune, he becomes popular with almost everybody, and his personality then becomes genuinely brighter and more engaging.

Prince Kuragin now succeeds in tricking Pierre into proposing to Ellen, Kuragin's daughter. Ellen is a great beauty, but has no vestige of honesty or scruples of any sort. She and Pierre live unhappily together for some time, but are separated when her husband suspects her of having an affair with another man. Later, out of sheer magnanimity, he becomes reconciled with her. But they are never happy together, and her death (late in the novel) comes as a great emancipation for Pierre.

In the meanwhile, important events have been taking place in the lives of the other two families. Prince Andrey Volkonsky, Pierre's friend, has joined the army in order to help fight against Napoleon. Andrey is aristocratic, humane, intelligent, and handsome, but very cynical. He leaves his wife Lisa in the care of his sister Marya and his old father. Lisa dies in childbirth while Andrey is away.

Pierre is also a friend of the Rostovs, rich and lovable people who, for Tolstoy, represent the typical Russian minor nobility of the period. The father is generous and indulgent to the point of fatuity and gradually sacrifices a considerable portion of the family fortune in order to raise enough cash to entertain his friends and grant every whim of his wife and children. His elder son Nikolay is a dashing youth, who goes to war for the glory and thrill of military life. Natasha, Nikolay's sister, is a charming and *spirituel* young girl. Sonya, a cousin of the young Rostovs, lives with them; she falls in love with Nikolay, and to some extent he returns her affection.

During a visit on official business to Count Rostov, Andrey Volkonsky (now a widower) sees Natasha; they fall in love with each other and become engaged. Andrey returns to the wars. During his long absence Natasha meets Anatole Kuragin (son of the Prince), a dashing and unscrupulous reprobate. He conceals from Natasha the fact that he is already married, and he persuades her to elope with him; the elopement is prevented by Sonya and Natasha's mother. Humiliated and broken in spirit, Natasha goes into a physical as well as spiritual decline. She writes to Andrey to release him from all his obligations to her. Somewhat later Andrey is wounded and is brought by chance to the Rostovs' house in the country, where Natasha nurses him and tells him that she still loves him. Andrey dies.

In the meanwhile, Nikolay Rostov has fallen in love with Marya, the homely but gentle sister of Andrey.

Count Pierre has suffered many vicissitudes. He has joined the Freemasons, feeling that devotion to their ideals will be a good purpose for his life, but he has been disappointed. Then he has tried to assassinate Napoleon, but he has been captured by the French and carried along as a prisoner in their retreat from Moscow. At length he is released by one of the many Russian attacks on the retreaters.

After the war Pierre marries Natasha, and Nikolay marries Marya. The two couples settle down to quiet domestic happiness.

In the "war" passages of the novel Tolstoy gives detailed and graphic accounts of several battles, including that of Borodino. He describes, too, the occupation of Moscow by the French and their disastrous retreat from Russia. He draws a satirical picture of most of the staff officers, especially of the German ones on the Russian side. He holds Napoleon up to ridicule as a vain and powerless puppet — thereby illustrating his own theory of history. He depicts the Russian general Kutuzov as a foil to Napoleon; the former is old, sluggish, and tired, but wise and honest. It is Kutuzov's policy of drawing the French deep into Russia and then allowing fate — and the lengthening of supply lines — to bring about Napoleon's downfall. The common soldiers and the noncommissioned officers are treated sympathetically. According to Tolstoy, they are brave people, and some of them are intelligent; but they have little idea why they are fighting. Tolstoy makes the peasant (especially as an infantryman) the "embodiment of everything Russian, everything good."[38]

War and Peace is panoramic and epic; it is a picture not only of the whole of Russia in the years 1805–1812, but also of human nature everywhere in periods of great emergencies.

ANNA KARENINA (1875–1877).   According to Phelps, "surely the most powerful novel written by any man of our time, and it would be difficult to name a novel of any period that surpasses it in strength."[39]   Its theme (which reflects the beginning of Tolstoy's development from Rousseauistic freedom to Tolstoyism) is the calamities a woman brings on herself and others by following her emotions rather than her moral impulses.   Anna leaves her phlegmatic husband Karenin for the dashing Vronsky, an officer who is engaged to her friend Kitty.   Anna and Vronsky live together without being married.   Kitty marries Levin,* a good and wealthy man who is interested in the improvement of the social order.   Anna's friends desert her; she becomes remorseful about her life of adultery; Karenin refuses her a divorce, which would permit her to marry Vronsky; Vronsky begins to be interested in other women; and Anna commits suicide by throwing herself under the wheels of a train.

Anna Karenina has a more centralized action and a more definite plot than *War and Peace*.   Although it has about a hundred and seventy-five characters, most of them are unimportant and appear only in episodes.   The later novel is less epic and less idyllic than *War and Peace,* but is more dramatic and more tragic.   The moralizing tendency is much stronger in *Anna Karenina* — to the detriment of pure artistry.   This didacticism is a harbinger of Tolstoy's third period; the epilogue to *Anna Karenina* has been called the prologue to his new life.

THIRD PERIOD.

THE DEATH OF IVAN ILYITCH (1886).   An excruciating novelette about a man who dies a long and lingering death as a result of an injury caused by a fall from a ladder.   There is much realistic observation of a man's mental processes as he nears death. He is egoistic and complaining, and his wife tries unsuccessfully to be sympathetic.   He and she — and the reader — are glad when Ivan finally dies.

RESURRECTION (1899–1900).   A sequel — or a complement — to Dostoevsky's *Crime and Punishment*.   Its ostensible theme is the regeneration of a worldly aristocrat, Prince Nekhludov, who has started a young and innocent servant girl (Katusha) on the road to

* All commentators agree that Levin is a portrait of Tolstoy himself.

prostitution.* He discovers the girl in prison, charged with a murder of which she is innocent. She is convicted through a court error, and Nekhludov decides to distribute his possessions among his peasants, follow Katusha to Siberia, and marry her. Sensing that his actions are motivated by pity rather than love, she rejects him and marries a fellow prisoner. The Prince accepts her decision and makes up his mind to lead a new, "resurrected" life according to the teachings of Christ.

Estimate. There is no question that Tolstoy was one of the two greatest authors of Russian prose fiction. He and Dostoevsky rise far above the others. Although some critics have censured his ethical and religious system, his ability as an observer and analyst of life is beyond dispute. ". . . [It] is absolutely certain that no man since the times of Rousseau has so profoundly stirred the human conscience as Tolstóy has by his moral writings."[40] "Humanly speaking, it is impossible to deny that he was the biggest man (not the best, nor perhaps even the greatest, but just morally the bulkiest) that trod the Russian soil within the last few lifetimes; the biggest man, if not the greatest artist, in all Russian literary history."[41]

* Spector (*The Golden Age of Russian Literature* [Caldwell, Idaho: 1943] pp. 171–172) holds that Nekhludov is not really regenerated, that "all [his] sacrifices [are] made from an egotistical motive — in order to achieve inner peace."

17

The Interim

(*1883–1917*)

Historical Background. As early as the 1840's there began to appear a sharp cleavage of opinion between the Slavophils (who espoused conservatism, religious orthodoxy, and nationalism) and the Westernists (who supported liberalism, secularism, and greater friendliness to foreign culture). Some of the more radical aristocratic youths formed groups whose purpose was the furtherance of a social revolution, and some advocated socialistic schemes. A member of one extremist organization, The People's Will, assassinated Alexander II (1881).

The reign of Alexander III (1881–1894) was relatively calm, but toward the end of the century new revolutionary movements gave evidence of the widespread discontent. The factory workers now joined the young idealists in assailing autocracy and in clamoring for a revolution which would result in the establishment of a socialistic regime.

General View of the Literature. Two literary trends are noticeable in the period between 1883 and 1917. One, represented chiefly by Chekov, Gorky, and Korolenko, is in the direction of social criticism and continues the realistic and naturalistic techniques of the novelists and dramatists of the Golden Age. The other trend, known as "modernism" is a revolt against realism and didacticism in the direction of aestheticism and symbolism. It is best represented by several minor poets.

VLADIMIR KOROLENKO (1853–1921) is most famous for his short stories showing sympathy for the oppressed. Best known are "Yom-Kipur" about the mistreated Jew and "Makar's Dream" about a poor Siberian peasant. He also wrote *The Blind Musician* (1886), a novelette which "is a psychologocal study born of the spirit of love for the afflicted."[1]

The most interesting figures of the "poetic revival" are VYACHES-

LAV IVANOV (1866–1945), IVAN BUNIN (1870–1953), VALERY BRYUSOV (1873–1924), MAXIMILIAN VOLOSHIN (1877–1932), ALEXANDER BLOK (1880–1921), and SERGEY YESENIN (1895–1925).

By far the most important authors of the Interim were Chekhov and Gorky, both novelists, dramatists, and short-story writers.

CHEKHOV

ANTON CHEKHOV (1860–1904), the son of an ex-serf, was born at Taganrog. His early schooling was received at the Gymnasium (preparatory school) there. He was graduated in 1879 and the same year enrolled in the University of Moscow, from which he received a medical degree in 1884. His first story was published in 1880. After practicing medicine for a short while, he gave it up so that he could spend all his time on literature. Novelettes, short stories, and plays appeared often from then till his death. A trip to Sakhalin (1890) to study the penal institutions there resulted in a series of sketches entitled *Sakhalin* (1893). In 1891 he visited Austria, Italy, and France. In 1901 he married the actress Olga L. Knipper. The tuberculosis from which he had suffered since his twenties now became worse. He spent his last years in the mild climate of Yalta. He died at a health resort in Badenweiler, Germany.

Works. Like Gogol, Chekhov had a wonderful sense of humor plus a profound sense of the tragedy of life. His earliest stories are little more than humorous sketches, but they show his powers of perception. Some critic said that "it was too bad that such a talented young man should spend all his time making people laugh."[2] Maturity, disease, and perhaps this advice changed his attitude, and most of the stories and dramas he wrote between 1888 and 1900 are darkly tragic. Then in his last four years he began to hold out a ray of hope for the deplorable situation in his country; he had no specific cure for its ills, but he diagnosed them accurately and foreshadowed the coming revolutions.

SHORT STORIES. His short stories are perhaps more descriptive than narrative. Many of the six hundred that he wrote are mere sketches of situations and have no real plot at all. His attitude is aloof and impersonal, and he has no lesson to teach. Like most of the other fiction-writers of Russia, he makes his stories abound in realistic details. He is never sentimental and rarely compassionate, and his stories appeal rather to the intellect than to the emotions.

One of his best known tales is "Ward Number Six" (1892), in which a doctor's pity for his insane patients leads his associates to conclude that *he* is deranged. They throw him in the loathsome cell with the madmen, and he dies within a few hours. Some other stories are "Vanka" (1886), "The Siren" (1887), "In the Cart" (1897), and "The Darling" (1899).

DRAMAS. All of Chekhov's essential characteristics are shown in his dramas. These are almost entirely formless and disconnected, but their very chaos is perhaps symbolic of society as he saw it.

IVANOV (1887). A tragedy of an "intellectual" with whom Sasha, a young girl, has fallen in love because she admires his high aspirations. Knowing that his former aspirations are really dead and that "the sacred fire is with him a mere reminiscence of the better years,"[3] he shoots himself immediately before the wedding is to take place.

THE CHERRY ORCHARD (1904). Chekhov's most characteristic drama. It is a tragedy of the decayed aristocracy of Russia, who recognize that their decadence and impracticality are leading to ruin but who are totally unable to act — to do anything about the situation. The drama is a masterpiece of portraiture; the aristocrats and the "intellectuals" are held up in contrast to the crude but businesslike ex-serf, who represents the new and effective social order. Madame Ranevskaya, a sentimental and extravagant land owner, is deep in debt and faces the loss of her estate. Lopahin, an ex-serf who is now a rich merchant, shows her a way out: she must cut down her vast cherry orchard and divide the land up into lots for leasing to those who want to build villas. The orchard, however, is a symbol of all she holds dear — the old order — and she is horrified at Lopahin's suggestion. She refuses to follow his advice even though it is perfectly clear that she will otherwise lose the orchard. The whole estate is sold at auction, and Lopahin is the buyer. The play ends with the sound of axes ringing against the cherry trees.

Summary of Criticism. Although Chekhov "lacks the tremendous force of Tolstoi, the flawless perfection of Turgenev, and the mighty world-embracing sympathy of Great-heart Dostoevski,"[4] he is an excellent interpreter of his time and country, and his subtle, objective, and nonsentimental plays and stories have enjoyed a great vogue in English-speaking countries.

GORKY

Maxim Gorky (pseudonym of Alexey Maximovich Pyeshkov, 1868–1936) was born at Nizhni Novgorod. His father, an upholsterer, died when the boy was only four, and his mother died when he was ten. After only a few years of elementary schooling, he was apprenticed to a shoemaker, and two years later he worked as a draftsman. When he was twelve, he ran away from home and became a cook's helper on a Volga steamboat. Smury, the cook, had a trunkful of books and imparted his enthusiasm for reading to the young boy. Maxim thereafter tried many jobs, including icon painting, acting, working in a bakery, serving as a porter, selling fruit, and clerking for a lawyer. In 1891 he engaged in revolutionary activity and was arrested three times. His first story (1892) was not especially successful, but he persevered, and by 1901 his works were widely read and frequently republished. He came to America in 1906 to raise funds for the revolutionary cause and was at first warmly received; but when it was discovered that his female companion was not his wife, he was turned out of his hotel and snubbed generally. He went to live on the isle of Capri, where in 1909 he set up a school for revolutionists; among his pupils was Joseph Stalin. In 1913 he was allowed to return to Russia. In the revolution of 1917 he at first opposed and then embraced the Bolshevik cause. A disagreement with Lenin in 1921 led to his leaving the country. He lived in Germany till 1928, when he was invited to return to his fatherland. He died at Gorky (a town near Moscow named for him).

Message. Gorky's contribution to Russian literature is that "he discovered a world in the underworld. His implication is clear enough — that tramps or hoboes with such beautiful souls should not be lost to humanity because they are victims of an unjust social order."[5] His ever recurrent theme "is the story of a mute soul that strives to become articulate; it is the story of innately sound human beings being thrown into primitive environments and groping their way upward to the light."[6]

Works. He wrote many short stories, of which the most notable are "Konovalov" (1896), "Orlov and His Wife" (1897), "Twenty-six Men and a Girl" (1899), and "Birth of a Man" (1912). His most memorable novels are *Foma Gordeyev* (1899), *Three of Them*

(1900–1901), and *The Mother* (1907). He left unfinished a huge —
and disappointing — four-volume novel, of which the separate titles
are *The Bystander* (1930), *The Magnet* (1931), *Other Fires* (1938), and
The Specter (1938). One of his best pieces of writing is his autobiographical trilogy: *My Childhood* (1913), *In the World* (1915), and
My University Days (1923). Among his best plays are *The Middle
Class* (1900), *The Lower Depths* (1902), and *The Last* (1908).

A glance at two of his works will suffice to show his message and
his method.

THE LOWER DEPTHS. A drama about several dregs of
society brought together in a cheap boardinghouse. Pepel, a thief,
has been having a love affair with Vasilisa, the proprietor's wife;
but he grows tired of her and becomes interested in her sister
Natasha. At first furious, Vasilisa calms down and agrees to help
him in his suit if he will kill her husband. When he refuses,
Vasilisa starts a scuffle, in which Pepel does kill her husband.
Vasilisa accuses Pepel of the crime, but Natasha succeeds in im-
plicating both her sister and Pepel, and the two are imprisoned.
One character dies of consumption, and a drunken actor hangs
himself.

THE MOTHER. A novel about a woman and her alcoholic son
who are the center of a group of socialists in a factory community.
When the son, Pavel, is arrested and sent to Siberia for inciting a
strike and for leading a May-Day parade, his mother assumes his
duty of distributing socialistic literature. Caught with the literature, she is choked and beaten to death.

Summary of Criticism. Although Gorky's narratives are shocking, it is extremely unlikely that they are literature which will live.
There is no doubt that Gorky had a message, but the message was
dated; and there is no doubt that he had a spark of genius, but he
had little art. His works repeat each other endlessly. His portraits are not realistic; they are idealizations or exaggerations. His
tramps are too clever and too learned; and the mother, for example,
in the novel of the same name, is not a real woman of the people,
but Gorky's ideal of what a proletarian mother should be. As a
technician he is guilty of "the incoherence and slipshod workmanship of Dostoevsky, without the latter's glow of brotherly love."[7]

Perhaps Phelps was right in saying that "Gorky went up like the
sky-rocket, and seems to have had the traditional descent."[8]

18
Soviet Literature[1]

Historical Background. A revolution in 1905 was entirely unsuccessful. A second, however, in 1917, led by members of the Bolshevik party (later called the Communist party), overthrew the government of Nicholas II (reigned 1894–1917). Civil war followed. Then in 1921 the semicommunistic system known as the New Economic Policy was adopted. The following year the Union of Soviet Socialistic Republics, a federation of sixteen autonomous states, was formed and a constitution approved (1923). After the death of the Bolshevik Lenin (1924), Joseph Stalin (1879–1953) eliminated all opposition and soon established himself as/dictator. In 1928 he announced the abandonment of the New Economic Policy and the beginning of the far more socialistic Five-Year Plan; three other such plans have been completed. Under these plans the U.S.S.R. has made tremendous industrial and military progress. After a brief war with Finland (1939–1940), the country was drawn into World War II by Germany's invasion of Russian territory in 1941. In 1946 the U.S.S.R. initiated a "cold war" on capitalistic nations all over the world.

General View of the Literature. Soviet literature has been principally occupied with glorifying the new regime, describing its struggles, and proclaiming the hope which it holds for the future. Novels, short stories, and poetry, have, of course, been under strict censorship since 1917 and have been for the most part propagandistic and didactic. The didacticism is almost certain to be social rather than personal or individual, and it often reflects an event or the official political bias of the moment.

Drama has been negligible, but poetry, novels, short stories, and satire have flowed copiously since 1917.

On the whole, Soviet literature thus far is of historical interest as a reflection of an epoch, but it is doubtful that its intrinsic merit is great enough to assure it a permanent place in world literature.

POETRY

Directly after the revolution of 1917, the world for the Soviets was a land of hope and enthusiasm; emotions ran high. Consequently it was an era for poetry. There were three main topics of this early poetry: the life of the working class, rural experiences, and joy over the complete break with the past and the establishment of a new order. ALEXEY GASTEV (1882–   ), represents the first group; SERGEY YESENIN (1895–1925), the second; and VLADIMIR MAYAKOVSKY (1893–1930), the third. The last named especially made literature a socialistic weapon.

Two poets who refused to devote their pen to utilitarian purposes were BORIS PASTERNAK (1890–1960) and ANNA AKHMATOVA (1889–   ).

Later poetry has sought to justify and popularize Soviet ideology and to immortalize Soviet struggles, particularly the tribulations and victories of World War II.

Other prominent poets are Alexander Bezymensky (1889–   ), Mikhail Matusovsky (1915–   ), and Yevgeny Dolmatovsky (1915–   ).

PROSE FICTION

The novel and short story have in general followed the same trends as poetry. The most eminent authors of short stories and novels are four. (1) YEVGENY ZAMYATIN (1884–1937) wrote "Cave," a short tale about the hardships which St. Petersburg suffered in the winter of 1918, and *We* (1924), a satirical fantasy about the twenty-sixth century. (2) ISAAK BABEL (1894–*ca.*, 1941), a careful artist, wrote *Red Cavalry* (1926), a volume of stories about Budyonny's battles in the Soviet-Polish War of 1920; he also wrote stories about the Jews of Odessa. He is a romantic, "whose attitude toward life can be described as purely sensuous and aesthetic."[2] (3) ALEXEY N. TOLSTOY (1882–1945), "the dean of Russian letters," is famous for his *Road to Calvary* (or *The Way through Hell,* completed 1941), a picture of Russian life between 1913 and 1918. He also wrote a charming semiautobiographic story entitled *Nikita's Childhood* (1921). (4) MIKHAIL SHOLOKOV (1905–   ), "the foremost of living Soviet authors,"[3] is best known for a monumental novel, *The Quiet Don* (*And Quiet Flows the Don,* 1942),[4] a chronicle of Cossack life during the period 1913–1922. Struve calls it "a Cossack *War and Peace*,"[5] and Spector adds that it is "a genuine contribution to classical Russian literature."[6] Sholokov wrote some war stories during World War II (e.g., "The Science of Hatred," 1942) and has begun *They Fought for Their Country*, a war novel of which only fragments have appeared so far.

Other outstanding Soviet novelists are Panteleimon Romanov (1884–1938), Valentin Katayev (1897–   ), Leonid Leonov (1899–   ), Yury Olesha (1899–   ), and Veniamin Kaverin (1902–   ).

HUMOR AND SATIRE

Although there is comparatively little humor in Soviet literature, there are a few, good funny-pieces, but even these are likely to be didactic.

ILYA ILF (1897–1937) and YEVGENY PETROV (pseudonym of Eugene Katayev, 1902–1944) collaborated first on *Twelve Chairs* (1928), a long but gay and satirical picaresque novel, which deals with Bender, a rogue, searching for some pre-Revolutionary diamonds hidden in a chair. Though Bender dies at the end of the novel, the authors revive him in *The Little Golden Calf* (1931), a more serious but more artistic satire. *Tonya* (1935) and *One-Storied America* (1936) are satires on the United States.

Finally there is MIKHAIL ZOSCHENKO (1895–   ), who has written many short sketches poking fun at Communist corruption, red tape, science, criticism, and the like. *Youth Restored* (1933) purports to be a novel, but is hardly more than a collection of brief stories and sketches in his usual vein. *The Light-Blue Book* (1934) is another group of stories, full of parody, irony, and laughing at the foibles of mankind — especially Communistic mankind. Zoschenko's fun-poking is not particularly humorous, and "the reader cannot help feeling uncomfortable."[7] His last work is *Before Sunrise* (begun serially in 1943, left unfinished), which is even less funny than usual. It contains some accounts of the author's earlier life but no satire — unless some passages praising the Soviet scientist Pavlov are ironical. For some reason the publication was interrupted, and it is significant that Zoschenko's works were attacked in the Communist press and that he was "purged" from Soviet literature in 1946.

Bibliography for Russian Literature

Brückner, Alexander. *A Literary History of Russia.* Translated by H. Havelock. New York: Charles Scribner's Sons, 1908.

Hapgood, Isabel F. *A Survey of Russian Literature, with Selections.* New York: Chautauqua Press, 1902.

Kropotkin, P. *Russian Literature.* New York: McClure, Phillips and Co., 1905.

Mirsky, D. S. *A History of Russian Literature.* Edited and abridged by Francis J. Whitfield. New York: A. A. Knopf, 1949.

Olgin, Moissaye J. *A Guide to Russian Literature (1820-1917).* New York: Harcourt, Brace and Howe, 1920.

Phelps, William Lyon. *Essays on Russian Novelists.* New York: Macmillan Co., 1926.

Spector, Ivar. *The Golden Age of Russian Literature.* Revised ed. Caldwell, Idaho: Caxton Printers, 1943.

Struve, Gleb. *Soviet Russian Literature, 1917-50.* Norman, Okla.: University of Oklahoma Press, 1951.

Thompson, Stith, and John Gassner. *Our Heritage of World Literature.* New York: Dryden Press, 1942.

Waliszewski, Kazimierz. *A History of Russian Literature.* New York: D. Appleton and Co., 1900.

Weatherly, Edward H., and Others. *The Heritage of European Literature.* Boston: Ginn and Co., 1949. Vol. II.

Notes

Notes to Chapter 1

1 There is little agreement among literary historians about the date of the beginning of the Renaissance, and any specific date is, of course, arbitrary. The year of Dante's death is about as logical and convenient a date as any other.

2 John Addington Symonds, *Renaissance in Italy*, Part I, *The Age of Despots* (New York: H. Holt and Co., 1881), I, 15 n. [Henceforth, this work will be referred to only by the title of the part.]

3 George Clark Sellery, *The Renaissance: Its Nature and Origins* (Madison, Wisconsin: University of Wisconsin Press, 1950), p. 260.

4 The term was derived from the phrase "*litterae humaniores*, or humane studies" (William Bradley Otis and Morriss H. Needleman, *Outline-History of English Literature*, 4th ed. [New York: Barnes & Noble, Inc., 1952], I, 111.)

5 Edward Maslin Hulme, *The Renaissance, the Protestant Revolution, and the Catholic Reformation in Continental Europe*, rev. ed. (New York: Century Co., 1920), p. 90.

6 Henry S. Lucas, *The Renaissance and the Reformation* (New York: Harper Brothers, 1934), p. 141.

7 Hulme, p. 66.

8 Lucas, p. 199.

9 Hulme, p. 61.

10 Edward H. Weatherly and Others, *The Heritage of European Literature* (Boston: Ginn & Co., 1948), I, 591.

11 Hulme, p. 62.

12 Francis Petrarch, *Some Love Songs of Petrarch*, ed. and intro. William Dudley Foulke (London: Oxford University Press, 1915), intro., p. 20.

13 He has been called " 'the last of the troubadours' " (Petrarch, ed. Foulke, p. 22).

14 Francis Petrarch, *Sonnets and Songs*, tr. Anna Maria Armi, intro. Theodor E. Mommsen (New York: Pantheon, 1946), intro. p. xxvii.

15 *Prologue to the Clerk's Tale.* Chaucer thought Petrarch the originator of the tale.

16 Petrarch, ed. Foulke, p. 126.

17 Richard Garnett, *A History of Italian Literature* (New York: D. Appleton & Co., 1898), p. 66.

18 Petrarch, tr. Armi, intro., p. xxxviii.

19 William Everett, *The Italian Poets since Dante* (New York: Charles Scribner's Sons, 1904), p. 21.

20 English translations by Foulke, Petrarch, ed. Foulke, pp. 242–244.

21 Quoted by Foulke, Petrarch, ed. Foulke, p. 194.

22 Stith Thompson and John Gassner, *Our Heritage of World Literature* (New York: Dryden Press, 1942), p. 579.

23 Garnett, p. 54.

24 Sellery, p. 74.

25 Levi Oscar Kuhns, *The Great Poets of Italy* (Boston: Houghton Mifflin Co., 1903), p. 120.

26 Jefferson Butler Fletcher, *Literature of the Italian Renaissance* (New York: Macmillan Co., 1934), pp. 68–69.

27 Everett, p. 20.
28 Everett, p. 23.
29 P. 66.
30 *The Sonnets of Petrarch* (London: Longmans, Green and Co., 1932), foreword, p. x.
31 Weatherly and Others, I, 590. For a definition of *Petrarchism*, see p. 57n.
32 Edward Hutton, *Giovanni Boccaccio* (London: Longmans, Green and Co., 1910), p. 291
33 Many of the dates given in connection with Boccaccio's life are matters of conjecture, including the dates of his birth and apprenticeship. Biographers differ.
34 Fletcher, p. 79.
35 Frederick J. Snell, *The Fourteenth Century* (New York: Charles Scribner's Sons, 1899), p. 265.
36 The word is taken from the Greek *deka* — "ten" and *hemera* — "days" (Webster's *New Collegiate Dictionary*, 1949).
37 All words in quotation marks are taken from Fletcher, p. 91.
38 Fletcher, p. 92.
39 Fletcher, pp. 94–95.
40 Symonds, Part IV, *Italian Literature* (New York: H. Holt and Co., 1888), I, 105.
41 Fletcher, p. 96.
42 Fletcher, p. 96.
43 Sellery, p. 86.
44 Symonds, *Italian Literature*, I, 117.
45 P. 269.
46 The date of *Filostrato* is uncertain. Joseph Wood Krutch ("Boccaccio," *Five Masters* [New York: J. Cape and H. Smith, 1930], p. 30) dates both the *Teseide* and the *Filostrato* before 1344 — while the author was still in Naples; Garnett (p. 91) dates the *Teseide* about 1341, the *Filostrato* about 1347.
47 Snell, p. 268.
48 Sellery, p. 78
49 Symonds, *Italian Literature*, I, 123.
50 Garnett, p. 93.
51 Sellery, p. 84.
52 Sellery, p. 87.
53 Symonds, *Italian Literature*, I, 135.
54 Fletcher, p. 95.
55 Symonds, *Italian Literature*, I, 103.
56 Garnett, p. 96.
57 Snell, p. 274.
58 Fletcher, p. 142.
59 The adjective was added to the original title of *Morgante* when Pulci added five extra cantos.
60 Fletcher, p. 148.
61 The usual date given for Boiardo's birth is 1434. Sellery (p. 113) and Fletcher (p. 154) give 1441; the latter historian cites Vittorio Rossi as his authority for the later date.
62 Symonds, *Italian Literature*, I, 478.
63 Symonds, *Italian Literature*, I, 479.
64 Symonds, *Italian Literature*, I, 464.
65 Symonds, *Italian Literature*, II, 9.

66 Everett, p. 83.   Perhaps this censure and that by Foligno and Sellery in the following paragraph is unjustly harsh.
67 Cesare Foligno, *Epochs of Italian Literature* (Oxford: Clarendon Press, 1926), p. 23.
68 P. 119.
69 Symonds, *Italian Literature*, II, 18.
70 Symonds, *Italian Literature*, II, 49.
71 Symonds, *Italian Literature*, II, 18.
72 Symonds, *Italian Literature*, II, 10.
73 Symonds, *Italian Literature*, II, 42.
74 P. 79.
75 Fletcher, p. 241.
76 Fletcher, p. 172.
77 Cesare Foligno, "Renaissance Literature," *Italy, a Companion to Italian Studies*, ed. Edmund G. Gardner (London: Methuen and Co., 1934), p. 99.
78 Sellery, p. 45.
79 Fletcher, p. 194.   The phrase means "arbiter of elegance."
80 Fletcher, p. 197.
81 Fletcher, p. 198.
82 Fletcher, p. 270.
83 Fletcher, pp. 288–289.   As Fletcher points out, the word *farce* (*farci*) derivatively means "stuffing."
84 Fletcher, p. 290.
85 Fletcher, p. 295.
86 Fletcher, p. 303.   The old belief that Tasso's mental disturbances were caused by an unrequited love for Leonora, sister of Duke Alfonso, and by cruelty at the hands of the Duke himself has been proved entirely false.
87 Garnett, p. 234.
88 Symonds, *Italian Literature*, II, 242.
89 Garnett, p. 249.
90 Everett, p. 110.
91 Everett, p. 111.

Notes to Chapter 2

1 The pope signed no formal treaty with Victor Emmanuel, and the papacy remained in a state of semihostility with Italy till 1929, when the Treaty of the Lateran gave the pope sovereignty over Vatican City; he renounced his temporal claims on all other territory.
2 Cesare Foligno, *Epochs of Italian Literature* (Oxford: Clarendon Press, 1926), p. 33.
3 Foligno, p. 35.
4 Foligno, p. 71.
5 Richard Garnett, *A History of Italian Literature* (New York: D. Appleton & Co., 1898), p. 323.
6 Levi Oscar Kuhns, *The Great Poets of Italy* (Boston: Houghton Mifflin Co., 1904), p. 262.
7 Lacy Collison-Morley, *Modern Italian Literature* (Boston: Little, Brown and Co., 1912), p. 72.
8 Foligno, p. 41.
9 Collison-Morley, p. 126.
10 Kuhns, p. 266.   The last sentence of the quotation is misleading inasmuch as Dante, Machiavelli, and others had long before dreamed of a united Italy.

11 Collison-Morley, p. 133.
12 Kuhns, p. 265.
13 See I Samuel 18–31.
14 Collison-Morley, p. 191.
15 Collison-Morley, p. 199.
16 Collison-Morley, p. 195.
17 Garnett, p. 348.
18 Collison-Morley, p. 210.
19 Collison-Morley, p. 229.
20 Kuhns, p. 292.
21 Kuhns, p. 293.
22 Kuhns, p. 292.
23 Collison-Morley, pp. 280–281.
24 Collison-Morley, pp. 328–329.
25 Garnett, p. 405.
26 Kuhns, p. 330.
27 Camillo Pellizzi, "Italy from 1870 to the Fascist Revolution," *Italy, A Companion to Italian Studies*, ed. Edmund G. Gardner (London: Methuen and Co., 1934), p. 250.
28 Collison-Morley, p. 334.
29 Pellizzi, p. 251.
30 Domenico Vittorini, *The Drama of Luigi Pirandello* (Philadelphia: University of Pennsylvania Press, 1935), p. 26.
31 *Italian Silhouettes* (New York: A. A. Knopf, 1924), pp. 119, 126–127.
32 P. 37.
33 *The Contemporary Drama of Italy* (Boston: Little, Brown, and Co., 1920), pp. 220–221.
34 Quoted by Phelps, p. 139.
35 Vittorini, p. 26.
36 Pp. xi–xiii.

Notes to Chapter 3

1 For a discussion of the origins and elements of the Renaissance, see pp. 3–6.
2 Paraphrased by Kathleen T. Butler, *A History of French Literature* (New York: E. P. Dutton & Co., 1923), I, 97.
3 Butler, p. 104.
4 Now known as the Collège de France.
5 Butler, I, 100.
6 P. 89.
7 Quoted (in French) by William A. Nitze and E. Preston Dargan, *A History of French Literature*, 3rd ed. (New York: H. Holt and Co., 1950), p. 150.
8 Butler, I, 112.
9 Nitze and Dargan, p. 152.
10 George Saintsbury, *French Literature and Its Masters*, ed. Huntington Cairns (New York: A. A. Knopf, 1946), p. 17.
11 Nitze and Dargan, p. 152.
12 Saintsbury, p. 18.
13 "The first of our books which one can call classic" (Butler, I, 109).
14 Butler, I, 110.
15 Nitze and Dargan, p. 179.
16 Nitze and Dargan, p. 179.

17 C. H. C. Wright, *A History of French Literature* (New York: Oxford University Press, 1925), p. 191.
18 George Saintsbury, *A Short History of French Literature*, 5th ed. (Oxford: Clarendon Press, 1897), p. 172.
19 Nitze and Dargan, p. 183.
20 Butler, I, 137.
21 Translated by Spenser with the title *The Ruines of Rome*.
22 "The Author to the Reader," quoted (in French) by Butler, I, 160.
23 Butler, I, 147.
24 Butler, I, 150.
25 Nitze and Dargan, p. 244.
26 I, 150.

Notes to Chapter 4

1 Stanley H. Schwarz, *An Outline History of French Literature* (New York: A. A. Knopf, 1921), p. 62.
2 Kathleen T. Butler, *A History of French Literature* (New York: E. P. Dutton & Co., 1923), I, 247.
3 J. B. Bury, quoted by Butler, I, 306.
4 William A. Nitze and E. Preston Dargan, *A History of French Literature*, 3rd ed. (New York: H. Holt and Co., 1950), p. 258.
5 Butler, I, 206.
6 *"Le sujet d'une belle tragédie, doit n'être pas vraisemblable"* (Preface to *Heraclius*).
7 Butler, I, 209.
8 Butler, I, 204.
9 Nitze and Dargan, p. 320.
10 Giles Lytton Strachey, *Landmarks in French Literature* (New York: Oxford University Press, 1912), p. 99.
11 Strachey, p. 106.
12 Nitze and Dargan, p. 316.
13 Quoted by C. H. C. Wright, *A History of French Literature* (New York: Oxford University Press, 1925), p. 354.
14 Nitze and Dargan, p. 318.
15 Nitze and Dargan, p. 318.
16 P. 320.
17 P. 359.
18 *A Short History of French Literature* (Oxford: Clarendon Press, 1897), p. 276.
19 *French Literature and Its Masters*, ed. Huntington Cairns (New York: A. A. Knopf, 1946), pp. 81–82.
20 Schwarz, p. 66.
21 Strachey, p. 102.
22 Strachey, p. 109.
23 *"L'affaire de la comédie est de représenter en général tous les défauts des hommes, et principalement des hommes de notre siècle"* (quoted by Wright, p. 368).
24 Wright, p. 375.
25 Title as translated by Stith Thompson and John Gassner, *Our Heritage of World Literature* (New York: Dryden Press, 1942), p. 663. The French title virtually defies literal translation.
26 Wright, p. 372.
27 Nitze and Dargan, p. 295.
28 Strachey, p. 88.
29 P. 297.
30 Wright, p. 373.

31 Nitze and Dargan, p. 297.
32 Nitze and Dargan, p. 304.
33 Butler, I, 273.
34 Edward Dowden, *A History of French Literature* (New York: D. Appleton and Co., 1898), p. 193.
35 Strachey, p. 113.

Notes to Chapter 5

1 Kathleen T. Butler, *A History of French Literature* (New York: E. P. Dutton & Co., 1921), I, 348.
2 Butler, I, 350.
3 Classification by Butler, I, 413–423.
4 Butler, I, 429.
5 Butler, I, 383.
6 H. Stanley Schwarz, *An Outline History of French Literature* (New York: A. A. Knopf, 1924), p. 84.
7 Butler, I, 388.
8 C. H. C. Wright, *A History of French Literature* (New York: Oxford University Press, 1925), p. 514.
9 Wright, pp. 514–515.
10 Wright, p. 515.
11 Wright, p. 515.
12 George Saintsbury, *A Short History of French Literature* (Oxford: Clarenden Press, 1897), p. 395.
13 Butler, I, 389.
14 Edward Dowden, *A History of French Literature* (New York: D. Appleton and Co., 1898), p. 292.
15 "*Il faut cultiver notre jardin.*"
16 Saintsbury, pp. 395–396.
17 Butler, I, 386.
18 William A. Nitze and E. Preston Dargan, *A History of French Literature*, 3rd ed. (New York: H. Holt and Co., 1950), p. 491.
19 Nitze and Dargan, p. 492.
20 Nitze and Dargan, p. 492.

Notes to Chapter 6

1 C. H. C. Wright, *A History of French Literature* (New York: Oxford University Press, 1925), p. 647.
2 Kathleen T. Butler, *A History of French Literature* (New York: E. P. Dutton & Co., 1923), II, 19.
3 Butler, II, 15.
4 Butler, II, 16.
5 Giles Lytton Strachey, *Landmarks in French Literature* (New York: Oxford University Press, 1912), pp. 203–204. See also Butler, II, 25.
6 Butler, II, 24.
7 William A. Nitze and E. Preston Dargan, *A History of French Literature*, 3rd ed. (New York: H. Holt and Co., 1950), p. 511.
8 Nitze and Dargan, p. 511.
9 Butler, II, 21.
10 Butler, II, 22.
11 Nitze and Dargan, p. 515.
12 Strachey, p. 204.

13 Émile Faguet, *A Literary History of France* (New York: Charles Scribner's Sons, 1907), p. 558.
14 Nitze and Dargan, p. 507.
15 Butler, II, 25.
16 Edward Dowden, *A History of French Literature* (New York: D. Appleton and Co., 1898), p. 353.
17 Wright, p. 716.
18 Butler, II, 117.
19 Wright, p. 718.
20 Nitze and Dargan, p. 575.
21 Faguet, p. 573.
22 Butler, II, 77.
23 Nitze and Dargan, p. 533.
24 Quoted (in French) by Butler, II, 75.
25 Butler, II, 91.
26 Butler, II, 90.
27 Nitze and Dargan, p. 548.
28 Butler, II, 111.
29 Nitze and Dargan, p. 540.
30 Nitze and Dargan, p. 542.
31 Butler, II, 81–82.
32 Butler, II, 85.
33 Nitze and Dargan, p. 558.
34 Butler, II, 108–109.
35 Butler, II, 109.
36 Strachey, p. 216.
37 Strachey, p. 214.
38 Pp. 377–378.
39 Nitze and Dargan, p. 543.
40 Butler, II, 87.
41 Dowden, p. 377.
42 Saintsbury, p. 503.
43 Nitze and Dargan, p. 544.
44 Nitze and Dargan, p. 561.
45 Dowden, p. 386.
46 Nitze and Dargan, p. 559.
47 Nitze and Dargan, p. 560.
48 Butler, II, 110.
49 Faguet, pp. 570–571.
50 Nitze and Dargan, p. 571.
51 Butler, II, 125.
52 P. 575.
53 Pp. 157–176. Michelet (quoted, in French, by Butler, II, 171) says: "Augustin Thierry has called history narration; Guizot, *analysis;* and I call it *resurrection.*"
54 Butler, II, 159.
55 Butler, II, 179.

Notes to Chapter 7

1 Kathleen T. Butler, *A History of French Literature* (New York: E. P. Dutton & Co., 1923), II, 206–207.
2 Butler, II, 206–207.
3 Butler, II, 227–228.

4 Butler, II, 235.
5 For the view that realism is simply a branch or outgrowth of romanticism, see Butler, II, 195–196.
6 The *de* was inserted by Balzac himself; it is misleading inasmuch as his family did not belong to the aristocracy.
7 H. Stanley Schwarz, *An Outline History of French Literature* (New York: A. A. Knopf, 1924), p. 111.
8 William A. Nitze and E. Preston Dargan, *A History of French Literature*, 3rd ed. (New York: H. Holt and Co., 1950), p. 587.
9 Nitze and Dargan, p. 587.
10 Quoted (in French) by Butler, II, 137.
11 Nitze and Dargan, pp. 591–592.
12 Nitze and Dargan, p. 591.
13 Giles Lytton Strachey, *Landmarks in French Literature* (New York: Oxford University Press, 1912), p. 225.
14 Strachey, p. 228.
15 Butler, II, 139.
16 Nitze and Dargan, p. 593.
17 C. H. C. Wright, *A History of French Literature* (New York: Oxford University Press, 1925), p. 712.
18 Butler, II, 119.
19 P. 410.
20 George Saintsbury, *A Short History of French Literature*, 5th ed., rev. (Oxford: Clarendon Press, 1897), pp. 515–516.
21 Nitze and Dargan, p. 616.
22 Pp. 761–762.
23 Nitze and Dargan, p. 617.
24 Strachey, p. 239.
25 Saintsbury, pp. 562–563.
26 Nitze and Dargan, p. 625.
27 Nitze and Dargan, p. 626.
28 Butler, II, 252.
29 Wright, p. 772.
30 Nitze and Dargan, p. 633.
31 Nitze and Dargan, p. 621.
32 Nitze and Dargan, p. 620.
33 *Guy de Maupassant* (New York: A. A. Knopf, 1926), p. 134.
34 Strachey, p. 244.
35 Quoted (in French) by Butler, II, 259.
36 Butler, II, 263.
37 A second and a third series were issued in 1871 and 1876, respectively.
38 Butler, II, 265.
39 Butler, II, 275.
40 Nitze and Dargan, p. 602.
41 A. Barre, *Le Symbolisme*, quoted (in French) by Butler, II, 302.
42 Nitze and Dargan, p. 603.
43 Butler, II, 304.
44 Quoted (in French) by Butler, II, 311.
45 II, 311.
46 Pp. 244–245.
47 Butler, II, 306.
48 Nitze and Dargan, p. 706.
49 Butler, II, 308.

50 Nitze and Dargan, p. 706.
51 Nitze and Dargan, p. 708.
52 Butler, II, 316.
53 Butler, II, 279.
54 Butler, II, 320.

Notes to Chapter 8

1 Kathleen T. Butler, *A History of French Literature* (New York: E. P. Dutton & Co., 1923), II, 323–324.
2 H. Stanley Schwarz, *An Outline History of French Literature* (New York: A. A. Knopf, 1924), p. 129.
3 William A. Nitze and E. Preston Dargan, *A History of French Literature*, 3rd. ed. (New York: H. Holt and Co., 1950), p. 694.
4 Quoted (in French) by Butler, II, 326.
5 Nitze and Dargan, p. 787.
6 Edward H. Weatherly and Others, *The Heritage of European Literature* (Boston: Ginn & Co., 1949), II, 691.
7 The English titles of the whole cycle and of each book (except the last one) are those used by Charles Scott-Moncrieff, who took the title for the cycle from Shakespeare's Sonnet XXX, 1–2.
8 Nitze and Dargan, p. 789.
9 Nitze and Dargan, p. 790.
10 C. H. C. Wright, *A History of French Literature* (New York: Oxford University Press, 1925), p. 879.
11 Butler, II, 328.
12 Butler, II, 328.
13 Van Meter Ames, *André Gide* (New York: New Directions, 1947), p. 143.
14 Ames, p. 143.
15 The English translation of the work bears the title *Beethoven the Creator*.
16 Nitze and Dargan, p. 785. This identification is part of his "unanimism" (see Romains, p 147).
17 Wallace Fowlie, *Clowns and Angels: Studies in Modern French Literature* (New York: Sheed and Ward, 1943), p. 62.
18 Denis Saurat, *Modern French Literature, 1870–1940* (New York: G. P. Putnam's Sons, 1946), p. 122.
19 Saurat, p. 122.
20 Nitze and Dargan, p. 781.
21 Butler, II, 340.
22 Nitze and Dargan, p. 759.
23 Nitze and Dargan, p. 760.
24 Mary Duclaux, *Twentieth Century French Writers* (London: W. Collins Sons and Co., 1919), p. 98.
25 Butler, II, 338.
26 Florian-Parmentier, quoted (in French) by Nitze and Dargan, p. 745.
27 Nitze and Dargan, pp. 800–801.
28 Wright, p. 895.

Notes to Chapter 9

1 According to most literary historians, the Renaissance in Spain extended from 1469 to about 1580 (the date of the beginning of the literary activity of Lope de Vega and Cervantes). The death of Calderón (1681) marks the end of the Golden Age (*El Siglo de Oro*). George Tyler Northup (*An Introduction to Spanish Literature* [Chicago: University of Chicago Press, 1925],

p. 124) suggests 1444 as a more logical date for the beginning of the Renaissance; that is the year in which Juan de Mena (1411–1465) published *The Labyrinth of Fortune* (*El laberinto de Fortuna*).   Inasmuch as several literary forms had reached a high degree of perfection before 1580, the distinction between the Renaissance and the Golden Age seems artificial and unnecessary.

2 Ferdinand did not succeed his father, Juan II, as king of Aragón till 1479. After Isabella's death in 1504 till his own in 1516, he was regent of Castile and León.   The three territories were not politically united till the accession of Charles I in 1516.

3 Ernest Mérimée, *A History of Spanish Literature*, tr. and rev. by S. Griswold Morley (New York: H. Holt and Co., 1930), p. 93.

4 The first of the Hapsburg rulers.   He was crowned Emperor Charles V of the Holy Roman Empire in 1519.

5 Barcelona in 1450, Valencia in 1499, Alcalá in 1508, and Sevilla in 1509.

6 For a list of some important later collections, see Jeremiah D. M. Ford, *Main Currents of Spanish Literature* (New York: H. Holt and Co., 1925), p. 48, and Northup, p. 214.

7 Northup, p. 134.

8 Northup, p. 137.

9 Mérimée, p. 266.

10 The term is Northup's (p. 160).

11 The earliest extant edition is dated 1499, but there are reasons to believe that there was a still earlier edition which has been lost.   Enlarged editions appeared in 1501, 1502, and 1526; these are said to be the work of Fernando de Rojas of Montalbán (*c.* 1475–1537).   For the disputed questions of authorship and texts, see Mérimée, pp. 141–142 and Northup, pp. 163–164.

12 The 1501 edition is entitled *The Comedy of Calisto and Melibea* (*Comedia de Calysto y Melybea*); later editions call it a tragicomedy.

13 Mérimée, p. 140.

14 Northup, p. 165.

15 P. 202.

16 P. 168.

17 Its simultaneous appearance in three places indicates an earlier (now lost) edition.

18 There is no hint of dishonesty — only incompetence.

19 The name is thought to be a pseudonym.   Many attempts to identify Avellaneda, however, have failed.

20 Joseph Wood Krutch, *Five Masters* (New York: J. Cape and H. Smith, 1930), p. 77.

21 P. 254.

22 James Fitzmaurice-Kelly, *A History of Spanish Literature* (New York: D. Appleton and Co., 1921), pp. 232–233.

23 Northup, 257.

24 See Northup, p. 229.

25 The dates of many of his works are uncertain.   It is believed that most of his best known dramas were written while he was in Italy between 1500 and 1519.   See Mérimée, p. 145.

26 Northup, p. 231.

27 All but two of Torres' comedies were published in his *Propaladia* (1517).

28 Northup, p. 233.

29 Northup, p. 275.

30 Mérimée, p. 251

31 Northup, p. 267.
32 Pp. 339–340.
33 Translation given by George Ticknor, *History of Spanish Literature*, 4th ed. (Boston: Houghton, Osgood & Co., 1879), II, 258.
34 Interpretation derived from a lecture at Harvard University by Professor Renato Poggioli, February, 1953.
35 Northup, p. 277.
36 Ticknor, II, 305.
37 Mérimée, p. 344.
38 Ticknor, II, 316.
39 Northup, p. 277.
40 Ford's translation, p. 141.
41 Ballads and folklore indicate that Don Juan may have been a historical personage, but Tirso "fixed it [the type] brilliantly and definitively as a dramatic figure" (Mérimée, p. 355).
42 Pp. 281–282.
43 Quoted by Mérimée, p. 355.
44 P. 356.
45 Northup, p. 280.
46 Unauthorized editions contained twenty-four. See Mérimée, p. 357.
47 Mérimée, p. 358.
48 For a discussion of the number and authenticity of his dramas, see Mérimée, p. 374.
49 Pp. 160–161. For a different categorization, see Mérimée, p. 374.
50 Mérimée, p. 376.
51 Ford, p. 166.
52 Northup, p. 193.
53 Mérimée, p. 267.
54 Quoted by Mérimée, p. 268.

Notes to Chapter 10

1 George Tyler Northup, *An Introduction to Spanish Literature* (Chicago: University of Chicago Press, 1925), p. 344.
2 Northup, p. 368.
3 Northup, pp. 399–400.

Notes to Chapter 11

1 George Madison Priest, *A Brief History of German Literature* (New York: Charles Scribner's Sons, 1932), p. 72.
2 Desiderius Erasmus, *In Praise of Folly* (New York: Peter Smith, 1941), p. 46.
3 Priest, p. 76.
4 Edward H. Weatherly and Others, *The Heritage of European Literature* (Boston: Ginn & Co., 1948), I, 688.
5 Calvin Thomas, *A History of German Literature* (New York: D. Appleton and Co., 1909), p. 143.

Notes to Chapter 12

1 George Madison Priest, *A Brief History of German Literature* (New York: Charles Scribner's Sons, 1932), p. 95. The title is also Priest's translation.
2 Calvin Thomas, *A History of German Literature* (New York: D. Appleton and Co., 1909), p. 198.
3 Thomas, p. 200.

Notes to Chapter 13

1 Edward H. Weatherly and Others, *The Heritage of European Literature* (Boston: Ginn and Co., 1949), II, 7.
2 George Madison Priest, *A Brief History of German Literature* (New York: Charles Scribner's Sons, 1932), p. 123.
3 Priest, p. 113.
4 Priest, p. 101.
5 Priest, p. 158.
6 Priest, p. 159.
7 Quoted (in German) by John G. Robertson, *A History of German Literature,* rev. ed. (Edinburgh: Blackwood, 1949), p. 289.
8 Calvin Thomas, *A History of German Literature* (New York: D. Appleton and Co., 1909), p. 235.
9 Priest, p. 149. Priest's words are almost a translation of Lessing's subtitle, *"ein bürgerliches Trauerspiel."* W. P. Friederich disagrees that this is the first bourgeois tragedy and claims that *Cardenio and Celinde* (Ch. 12) is.
10 Robertson, p. 279.
11 As quoted by Priest, p. 150.
12 Robertson, p. 279.
13 Priest, p. 143.
14 P. 148.
15 Robertson, p. 286.
16 L. A. Willoughby, *The Classical Age of German Literature, 1748–1805* (Oxford: Oxford University Press, 1926), p. 52.
17 Willoughby, p. 52.
18 Willoughby, p. 60.
19 Priest's translation of the German title, p. 161.
20 Willoughby, pp. 54–55.
21 Priest, p. 164.
22 Priest, p. 167.
23 Priest, p. 130.
24 Robertson, p. 265.
25 Priest, p. 181.
26 The sincerity of Goethe's remorse has been questioned. See, for example, William Cleaver Wilkinson, *German Classics in English* (New York: Funk and Wagnalls Co., 1900), pp. 165–169.
27 Karl Viëtor, *Goethe: The Poet,* tr. Moses Hadas (Cambridge, Mass.: Harvard University Press, 1949), p. 108.
28 P. 199.
29 See pp. 160–221, *passim.* Wilkinson is prejudiced and does not thoroughly understand Goethe.
30 Quoted by Wilkinson, p. 177.
31 Robertson, p. 374.
32 P. 196.
33 Wilhelm Scherer, *A History of German Literature,* tr. Mrs. F. C. Conybeare, 3rd ed. (New York: Charles Scribner's Sons, 1899), II, 322, says that Faust's "repentance falls between the first and second parts of the (book." Wilkinson disagrees and thinks that Faust never repents — that he remains an "irredeemable egoist" (p. 220) to the end.
34 Robertson, p. 448.
35 Weatherly and Others, II, 8.
36 Stith Thompson and John Gassner, *Our Heritage of World Literature* (New York: Dryden Press, 1942), p. 808.

37 P. 320.
38 *Modern German Literature* (Boston: Roberts Brothers, 1897), p. 181.
39 P. 200.
40 Quoted by Wells, p. 111.
41 "Memorial Verses, April 1850."
42 P. 316.
43 P. 451.
44 Quoted by Wilkinson, p. 208.
45 Priest, p. 230.
46 Willoughby, p. 107.
47 Willoughby, p. 109.
48 Priest, p. 234.
49 *A Short History of German Literature*, rev. ed. (New York: Charles Scribner's Sons, 1910), pp. 414–415.
50 P. 264.
51 P. 395.

Notes to Chapter 14

1 George Madison Priest, *A Brief History of German Literature* (New York: Charles Scribner's Sons, 1932), p. 246.
2 John G. Robertson, *A History of German Literature*, rev. ed. (Edinburgh: Blackwood, 1949), p. 425.
3 The first volume of *Capital* was published in 1867; the last two volumes edited by Engels, were brought out in 1885 and 1895 respectively.
4 Priest, p. 245.
5 Edward H. Weatherly and Others, *The Heritage of European Literature* (Boston: Ginn & Co., 1949), II, 270.
6 Robertson, p. 406.
7 P. 467.
8 Robertson, p. 503.
9 Robertson, p. 500.
10 Weatherly and Others, II, 277.
11 Priest, p. 272.
12 Calvin Thomas, *A History of German Literature* (New York: D. Appleton & Co., 1909), p. 362.
13 Robertson, pp. 533–534.
14 Priest's translation, p. 248.
15 Priest, p. 255.
16 Robertson, p. 431.
17 Thomas, p. 350. Other critics disagree with Thomas; one commentator calls it "awful."
18 Robertson, p. 432.
19 Priest's translation, p. 279.
20 Thomas, p. 372.
21 Priest, p. 278.
22 Priest, p. 242.
23 Robertson, p. 403.
24 Quoted (in French) by Robertson, p. 477.
25 Thomas, p. 396.
26 Robertson, p. 557.
27 Priest's free translation (p. 302); the literal rendering is "From the Rain into the Trough."
28 Otto Heller, *Henrik Ibsen: Plays and Problems* (Boston: Houghton Mifflin Co., 1912), p. 106.

29 Compare Sophocles' *Oedipus the King*.
30 Heller, p. 183.
31 The very important problem of Ibsen's symbolism is too complex to be discussed adequately here. For further comment, see Heller, pp. 188–189 and 270; Jenette Lee, *The Ibsen Secret* (New York: G. P. Putnam's Sons, 1907), pp. 37–138; and Montrose J. Moses, *Henrik Ibseb: The Man and His Plays* (New York: M. Kennerley, 1908), pp. 439–469.
32 See Heller, p. 188.
33 Weatherly and Others, II, 366.
34 Heller, p. 110.
35 For discussions of this question, see Heller, pp. 110, 135, 202–208, and 316; Lee, pp. 179–207; Weatherly and Others, II, 366; and Herman J. Weigand, *The Modern Ibsen: A Reconsideration* (New York: H. Holt and Co., 1925), pp. 403–404.
36 See Weatherly and Others, II, 366; Lee, pp. 114–125; Moses, pp. 470–482; Heller, pp. 269–286; and Weigand, pp. 274–309.
37 See Lee, pp. 161–207; Heller, pp. 308–322; Moses, pp. 492–498; Weigand, pp. 378–410; and Theodore Jorgenson, *Henrik Ibsen: A Study in Art and Personality* (Northfield, Minn.: St. Olaf College Press, 1945), pp. 501–515.
38 Priest, p. 326.
39 Otto Heller, *Studies in Modern German Literature* (Boston: Ginn & Co., 1905), p. 31.
40 Robertson, p. 490.
41 Priest's translation, p. 303.
42 P. 571.
43 P. 389.

Notes to Chapter 15

1 John G. Robertson, *A History of German Literature*, rev. ed. (Edinburgh: Blackwood, 1949), p. 607.
2 Edward H. Weatherly and Others, *The Heritage of European Literature* (Boston: Ginn & Co., 1949), II, 641.
3 Robertson, p. 622. George Madison Priest, *A Brief History of German Literature* (New York: Charles Scribner's Sons, 1932), p. 327, says that George "had an aristocratic aversion to real life. . . ."
4 Weatherly and Others, II, 641.
5 Priest's translation, p. 327.
6 Robertson, p. 623.
7 Victor Lange, *Modern German Literature, 1870–1940* (Ithaca, N. Y.: Cornell University Press, 1945), p. 39.
8 Lange, p. 70.
9 Richard Samuel and R. Hinton Thomas, *Expressionism in German Life, Literature and the Theater* (Cambridge, England: W. Heffer and Sons, 1939), p. 14.
10 Samuel and Thomas, p. 39.
11 Lange, p. 120.
12 Lange, p. 100.
13 Pp. 88–89.
14 Literally, "*Nothing New in the West.*"
15 Lange, p. 73.
16 Pp. 73 and 74.
17 P. 637.

18 *The Reader's Encyclopedia* (New York: Thomas Y. Crowell Co., 1948), IV, 1190.
19 Comment made to the author of this outline.
20 Weatherly and Others, II, 646.
21 Bayard Q. Morgan's translation, quoted by Weatherly and Others, II, 658.
22 Benét, III, 673.
23 Benét, II, 567.
24 P. 86
25 Quoted by Samuel and Thomas, pp. 38–39.
26 Robertson, p. 635.

Notes to Chapter 16

1 Isabel F. Hapgood, *A Survey of Russian Literature, with Selections* (New York: Chautauqua Press, 1902), p. 1.
2 So it has been styled by K. Waliszewski, *A History of Russian Literature* (New York: D. Appleton & Co., 1900), p. 47, and others.   In Russia's case, however, the event is perhaps more accurately termed a mere "birth" than a "rebirth."
3 Edward H. Weatherly and Others, *The Heritage of European Literature* (Boston: Ginn & Co., 1949), II, 55.
4 D. S. Mirsky, *A History of Russian Literature*.   Edited and abridged by Francis J. Whitfield (New York: A. A. Knopf, 1949), p. 40.
5 Mirsky, p. 42.
6 Leo Tolstoy continued to write for several years after the end of this period, but most of the work on which his reputation is built was published before 1883.
7 Stith Thompson and John Gassner, *Our Heritage of World Literature* (New York: Dryden Press, 1942), p. 909.
8 Mirsky, p. 224.
9 Mirsky, p. 90.
10 P. Kropotkin, *Russian Literature* (New York: McClure, Phillips and Co., 1905), p. 47.   Waliszewski (p. 164) dissents and says: "The subject is like those landscapes on the steppes, into which God put so little and in which men who know how to dream can see so much."
11 Mirsky, p. 91.
12 Kropotkin, p. 40.
13 P. 177.
14 Moissaye J. Olgin, *A Guide to Russian Literature* (1820–1917) (New York: Harcourt, Brace and Howe, 1920), p. 14.
15 *The Golden Age of Russian Literature*, rev. ed. (Caldwell, Idaho: Caxton Printers, 1943), p. 30.
16 Weatherly and Others, II, 418.
17 Mirsky, p. 134.
18 Quoted by Kropotkin, p. 58.
19 Olgin, p. 26.
20 P. 149.
21 Olgin, pp. 42–43.
22 Mirsky, p. 148.
23 Weatherly and Others, II, 443.
24 Olgin, p. 46.
25 Spector, p. 92.
26 A. E. Gruzinsky (quoted by Olgin, p. 81), Olgin himself (p. 81), and Spector (p. 106) think he succeeded.   Mirsky (p. 195) disagrees and calls the novel

"a complete failure" because Turgenev had been out of the country and did not know what he was writing about.

27 Mirsky, p. 175.
28 Spector, p. 114.
29 Mirsky, p. 278.
30 William Lyon Phelps, *Essays on Russian Novelists* (New York: Macmillan Co., 1926), p. 141.
31 Phelps, pp. 140 and 169.
32 Spector, p. 158.
33 Spector, p. 159.   Spector goes on to show that Tolstoy's philanthropy and whole ethical scheme are founded on selfishness — that the ultimate aim of his humanitarian and spiritual endeavors is his own "inner peace."
34 Mirsky, pp. 252–253.
35 Mirsky, p. 251.
36 Many of the facts and opinions about this novel and *Anna Karenina* have been drawn from a series of lectures given in a survey of Russian literature by Professor Michael Karpovich at Harvard University in the spring term, 1953.
37 Spector, p. 166.
38 Karpovich.
39 P. 198.
40 Kropotkin, p. 148.
41 Mirsky, p. 246.

Notes to Chapter 17

1 Moissaye J. Olgin, *A Guide to Russian Literature (1820–1917)* (New York: Harcourt, Brace and Howe, 1920), p. 153.
2 Quoted by William Lyon Phelps, *Essays on Russian Novelists* (New York: Macmillan Co., 1926), p. 236.
3 P. Kropotkin, *Russian Literature* (New York: McClure, Phillips and Co., 1905), p. 315.
4 Phelps, p. 247.
5 Ivar Spector, *The Golden Age of Russian Literature*, rev. ed. (Caldwell, Idaho: Caxton Printers, 1943), p. 246.
6 Olgin, p. 224.
7 Phelps, p. 221.
8 P. 215.

Notes to Chapter 18

1 This chapter is based in part on Edward H. Weatherly and Others, *The Heritage of European Literature* (Boston: Ginn & Co., 1949), II, 710–766.
2 Gleb Struve, *Soviet Russian Literature, 1917–50* (Norman, Oklahoma: University of Oklahoma Press, 1951), p. 66.
3 Weatherly and Others, II, 711–712.
4 Published earlier in four volumes, 1928–1940.
5 P. 131.
6 *The Golden Age of Russian Literature* (Caldwell, Idaho: Caxton Printers, 1943), p. 257.
7 Struve, p. 153.

Quiz and Examination Questions

Quiz and Examination Questions

[The following questions may perhaps be found useful as a study-guide to students and as a list from which teachers may select questions for quizzes and examinations. Discussion Questions 1–93 and Definitions and Identifications 1–100 cover the literary works discussed on pages 3–153 of the text. Discussion Questions 94–200 and Definitions and Identifications 101–200 cover the works discussed on pages 154–301 of the text. This division may prove convenient in preparing separately for a mid-term test and for the final examination.]

Part A. Discussions

Write an essay on each of the following topics. *Think* before you *write*. Use only complete sentences. Illustrate your discussions whenever possible with direct references to (or quotations from) the literary works under consideration.

1. The "constituent elements" of the Renaissance.
2. The meaning of Renaissance humanism.
3. The relationship between the Renaissance and the Reformation.
4. The course of Petrarch's love for Laura as reflected in *The Song-Book*.
5. The identity of Petrarch's Laura.
6. Reasons why Petrarch has been called "the first humanist" and "the first modern man."
7. The patriotism of Petrarch.
8. The literary characteristics of Petrarch's sonnets.
9. Autobiography in Boccaccio's *Filocolo* and *Filostrato*.
10. Plan, tone, style, and humor of *The Decameron*.
11. The origin of the romantic epic in Italy.
12. The significance of Pulci's *The Greater Morgante*.
13. A comparison and contrast of Boiardo's treatment of Orlando's love affair with the treatment by Ariosto.
14. The main themes of Ariosto's *Orlando Insane*.
15. Sannazaro and the pastoral romance in Renaissance Italy.
16. Machiavelli's political philosophy as set forth in *The Prince*.
17. The morality or immorality of Machiavelli's *The Prince*.
18. Castiglione's portrait of the perfect courtier — the "universal man."
19. Characteristics of Italian pastoral drama.
20. Characteristics and importance of the *commedia dell' arte*.
21. Theme and plot of Tasso's *Jerusalem Delivered*.
22. Criticism of *Jerusalem Delivered* as a romantic epic.
23. Subject matter and literary characteristics of Alfieri's tragedies.
24. Theme and philosophical implications of Manzoni's novel *The Betrothed*.

25. Compare the attitudes of Leopardi with those of Keats concerning love, beauty, and happiness.
26. The combination in Leopardi of classicism and romanticism.
27. Carducci's humanism.
28. The combination of primitivism and decadence in D'Annunzio's works.
29. *Six Characters in Search of an Author* as an embodiment of Pirandello's philosophy and as an example of his dramatic method.
30. Genesis and publication of Rabelais' works.
31. The meaning of *Pantagruelism*.
32. Rules and ideals of the Abbey of Thélème.
33. Merits and shortcomings of Rabelais' works.
34. Contents and significance of *The Defense and Glorification of the French Language*.
35. Evaluation of the poetry of Ronsard.
36. Montaigne's mental attitude as shown in his *Essays*.
37. Nature of French tragedy before 1600.
38. The importance of the *salon* for French literature during the seventeenth century.
39. The meaning of *Jansenism*.
40. Malherbe's influence on French literature in the early seventeenth century.
41. Boileau's role in effecting the triumph of neoclassicism in France.
42. The dramatic theories of Corneille.
43. The significance of the "Quarrel of *The Cid*."
44. Racine's techniques as an author of tragedy.
45. Comparison of the dramatic theories and techniques of Corneille with those of Racine.
46. Evaluation of Racine as an author of tragedy.
47. Molière's attacks on the hypocrisy of the medical profession.
48. Molière's attacks on the affectation of the literary *salons*.
49. *The Miser* as a satire on avarice and parental autocracy.
50. *Tartuffe* as an attack on religious hypocrisy.
51. Merits and defects of Molière's comedies.
52. La Fontaine's transformation of the fable into a satirical *conte*.
53. Voltaire's theory of history.
54. Voltaire's religion.
55. *Candide* as an attack on Leibnizian optimism.
56. Rousseau's fundamental doctrine concerning the nature of man.
57. Rousseau's socio-political beliefs.
58. Rousseau's theories about education.
59. Rousseau's theories about religion.
60. The significance of Madame de Staël as a literary critic.
61. Romanticism in Chateaubriand's works.
62. Comparison of Chateaubriand's René with Goethe's Werther.
63. Chateaubriand as a religious author.
64. George Sand's debt to Rousseau for her theories about love.

65. Topics, characteristics, merits, and defects of the poetry of Lamartine.

66. Alfred de Vigny's stoical pessimism.

67. Comparison of the life and poetry of Vigny with those of Leopardi.

68. Criticism of Victor Hugo as a lyricist.

69. The contents and the significance of Hugo's preface to *Cromwell*.

70. Autobiography in Alfred de Musset's "Night" poems and in his *Confession of a Child of the Century*.

71. Dumas the Elder as the author of "cloak-and-sword" novels.

72. Gautier's literary theories, especially as set forth in the preface to *Mademoiselle de Maupin*.

73. The critical method of Sainte-Beuve.

74. Aims and techniques of the Parnassians.

75. The plan and content of Balzac's *Human Comedy*.

76. The combination in Balzac's works of romantic and realistic elements.

77. Flaubert's three cardinal literary principles.

78. Methods and techniques of Zola and the other Naturalists.

79. Shortcomings of Zola as a literary artist.

80. *Tartarin de Tarascon* as an illustration of Daudet's characteristics as an author of humorous novels.

81. Comparison and contrast of the works of Maupassant with those of Flaubert as to subject matter, style, and tone.

82. Maupassant's literary treatment of the people of Normandy.

83. Maupassant's depiction of horror, madness, and the supernatural.

84. Baudelaire as a transitional figure between the Parnassians and the Symbolists.

85. The characteristics of Symbolist poetry.

86. Claudel as the author of religious dramas.

87. *Cyrano de Bergerac* as a typical neo-romantic drama.

88. Proust's psychological system and its effects on his literary style.

89. Exoticism and melancholy in the novels of Loti.

90. The dilettantism, cynicism, and aestheticism of Anatole France.

91. Gide's *Journals* as a commentary on twentieth-century problems.

92. Duhamel's attacks on the inhumanity of war.

93. Comparison and contrast of Verhaeren and Jammes as nature poets.

94. Historical background of the age of the Renaissance in Spain.

95. The characteristics of baroque literature (cf. Marinism, euphuism, Gongorism, and *préciosité*.

96. St. John of the Cross as a religious lyricist.

97. *The Lusiads* as a national epic of Portugal.

98. Ercilla's treatment of contemporary events in his *Araucana*.

99. Characteristics and defects of the Spanish romance of chivalry.

100. Ostensible purpose, contents, and merits of the *Celestina*.

101. The importance of *Lazarillo de Tormes* as the first picaresque novel.

102. The evils satirized by Guevara in *The Lame Devil*.

103. A brief biography of Cervantes.

104. Three different interpretations of the meaning of *Don Quixote*.

105. Genesis, composition, and publication of the two parts of *Don Quixote*.

106. Encina's secularization of the drama.

107. Lope de Vega's innovations in the drama, especially as set forth in *The New Art of Making Comedies*.

108. *Sheep's Well* as a "point of honor" drama.

109. *The Doubter Damned* as a treatment of the problem of faith versus good works.

110. Tirso de Molina's portrait of Don Juan.

111. Alarcón's "concern for ethics."

112. Calderón's *Life Is a Dream* as a treatment of the problem of freedom of the will.

113. Saint Teresa's ability (as in *The Inner Castle*) to put into words the subjective emotions of the religious mystic.

114. Targets of Erasmus' satire in *The Praise of Folly* and in *The Colloquies*.

115. The literary significance of Luther's translation of the Bible.

116. The principal merits of the dramas of Hans Sachs.

117. *Cardenio and Celinde* as the first "bourgeois tragedy."

118. The literary "reforms" of Gottsched.

119. Elements of the Storm and Stress.

120. Wieland's contributions to the development of the German novel.

121. Lessing's principal theories about literature contained in *Laocoön* and *Letters Concerning the Latest Literature*.

122. *Miss Sara Sampson* as a "bourgeois tragedy."

123. The political implications of *Minna von Barnhelm*.

124. Lessing's religious beliefs as set forth in *Nathan the Wise*.

125. Herder's influence on later German literature.

126. Herder's literary and philosophical beliefs.

127. Klopstock's greatest contribution to the growth of German literature.

128. The influence on Goethe's life and works of *three* of the following: Herder, Charlotte von Stein, Friederike Brion, Schiller, Christiane Vulpius.

129. *The Sorrows of Young Werther* as the "presentation of a soul in travail."

130. Wilhelm Meister's struggle to find life's meaning.

131. The philosophical significance of the changes Goethe made in adapting Euripides' *Iphigenia at Tauris*.

132. Autobiography in Goethe's *Torquato Tasso*.

133. The sincerity of Faust's repentance for his treatment of Margaret.

134. The meaning and philosophical conclusion of *Faust*.

135. Evaluation of Goethe as one of the world's five greatest poets.

136. Schiller's opinions about the relation between art and morality, especially as set forth in *Philosophical Letters* and in *On Grace and Dignity*.

137. Schiller's love for liberty as illustrated in any *two* of the following dramas: *The Robbers, Don Carlos, Wallenstein, William Tell*.

138. A brief summary of Hegel's "absolute idealism."

139. Schopenhauer's opinions about misery and the human will.

140. Nietzsche's doctrine about the "will to power" and the superman.

141. The main tenets of Marx and Engel's *Communist Manifesto* and *Capital*.

142. The nature poetry of Joseph von Eichendorff.

143. Estimate of Heine as an author of lyrics and ballads.

144. The combination of romantic, classical, and realistic elements in the dramas of Heinrich von Kleist.

145. Grillparzer's ability as a portrayer of character as shown in *Waves of the Sea and of Love*.

146. E. T. A. Hoffmann as the author of tales of horror.

147. An analysis of *Agnes Bernauer* and of *Gyges and His Ring* as illustrations of Hebbel's "penchant for the violent and the abnormal."

148. Ibsen's innovations in plot construction and characterization.

149. Ibsen's use of symbolism in *A Doll's House* and *When We Dead Awaken*.

150. Ibsen's interest in self-realization.

151. Keller's reflection in his stories and novels of his "own engaging . . . and robust personality."

152. The treatment of various conceptions of honor in Suderman's *Honor* and *Magda*.

153. Hauptmann's *The Weavers* as a typical Naturalistic depiction of a socio-economic problem.

154. Keller's reflection in his stories and novels of his "own engaging . . . and robust personality."

155. Contrast of Dehmel and Stefan George as to philosophy and technique.

156. Methods and beliefs of the German Expressionists of the twentieth century.

157. Thomas Mann's treatment of the role of aesthetics in *Buddenbrooks*, *Tonio Kröger*, and *The Magic Mountain*.

158. Summary and significance of *The Tale of the Band of Igor*.

159. The content and status of Russian literature prior to 1700.

160. Topics and characteristics of the dramas of Denis Fonvizin.

161. Biography of Alexander Pushkin.

162. Classicism versus romanticism in the works of Pushkin.

163. *Eugene Onegin* as a picture of Russian aristocratic life in the nineteenth century.

164. Byronic influences on Pushkin.

165. *Boris Godunov* as a romantic tragedy.

166. Comparison and contrast of the works of Pushkin and those of Lermontov as to topics, emotion, depth, pessimism, and universality.

167. *The Hero of Our Times* as a portrait of the vices of Lermontov's generation.

168. The strange combination of sympathy, realism, and humor in the works of Gogol.

169. Gogol as a reformer of the social order.

170. Plot and characterization in *Dead Souls*.

171. Humor and satire in *The Inspector-General*.

172. *The Cloak* and *The Inspector-General* as attacks on the evils of Russian officialdom.

173. The attitude of Turgenev toward Nihilism as implied in *Fathers and Sons*.

174. *Smoke* as a picture of the "chaos and meaninglessness . . . of everything Russian."

175. Turgenev's attitude toward revolutionary violence as shown in *New Earth*.

176. Autobiography in Dostoevsky's *Memoirs of the House of the Dead*.

177. The problem of guilt and rehabilitation of criminals as treated in *Crime and Punishment*.

178. The "idiocy" of Prince Myshkin.

179. The effects of crime on each of the four Karamazov brothers.

180. Merits and shortcomings of Dostoevsky as a novelist.

181. Tolstoy's conversion.

182. The meaning of Tolstoyism.

183. Tone, style, and techniques of Tolstoy as a novelist.

184. Tolstoy's attitude (or theory) of history as illustrated in *War and Peace*.

185. A brief synopsis of *War and Peace*.

186. Count Rostov as a typical, indulgent father of a family of the minor Russian nobility of the nineteenth century.

187. *Anna Karenina* as a study of moral degeneration and its results.

188. Tolstoy's *Resurrection* as a philosophical sequel to Dostoevsky's *Crime and Punishment*.

189. Commentary on the assertion that Tolstoy was "the biggest man, if not the greatest artist, in all Russian literary history."

190. The social and economic revolution in Russia from 1883 to 1917.

191. Plot versus description in Chekhov's short stories.

192. *The Cherry Orchard* as a picture of the impotence and decay of the Russian aristocracy about 1900.

193. *The Lower Depths* and *The Mother* as illustrations of Gorky's "message" and his method.

194. Summary of criticism of Gorky as a literary artist.

195. Brief summary of Soviet poetry, with special emphasis on its topics, characteristics, merits, defects, and principal authors.

196. Isaak Babel as a "romantic aesthetic."

197. Alexey N. Tolstoy's picture of pre-Soviet Russia in *The Road to Calvary*.

198. Sholokov's *The Quiet Don* as "a Cossack *War and Peace*."

199. Objects of satire in *Twelve Chairs*.

200. Zoschenko as a satirist.

Part B. Identifications and Definitions

Identify briefly but unmistakably each of the following:

1. Matteo Bandello
2. A *novella*
3. Giraldi Cinthio
4. Galileo
5. Griselda
6. Fiammetta
7. *Ottava rima*
8. Palemone
9. Margutte
10. Bradamante
11. Rinaldo
12. Amaranta
13. Callimaco
14. "Courtesy" literature
15. Benvenuto Cellini
16. Angelo Ambrogino Poliziano
17. Battista Guarini
18. Aminta
19. Tancredo
20. Uliviere
21. Carlo Goldoni
22. The Risorgimento
23. *Barbaric Odes*
24. *Right You Are if You Think You Are*
25. Andrea del Sarto
26. Catherine de' Medici
27. Clément Marot
28. *The Heptameron*
29. *The Institutes*
30. The Pleiad
31. Cassandre Salviatti
32. Étienne Jodelle
33. Joachim du Bellay
34. Robert Garnier
35. René Descartes
36. Jacques Bossuet
37. Blaise Pascal
38. *Polyeucte*
39. Athalie
40. Bérénice

41. Oreste
42. Poquelin
43. Sganarelle
44. Alceste
45. Orgon
46. Harpagon
47. Valère
48. Diderot
49. Montesquieu
50. Marivaux
51. *The Lame Devil*
52. Manon Lescaut
53. *The Henriade*
54. Zadig
55. Julie
56. *Paul and Virginia*
57. Saint-Pierre
58. Émile
59. Auguste Comte
60. Charles Fourier
61. Proudhon
62. Corinne
63. Chactas
64. *Mauprat*
65. *A femme incomprise*
66. Monsieur Antoine
67. *The Poetic Meditations*
68. Cinq-Mars
69. Quasimodo
70. Jean Valjean
71. D'Artagnan
72. "The Mummy's Foot"
73. Alfred Dreyfus
74. Ernest Rénan
75. Henri Beyle
76. Julien Sorel
77. *Colomba*
78. Emma Bovary
79. Salammbô
80. Leconte de Lisle
81. Paul Verlaine
82. "The Swan"

83. Eugène Scribe
84. *Lady of the Camellias*
85. Henri Becque
86. *The Blue Bird*
87. Charles Vildrac
88. Vaudeville
89. *Promised Land*
90. Henri Bergson
91. Bernard Profitendieu
92. Pontius Pilate
93. Sylvestre Bonnard
94. Jean Christophe
95. Unanimism
96. Salavin
97. André Malraux
98. Colonel Bramble
99. Paul Fort
100. Poet of the French Resistance
101. Luis Vives
102. Boscán
103. *Songbook of Ballads*
104. Luis de León
105. "Calm Night"
106. Vasco da Gama
107. Calisto
108. *Diana*
109. Pablo
110. The Ingenious Elena
111. Alemán
112. Dulcinea
113. Rozinante
114. *Galatea*
115. Pipota
116. *Kitchen Comedy*
117. *Dragontea*
118. Doña Maria
119. Juana
120. Pedro Crespo
121. Andrenio
122. Pío Baroja

123. Juan Ramón Jiminez
124. "A Mighty Fortress"
125. The Wittenberg Nightingale
126. Martin Opitz
127. Johann J. Bodmer
128. Christian F. Gellert
129. Agathon
130. Oberon
131. Winckelmann
132. Emilia Galotti
133. *Voices of the Nations*
134. Lotte
135. Mignon
136. Johann G. Fichte
137. Friedrich Engels
138. Wilhelm Müller
139. Ludwig Tieck
140. Bancban
141. Jean Paul
142. *The Devil's Elixir*
143. *The Hereditary Forester*
144. Torvald Helmer
145. Solveig
146. Halvard Solness
147. *Dame Care*

148. Hannele
149. Judge Wehrhahn
150. Theodor Storm
151. *The Cavalier of the Rose*
152. Rainer M. Rilke
153. Hans Grimm
154. Hans Castorp
155. Bernadette
156. The Tatars
157. The Decembrists
158. Deacon Gregory
159. *The Chronicle of Nestor*
160. Prince Antioch Cantemir
161. Vasily Trediakovsky
162. Ivan Krylov
163. Alexey K. Tolstoy
164. Tatyana Larin
165. Alexander Griboedov
166. Tamar
167. Ilya Ilf
168. Oblomov
169. Alexey Gastev
170. Chichikov
171. Isaak Babel

172. Akaky Akakyevich
173. Pavel
174. Bazarov
175. Irina
176. *Rudin*
177. Solomin
178. Bwikov
179. *The Gambler*
180. Raskolnikov
181. Agila
182. Stagrovin
183. Verkhovensky
184. Smerdyakov
185. *Sevastopol*
186. Olenin
187. Pierre Bezukhov
188. Andrey Volkonsky
189. Natasha Rostov
190. Anatole Kuragin
191. Vronsky
192. Levin
193. Ivan Ilyitch
194. Slavophils
195. Nekhludov
196. Katusha
197. Korolenko
198. Lopahin
199. Pepel
200. Bender

Indexes

General Index

[Note: Literary works are listed by title only, not by author.]

Index to Characters

[See the General Index for characters whose names appear in the titles of literary works.]

Abelard, 87
Abner, 70
Achille, 17
Achilles (*Filostrato*), 17
Achilles (*Penthesilea*), 235
Adam, 18
Aeneas, 161
Affrico, 17–18
Africanus, Scipio, 9
Agathon, 204
Agila, 285
Agnes Bernauer, 239
Agramante, 22
Ahab, 70
Ahaziah, 70
Akaky Akakyevich, 280–281
Akakyevich, Akaky, 280–281
Alceste, 73
Alcinous, 161
Alving, Oswald, 245
Alyosha Karamazov, 285–286
Amalia, 223
Amaranta, 24
Amarilli, 29–30
Aminta, 30–31
Ana, Doña, 177–178
Anatole Kuragin, 291
Andrenio, 180–181
Andrey Volkonsky, 290–291
Andromaque, 69
Anfriso, 173
Angelica, 22
Anitra, 244
Anna Karenina, 292
Anselme, 73–74
Antonio, 218
Appiani, Count, 208
Appius, 208

Archytas, 204
Arcita, 16–17
Arcite, 17
Ariosto, 22–24
Arkady, 282
Arlecchino, 29
Armida, 31–32
Artagnan, D', 109
Arthur, King, 19, 52, 204
Astarotte, 20
Astolfo, 22
Astyanax, 69
Atala, 94
Athaliah, 70
Athalie, 70
Athene, 217

Bacchus, 161
Banchan, 237
Barbara Dobroselova, 284
Barca, Hamilcar, 124
Barnhelm, Minna von, 208
Bazarov, 282
Beate, 245
Beatrice (*Bride of Messina*), 225
Beatrice Portinari, 10, 12
Becket, St. Thomas à, 253
Belardo, 173
Bell, Kitty, 102
Bembo, Cardinal Pietro, 27
Bender, 301
Beppo, 20
Bérénice, 69
Berganza, 170
Bergerac, Cyrano de, 140

Bergeret, 145
Berlichingen, Götz von, 217, 223, 236
Bernauer, Agnes, 239
Bernick, Karsten, 244–245, 247
Bette, Cousine, 119
Bezukhov, Pierre, 290–291
Blanchefleur, 13
Bonifacio, Carmosina, 24
Bonnard, Sylvestre, 144
Bovary, Madame Emma, 124
Bradamante, 22
Brand, 244
Bruto, 36
Brutus, 36
Buddenbrooks, Hanno, 262
Bussone, Francesco, 37
Buttler, 224
Buttonmolder, 244
Bwikov, 284

Caesar, Augustus, 67
Caesar (*Bride of Messina*), 225
Caesar, Julius, 36
Calisto, 163
Callimaco, 25
Candide, 84
Carlo (Charlemagne), 19, 20, 37, 204–205
Carlos, Don, 223–224
Carmosina Bonifacio, 24
Carrasco, 168
Castorp, Hans, 263
Celestina, 163
Célimène, 73
Chactas, 94, 95

369